THE BOSTON IRISH

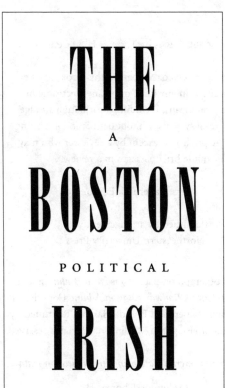

THE

A

BOSTON

POLITICAL

IRISH

HISTORY

THOMAS H. O'CONNOR

BOSTON   NEW YORK   TORONTO   LONDON

First Paperback Edition

Published by arrangement with
Northeastern University Press

The photograph on page 179 is from *Brahmins and
Bullyboys: G. Frank Radway's Boston Album.* Copyright 1973
by Stephen Halpert and Brenda Halpert. Reprinted by
permission of Houghton Mifflin Co. All rights reserved.

Library of Congress Cataloging-in-Publication Data

O'Connor, Thomas H.
The Boston Irish : a political history / Thomas H. O'Connor.
p.   cm.
Includes bibliographical references (p.) and index.
ISBN 1-55553-220-9 (hc)   0-316-62661-9 (pb)
1. Irish Americans—Massachusetts—Boston—Politics and
government. 2. Boston (Mass.)—Politics and government. I. Title.
F73.9.I6O28   1995
974.4'610049162—dc20   94-24984

10   9   8   7   6   5   4   3   2   1

Published simultaneously in Canada by Little, Brown & Company
(Canada) Limited

Printed in the United States of America

To my grandsons,
MATTHEW and BRIAN

CONTENTS

❧

ILLUSTRATIONS

BOSTON'S IRISH MAYORS

⦿

HUGH O'BRIEN	1885–1889	*b. Ireland*
PATRICK COLLINS	1903–1905	*b. Ireland*
JOHN F. FITZGERALD	1906–1908 1910–1914	*b. North End*
JAMES M. CURLEY	1915–1919 1922–1926 1930–1934	*b. Roxbury*
FREDERICK W. MANSFIELD	1934–1938	*b. East Boston*
MAURICE J. TOBIN	1938–1942 1942–1944	*b. Roxbury*
JOHN E. KERRIGAN (Acting Mayor) 1945		*b. South Boston*
JAMES M. CURLEY	1946–1950	*b. Roxbury*
JOHN B. HYNES	1950–1952 1952–1956 1956–1960	*b. Dorchester*
JOHN F. COLLINS	1960–1964 1964–1968	*b. Roxbury*
KEVIN H. WHITE	1968–1972 1972–1976 1976–1980 1980–1984	*b. West Roxbury*
RAYMOND L. FLYNN	1984–1988 1988–1992 1992–1993	*b. South Boston*

ACKNOWLEDGMENTS

❧

In undertaking a historical synthesis that covers so many topics over such a long period of time, it is almost impossible to single out any one particular authority from all those whose valuable research on the subject of the Irish in America has made this work possible. I would, however, like to acknowledge a special indebtedness to the late John T. Galvin, a devoted civic leader and avid historian, for his pioneering studies on the role of the Irish in Boston politics.

I benefited greatly from the personal friendship and the professional expertise of William A. Frohlich, Director of the Northeastern University Press, who suggested this particular topic and who worked closely with me on its development. I am grateful to Ann Twombly, production director at Northeastern University Press, for her great skill in transforming my manuscript into a book, and to Martha Yager for her expert copyediting.

Chestnut Hill, Massachusetts
September 1994

I should state plainly at the outset that I begin this study with a personal assumption with which many readers may agree, but to which others may take strong exception. It is that the Boston Irish are *different*. I regard them as different from the New York Irish, the Philadelphia Irish, the Chicago Irish, and from most clearly identifiable groups of Irish Americans in other parts of the United States. Moreover, I find them different from the Irish in Springfield, Worcester, and most other cities in the Commonwealth of Massachusetts. I have always felt that during Boston's terrible conflict over school desegregation and court-ordered busing, the fact that Judge W. Arthur Garrity came from an Irish-Catholic family in Worcester, while Mayor Kevin H. White was an Irish Catholic from West Roxbury, did nothing at all to ease tensions or encourage an amicable solution. The two men simply did not understand each other. The essential nature of this difference was captured by the perceptive prizewinning author J. Anthony Lukas in a lecture at the John F. Kennedy Library commemorating the 350th anniversary of the founding of Boston. Boston's busing struggle, he observed, was "a feud within the Irish political family," with the struggle in Judge Garrity's courtroom taking on all the aspects of an "Irish morality play" fought out between "various conceptions of what it meant to be Irish in contemporary Boston."[1]

The reason for this "difference," at least according to my own preliminary assumption, is not that the Irish who came to Boston were significantly different from other Irish immigrants who came to American cities during the greater part of the nineteenth century. Rather, it lies in the unique surroundings in which the Irish found themselves when they first arrived in Boston. If there had existed in the nineteenth century a computer able to digest all the appropriate data, it would have reported one city in the entire world where an Irish Catholic, under any circumstance, should never, *ever*, set foot. That city was Boston, Massachusetts. It was an American city with an intensely homogeneous Anglo-Saxon character, an inbred hostility toward people who were Irish, a fierce and violent revulsion against all things Roman Catholic, and an economic system that precluded most forms of unskilled labor. Boston was a city that rejected the Irish from the very start and saw no way in which people of that ethnic background could ever be fully assimilated into the prevailing American culture. Other major American cities, to be sure, shared many of Boston's social, cultural, and religious characteristics, but few to the same extent and none to the same degree. Yankee Boston was unique in the depth and intensity of its convictions. The generations of bitter and unyielding conflict between the natives of Boston and the newcomers from Ireland would forever mold the social and political character of the Boston Irish in ways not found elsewhere.

The awkward twists and convoluted turns that developed in the character of the Boston Irish, combining the attributes and idiosyncrasies they bought from Ireland with the eccentricities they developed as a result of their abnormal relations with the natives of Boston, were nowhere more evident than in the role the newcomers played in the city's celebrated political life. Unfortunately, however, most Bostonians have only an incomplete and highly eclectic knowledge of their city's history. This is especially true of residents whose ancestors came from the Emerald Isle. To a great extent the Irish, like many other European immigrants, are an oral people. They have not always provided either a written or an accurate record of their long and fascinating role in American history. The Boston Irish, particularly, have generated no end of marvelous stories and delightful anecdotes, incredible myths and exciting legends, rollicking songs and uproarious jokes. Unfortunately, very little of this tradition has been recorded as permanent history.

In the past, the obvious and generally accepted explanation was that Irish immigrants were simply too poor, too tired, and too preoccupied with the time-consuming drudgery of everyday life to write down the details of their existence. When a people have been uprooted from their past and look forward to an uncertain future, an image of history is only dimly perceived. Newcomers in a strange and often hostile land, without permanent homes or substantial incomes, Irish immigrants were destined to spend most of their lives in a desperate quest for security. Unfortunately for the historian, a people forced to engage in backbreaking work from sunrise to sunset had neither the time nor the luxury to document the complexity, the diversity, and the richness of their daily lives, much less reflect upon their place in the grand scheme of things.

I am not at all convinced, however, that this economic explanation provides a satisfactory answer. Many other immigrant peoples were just as poor as the Irish and faced just as many problems, but were able to keep records and provide welcome histories of their colonies and settlements. There must be additional explanations, therefore, having more to do with the social, political, and religious background of Irish Catholics than with the depressing nature of their physical circumstances. For one thing, the Irish were not raised in the Calvinist or Puritan tradition of their Anglo-Saxon counterparts which otherwise might have caused them to examine their consciences nightly and record in painful detail the minutiae of their faults and failings. It is certainly no coincidence that, as Roman Catholics, the Irish were raised in a tradition of auricular confession that encouraged them to *speak* to their confessors about their mortal sins and venial shortcomings. Nor did the Irish adopt the custom of confiding their innermost thoughts, their personal experiences, the stories of their families, or the events of their neighborhoods to the pages of a diary or a memoir. They seldom encouraged their children to adopt the practice of record keeping so that family histories could be traced from one generation to another without reliance on the encyclopedic memory of some elderly grandmother or maiden aunt who kept it all in her head, and who took it all with her when she passed to her eternal reward.

Then, too, there seems to have been a strong element of humility or self-abnegation in the typical Irish-Catholic upbringing that discouraged individuals from feeling that they were important enough to record their own stories or that any project in which they were engaged was of sufficient consequence to warrant being set down for future generations. Fear of the unpardonable sin of pride was still strong enough to preclude seeing one's small and insignificant self as an important element in the great eternal scheme of things. As a result, most Irish people had an acute, often ironic, and usually comical sense of the present but seldom a personal sense of the past. They harbored the conviction that they were not good enough, important enough, deserving enough, influential enough to be considered part of real history. In the subtle form of Irish Jansenism that, ironically, made them similar in many ways to the New England Puritans they so thoroughly despised, the Boston Irish had come up with their own form of predestination, which caused them to view themselves as loving and obedient children who would be carried on the tides of history wherever the Almighty dictated. Many everyday expressions, such as "We'll be there tomorrow, God willing," inadvertently conveyed the idea that the Irish were not the shapers of their own history: they were the passive recipients of whatever God's grand design held in store for them.

As the Irish came to play an influential role in Boston politics, however, the earlier traditions of modesty, humility, and taciturnity took on aspects of suspicion, secrecy, and duplicity. Old-time politicians—and quite a few young ones, too—generally observed the well-known dictum of Martin Lomasney, legendary boss of the West End's Ward 8, to the effect that a wise politician never puts anything in writing. "Don't write when you can talk; don't talk when you can nod your head," he admonished his lieutenants. And so it went. Important discussions went unheard and unrecorded at late-night dinners, at noontime lunches, during whispered telephone conversations, and on those quiet strolls between the State House on Beacon Hill and the City Hall on School Street. More often than not, a wink of the eye, a knowing glance, a casual gesture, were enough to set the wheels in motion for an appointment to be made, a contract to be signed, a deal to be closed. Written words were usually superfluous in these matters. We lack papers or records of prominent political figures from even as late as the first half of the twentieth century. Not only Hugh O'Brien, Patrick Collins, Martin Lomasney, Patrick Kennedy, and John F. Fitzgerald, but even such recent mayors as James Michael Curley, Maurice Tobin, and John B. Hynes have left behind no compilations of official documents or personal papers.

But it was difficult for the Irish to be quiet for long, and on those occasions when they did take pen in hand, their passion for the romantic and the colorful, the literary and the poetic, led them to take charming but unconscionable liberties with the truth. Inveterate storytellers, they were never ones to let anything as prosaic as facts get in the way of a delicious anecdote or a wonderful tale. It was not so much that they were trying to hide the truth or tell deliberate lies; they were simply exercising what Sean O'Faolain once described as the Irish genius for "reservations, loopholes, and wordy discrimination"—for "anything on earth and under heaven, except a clear statement of fact or intent."[2] In the absence of factual records, informative documents, and reliable autobiographies, it is little wonder that modern readers have been forced to rely so long on the fertile imaginations of creative novelists like Joseph Dinneen and Edwin O'Connor for what they know about the political history of the Boston Irish.

I hope this volume will supply for the general reader as well as for the specialist an accurate historical synthesis of the major Irish influences on the political history of Boston. This book is also an attempt to explain the many ways in which Boston has helped to shape its Irish immigrant population over the course of nearly two centuries. A political history of this sort should provide a lens that gives us a microscopic view of the way a specific immigrant people developed as an identifiable and comprehensive ethnic community. By examining the shortcomings and weaknesses of the Boston Irish, their strengths and achievements, their abilities to adapt and to survive, their tendencies to procrastinate and to excuse, their sincere religious fidelity and their propensity for political chicanery, we may better understand the fascinating contradictions so apparent in their character as they have made their way through the long tortuous maze of Boston politics.

1

WILD GEESE AND

TRAGIC EXILES

IN THE COURSE of the late nineteenth century Mr. George Apley, that fictional but quintessential stereotype of the Beacon Hill Brahmin, had just been asked to serve with a new organization called the Save Boston Association. His sister, Amelia, pleaded with him to do so in light of the alarming changes that were taking place in the old city. "We must and we shall clean up Boston," she wrote. "If we do not, this will become an Irish city run by the Roman Catholic Church."[1]

This was an appeal no native-born Anglo-Saxon, Protestant-reared Bostonian could possibly ignore. Although the theoretical threats of Papism, of Jesuit wiles, and of more inroads by the Irish had been an integral to the Puritan legacy from time immemorial, they had never loomed large as a practical reality until the first quarter of the nineteenth century. For generations it had been comforting for the "better elements" of the city to reflect upon the purity of their culture and the homogeneity of their blood. They could take great pride in the fact that no Irishmen or members of any other "lesser breeds" had intruded upon their illustrious heritage. Successions of Harvard-trained, New England–bred historians had assured their readers quite categorically that no Irish were to be found in North America before 1830. The inhabitants of New England at the time of the Revolution, according to John Gorham Palfrey in his *History of the Revolution* (1865), were "wholly English"; Palfrey held that probably not a single county in all England had "purer English blood than theirs." Some twenty-five years later the eminent historian John Fiske, writing in *The Beginnings of New England* (1889), also agreed that the Puritan exodus had been "purely and exclusively English. There was nothing in it that was either Irish or Scotch," he wrote, "very little that was Welsh." Occasionally, he conceded, New England did receive a "slight infusion" of non-English blood: In 1652, for example, Oliver Cromwell shipped more than 270 of his Scottish prisoners to Boston; in 1685 some 150 French Huguenot families arrived in the Bay Colony; and in 1719 a group of 120 Presbyterian families from northern Ireland settled in Londonderry, New Hampshire. But these were exceptions, Fiske wrote reassuringly. Nowhere was the population more purely English than in New England at the end of the eighteenth century. "In all history," he concluded, "there has been no other instance of colonization so exclusively effected by picked and chosen men."[2] A short time later, in *The Story of the Revolution* (1898), Henry Cabot Lodge agreed with his colleagues that those American colonials who fought for independence were "almost of pure English blood, with a small infusion of Huguenots and a slight mingling, chiefly in New Hampshire, of Scotch-Irish from Londonderry."[3]

In fact, however, many immigrants from Ireland came to New England as early as the seventeenth century. Contemporary shipping records, passenger lists, town records, minutes of town meetings, church registers, and graveyard epitaphs list family names that are distinctively Irish. On the basis of sources such as these and data taken from the 1790 federal census, modern historians estimate that the total population of those who had come from all parts of Ireland to America by the time of the Revolution was somewhere between 350,000 and 400,000.[4] As far back as the 1620s, ships sailed regularly from such southern Irish ports as Cork and Kinsale, on their way to the West Indies or the Chesapeake Bay to bring back sugar and tobacco in exchange for provisions, textiles, and Irish servants. At first it was Catholics who left, in small numbers as indentured servants, pledged to complete several years of bonded labor in return for free passage across the Atlantic. Most of them headed for the West Indies, where their services were in great demand in the early years before the expansion of slavery; but smaller groups shipped out to American colonies such as Maryland and Virginia, and later to the Carolinas. A sizeable number of Catholics made their way from Waterford and Wexford to Newfoundland. Many traveled back and forth between Ireland and America on a fairly regular basis to work at seasonal jobs as laborers and fishermen in the Grand Banks; but as time went on, an increasing number settled down as permanent residents.[5]

In the last decades of the 1600s, however, the number of non-Catholics emigrating from the northern ports of Ireland greatly exceeded that of Catholics from the southern regions, and by the beginning of the eighteenth century, Protestants constituted the major source of Irish emigration to the New World. "Both in size and relative proportion," concludes the modern historian Kerby Miller, "Ulster Presbyterians far outshadowed all other population movements from Ireland to Colonial America."[6] Most of these northern Protestants were the descendants of the original Scottish settlers who had been planted on confiscated lands in rebellious Ulster by King James I in the early 1600s and whose numbers had been augmented by some 50,000 families that came from Scotland later in the century.[7] Life in Ireland was difficult for these transported people, who lived on lands they had taken over from the native peoples. Because they did not subscribe to the prevailing Roman Catholic religion and because they were seen as an overseas arm of English oppression, the Ulster Irish were hated and despised by the Catholic majority. That was to be expected. What was not expected was the shabby treatment they received from an English government to which they were loyal. As fundamentalist Protestants, mainly Presbyterians, who dissented from the official tenets of the Church of England, they found themselves subject to many of the High Church pressures exerted against the various Puritan sects, as well as to the penal laws leveled at recalcitrant Roman Catholics. As landowners, artisans, craftsmen, hardworking proprietors, and enterprising merchants who contributed to the wealth of the empire, they were appalled to find themselves regarded as potential rivals to their English counterparts. Year after year they struggled with high rents, coped with repressive taxes, and suffered periodic famines. During the 1600s the Ulster Irish also took the brunt of a series of discriminatory English trade laws and commercial regulations that benefited England but weakened the economy of Ireland. Bitter, disillusioned, and disheartened about their prospects for the future, the dissenting Protestants of northern Ireland began seeking greater religious freedom, political independence, and economic opportunity across the Atlantic Ocean.[8]

By the early 1700s, Irish from the north had already begun emigrating to America, and as the century advanced, so did their numbers. During 1715–20, a succession of misfortunes—high rents, bad weather, crop failures, and livestock diseases—produced a period of heavy emigration from Ulster; another followed in 1725–29 as a result of disastrous harvests, food shortages, and inflationary prices. One Ulster official, alarmed when he saw as many as 4,000 of his Protestant friends and neighbors depart in the year 1728 alone, expressed the fear that if emigration kept up at that rate the only ones left in northern Ireland would be Roman Catholics.[9] Between 1730 and 1769, perhaps as many as 70,000 Presbyterians sailed away to the colonies—this time including a poorer class of workers, such as small landholders, artisans, cottier-weavers, and common laborers. In 1770–75 emigration from northern Ireland reached a peak, with some 30,000 Ulster Presbyterians leaving behind them high rents, wholesale evictions, and a depressed linen industry. They also took with them a number of rebellious countrymen, members of groups like the "Steelboys" and other secret farm organizations escaping English reprisals for engaging in guerrilla warfare against local landowners. Scholars estimate that during the Colonial period a total of between 200,000 and 250,000 Ulster Irish emigrated to North America, with about half that number arriving during the sixty years between 1717 and 1776.[10]

The number of Irish coming to the New England region in the period before the American Revolution was never as great as the number of those who went to such Middle Atlantic colonies as Pennsylvania, New York, and Maryland or to the western parts of Virginia, the Carolinas, and Georgia. Because they knew that the hard-nosed Congregational establishment in the Boston area was notoriously inhospitable to persons with other social and religious backgrounds, the early arrivals from Ireland tended to settle in the less populated regions of New England—places such as Bangor, Belfast, and Limerick in Maine; Dublin, Londonderry, and Hillsboro County in New Hampshire; and Orange County in Vermont. In addition to those who sailed directly to the port of Boston, perhaps an equal number headed for northern Nova Scotia and Newfoundland and subsequently made their way south.[11]

Early Irish emigrants did well to stay clear of the Boston area, whose inhabitants were predominantly Anglo-Saxon, who generally regarded all Irish as members of a barbaric, inferior, and unmanageable race, and who saw themselves as representatives of a superior English culture. Although their own Puritan forebears had been forced to leave England in the early 1600s in the face of Anglican intolerance and Stuart political oppression, the early settlers in the Massachusetts Bay Colony maintained a genuine affection for England. When the Reverend Francis Higginson set sail from England in April 1629 with some three hundred colonists headed for Salem, he made a point of taking his children to the stern of the ship to cast one long last look at their homeland and cry out: "Farewell dear *England!*"[12] And when John Winthrop prepared to sail with an even larger group the following year, he had the leaders sign a formal document emphasizing that the future settlers of what would become Boston would not adopt "separatist" policies like those of the extremists who had settled in the Plymouth colony. Such Puritan spokesmen as Winthrop, Richard Saltonstall, Edward Johnson, and Thomas Dudley acknowledged the Church of England as their "Dear Mother" and expressed gratitude for the salvation they had "received in her bosom" and which they had sucked "from her breasts."[13]

Later generations would create serious divisions between the American colonists and their English motherland, but there always remained a significant strain of admiration for English ways. Bostonians, in particular, continued to regard their English heritage as an invaluable source of moral inspiration and cultural security. The similarities in language and literature, in constitutional rights and representative government, in private civilities and public ceremonies, all combined to form an enduring bridge between the Old World and the new. But as Bostonians continued to imbibe the heroic legends of their Anglo-Saxon past—the colorful sagas of King Arthur, Richard the Lion-Hearted, Bluff King Hal, Good Queen Bess—they also absorbed many age-old stereotypes and prejudices, which may have been less inspiring but were equally influential in establishing the subliminal assumptions upon which they based their outlook on life and their judgments about people. Among these was an almost universal Anglo-Saxon attitude attributing inferior status to the Irish people, an attitude that would color relationships between native Bostonians and immigrants from Ireland for generations to come.

In part, this attitude was based upon centuries of bitter political conflict and savage military struggles between the English and the Irish dating back at least to the twelfth century, when King Henry II of England brought his warriors across the sea to impose law and order on the "disordered and undisciplined Irish." Although the English eventually were forced to withdraw from their island garrisons, the fourteenth century saw Edward III, and later Richard II, launch new campaigns to tame the "wild Irish," take over their lands, and superimpose English political culture on that native Celtic form the English viewed as primitive and unprogressive. Still, the Irish refused to accede to the demands of the invaders. After the War of the Roses, King Henry VII impatiently rejected previous ideas for governing rebellious Ireland from within and set about imposing "direct rule" on what he regarded as a backward population for which he had little but contempt. This policy was continued by his son, Henry VIII, who sent in more troops to put down the last vestiges of "native rule" and bring the island under total English domination. With his officials exercising their authority from Dublin Castle, the Tudor king was confident that he had achieved his goal of subduing the country. The interior of Ireland, beyond the Pale, was still ablaze with defiance, however, especially after the English monarch added a volatile religious issue to what was already an insoluble political conflict. As a result of his matrimonial adventures, Henry VIII had broken with the Church of Rome and subsequently established his own authority as head of the Church in England. In October 1537, Parliament passed an act denying papal authority in Ireland and prescribing an oath acknowledging royal supremacy. To the staunchly Roman Catholic people of Ireland, the substitution of royal supremacy for papal authority was unthinkable and abominable, and the resulting religious schism only added to the ferocity with which the native population renewed its opposition to English rule. The English, in turn, first under Henry VIII and then under Elizabeth I, now viewed continued Irish resistance not only as a particularly barbarous form of political subversion but also as a diabolical conspiracy to restore the Whore of Babylon and establish the dominion of the Anti-Christ. During the reign of Elizabeth, there was a marked increase in military activity, with incredible slaughters, massacres, and brutality on both sides. In August 1598, Irish forces killed or wounded more than two thousand English troops sent to subdue them. In February 1600 Lord Mountjoy retaliated with a scorched-earth offensive that blackened the fields of Ireland: His men burned cottages, destroyed livestock, and slaughtered inhabitants without regard to age or sex. By the time the reign of the last Tudor had come to an end, hatred between the Irish and the English had reached a new and more terrible level of intensity.[14]

The coming of the Stuarts and the accession of James I to the throne of England did little to improve relations between the two peoples. Indeed, tensions rose to new heights in 1605 when a group of disgruntled Catholics, led by Guy Fawkes, conspired unsuccessfully to blow up king, lords, and commons in one spectacular explosion. This so-called Gunpowder Plot made the English more convinced than ever of the existence of a vast Papist conspiracy. It brought new recriminations against Catholics and made the authorities determined to reduce the Irish to total oblivion. James I sent English and Scottish settlers into the conquered sections of northern Ireland to live on lands completely cleared of native inhabitants. Thenceforth, the native Irish of the region were permitted to reside only on "lands granted to favoured Irishmen, to the Church, and to military officers who had served during the late war." These nearly five hundred years of bloody massacres and ruthless reprisals—reaching a new peak of cruelty in the mid-1600s with the military excesses of Oliver Cromwell, who visited his merciless vision of divine retribution upon thousands of innocent Irish noncombatants—created the kind of barrier between races that was almost impossible to breach.[15]

After the death of Cromwell, when Charles II was invited to return from France and take his place on the throne of England, Catholics in Ireland hoped for a better relationship. But it was not to be. Charles may have allowed a handful of noble Catholic families to regain their estates, but strict Protestant rule remained in effect throughout the land. The Irish House of Commons was exclusively a Protestant body; Dublin, a Protestant capital. The result was two Irelands: an official Protestant one, and a disenfranchised Catholic one. Persistent fears that Irish plots and "risings" would emerge from beneath the surface of sullen discontent gained credibility when James II succeeded his brother in 1685 as an avowed Roman Catholic. The prospect of a Catholic dynasty was too much for the leaders of England, however. They drove the Stuart monarch from the throne and replaced him with his Protestant daughter, Mary, and her husband, William of Orange.[16]

Unwilling to abandon either the king or their cause without a struggle, Catholics in Ireland rose up in rebellion, championed the Stuart cause, and looked to Louis XIV of France to come to their aid and strike a blow against England. Irish forces took control of Dublin, and the exiled James II returned to Ireland in triumph to meet with a newly formed Irish Parliament. But this proved to be only another glorious disaster the bards and minstrels would sing about in years to come. King William landed in Belfast, marched south, and met the Irish supporters of James II—the Jacobites—at the river Boyne, some forty miles north of Dublin. Here, with a superior force, the English inflicted a major defeat on the Irish rebels on July 1, 1690, and sent James fleeing once more to sanctuary in France. Although fighting persisted for some time in the western counties, English forces pressed on and put down the rebel resistance. By 1691 the rebellion was finished, no further outside aid was possible, and all property that had once belonged to Irish Catholics was transferred to English and Scottish Protestants. The "Protestant Ascendancy" was complete.[17] The remnants of the Irish nobility and the surviving rebels fled abroad and offered their services to the courts of England's enemies in France, Austria, and Spain. In time, many of these professional soldiers of fortune, frequently called "the Wild Geese," would catch the currents across the Atlantic. Nearly a century later their descendants, including Bernardo O'Higgins in Chile, took up arms in various wars of liberation that broke out in Latin American countries.[18]

But what many observers feel was even more devastating than the military defeats in bringing about the final and total demoralization of the Catholics in Ireland was the passage by the British government of the Penal Laws in 1691. These laws established regulations that forbade the teaching of the Irish language and denied Catholics the opportunity to vote, to serve on juries, to enter universities, to become lawyers, and to work for the government. The Irish became "beggars in their own land," writes William V. Shannon, "deprived of civil rights, mercilessly exploited, and subject to hanging or deportation for trivial offenses."[19] In the twentieth century, people would find it difficult to understand why the Boston Irish continued to be highly insecure and militantly defensive at a time when they were clearly a majority force in the city. But centuries of experience had demonstrated to the Irish what the black people of South Africa would come to learn: A race of people can have vast superiority in numbers and yet be subjugated and oppressed in their own land. Early on, the discovery by Irish Catholics that numbers alone did not guarantee power or protection created what seemed to be a permanent and, at times, almost paranoid sense of insecurity.

Five centuries of mutual hatred certainly accounted for the cold, even violent, reception faced by the first Irish people who ventured ashore on the Shawmut Peninsula in the Massachusetts Bay Colony. At first, even Ulster Presbyterians, for all their staunch Protestant virtues and equally strong anti-Catholic prejudices, were regarded by New England Puritans as "unclean, unwholesome, and disgusting"—little better than their Catholic countrymen.[20] Because the Irish had a reputation for shiftlessness, local residents viewed immigrants from that country as paupers who would undoubtedly cause trouble and become a drain on the colony's meager resources. In 1723, for example, Boston authorities complained

Life was poor and primitive in western Ireland, along the Atlantic seaboard from west Cork to Donegal. Most dwellings were one-room cabins or huts made of mud, turf, or dry stones. Because of the rising population and the fierce competition for land, more than half the farms in Ireland were too small to provide more than a bare subsistence. John F. Kennedy Library (Library of Congress photo).

that "great numbers of Persons have lately bin Transported from Ireland into this Province" and expressed considerable concern that too many of these newcomers would "become a Town Charge." The General Court subsequently passed a law requiring all persons who arrived in Boston, especially those coming from Ireland, to register within five days. Obviously, the fact that most of the newcomers were Protestants did little to soften the attitudes of the local Congregational population. In July 1729, the police watch had to be called out to put down a disturbance caused by a mob of angry townspeople who tried to prevent a group of Irish immigrants from landing. In 1736 the town authorities summoned Robert Boyd, captain of the brigantine *Bootle* out of Cork, made him promise not to let any of his Irish passengers "come on Shoar," and kept a strict watch on his vessel to see that he did not violate that stricture.[21]

Despite a cool reception and early difficulties, the Ulster Irish gradually achieved a greater degree of comfort and prosperity than would have been possible back in Ireland. The new charter issued to the Massachusetts Bay Colony in 1691 by William and Mary, prescribing that political representation be based not on religious affiliation but on income and property, worked to the advantage of the newcomers. The fact that most of them had been brought up to speak English rather than Gaelic made them more acceptable in the community. And as merchants and shopkeepers, craftsmen and artisans, country traders and commercial farmers, their enterprising spirit was found to be compatible with the Puritan work ethic. Their efforts in establishing local benevolent societies to look after the needs of their own people did much to remove the stigma of pauperism and to reduce the fear that they would become public charges. As early as 1657, a Scots Charitable Society was formed to assist in the relief of the poorer members of their community, and in 1724 the Irish Charitable Society was created for similar purposes. Defining themselves quite specifically as members "of the Irish Nation" and starting their organization on St. Patrick's Day "in observance of the Feast Day of Ireland's National Apostle," the founders of the Irish Charitable Society determined that all officers were to be "natives of Ireland," "Protestants," and "inhabitants of Boston."[22] Three years later, immigrants from Ireland made their presence further known by establishing the Irish Presbyterian Church in an old building not too far from the waterfront. In 1744 they moved to more spacious quarters on Long Lane, only a short distance from the Town House, the seat of British government, in a meetinghouse that would later be the site of the 1788 Massachusetts convention that ratified the federal Constitution.[23] These activities seem to have mollified the local population and helped to make the newcomers more acceptable. In September 1750, for example, some two hundred Irish immigrants landed in Boston, but this time they were welcomed because the townspeople had been assured that their numbers included "Persons of Considerable Substance" who would make no demands on public charity. Records from a decade later indicate that the town's poor population was likely to include fewer persons of Irish extraction than vagrants who had gravitated to Boston from nearby towns or neighboring seaports.[24]

Although by 1776 Irish Presbyterian immigrants and their descendants were still characterized as "Scotch-Irish" or as "Ulster-Americans," most of them, in their speech, their attitudes, their conduct, and their economic enterprises, had adapted to American ways and become largely assimilated into predominantly Anglo-Saxon patterns. By throwing themselves vigorously into the Colonial rebellion against acts of British oppression similar to the restrictive laws that had forced them to leave Ireland in the first place, and then by participating actively and in great numbers in the subsequent Revolution, the Irish Presbyterians finally won recognition as loyal and patriotic Americans. Even back in the northern parts of Ireland, the people showed themselves so sympathetic to the American rebellion that the lord lieutenant informed London that Irish Presbyterians were Americans "in their Hearts" and were openly expressing their views in such a way that "if they are not rebels, it is hard to find a name for them."[25]

The political ascendancy of the first wave of Irish Protestant immigration to New England was perhaps most dramatically demonstrated in 1807 when an Ulster Protestant named James Sullivan was elected governor of Massachusetts. James was the grandson of Major Philip O'Sullivan of Limerick, a Catholic rebel who had fled to France in 1691 along with other "Wild Geese" after the victory of William of Orange. The major's son John returned to Ireland, where he intended to study for the priesthood, but gave up the idea, set sail for America in 1723, and put ashore at York, Maine. Following the pattern set by so many other Irish immigrants during this period, Sullivan lost touch with his Catholic roots and became a Protestant. Of his five sons, Benjamin served as an officer in the British navy, while Daniel, Eben, and John held commissions in the Continental army. John rose to the rank of brigadier general, served under General George Washington during the evacuation of Boston, and, according to long-established local legend, was authorized to use "St. Patrick" as the official password of the day when he led Colonial troops into Boston after the British had vacated the town.[26] In the meantime, James Sullivan, the fifth brother in this remarkable family, rose to prominence in politics. First practicing law in Maine, he moved to Massachusetts, where he became one of the most influential lawyers in the state. The author of several legal and historical studies, James Sullivan served as governor of Massachusetts from 1807 to 1808.[27]

As Protestant Irish from the northern counties dominated the exodus from Ireland during the 1700s, by contrast the number of Catholics from the southern counties was surprisingly small, considering that social discrimination, religious segregation, and economic deprivation during the same period were even more oppressive for them than for their countrymen in the north. According to Kerby Miller, it is likely that during the period from 1700 to 1776 only one-fifth to one-fourth of the emigrants from Ireland were Roman Catholics.[28] This apparent reluctance to emigrate can be explained in part by certain obvious and very tangible circumstances that were part of the early Catholic experience in southern parts of Ireland. Extreme poverty, of course, was a major reason for the lack of mobility. Mainly poor subtenants, sharecroppers, migrant workers, rural farmers, and unskilled urban laborers, Catholics were subject to periodic upheavals, dislocations, famines, and evictions. They were often seen roaming the countryside, hungry and ragged, in search of land, food, and jobs. Many moved into towns like Dublin, where they swelled the native populations; others went so far as to cross the Irish Sea to seek work in the slums of London and other industrial cities, where Irish Catholics were among the lowest-paid laborers. By the early nineteenth century, between one-fifth and one-third of the working population of Liverpool and Manchester was estimated to be Irish.[29] However, few had the money or resources for the longer and much more hazardous passage across the stormy Atlantic.[30]

Then, too, many were discouraged by pessimistic reports coming back from North America describing the extent and intensity of anti-Irish and anti-Catholic feeling among the Anglo-Saxon settlers, and warning prospective emigrants that they would be better off staying home. Accounts of abusive treatment of indentured servants—long terms of service, cruel punishments, overwork, insufficient food, and inadequate clothing—dampened any enthusiasm for wholesale emigration to America on contract. Reports concerning the virulent hatred and open hostility of New England Puritans toward Roman Catholics in general and toward Irish Catholics ("St. Patrick's Vermin") in particular, ruled out any interest in heading to the shores of Massachusetts Bay. In Massachusetts at that time, the Irish Catholics were seen as potential allies of their French coreligionists who were in the process of colonizing neighboring Canada.[31] Bostonians were especially concerned about the Jesuits who were working among the Abenakis and the other Indian tribes along the Kennebec River in Maine—fearful that in converting the Native Americans to Catholicism the priests would also make them allies of the French. Convinced that the Jesuits would "debauch, seduce, and withdraw the Indians from their due obedience unto his Majesty and stir them up to sedition, rebellions, and open hostility against his Majestie's government," in June 1700 the Massachusetts General Court passed a law forbidding any Catholic priest to be present in Massachusetts territory, under penalty of life imprisonment or—if he escaped and was recaptured—death.[32] During the winter of 1731–32, Boston was thrown into a minor panic when the rumor circulated that a Roman Catholic priest in town was planning to celebrate a Mass for the local Papists on Friday, March 17—"what they call St. Patrick's Day." Governor Jonathan Belcher immediately prepared to put into force the Massachusetts antipriest law. He issued a warrant to the sheriff, the deputy sheriff, and the constables of Suffolk County authorizing them to break into houses, shops, and all other "Places or apartments" in tracking down and apprehending any "Popish Priest and other Papists of his Faith and Perswasion."[33]

Although no such priest was ever located, fear of the Catholics, the French, and their Indian allies continued to permeate the town of Boston, and when residents became aware that there were several persons identified as "Roman Catholicks" living in their town, they decided it was hazardous to have such persons walking around unsupervised and unguarded, "in Case we should be attack'd by an Enemy." At a town meeting on September 22, 1746, they voted that a three-man committee be appointed to make "strict Search and enquiry" into the activities of these Catholics in order to prevent any possible danger to the town.[34] This type of hostility and suspicion continued undiminished for years: even as late as 1772, when town leaders voted to extend "liberty of conscience" to most Christian denominations, they excluded "Catholics or Papists" from such toleration because their doctrines were considered "subversive of society." The leaders reminded the townspeople that, besides recognizing the Pope in "an absolute manner," Catholics taught that heads of state who were excommunicated could be deposed and that those the Catholics called "Hereticks" could be destroyed without mercy.[35] The spectre of the pope and the stereotype of every Catholic as a potential subversive and terrorist continued to inflame Puritan emotions, and for generations on Guy Fawkes Day, every November 5, the Protestants of Boston took part in a public demonstration called "Pope's Night," marked by processions of floats and wagons, tableaux, and other antipopery exhibits, climaxing with the burning of the pope in effigy. Often the night ended in a pitched battle, fought with clubs, staves, bricks, and cobblestones, between rival gangs from the North End and the South End.[36]

The defeat of France in the Seven Years' War in 1763 brought to an end, once and for all, any prospects of French domination in North America. As a result, the government of Great Britain relaxed its official anti-Catholic policies to accommodate its newly acquired French-Catholic population in what had now become British Canada. Indeed, the British king assured his new Roman Catholic subjects in the former French colony that they would be allowed to profess their religion "according to the rites of the Romish Church, as far as the laws of Great Britain permit." In Massachusetts, however, it was clear that Puritan leaders had no idea of letting down their guard or changing their traditional anti-Papist attitudes. Delivering a Dudleian lecture "against popery" in the chapel of Harvard College on May 8, 1765, the Reverend Jonathan Mayhew, pastor of West Church and champion of old-time Puritanism, expressed his regrets that some people calling themselves Protestants (obviously, the king and his Anglican supporters) now looked upon "popery" as "a harmless and indifferent thing." Referring scornfully to members of the Church of England as "half-Papists" who conducted "Masses" instead of "Meetings," he questioned where this new type of liberal and reckless thinking would lead. "May this seminary of learning, may the people, ministers, and churches of New England," he pleaded, "ever be preserved from popish and all other pernicious errors. . . ."[37] John Adams, a thirty-year-old lawyer from Braintree, also viewed "popery" as incompatible with liberty and agreed with Mayhew that Catholicism had no right to recognition or toleration. After all, he asserted, it was the "Roman system" that had kept human nature in chains "for ages, in a cruel, shameful, and deplorable servitude." It was clear that Boston was a place that still held few attractions for Catholics, no matter how difficult things were for them back in Ireland.[38]

It was the coming of the American Revolution that brought about remarkable and totally unexpected changes in the attitude of Bostonians toward Roman Catholics. In the early stages of the Revolution, the American rebels saw the strategic advantages of developing good relations with the French population of neighboring Canada, not only as a convenient source of provisions and materiel but also as a potential military ally in their war against Britain. This concern for friendship and alliance with the French Canadians was one of the main reasons that General George Washington, when he arrived in Cambridge in November 1775 to take command of the Continental army, issued an order prohibiting his officers and men from taking part in that "ridiculous and childish" custom known as "Pope's Night." He pointed out the "impropriety" of insulting the religious beliefs of their French Canadian allies in such a "monstrous" and inexcusable fashion.[39] These were days, too, when the crisis of the war took many provincial Bostonians to other cities and other parts of the country, where they began to meet people with whom they had never before been associated. After meeting Charles Carroll of Carrollton, for example, John Adams was greatly impressed not only by the gentleman's liberal education and his ability to speak French but also by the fact that, although he was a dedicated Roman Catholic, he appeared to be a patriotic American. Adams also went so far as to approve the sending of Carroll's brother John, "a Roman Catholic Priest and a Jesuit," to work among the people of Canada.[40] While there was undoubtedly a great deal of pragmatic maneuvering in these associations, personal contact went a long way toward reducing many old stereotypes.

Religious attitudes in Boston showed signs of even greater toleration in the spring of 1778, when news arrived that France itself had concluded a major military and commercial alliance wih the newly formed United States of America after the British defeat at Saratoga the previous fall. This treaty was of such "extraordinary importance," according to the local church historian, "that it rightfully dominates the whole history of that time."[41] The Puritan city's traditional antipathy to things French and Catholic was now further subordinated to the necessity of aid in the life-and-death struggle for independence. Local dignitaries became downright fulsome in their praise for the French and in their hospitality to French officers and men whose naval vessels were tied up at Boston harbor. Although there was still a nasty undercurrent of distrust and resentment among the common people, many of whom still regarded the French as "odious" and occasionally engaged in street brawls with sailors on shore leave, most Bostonians generally went out of their way to be kind and polite to French visitors on public, formal, and official occasions.[42] There was not much mixing, and few serious friendships resulted from these occasions, but the presence of so many Frenchmen in town gave curious local Puritans an opportunity to witness at first hand some of the "dreadful" religious rituals they had heard so much about. French chaplains celebrated Mass in public on many occasions and in many different settings—aboard ships, in barracks, in military hospitals—undoubtedly helping to reduce the level of apprehension with which such practices were traditionally viewed in Boston.[43]

These various changes in the local religious climate help explain why, when Massachusetts delegates met in September 1779 to draw up the draft of a constitution for their newly organized state, they composed a Bill of Rights that guaranteed liberty of conscience and freedom of worship to all men. The Bill of Rights made unconstitutional the passage of any further legislation in Massachusetts against members of the Roman Catholic religion. In view of the circumstances of the war and the presence of so many of their Continental allies, the French residents of Boston were the first to react to the new climate of toleration and begin practicing their religion openly. There weren't many Catholics in town, only a handful of French and Irish, but when a French chaplain, l'Abbé de la Poterie, organized a small congregation in the West End, they gathered in an old Huguenot church on School Street and, on Sunday, November 2, 1788, celebrated what is recorded as the first official Mass in Boston. The French abbé remained about a year before leaving for other parts and was followed by another French priest, Father Louis de Rousselet, who tried to hold the small congregation together despite a heavy accent and the indifference of most of his Irish parishioners, who were hoping for the arrival of an American priest reported to be on his way to Boston.

On January 2, 1790, the American priest finally arrived in Boston, paid his respects to Father Rousselet, and said his first public Mass on January 10. John Thayer had been born in Boston of staunch Congregational parents, attended Yale College, and traveled to France and to Italy, where in 1783 he was converted to Catholicism. In 1787 he was ordained a Catholic priest and decided to return to America as a missionary after extensive preparation in London and Paris. Thayer's long-awaited arrival brought an almost immediate increase in the size of the small French and Irish congregation. The Irish, especially, were pleased finally to have an English-speaking curate at their disposal. They began to attend church services in greater numbers, brought their children (some as old as sixteen) to be baptized, and had their Protestant marriages solemnized in the Catholic Church.[44]

According to the Boston Directories for 1789 and 1796, there were Callahans, Cavanaghs, Dohertys, Doyles, Driscolls, Duggans, Fitzpatricks, Kennys, Lynches, Mahoneys, McCarthys, O'Briens, O'Donnells, Ryans, Sullivans, and Walshes living in Boston during the 1780s. One of the first and most active members of Father Thayer's congregation was Mrs. Mary Lobb (née Connell), widow of a sea captain, who in 1779 had married a propertied resident named George Lobb. John Magner, from County Waterford, was a local blacksmith who was also active in parish affairs, as was Patrick Campbell, a blacksmith and veterinarian, who became one of the church's first wardens. Joseph Harrington worked as a cooper; Michael Mellony made his living as a chimney sweep. Francis Mulligan and Daniel Hay owned rental property in the town; Joshua Farrington was a merchant. John Boyle and his sons were booksellers; Anna McClure was a schoolteacher; Patrick Duggan and his brother John were lemon dealers; John Larkin sold tea; and Michael Burns was a liquor dealer. Most of these Irish Catholics were not fresh off the boat; they had been residents of the town for many years, living quietly and unobstrusively among their neighbors, following local customs, and passing easily as northerners from Ulster. Lacking churches and priests of their own, they had married young Congregational women, had recorded the births of their children in the town register, and as often as possible on the Sabbath attended the more familiar Anglican ceremonies where, as the Reverend Mayhew had sourly observed, they held "Masses" instead of "Meetings." With the warm air of change wafting through Boston, these Irish Catholics slowly lifted their heads, cautiously sniffed the air, and tentatively came out in public to declare themselves members of the previously outlawed sect.[45]

Still, the number of Irish Catholics in Boston was small, and there were few signs that larger numbers would be forthcoming any time in the near future. Despite hardship and oppression, the Irish in the southern counties still showed great reluctance to leave the Old Country and emigrate to America in anything like the huge numbers that had come from the northern counties. Beyond the woeful lack of money, the continued presence of bigotry, and the very real fear of the unknown, there were certain more subtle social and psychological factors that help explain the particular reluctance of the Irish Catholics to uproot themselves permanently from their native soil. Generally speaking, the Catholics of Ireland were more rural, less literate, more parochial, more closely tied to home, family, and religion than their Presbyterian neighbors to the north. They tended to be more influenced by the appeals of continuity and tradition than by calls for change and innovation. They were more passive and fatalistic, more comfortable with the status quo, more inclined to accept their lot in life than to try to rise high or achieve much. The inbred reluctance to see a countryman advancing beyond what appeared to be his natural abilities or his cultural limitations was another one of the characteristics the Irish would bring with them to America. "The Irish must be a fair race," observed Dr. Samuel Johnson caustically in the eighteenth century; "they never speak well of one another." Some two centuries later, from his vantage point as a member of one of Boston's most prominent Yankee families, Henry Cabot Lodge made a similar observation concerning the Irish of his city: "Ah, the Irish. The minute one of them accomplishes anything, there's always another one behind him with a rock, waiting to bring him down." In short, in light of what Kerby Miller describes as their "worldview," Irish Catholics as a group were apt to endure pain and suffering as long as possible, relying on the love of their family, the comfort of their friends, and the consolation of their sacraments. "Catholics never went," noted Arthur Young, an eighteenth-century English expert on Ireland. "They seemed not only tied to the country, but almost to the parish where their ancestors were born."[46]

It was this reliance on home and family, this dependence on faith and friendship, that gave Irish Catholics the unyielding determination to support lost causes and leaders long after all hope had been lost, all efforts had failed, and all others had abandoned the struggle. In the course of their own national history, they had seen every military rebellion defeated, every social movement collapse, every appeal for justice denied, every effort to rise above their squalid conditions suppressed. And yet the Irish did not break. Against all odds, in the face of irrefutable logic, contrary to the rules of law and the dictates of society, the Irish would refuse to accept any measure or policy they felt conflicted with their faith, their values, or their ideals. Forming in solid ranks with the members of their respective clans, and dedicated only to holding together the basic family unit at all costs, the Irish would continue to resist. With a sense of themselves as what Shannon calls a "fated race"—but a race destined to survive the most terrible of disasters, to outlast the most depressing of failures—they would bring with them to America a fierce stubbornness and an unyielding pride that would continually frustrate their enemies, but never fail to delight their friends.[47]

In the Catholic community that served as the spiritual foundation upon which this sense of destiny was based, the literature of the soul and the spirit was usually seen as much more desirable than the literature of the mind and the intellect; the emotional and the spiritual were regarded as more important than the rational and the material. The repetitive strains of catechetical instruction, painfully memorized in childhood and continued literally unchanged into old age, provided the constancy of religious belief regarded as essential for salvation. The Catholic was encouraged to avoid the complicated, the speculative, and the theoretical in favor of the secure, the simple, and the traditional. There were definite limits beyond which the human intellect should not venture and beyond which success could lead to the kind of overweening vanity and pride that would cause friends and neighbors to refer to a person as "full of himself." It is not at all coincidental that the cautionary words of St. Francis Xavier—"What doth it profit a man if he gain the whole world and suffer the loss of his immortal soul?"—were graven on the mind of every young Irishman. Enterprises involving speculation about the character of the human personality and the nature of the rational being, therefore, were seen as leading to the errors of relativism and subjectivism; too many inquiries into hypothetical theological questions could well produce the kinds of doubts and confusion that undermine one's religious faith. Investigations into the origins and structure of the social order could upset prevailing notions of political and social hierarchies; intensive research into the intricacies of the physical sciences or the complexities of the universe would only bring frustrating questions that could never be answered and that would always lead to dissatisfaction and disillusionment. Most Catholics were encouraged to cling to the comfortable and the familiar, to seek security within those natural boundaries God had ordained for each individual.

The literature of the spirit, in contrast to the literature of the intellect, was less speculative and explorative—more repetitive and familiar. Irish literature emphasized the nostalgic and the romantic, playing on themes out of the Celtic past. Legends, fables, stories, and anecdotes provided variations on ancient themes that reminded the Irish people of their rich and glorious heritage at a time when they suffered in abject poverty and subjugation under an alien rule. The glories of the Gaels, the bravery of their heroes, the beauties of their countryside, the loveliness of their women, and dreams of future freedom were celebrated again and again in the songs that were sung, the poetry that was read, and the music that was played in homes and taverns throughout the countryside. This history was written not so much to furnish new documents or to provide new evidence as to offer moral lessons from the Gaelic past of courage, integrity, loyalty, and patriotism to serve as inspiration for generations to come. The commanding presence of the powerful orator and the spellbinding art of the skillful storyteller were especially valued by a people who often could neither read nor write. Out of this tradition, the Irish brought with them to America an exalted regard for the man with the gift for words, the man who could sway audiences, reach the hearts of the people, and conjure up visions of past glories and future accomplishments. Even generations later, the turn-of-the-century Irish nationalist Maude Gonne could rhapsodize about the glorious Celts, who worshipped "an ideal purer, more spiritual, higher than themselves" while their historic enemies, the English, were nothing less than "the outward symbol of Satan in the world."[48]

Despite their determination to suffer the insufferable, occasionally things got so bad that many Catholics did make the effort to leave their native land. In 1789, the outbreak of the French Revolution seemed to offer the bright promise of exactly the kinds of political freedom and personal liberties the Irish people wanted for themselves. A revolutionary society was organized by Wolfe Tone, and for many years groups of idealistic Irish rebels looked to the French for moral support as well as military assistance. At a time when the Bank of England had collapsed, when the Royal Navy faced mutiny, and when the French were overrunning the European continent, a fearful British government was in no mood for an Irish rebellion. In the northern counties, the unruly Protestant militia was turned loose to suppress all signs of insurrection, and it used the opportunity to settle old scores with local Catholics. Men and women were beaten, flogged, hanged, or shot down in cold blood for wearing even a ribbon of the revolutionary green. (In the words of a popular song: "It's the most distressful country that ever I have seen/ They're hanging men and women for the wearin' of the green.") In the southern counties, full-scale armed rebellion broke out in 1798 as a powerful French fleet approached the Irish coast and threatened to land a substantial body of French troops to provide much-needed firepower for the Irish rebels. A series of violent gales drove the enemy vessels out to sea, however, and British regular army forces under the command of Lord Cornwallis made short work of the poorly equipped insurrectionists, who were hacked to pieces on the slopes of Vinegar Hill.[49] In the wake of this abortive "United Rising," several thousand Irish fled to safety across the sea, carrying with them to America their undying hatred of the British authorities and of their own Protestant countrymen.

Hard on the heels of this terrible military disaster, the passage of the Act of Union provided even further reason for the Irish to despair of any possibility for the independence of their land and the freedom of their people. Just as Wales and Scotland had been "united" with England in 1536 and 1797, respectively, so in 1800 Ireland was officially absorbed into the United Kingdom. The Act of Union abolished the separate Irish Parliament and moved political power over Ireland to a Union Parliament sitting at Westminster. Exactly 100 Irish-elected MPs would now sit in a House of Commons of 658 members, meaning that thenceforth matters relating to Ireland would be disposed of by a body of which Irish representatives constituted only one-sixth.[50] Deprived of political self-determination, still subject to the obnoxious Penal Laws, and facing a heavy burden of taxation, an increasing number of Irish Catholics saw little chance for an independent future and began emigrating to America during the late 1790s and early 1800s.

The number of Irish Catholics in Boston, though still small by later standards, showed definite signs of increasing, nearly reaching five hundred by 1790. The new American priest, however, proved incapable of handling the growing numbers and reconciling the interests of his French parishioners with those of the Irish. Despite high hopes at the start, Father Thayer was a disappointment. His feudings with Father Rousselet alienated the French members of the parish, while his provocative theological disputes with local Protestants threatened to turn public opinion against the small Catholic group. Bishop John Carroll wisely reassigned both priests to other parts of the country and in August 1792 sent in a new French priest, thirty-eight-year-old François Matignon, who had recently fled the revolutionary government in his native country. A kind, gentle, personable man who made friends easily and listened to both sides of an issue, Matignon slowly brought order out of chaos: He mended the schism beween the French and the Irish, made some needed repairs on the old church, and gradually acquired the respect and affection of his parishioners. With the arrival in October 1796 of twenty-eight-year-old Jean Lefebvre de Cheverus, a young friend and former student of Matignon, Boston acquired another curate of rare personal charm and distinctive abilities. Working tirelessly together in a spirit of harmony and brotherhood, the two priests not only presided over a growing congregation but also made a remarkably good impression on the leading members of Boston's Protestant community.[51]

On March 31, 1799, members of the congregation met to consider raising money to purchase a piece of land for the construction of a church. John Magner, Patrick Campbell, and Michael Burns, the three wardens of the group, assumed leadership roles in the enterprise and were joined by Edmund Connor, John Duggan, and Owen Callahan. The fact that the names of all these men are clearly Irish is dramatic evidence that, by this time, most of the French had moved away and the great majority of the Boston congregation was Irish. As the number of communicants grew from a mere handful to nearly one thousand, the members agreed that a new church was desperately needed and that fund-raising should begin immediately. They selected a site in the heart of Boston at the end of Franklin Street and were pleased to accept an architectural design drawn up by the young Charles Bulfinch, who had only recently designed the new State House on Beacon Hill. Raising money for the new project was a difficult and time-consuming task, and the construction work progressed haltingly, with a frustrating series of delays while more funds were acquired through monthly collections, special collections, sales of pews, and appeals to the general public. A number of prominent non-Catholics in the town added their names to the subscription list, and thanks to their generosity the construction was completed in the fall of 1803. Bishop John Carroll came up from Baltimore for the occasion. On Thursday, September 29, the feast of St. Michael the Archangel, he formally dedicated the Church of the Holy Cross with a Pontifical High Mass attended by an overflow crowd of parishioners, members of Boston society, and visiting clergy from Maine and Connecticut. Looking around him at the gathering, Father John S. Tisserant, up from Connecticut, observed that the congregation was composed largely of Irish folk "who were drawn here by the miserable conditions that existed in their native country."[52]

It was precisely the recollection of those "miserable conditions" back home in Ireland that helped shape the political choices of the newcomers at a time when political parties were just beginning to emerge on the

Dramatic evidence of how death came to early Irish immigrants at a tragically young age can be seen by the dates on the gravestones at St. Augustine's cemetery in South Boston. The land for this burial ground for the town's Catholic population was purchased in 1818, and the building is the oldest Catholic structure in the Archdiocese of Boston. St. Augustine Church Archives.

American scene. These were changing times in Boston, as throughout the young Republic. Although, originally, no provisions had been made for political parties in the United States—indeed, many Americans hoped they would never need the troublesome things—by 1794, the controversies generated between Alexander Hamilton of New York, who was President Washington's Secretary of the Treasury, and Secretary of State Thomas Jefferson of Virginia had produced two separate and recognizable political factions. Hamilton and his followers favored a strong, centralized federal system of government with an active program of business and financial enterprises. They preferred the stability of an English parliamentary system and looked with horror at the excesses of the French Revolution. Jefferson and his supporters, on the other hand, supported a traditional system of states' rights, clung tenaciously to the ideal of a small nation of yeoman-farmers who had left their oppressive "workshops" behind in Europe, and sympathized with the democratic aspirations of the French revolutionists, whose Declaration of the Rights of Man they found reminiscent of their own Declaration of Independence.[53]

In Boston the two political groups vied for the favor and support of the small but growing number of Irish voters. Upper-class Federalists urged the immigrants not to listen to the hypocritical appeals of the Jeffersonian Republicans, who had never lifted a finger to help them. They cautioned the Irish to remember who was running the state of Massachusetts, who had given them their religious liberty, and who had helped them build their "handsome house of worship." They suggested that with the Jeffersonians the Irish might not find the degree of liberty and tolerance they currently enjoyed.[54] The Jeffersonian Republicans, however, commiserated with "the unhappy situation of the Catholics in Ireland" and presented themselves as the true friends of the immigrants in America. Playing on the recently enacted Act of Union, which had ended any hopes for self-rule in Ireland, they deplored the "miserable state of the millions in Ireland" and made political capital of the fact that the Federalists were on record as supporting the British "in all their measures."[55]

Generally speaking, the rank and file of the Irish in Boston did not need too much persuasion to become staunch supporters of the Jeffersonian

Republicans. The homespun image of Jefferson himself, the agrarian nature of his political ideal, and the opportunity to support the French rebels and strike a blow at Great Britain were all factors that appealed to immigrant Irish Catholics, who usually found the aristocratic Federalists painful reminders of the supercilious English gentry back home. Interestingly enough, church leaders like Father Matignon and Bishop Cheverus (named Boston's first bishop in 1808), both of whom had escaped from a revolutionary and ostensibly "republican" regime that had secularized their church, executed members of the clergy, and forced dissenters like themselves to become homeless exiles, had a different view. They came out in support of the conservative principles of Hamilton, opposed the liberalism of Jefferson, and subscribed to the Federalist denunciation of extremist violence.[56] As a result, in a pattern that would last long into Boston's future, the political ideals of the common people were at complete variance with those of the members of their church hierarchy. Fortunately for all concerned, the American principle of separation of church and state made it possible for the Irish to hold completely different and sometimes conflicting political views from those of their bishops, while continuing to submit loyally and obediently to their ecclesiastical authority in religious matters. Outsiders often found this kind of arrangement confusing and contradictory, but that was only one of the many peculiarities inherent in Irish-Catholic politics in Boston.

The split between Federalists and Irish Americans widened considerably during the first years of John Adams's administration, as the naval conflict between England and France brought the United States closer and closer to war with the French. As they built up military and naval forces in anticipation of full-scale conflict, Federalist leaders like Alexander Hamilton used the "quasi-war" for their own political purposes. Disturbed by the movement of large numbers of Irish, French, Germans, and other "malcontents" into the ranks of a Democratic-Republican party that stood for "Gallomania and democracy," the Federalists sought to make it more difficult for aliens to become citizens and voters.[57] Using the French war scare as political leverage, in 1798 the Federalist-dominated Congress passed a series of Alien Acts to counteract the influx of the "hordes of Foreigners immigrating to America." Harrison Gray Otis warned that, unless some means were adopted to prevent "wild Irishmen & others" from being allowed to vote, there would "soon be an end to liberty and property." Otis had already introduced a bill into Congress calling for a twenty-dollar tax to be levied on all certificates of naturalization. He said he didn't mind letting "honest and industrious people" come into the country, but he didn't want "hordes of wild Irishmen" and other "disorderly people" from all parts of the world coming in to "disturb our tranquility" after having overthrown governments in their own countries.[58] Otis's colleague from nearby Dedham, Fisher Ames, agreed that the country's welfare plainly required the power of "expelling or refusing admission to aliens and the rebel Irish."[59] The subsequent Alien Acts increased the residency requirement for citizenship from five to fourteen years; they authorized the president to deport any alien considered "dangerous"; and they empowered the president to arrest, imprison, or banish any alien whose country was at war with the United States. At the same time, the Federalists also passed the Sedition Act, which provided that anyone who spoke or wrote "false, scandalous, or malicious" attacks on the president, the Congress, or any federal official would be liable to fine and imprisonment.[60]

The Alien and Sedition Acts were intended to help the Federalist cause by reducing the constituency of the Republican party, but they boomeranged against the Federalists. The major political attacks came from the pens of Thomas Jefferson and his colleague James Madison, who drew up formal protests known as the Kentucky and Virginia Resolutions denouncing the acts as dictatorial, unconstitutional, and in violation of states' rights. On the grass-roots level, too, opposition to the Alien and Sedition Acts produced exactly the kind of Republican expansion the Federalists had feared. The mean-spirited stand the Federalists had taken against immigrants and foreign-born citizens, and especially the unwarranted increase in the residency requirements for naturalization, elicited a strong reaction from the Irish and caused them to gravitate toward the Democratic-Republicans in even greater numbers than before.[61] Despite the efforts of the Federalists to forestall the inevitable, they lost the election of 1800. The victory of Thomas Jefferson and his inauguration in March

1801 were greeted by the Irish with great joy, especially when the new Republican administration changed the naturalization requirement and reduced the residency period from fourteen back to five years. This was clear evidence to the Irish that they had made the right political decision in casting their lot with the Republicans.[62]

Although President Jefferson stated in his inaugural address that he intended to focus primarily on domestic issues, he was forced by circumstances to deal with complicated international affairs. During his first administration he was preoccupied with negotiations with Napoleonic France that eventually led in 1803 to the purchase of the vast Louisiana Territory. During his second administration he was forced to confront the consequences of naval warfare between the British and the French, whose warships were attacking neutral American vessels on the high seas.[63] At first, Jefferson tried to avoid the problem in 1807 with an embargo that prevented American vessels from sailing into foreign ports. As a strategy, however, the embargo proved extremely unpopular and clearly ineffective: the United States suffered heavy commercial losses while England and France found other nations with which to conduct essential trade. On March 1, 1809, only a few days before retiring from office, Jefferson repealed the embargo and allowed the reopening of international trade.[64]

After 1809, the balance of power shifted. With the French navy growing increasingly weak and ineffective, Great Britain emerged as the villain. The Royal Navy was capturing American ships, impressing American sailors, and confiscating American cargoes at an even greater rate than before. The American public quickly forgot about the French and turned decidedly against the English. After 1810, new congressional representatives from the South and the West, known collectively as "the War Hawks," began to clamor for an all-out war to avenge the numerous British insults against the nation's honor. New England Federalists, with their pro-English leanings, strongly opposed a war with Great Britain because of the damage it would do to the Bay State's mercantile economy. Many Irish immigrants, however, favored war, which they viewed as an appropriate response to the depredations of an arrogant foreign power they hated. They were delighted at anything that would cause problems for the

British and upset relations between the two countries. August John Foster, the young British minister to Washington during the crisis, later testified before Parliament that Irish "exiles" had been the ones who kindled the fires that inflamed Americans against the British people.[65]

On June 1, 1812, President James Madison finally gave in to public pressure and sent a message to Congress demanding war with Great Britain to avenge the impressment of American seamen, the violation of neutral rights, the blockade of American ports, and the inciting of hostile Indians on the frontier. Within three days, the House of Representatives voted in favor of war; on June 18 the Senate followed suit.[66] With that, America's second War of Independence was on. Although Massachusetts troops did not enter the service of the federal government and assumed they would not be required to serve outside the borders of their own state, Bay Staters were always conscious of the possibility of naval attacks along their coastlines. The inhabitants of Boston, especially, were in constant fear of invasion, and a wave of panic swept through the town whenever a British ship was sighted in New England waters. Local troops were drilled every morning and afternoon, and sentries were stationed at intervals along the stretch of unprotected beach running from Dorchester Neck (South Boston) to Dorchester. When reports filtered down in September 1814 that British troops out of Canada would be advancing southward along the Maine coast, Boston selectmen issued appeals for help in fortifying the harbor. In response, a number of volunteer organizations representing civic, fraternal, and religious groups worked from the middle of September to the middle of October at various military installations in and around the town. Even the popular Catholic bishop Jean Lefebvre de Cheverus accompanied a group of 250 of his predominantly Irish parishioners to Dorchester Heights, the site of the evacuation of Boston in 1776, to rebuild and reinforce the old Revolutionary fortifications. They constructed a new powderhouse near the redoubts and erected platforms to hold a number of cannon in case they were needed to repulse British warships coming into Boston harbor.[67]

Fortunately, these elaborate precautions proved unnecessary. By the closing months of 1814, British and American negotiators were conducting serious peace talks in the little Belgian town of Ghent. Early in 1815, while celebrating the news of General Andrew Jackson's dramatic victory over the British at New Orleans, the American people learned that a peace treaty had been concluded some six weeks earlier. The war was over, and the United States was about to embark upon a new and decidedly different phase of its national history.

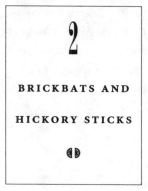

2

BRICKBATS AND

HICKORY STICKS

THE YEAR 1815 was one of those moments in history that mark the end of one clearly identifiable period and the beginning of another. The modern English historian Paul Johnson has gone so far as to describe that particular year, and the fifteen years that followed it, as "the matrix of the modern world."[1] It was a year of bright auguries and exhilarating promises. In America, Andrew Jackson's stunning victory at New Orleans in January, followed by the news of the Treaty of Ghent, ushered in a burst of national pride that caused the young Republic to sever its last remaining ties with the Old World and to embark upon a new and self-consciously independent course. In Europe, Wellington's victory at Waterloo put a final end to the overarching ambitions of Napoleon and introduced an era of general European peace that was destined to last a century.[2]

But 1815 had its dismal prospects as well. Great Britain, it is true, had won a decisive military victory on the continent and had established herself as undisputed mistress of the seas. As long as the war was in progress, the British economy was productive and profitable. Men who were not serving in the army or the navy were gainfully employed; manufacturing had expanded enormously to supply the sinews of war; and the nation's farmlands were cultivated extensively to feed both the civilian population and members of the armed forces. To increase the production of foodstuffs and cattle, great landowners and farmers of broad acreages adopted new methods of "scientific" agriculture. Mechanical cultivators, seed drills, new methods of crop rotation and fertilization, and experiments in the breeding of sheep, horses, and cattle made agriculture more efficient, more productive, and more profitable.

But the long and costly war took a heavy toll. Once it was over, the British people found their treasury empty, their taxes skyrocketing, and their national debt colossal. Overstocked with finished products, manufacturers hastily dumped their unsold inventories on the open market at rock-bottom prices. Firms collapsed, factories shut down, and unemployment became widespread in the industrial towns of England. And in the outlying agricultural areas the situation was even worse. In the wake of world peace and the reopening of international trade, farm prices declined and the war-generated prosperity came to an end. There was no question that the large landholders had to move quickly to make their fields more productive, in order to drive deflated prices back up and increase the rental value of their property. Many turned to the government for help, demanding that new tariffs in the form of Corn Laws be passed to protect English agriculture from the grain that was then pouring in from foreign countries. Seeing that new scientific methods were revolutionizing the haphazard and inefficient methods of old-fashioned village farming, large landowners pressed for passage of the new Acts of Enclosure. These laws allowed them to fence off their lands and use the open fields either for large-scale scientific agriculture or for the more efficient production of sheep and livestock. The Acts of Enclosure resulted in the wholesale eviction of thousands of small yeomen farmers, leaseholders, cottagers, and sharecroppers who could not afford to enclose their own meager holdings and who did not have money to buy new livestock or machinery. Throughout England and Ireland poor farmers lost the right to till the soil and grow food; they lost the right to pasture their animals and gather fuel on the common land. "Enclosure had the effect of making the rich richer, the poor poorer," wrote historians of the Commonwealth. "It struck particularly at the yeoman, the man who had control of enough land to support himself and his family in decent comfort."[3] Many cottagers and small leaseholders sold off their farms and became hired men or tenant farmers on the great estates. Others became part of the new proletarian army of wage earners making its way into the industrial towns in search of factory work. Still others gave up all hope and began contemplating a move to America.

In Ireland, the passage of the Corn Laws that kept up the prices of local grains, the protective tariffs that made it impossible for manufacturers to maintain full-scale production, and the far-reaching Acts of Enclosure that turned poor farmers off the land all had crippling effects on an already depressed economy. Despairing of a prosperous future, growing numbers of craftsmen, tradesmen, shopkeepers, and small businessmen decided to abandon their shops and their workrooms, gather up their meager savings, and move with their families to America. During the late teens and early 1820s, many of these Irish emigrants arrived in Boston, where they took work as weavers and cutters, drapers and tailors, millwrights and tanners, leatherworkers and glassblowers, blacksmiths and stonemasons, storekeepers and tavern keepers. Most of the newcomers were Protestants from the northern counties, and the fact that many of them were traveling in family groups, observes Kerby Miller, was a "sure indication of relative affluence."[4] But a growing number of Catholic artisans from the south also made the crossing after 1815, adding to the number of Irish in America. Determined to make good in their adopted country, they worked hard at their trades, saved their money with an eye to eventually owning their own shops, and even put aside small savings for future investments.

Joining their countrymen in the postwar exodus came a number of emigrants from the farming areas of the south, many of them young men in their twenties and thirties who could see little future in a country where an acute population explosion was leaving little room for new farms and little opportunity to marry and raise families.[5] The exodus rose measurably in 1821 when the potato crop failed—an ominous prelude to things to come. The following spring, in order to avoid wholesale famine in Ireland, the British government tried to organize a mass emigration movement from the southern countries to Canada. In Mayo, Clare, Kerry, and Cork, where emigration had not yet become the accepted pattern, the idea of going to America at government expense caught on among the predominantly Catholic population. At first, most of the emigrants had no particular desire to travel on vessels headed for British-controlled Canada, which they assumed was still militantly Protestant. But when the first wave of emigrants wrote home to their friends and relatives, telling them how easy it was to slip away from Canada to the United States, and how the passage of new laws and state constitutions in that young republic enabled Roman Catholics to enjoy equal rights, the rush was on to leave Ireland and go to America. In 1825, no fewer than 50,000 Irish Catholics from the southern counties, most of them from the depleted farming areas, applied for a mere 2,000 places on a British Colonial Office overseas program—a foretaste of the mass exodus that would eventually bring a third of the Irish population to America.[6]

While most of these able-bodied refugees from the farms and the fields of Ireland had few technical skills to offer, their strong muscles and hardy physiques qualified them for jobs as day laborers on the numerous construction projects under way in Boston during the 1820s. When the newcomers arrived, Boston had recovered from the disruptive effects of British occupation during the War of Independence and was in the process of transforming itself from a small colonial town into a substantial metropolis. Shortly after young Charles Bulfinch completed his new State House on the crest of Beacon Hill in 1798, alert real-estate developers calling themselves the Mount Vernon Proprietors bought up extensive property in the vicinity and transformed what had been a small, rustic area into a fashionable residential district. In addition to cutting down hills and constructing townhouses on Beacon Hill, developers were busy in other parts of town erecting private residences, public buildings, marketplaces, warehouses, and churches. To provide even more room for a rapidly expanding population, investors dumped tons of gravel into the muddy waters along the south side of the thin "neck" that connected the Shawmut peninsula with the mainland of Roxbury. As early as the 1830s this district, called the South End, began to take shape as an attractive community where wealthy Bostonians could move when there was no more room on Beacon Hill.

Many of the early Irish immigrants settled with their relatives and friends along the Boston waterfront, where the men were able to get temporary jobs cutting fish and unloading ships, while their wives and daughters obtained better-paying jobs as domestics and servants in hotels and private homes. This painting shows a view of the city from South Boston in the early nineteenth century. The Bostonian Society.

The old town meeting system proved incapable of handling the complex problems created by the physical expansion of the town and its rapidly growing population. By 1822 Boston had changed from a town into a city, complete with a mayor, an eight-man Board of Aldermen, and a Common Council of forty-eight members. Only a short time after becoming the city's second mayor, Josiah Quincy undertook an extensive program of urban renewal to refurbish the old parts of the city, which had deteriorated badly over the course of two centuries. Working with energy and determination, the "Great Mayor," as he later came to be called, saw that rubbish was collected regularly, streets cleaned effectively, and sewers brought under public control. He filled up Mill Creek, drained the putrid old Town Dock, moved the sewer outlets to the mudflats, and brought in landfill to create an expanse of land on which he created a new business district including an impressive new Market House directly behind Faneuil Hall.

These construction projects continued to provide work for Irish laborers, who were in great demand as long as their numbers were small and they did not take jobs away from local workmen. During the summer of 1835, Patrick Tracy Jackson, one of the founders of the Lowell textile mills, recruited a work force consisting of no fewer than 190 Irishmen, along with 60 Yankees, to create another profitable development on the southwest slope of Beacon Hill.[7] Working from May to October 1835, the workers reduced Pemberton Hill, leveled the adjacent land, and cleared a fashionable residential area for retired merchants and successful businessmen. Continuing the landfill process, the workers emptied the diggings into the waters on the north side of Causeway Street, creating land for North Station, where railroad lines came in from the textile centers to the north.[8] This decade of almost feverish investment, development, construction, and expansion provided more than enough pick-and-shovel jobs, not only for native-born American workers but also for the modest number of unskilled Irish-Catholic laborers who had settled in the town.

From only a few hundred when the first official congregation was formed, the number of Irish Catholics in Boston had risen to some two thousand by 1820 and to more than five thousand by 1825; by 1830 it had passed the seven thousand mark. Despite the increase in their numbers, however, the Irish were remarkably slow in becoming politically active. As late as 1834, for example, there were only two hundred Irish residents registered as voters in Boston. Certainly a factor in promoting what seems, at first glance, to have been a case of political indifference was the changing and rather confusing character of the American party structure immediately after the War of 1812. Because of its public opposition to the war against Great Britain, the Federalist party ceased to exist as a functioning political organization. For all practical purposes, after 1815 the nation had only a single political party, dramatizing the new sense of national unity and harmony that caused the postwar decade to go down in history as the Era of Good Feeling. With the growth of nationalistic pride, Jefferson's old states'-rights, agrarian, hard-money party was transformed almost overnight into a much more modern and federalized organization, advocating central banking, high tariffs, manufacturing, and strong national security. Now called the National Republican Party, it drew old-time Southern Democratic-Republicans into an uneasy and unnatural alliance with advocates of national planning, paper currency, and commercial prosperity.

The Era of Good Feeling did not survive the election of 1824, however, as the supporters of the defeated candidate from Tennessee, Andrew Jackson, denounced the "corrupt bargain" between John Quincy Adams and Henry Clay that had deprived Jackson of the presidency. Determined to set things right, vocal supporters of Old Hickory denounced the improper machinations of the elite Virginia-Massachusetts dynasty and proceeded to create a new "Democratic" party, tailor-made to fit the slim, erect figure of the Hero of New Orleans. Perceived as a candidate of the yeoman farmer, the frontier pioneer, and the self-made man, Jackson had no trouble drawing opponents of banks and tariffs, advocates of hard money and low taxes, and other supporters of Jefferson's agrarian tradition into the new party.

Along with their countrymen in other parts of the United States, the Boston Irish hailed Jackson's entrance into national politics, not only because he seemed to represent many of Jefferson's appealing rustic virtues, but also because they could identify closely and comfortably with those "real people" with whom Jackson associated himself and with his frontier political philosophy. Planters, farmers, mechanics, and laborers—these included most immigrants—were "the bone and sinew of the country," insisted the new candidate. Jackson honored the people whose ultimate success depended upon their own "industry and economy" and who understood that they must not expect "to become suddenly rich by the fruits of their toil." In praising those farmers and laborers who earned their living with the strength of their muscles and the sweat of their brows, and in denouncing those bankers, lawyers, and industrialists who enjoyed monopolies, special favors, and "exclusive privileges" without engaging in manual labor and who prospered at the expense of others, Jackson was appealing directly to a deep and abiding mistrust on the part of immigrants toward the upper-class business community whose arrogance and paternalism often reminded them of the behavior of their English overlords. Emphasizing this distinction between the party of the workingman and the party of the businessman, Jackson created a political and social alliance that would keep the Irish in the Democratic party for generations to come.[9]

And if that were not sufficient, there was the fact that Andrew Jackson was a self-proclaimed Irishman—a theme the old general played upon with great political savvy. Already, local supporters of John Quincy Adams, who were becoming conscious of the growing number of Irish Catholics in the city and nervous about their increasing political visibility, commented unfavorably about the appeal of the new Jackson party among immigrant voters. Native Bostonians continued to sing the old Federalist tune that only "men of affairs should run society" and complained about the way working-class Irishmen were adding their voices to "the clamor for change at the expense of the privileged class." The natives expressed disgust that Jackson leaders had moved into town and were welcoming the immigrants "with open arms."[10] Referring to the way in which Democratic organizers were operating in the Irish sections of town near the waterfront in preparation for the upcoming 1828 election, one critic made the acerbic comment that the Jackson campaign managers were looking for new recruits "in the kennels and the gutters." The writer observed that Jackson's followers, proclaiming him to be an Irishman, had marched through the downtown streets waving their shillelaghs as "hickory sticks" and planting their flag in "the ménage of Broad Street." They received with "hugs fraternal," he sneered in obvious distaste, "the tenants of poorhouses and penitentiaries."[11] In a St. Patrick's Day oration a short time later, however, David Henshaw, a Boston druggist who was leader of the Boston Democrats, turned the charge around to the old general's advantage. Andrew Jackson, he said proudly, was indeed "the champion of the poor against the rich" and a man who welcomed poor tenants and offered them compensation and assistance.[12] To further enhance their hold over the Irish vote, the Democrats published letters from the Ursuline Sisters of New Orleans testifying to the gratitude they felt for the protection Jackson had given them against British attack in 1814 and contributing the sum of fifty dollars for his presidential campaign.[13]

Massachusetts had set aside Monday, November 3, 1828, as election day, and as the time approached the various newspapers came out with their endorsements and predictions. The *Bunker Hill Aurora* saw an inevitable victory for John Quincy Adams, certain that he would sweep all the New England states and most of the Middle Atlantic states, although conceding that a number of the southern states would probably go for Andrew Jackson.[14] The *Boston Courier*, too, predicted a victory for Adams, pledging a solid conservative vote for the Massachusetts candidate. "Politically speaking," wrote editor and publisher Joseph T. Buckingham, "we are Federalists to the backbone, Hartford Convention to the core!"[15] On November 4, the day after the election, the *Boston Daily Advertiser* proudly announced that Adams had taken the city of Boston by a wide margin, receiving 3,112 votes to Jackson's meager 838. On November 14, the *Advertiser* was able to report to its readers that Adams had carried all of Massachusetts; the editors hopefully awaited similar results from the other states. When the shocking news arrived that Andrew Jackson had defeated John Quincy Adams for the presidency of the United States, the conservatives of Massachusetts could hardly believe what had happened. In the weeks that followed, distraught Republicans of every stripe were already complaining loudly about the hordes of ill-bred followers the uncouth westerner would inevitably bring into his administration. After the first of the year, one disgruntled Adams supporter remarked upon the fact that "all Broad Street" (the street where large numbers of Irish lived) had been invited to come to Washington to attend the presidential inauguration, since they were regarded as the "peculiar favorites of the Irish President."[16] Republican newspapers declared it to be a "curse" that foreigners who, "though legally naturalized," were "naturally and morally alien to our feelings, manners, and institutions," should not only be allowed to vote, but also be allowed the right to be elected to public office. As far as one writer was concerned, he would not want to see a foreign-born person in any office "above that of door-keeper in a public building."[17]

Despite the growing and perceptible animus against their race, there was little that could cool the enthusiasm of Irish Democrats in Boston, and nothing that could diminish their joy several years later when they learned that their hero, President Jackson, was coming to visit their city during the summer of 1833. This was part of a Grand Triumphant Tour, following the general's reelection the previous November, that would take the victorious Democratic leader through the major cities of the Atlantic seaboard. After visiting Baltimore and then Philadelphia, Jackson made his entry into New York City to wild rejoicing and three days of banquets, speeches, and continual celebrations. As he traveled on to Connecticut and then to Rhode Island, the sixty-six-year-old veteran, suffering from chronic pain and bleeding abscesses, was showing clear signs of exhaustion, and by the time he arrived in Massachusetts he was on the point of collapse. Nevertheless, he pressed on with rugged determination and good humor and, while resting at Boston's Tremont House, met with the various delegations that came to see him.

One of these delegations consisted of members of the Boston Charitable Irish Society, about a hundred strong, who marched in a body on June 22 to pay their respects to the visiting dignitary. Colonel William Prescott, president of the society, introduced the members to Jackson, first collectively and then individually, and the president greeted them warmly.[18] Delivering a brief speech for the occasion, Mr. James Boyd described the society as consisting "exclusively of Irishmen and their direct descendants" who were "industrious," hard at work like "bees in a hive," and supportive of the Constitution, the laws, and magistrates of "this our adopted country." Acknowledging that he was taking the opportunity to indulge in "some feelings of pride as well as of patriotism," he expressed the organization's "highest admiration" for the nation's chief magistrate—especially since he was the "son of an Irishman."[19] President Jackson thanked the society for its respectful greeting and expressed his pleasure at seeing so many "of the countrymen of my father." "I have always been proud of my ancestry and of being descended from that noble race," he told the assembled members. "Would to God, sir, that Irishmen on the other side of the great water enjoyed the comforts, happiness, contentment, and liberty that they enjoy here."[20] Following a day of enforced bed rest after an abscess ruptured and hemorrhaged, Jackson was ready to travel to Cambridge, where he was to be awarded an honorary Doctor of Laws degree by Harvard University. This was not at all to the liking of former president John Quincy Adams, an alumnus (class of '87), who told Harvard president Josiah Quincy that he could not bear to see his alma mater disgrace herself by conferring a degree upon a "barbarian" who couldn't write a grammatical sentence and "hardly could spell his name." But President Jackson accepted the degree, reportedly rattled off something like "*e pluribus unum*" as his response to the Latin part of the ceremony, and totally captivated the crowds that had come to see him.[21] Even young Josiah Quincy, son of Harvard's president, was forced to admit that he found Jackson "a knightly personage." Fully prepared to encounter an illiterate frontiersman who was "simply intolerable to the Brahmin caste of my native State," Quincy found the old general "a gentleman" in his "high sense of honor" and in the "natural straightforward courtesies" he displayed toward everyone.[22]

The increasing number of Irish Catholics in the city during the late 1820s and early 1830s, combined with what some observers saw as their expanding influence in political affairs — especially after Jackson's triumphant visit—was more than enough to rekindle old fears about the supposed threat of Roman Catholicism to Anglo-Saxon traditions, American freedoms, and democratic institutions. Samuel F. B. Morse, the famous artist-inventor, took up the pen in hopes of saving his country from what he perceived as a subversive papal conspiracy, insisting that every Catholic immigrant was a potential secret agent of a plot to take over America. The only way to prevent this catastrophe, he wrote, was to put an end to immigration itself. "Awake! To your posts! Place your guards . . . shut your gates!" he cried in alarm.[23] The same year, the Reverend Henry Ward Beecher, a well-known evangelist preacher, published a collection of sermons in which he elaborated upon the warnings of Morse and pointed to the Mississippi Valley as the immediate danger zone in the aggressive Catholic conspiracy to conquer America. Protestants everywhere must be constantly on guard against alien designs, he warned, and should be especially determined to offset the subversive influence of the growing number of Catholic schools in the United States.[24]

During the late 1820s, there had been sporadic outbreaks of violence against persons and property in Ann Street, Broad Street, and other Irish sections of the city near the waterfront. Throughout the summer months of July and August 1825, for example, the *Advertiser* reported "disgraceful riots" taking place almost every night by gangs who broke windows, damaged furniture, and destroyed "several small houses." The mayor and aldermen finally stationed six constables in the Irish district from ten o'clock at night until morning in an attempt to keep the peace.[25] By the 1830s, however, the forces of anti-Catholicism began to take a broader and more systematized offensive, directed by leading Protestant church groups in the area. During the early 1800s, a number of orthodox Protestant sects had banded together to form an evangelical opposition to what they regarded as the secularist and humanistic views of such new Protestant groups as the Unitarians and the Universalists. Soon, however, as the number of Roman Catholics began to increase substantially, this conservative association saw itself as an organized force capable of challenging a worldwide conspiracy to reestablish the menacing power of the Roman Catholic Church. The various agencies the association had formed to disseminate the Gospel, promote Anglo-Saxon virtues, and preserve the fundamental orthodoxy of Protestant teachings—the tract societies, the Bible societies, the missionary societies, the Sunday school societies—also took on the responsibility of pointing out the dangers of a resurgent "Romanism." Local weekly publications such as the *Boston Recorder* and the *Christian Watchman*, working in close association with a variety of New York–based newspapers and magazines such as *The Protestant*, the *New York Observer*, the *Christian Spectator*, and the *Home Missionary*, launched an all-out assault against what they saw as the insidious ideologies and the alien influences of "popery." By the late 1820s and early 1830s, a regular campaign of vituperation was being carried out in religious newspapers and journals, as well as in sermons, lecture programs, and public speeches. So-called native Americans denounced the "blasphemy" of Roman Catholic doctrine, the "immorality" of the Roman religion, the "idolatry" of the sacraments, the "cruelty" of the priests, and the "subversive" nature of papal authority.[26]

Catholic leaders in various parts of the country tried to answer the attacks on their religious beliefs and practices. They established newspapers of their own, set up tract societies to publish pamphlets explaining their beliefs, and organized public lectures to demonstrate the false and ridiculous nature of the charges being brought against them. In Boston, Bishop Benedict Fenwick, a Jesuit from Maryland who had taken over in 1825 as Bishop Cheverus's successor, authorized a weekly newspaper called *The Jesuit, or Catholic Sentinel,* which began publication in September 1829, in order to "explain, diffuse, and defend the principles of the One, Holy, Catholic, and Apostolic Church."[27] However, these new undertakings were too few in number to compete effectively with the large-scale efforts of the anti-Catholic press. In many cases, too, the Catholics' methods proved counterproductive. Too often, their newspaper articles assumed the shrill and argumentative tones of their adversaries. The influence of their publications was pretty much confined to their own constituencies, and their lecture programs all too frequently degenerated into raucous shouting matches. Even Fenwick's choice of *The Jesuit* as the title for his newspaper proved a serious tactical error, since the very word "Jesuit" symbolized to most Bostonians the worst excesses they associated with Catholicism. Nativists of the period usually singled out Jesuits as wily secret agents "prowling about" in all parts of the country "in every possible disguise," looking for effective ways to carry out the conspiracies of the Vatican and concocting schemes to "disseminate Popery."[28] The bishop eventually changed the name of the newspaper to *The Pilot,* which became a successful weekly publication catering to a predominantly Catholic readership.[29]

The newspaper competition became a secondary issue, however, as the anti-Catholic crusade spread rapidly beyond the printed page and the lecture platform. Rhetoric was replaced by innuendo as critics moved from condemning the doctrinal dangers of the Catholic Church to questioning its ecclesiastical practices which they maintained bred all sorts of personal vice and immorality. During the 1830s several American publishing houses revived a series of older anti-Catholic polemics, originally published in Europe a century earlier, whose suggestive titles and salacious subtitles represented a more subtle and even more vicious trend in the nativist crusade. While most of these works purported to expose the secret rites and elaborate intrigues of the "Popish religion," many of them actually made a special point of bringing to light the supposed licentious character of convents and nunneries where "lecherous" priests and "complaisant" nuns engaged in almost continuous acts of unspeakable sexual depravity. During the 1830s a rash of exposé literature made its appearance on the American scene, much of it designed to paint, in lurid details, the "real" "inside" story of what went on behind convent walls. "Escaped nuns" like Maria Monk, who published a totally fabricated story called *Awful Disclosures*, describing the terrible things that supposedly had happened to her at the Hôtel Dieu Nunnery at Montreal, found a ready-made market for their lascivious accounts of Catholic crime and abuse. "The traditional English image of the rude and undisciplined 'wild Irish,'" writes Dale Knobel, "nicely supplemented the notion that the immigrants were frightfully continental in their debauchery and self-indulgence."[30] Indeed, Boston experienced its own local version of this type of what one historian has called "the pornography of the Puritan" when a woman named Rebecca Reed made her appearance in town, claiming she had escaped from the Ursuline convent in nearby Charlestown, a large brick building where a small group of nuns lived and conducted a rather fashionable school for girls.[31] Miss Reed's harrowing tales of convent life, replete with cruel punishments and barbaric penances, provoked such excitement and consternation in the community that a group of enterprising citizens immediately exploited the situation. Putting the young woman's fantasies between the covers of a book entitled *Six Months in a Convent*, they produced within a year a best-selling novel. According to historian Ray Allen Billington, more than ten thousand copies were sold within the first week after publication, and some two hundred thousand copies were disposed of within the month, a remarkable demonstration of the popular market for such salacious literature.[32] When in late July 1834 one of the resident nuns suffered a nervous breakdown, wandered away from the Charlestown convent in a confused state, and had to be returned, local anti-Catholic groups were more certain than ever that Rebecca Reed's charges were true. Despite attempts by Bishop Fenwick to clarify the events connected with the nun's "disappearance," wild rumors circulated throughout Boston that helpless women were being forced to remain behind convent walls against their will. To people who had been brought up on a traditional Anglo-Saxon diet of Spanish inquisitions, Jesuit threats, Irish uprisings, gunpowder plots, and papal schemes, these terrifying stories seemed plausible.

By the first week in August, anti-Catholic feeling in Boston and Charlestown was running so high that it was uncertain how much longer the situation could be kept under control. In the midst of this excitement, the Reverend Lyman Beecher, who had recently left his post at the Hanover Street Church to accept the presidency of Lane Theological Seminary in Ohio, returned to Boston on a fund-raising tour. On Sunday night, August 10, Beecher delivered a series of thunderous anti-Catholic sermons in three Protestant churches in the area, repeating his earlier denunciations of Catholicism and calling upon his listeners to take decisive action against its resurgence in America.[33]

Given the general anti-Catholic sentiment of the times, the prolonged newspaper campaign, the vituperation of preachers like Reverend Beecher, the rash of shocking exposé literature, the dreadful stories of Rebecca Reed, and the persistent rumors about what was going on behind the walls of the Ursuline convent in Charlestown, the situation in Boston was primed for an explosion of violence. It came on the night of Monday, August 11, 1834, when a mob of forty or fifty laborers and truckmen smashed their way into the convent. After allowing the nuns and their students time to escape, the attackers set fire to the building while fire companies and a large crowd of people stood by and watched the structure burn to the ground. Prominent Bostonians publicly denounced the burning of the Ursuline convent, and leading Protestant journals officially protested against the use of violence in the anti-Catholic crusade. But there was little indication that such sentiments of regret reflected any basic change of attitude, and many were obviously glad to see the offensive

Nativist reaction against the influx of Irish Catholics to the Boston area finally erupted into violence on the night of August 11, 1834. An angry band of workingmen set fire to the convent in Charlestown, where a small group of Ursuline nuns operated a boarding school for children of local families.
Archdiocese of Boston.

convent gone. Although eight people eventually were brought to trial for the capital offense of arson, all were found not guilty—a verdict greeted with cheers of delight by their friends and neighbors who had packed the courtroom.[34]

As the Boston Irish had already learned from bitter experience under British rule, when intense social pressures create personal fears and financial insecurities, the upper class may provide the high-sounding polemics but it is the working class that throws the rocks and sets the fires. Over the years, local Yankee workmen in Boston representing a wide range of occupations—farmers, foresters, blacksmiths, masons, shopwrights, ropemakers, painters, carvers, and carpenters—had formed a strong and highly unified association. It was a close-knit society that frequently displayed its numbers and its solidarity by marching in public celebrations to commemorate such notable events as the ratification of the Constitution in 1788 and the fiftieth anniversary of the Declaration of Independence in 1826.[35] For a brief period, when jobs were plentiful and extra laborers were needed, local guilds tolerated Irish immigrants as part of the work force, either because they posed no threat to the local workers or because there were sufficient unskilled jobs to go around. But as the number of construction projects declined and as the rate of immigration went up noticeably, local workers became fearful that the impoverished and undesirable newcomers, with the brogue on their lips and mud on their boots, would work for slave wages and take away their jobs.

It was not the doctors or the lawyers, the merchants or the bankers, who feared the loss of their positions. They might have regarded the growing influx of foreigners as both distasteful and alarming, but they certainly did not anticipate losing their homes, their businesses, or their incomes. However, the same was not true of the day-laborer, the street sweeper, the lamplighter, the stableman, the gardener, or the truckman. Poor workingmen who made a meager living from unskilled occupations could easily see the Irishman as a potential rival, whose depressed standard of living would impel him to take the native worker's livelihood. Even members of the police and fire departments, whose uniformed ranks were reserved for able-bodied "American" candidates, could foresee the obvious economic consequences when immigrants eventually moved up the social ladder and demanded their rightful place on the city payroll.[36] Men confronted with such frightening possibilities were ready to lash out at any tangible evidence of growth or increasing prosperity in the immigrant population.

In the weeks and months that followed the burning of the Ursuline convent, Irish Catholics in Boston continued to be subjected to a relentless campaign of verbal abuse and physical harassment. Nativist attacks on Catholic property, not only in the city but throughout the state, became so frequent that many congregations were forced to place armed guards around their churches. And the first anniversary of the burning of the convent was commemorated with several public celebrations in Boston reminiscent of the old "Pope's Night" of Colonial days.[37] The level of hatred between Catholics and Protestants remained extremely high, and before another year had passed mob violence broke out in an incident that for a moment threatened to engulf the entire city. On June 11, 1837, a hot Sunday afternoon, a company of Yankee firemen, returning from a call, clashed at a downtown intersection with a Catholic funeral procession that was moving along Broad Street in the opposite direction. In a matter of minutes what started out as a fistfight had mushroomed into a full-scale riot. Nearly all the fire-engine companies in the city rushed to assist their comrades as fire bells sounded the alarm, while friends and relatives of the Irish mourners spilled out of their lodgings into the streets in order to help their own fighters. For more than two hours the battle raged up and down the streets of the lower part of the city where the immigrants lived, with an estimated ten thousand people watching eight hundred men fight it out with sticks and stones, bricks and cudgels. The so-called Broad Street Riot was finally halted only when Mayor Samuel Eliot brought in the National Lancers, followed by some eight hundred of the state militia, with fixed bayonets, to disperse the rioters and restore order to the city. Although fourteen Irishmen and four native Bostonians eventually were brought to trial, not a single Yankee was found guilty, while three of the four Irishmen were given jail sentences for their part in the riot.[38]

Even while the Broad Street Riot was still a topic of heated discussion, the Boston Irish suffered an even more insulting blow to their pride in an incident involving the militia. As the United States Army regular forces were greatly reduced after the War of 1812, volunteer militia companies were encouraged as a means of maintaining a basic line of defense and reviving popular interest in a citizen army. Throughout the nation, the number of volunteer companies greatly increased, reflecting both pride in the martial arts and enthusiasm for the companionship of friends and neighbors. The volunteers performed weekly drills, conducted periodic inspections, held annual tours of duty, designed their own fancy uniforms, and frequently put on military displays at their own expense. In addition to their soldierly duties, volunteers enjoyed a steady round of social activities in the form of gala banquets and military balls, where the elaborately uniformed soldiers were envied by the men and "beloved by the ladies."[39]

Volunteer militia companies of this kind were particularly appealing to Irish Americans, who were attracted by the uniforms, the parades, and the frequent social functions, as well as by the opportunity to put on public display their patriotism and their devotion to their newly adopted country. In cities like New York, Philadelphia, and New Orleans, newcomers formed Irish militia companies named after Richard Montgomery, an Irish-born brigadier general in the Continental army who had died leading an attack against English forces at Quebec. In January 1837, a group of Irish Americans in Boston, among whom were included Andrew Carney, Thomas Mooney, and Edwin Palmer, petitioned the Governor's Council for a charter to form such a militia company in Boston. The petition was duly granted, and the group became the Tenth Company of Light Infantry, Regiment of Light Infantry, Third Brigade, First Division, Massachusetts Volunteer Militia—better known as "the Montgomery Guards." Making their first appearance, ironically, as part of the military force that was sent in to put down the Broad Street Riot, the new organization was greeted with approval by most city officials. On June 17, only about a week after the riot, Governor Edward Everett himself reviewed the Montgomery Guards' first parade, which ended with a formal banquet at the Concert Hall, followed by a "collation" at the home of Andrew Carney on Ann Street. The *Boston Morning Post* reported that the ranks of the Irish company were full, their discipline good, and their maneuvering "excellent." The *Boston Daily Atlas* welcomed the new militia unit as a good example to the other Irish of the city—and a useful force in case of any further disturbances.[40]

There were many other Bostonians, however, in whom the sight of a green uniform trimmed in scarlet and gold and a military cap with the harp of Erin surmounted by the American eagle provoked feelings of anger and revulsion. Already alarmed by the flood of anti-Catholic literature depicting Irish immigrants as the dangerous vanguard of a new Papist conspiracy to take over America, nativists were appalled at the idea of providing these outsiders, who had "no sense of Union with America," with both weapons of war and the military training to use them. Charges were made that the governor had authorized the Irish company in response to intense political pressure, and rumors of "foreign influence" began to circulate through the city. Before long, the other militia companies in the Regiment of Light Infantry were seething with anger at the governor for admitting "low foreigners" to their ranks.[41] Rising tensions finally exploded in an embarrassing display of public bigotry on the day of the annual Fall Muster on Boston Common.

Early in the morning of September 12, 1837, the ten companies that made up the infantry contingent of the Boston Brigade gathered at their armories and then marched through the streets of the city to form their traditional brigade line on the Common. In order of precedence, the oldest companies took the lead, with the newest company—the Montgomery Guards—bringing up the rear. Just as the companies finished moving into line, a prearranged signal was given and the enlisted men of the City Guard proceeded to march off the field with the American flag flying, the band playing "Yankee Doodle," and their officers still standing at attention on the line. It was a planned insult to the new Irish company. One by one, five other infantry companies—the Lafayette Guards, the Independent Fusiliers, the Washington Light Infantry, half the Mechanics Rifles, and finally the Winslow Guards—marched off the field and returned to their armories. This left the Montgomery Guards to go through the prescribed maneuvers with only three remaining infantry companies for the rest of the afternoon, to the taunts and jeers of spectators who were enjoying the humiliating spectacle.[42]

When the brigade was finally dismissed about 6 P.M., the green-clad Montgomery Guards were forced to march across town to their armory through streets lined with hostile crowds, which subjected them to verbal abuse and physical attacks. As they marched along Tremont Street, past St. Paul's Church, they were pelted with bottles, rocks, and pieces of coal. One man was tripped, his weapon taken and broken; another was struck with a paving stone. The constables of the city made no effort to intervene, and at no time did any of the other militia companies came to the assistance of their Irish comrades. By the time the Montgomery Guards arrived at Dock Square, near Faneuil Hall, an estimated 3,000 people had surrounded their armory and threatened to storm the building. Only the appearance of Mayor Eliot and a number of prominent citizens caused the rioters to disperse and prevented any further trouble.[43]

Although the city newspapers censured the six militia companies that had walked off the field, denounced the "miserable vagabonds" who had rioted in Dock Square, and praised the Montgomery Guards for their discipline and forbearance in the face of such a "dastardly outrage," the final results were far from encouraging to the Boston Irish.[44] While three civilian rioters were sent to jail, none of the militia officers was prosecuted, and the offending infantry companies celebrated what they had done with a highly publicized routine of parades, banquets, and shooting matches, while city and state authorities argued among themselves about what official action to take. Under intense pressure from all sides, Governor Everett finally resorted to a strategem intended to uphold the letter of the law and prevent further disorder. First, in February 1838, he ordered the disbandment of the six mutinous infantry companies for publicly deserting their duties and provoking the riot. Three months later, in April, he ordered the disbandment of the Montgomery Guards on the grounds that the reappearance of the Irish company would be a signal for "outrages of a dangerous character." Within six months, all six of the mutinous companies had been rechartered under different names but with the same officers and the same enlisted personnel. The Montgomery Guards, on the other hand, made no such reappearance.[45] The people of Boston could now sit back and take comfort in the knowledge that an armed militia company of Irish Americans—a "distinct foreign corps," as the other companies referred to it—would no longer threaten the peace and safety of their community.

There were many who wondered why the Irish had come to Boston, and in light of the increasing harassment directed at the small immigrant community, many wondered why they stayed. Why didn't they move west as so many other immigrant groups had done, as Horace Greeley so emphatically urged, and as so many Bostonians suggested? Edward Everett, for example, in a letter to the Anglican archbishop of Dublin discussing the problems created by the unprecedented number of immigrants, described the vast expanse of the West as a gigantic "safety valve" that could easily funnel off the surplus supply of unskilled labor that plagued East Coast cities like Boston.[46] And Everett's nephew, Edward Everett Hale, a young Unitarian clergyman, also argued that westward migration would not only lessen the economic problems of the Irish but also ease the anxieties of the Yankees by greatly reducing the dangers of a Papist revival in America.[47] Benedict Fenwick, who had succeeded Cheverus as Roman Catholic bishop of Boston in 1825, was also sympathetic to the idea of moving the Irish out of the dismal hovels and cellars of their unsanitary waterfront location and sending them off to the fresh air and green fields of the country. At a time when a general reaction against the crowding and pollution of an industrial urban environment had produced throughout America utopian communities like New Harmony in Indiana, the Amana Community in New York, and the transcendentalist experiment at Brook Farm just outside Boston, Bishop Fenwick purchased a tract of eleven thousand acres in Aroostook County, Maine, where he planned his own utopian community called "Benedicta." He visited the site frequently, personally supervised the dredging of a canal, constructed a sawmill, and designed a Catholic college and seminary. But his parishioners never came. The Irish immigrants, despite all their difficulties in the city, showed no enthusiasm for living out their lives in the isolated woodlands of Aroostook County, and the utopian experiment collapsed.[48]

The traditional explanation for the reluctance of the Irish to abandon Boston's crowded waterfront in favor of a better life in the West is that the immigrants were so desperately poor that they could not afford even the nominal transportation rates of the period. But Fenwick's offer to help the Irish move to Maine and the encouragement his successor, Bishop John Fitzpatrick, gave the local Irish Immigrant Society in helping immigrants move to the western territories clearly indicate that, while the lack of money was certainly a consideration, it is not the ultimate explanation.[49] Basically, the Irish were a gregarious people, devoted to clan, family, and religion, with little experience in large-scale farming and no inclination to see their sons and daughters scattered to the four winds. They preferred to remain in Boston, close to their friends, their relatives, their priests, their sacraments, and their pubs. As a people, they had already lost so much by uprooting themselves from their native soil and leaving behind their beloved cultural traditions that they were determined not to

A sketch that appeared in Ballou's Pictorial Drawing-Room Companion *in 1857 shows the arrival of Irish immigrants at the port of Boston. The newcomer and his family are being met by relatives with whom they will probably stay until they can afford lodgings of their own. During this period, the Irish immigrant population was still concentrated along the Boston waterfront, from Fort Hill to the North End.*

lose any more. In the unity of togetherness, there was not only the strength and security they desperately needed in a hostile environment, but also the last opportunity to preserve whatever remained of their Celtic identity. The small piece of turf they had carved out along the shabby waterfront might be unsightly and unsanitary, but it was *theirs*, and they did not intend to give it up. They had fled the poverty of Ireland, survived the terrible Atlantic crossing, made it safely ashore, and established new roots in a new land. Like it or not, they were going to stay right where they were, and no one was going to make them leave. This was their beachhead for tomorrow.

The determination of the Irish to remain in Boston and the appearance there of more and more Irish faces raised the level of anxiety among natives of the city—especially as the number of registered Irish voters grew, reaching one thousand by 1840. Leading members of the anti-Jackson forces, who now called themselves "Whigs," used the potential threat of

Irish political power to bolster support for their own party and urged that steps be taken to monitor political recruitment by the rival party. Without mentioning the Irish by name, the conservative *Boston Daily Atlas* urged city officials to "purify the lists" by removing the names of dead people, aliens who were not naturalized, tax evaders, and people who had moved out of the city.

Tangible signs that the Irish were, indeed, becoming a political force to be reckoned with appeared in 1843, when *The Pilot*, now the city's principal Catholic weekly, undertook a campaign to defeat certain members of the state legislature. For several years after the burning of the Ursuline convent, *The Pilot* had regularly denounced that act of violence as unparalleled in the "annals of riot and rapine" and had repeatedly demanded that the victims be indemnified for their losses.[50] Leading citizens of Boston, many of them prominent Whigs, had also denounced the attack on the convent and urged the state legislature to pay damages to the Sisters. These efforts proved fruitless, however, and even a bill introduced by the businessman Abbott Lawrence calling for an inquiry into the facts of the case was defeated. *The Pilot* concluded on March 18, 1843, that the power of "mob law" had been sanctioned "in the most solemn and emphatic manner."[51] One week later, the newspaper urged its Catholic readers to take refuge in the ballot box, claiming that otherwise they would be deprived of protection, government, and country.[52] *The Pilot* had been hammering at this point for some time. Consistently, it expressed disappointment at the failure of many Irish to become registered voters, complaining that only one-third of the eligible Irishmen had become naturalized citizens. If more Irishmen had been going to the polls, the paper insisted, the community might have been spared the violence of the 1830s.[53] Frustrated at the outcome of the indemnity proposals, on April 1, 1843, *The Pilot* called upon its estimated 7,000 subscribers to organize a political campaign to elect a new slate of state legislators who would be sympathetic to the Catholic position on this issue. The paper urged its readers to put aside their political differences and work together to achieve this result. Since more conservative, upper-middle-class, property-minded Whigs were generally less hostile to the Catholic position than most rural Democrats, The Pilot was actually calling upon its Irish readers to renounce their usual Democratic loyalties and to cast their votes for the Whig candidates in the November elections. There were, said the editor, in an effort to rationalize the paper's position, "bigots in both parties"; he observed that Democratic governors had been no more helpful than Whig governors in helping the Catholic cause.[54] "There cannot possibly be any skulking the issue next fall," concluded The Pilot in urging this bipartisan effort, adding that "the man who is not with us must expect to be denounced as against us."[55]

But this single-issue approach to bipartisan politics proved a complete failure. Only five of the legislative candidates who had been labeled "bigots" and targeted by The Pilot for defeat lost their reelection bids in November. The Irish voters had either continued to vote for their Democratic favorites or stayed away from the polls entirely.[56] The failure of The Pilot's campaign to organize an Irish voting bloc revealed the political weakness of the Catholic population in Massachusetts, but it also revived old-time fears among those who saw the not-too-subtle hand of Roman Catholic clerical influence behind the scenes—fears further inflamed the following year by events associated with the presidential campaign of 1844. When the Whig candidate, Henry Clay, went down to defeat along with his vice-presidential candidate, Theodore Frelinghuysen, an outspoken opponent of Catholicism, the defeated Whigs angrily blamed Clay's defeat on the Irish vote. They claimed that a large bloc of fraudulent alien voters in New York was responsible for swinging that state's critical electoral votes to the Democratic victor, James K. Polk.

Locally, the Boston Courier picked up the theme and led the attack on Irish Catholic influence in the city in the aftermath of the election. The paper argued that the recent increase in riots and taxes in Boston was due to the types of Irish who were residents of the city, claiming that the more intelligent and industrious immigrants were those who had moved into the interior of the country.[57] It warned foreigners who made their homes in Boston that there was still a large enough number of native-born Americans around to bring to "a just punishment" those who attempted to disturb the peace of the community. While it insisted that it had no desire to awaken "sectarian animosity," the *Courier* nevertheless resurrected the old spectre of clerical influence by reminding its readers that politically active Catholics of foreign birth would vote "precisely as their spiritual guides shall dictate." The paper blamed the election of Polk on the influence of Catholic priests who were out to secure the dominion of that "arrogant blasphemer," the pope—as part of a "well-connected scheme" among the Catholic powers of Europe to bring the United States "under subjection to the Holy See."[58] Nothing less than the absolute exclusion of everyone born on foreign ground from the privilege of voting, it concluded, "would ever secure the people of this country from foreign domination."[59]

In the face of such onslaughts from the Whigs, the Irish became wedded more solidly than ever to the Democratic party. But while allying themselves to the Democrats might have been emotionally satisfying, it did little to enhance the political position of the Irish, who were part of what was, for all practical purposes, a minority party. Throughout the 1830s and 1840s, it was the Whig party that occupied the governor's office, controlled both houses of the state legislature almost without interruption, and managed the city of Boston, as one disgruntled Democrat put it, with "its overwhelming Whig majority, Whig money, and Whig influence."[60] The success of the Whigs' consistently probusiness policies of financial planning, credit financing, and diversified investment had produced an economic growth rate that earned the Bay State a reputation as "the model Commonwealth" and ensured the party's political acceptance among the voters. With virtually all forms of state and local patronage securely in Whig hands, there was little incentive for the ordinary Irishman to become a naturalized voter and an active citizen. Furthermore, the Democratic party was, in the words of one recent historian, "an establishment party" itself, with an an ideology as basically probusiness as that of the Whigs. Called "Hunker" Democrats because they hunkered after office, Democratic leaders like wealthy businessman David Henshaw, *Boston Post* publisher Charles Greene, and Boston lawyer Benjamin Hallet seldom carried their rhetorical denunciations of special favors or promises of economic reforms into legislative practice.[61] Nor did they provide much opportunity for their Irish Catholic supporters, whose votes they courted, to move up in the ranks of party hierarchy. Occasionally, Democratic party leaders nominated an Irish Catholic for some minor office as a gesture of appeasement, but usually there were enough Protestant members of the party to make sure no Irish-Catholic names appeared on the final ballot.[62] Although the local Democrats regularly lost out on the benefits of state patronage because of their failure to win state elections, by holding their organization together and conforming to the dictates of the national Democratic party the Hunkers were able to reap the substantial rewards of federal patronage. "There are Democrats in Massachusetts who have done nothing else but work in aid of the Whig party," complained one perceptive rural activist. "They want to keep the Democratic party conveniently small so that they and their friends may absorb all the spoils which fall to the State."[63] There may have been two major political parties in Boston at this time, but Irish Catholics were not an influential force in either one of them.

3

KNOW-NOTHINGS

AND UNIONISTS

IF THE INFLUX of Irish Catholics alarmed native Bostonians during the 1820s and 1830s, the unprecedented flood of immigration from Ireland during the late 1840s and early 1850s shocked local residents into even greater expressions of fear and apprehension. Late in 1845, American newspapers reported that a strange disease had attacked the Irish potato crop, the mainstay of the poor people's diet. At first, few appreciated the seriousness of the disease, and in anticipation of a mild and pleasant spring many American publications calmly assured their readers of an "abundant" crop and a "luxuriant" harvest.[1] But early in 1846 the deadly fungus broke out again, and by the end of the summer Ireland's entire crop of potatoes lay in ruins. By the end of September, many Irish towns had not a single loaf of bread or pound of meal to feed their hungry people. During a terrible winter, drenching rains and icy gales made outdoor work impossible; snowstorms blanketed the fields and closed the roads. Without land to work, firewood to burn, or food to eat, the poor people of Ireland died by the tens of thousands of hunger, exposure, and disease.[2] For many, especially in the Catholic southern counties where the devastation was the worst, there seemed to be no future at all. The land was ruined; food was unobtainable; work was unavailable; and eviction was inescapable. Scraping together what little money they could, the Irish booked passage to America in unprecedented numbers—many leaving in vessels so poorly constructed they were called "coffin ships."[3]

The city of Boston, with its large Irish-Catholic population, was one of the first American communities to respond to the disaster that had befallen the poor people of Ireland. Bishop John Bernard Fitzpatrick who had succeeded Fenwick as bishop of Boston in 1846, called upon his congregation to share their "last loaf of bread" with those unfortunate souls whose "wild shrieks of famine and despair" could be heard across the Atlantic.[4] In addition to the generous gifts of money sent to Ireland by the Catholics of Boston, estimated to have reached $150,000 before the famine was finally over, the city's non-Catholic residents also made substantial contributions toward the relief of the Irish people. In March 1847, several Boston merchants succeeded in getting the United States Congress to let them use the *Jamestown*, a sloop of war at the Charlestown Navy Yard, to transport provisions to the famine-stricken country. The ship was commanded by Captain Robert Bennet Forbes, a member of one of Boston's best-known families. A volunteer crew was enlisted, and on St. Patrick's Day the all-Irish members of the Boston Laborers' Aid Society turned out to load the vessel free of charge. On March 27, carrying eight hundred tons of grain, meal, potatoes, other foodstuffs, and clothing, the *Jamestown* set sail from Boston Harbor. Fifteen days later, the ship put into Cork Harbor to the cheers of throngs along the shore, who shouted greetings to their American benefactors while a band played "Yankee Doodle."[5]

Although most Americans must have expected some increase in Irish immigration as a result of the famine, it is clear that they did not anticipate the huge tidal wave that engulfed them. In 1847, for example—in a single year—the city of Boston, which had been absorbing immigrants at the rate of 4,000 or 5,000 a year, was inundated by 37,000 new arrivals. "This transfer of immense bodies of people, from one climate, government, and state of society, to another wholly different," observed Edward Everett Hale, "is the most remarkable social phenomenon of our times." Reverend Theodore Parker remarked that in a single decade Suffolk County had become a "New England County Cork," and the city of Boston, he said, had turned into "the Dublin of America."[6] Bostonians had never found it easy to accept foreign immigrants, especially the Irish, but at least those who had arrived during the 1820s and 1830s had been robust—strong enough to cut down the hills and fill in the coves. Most of the "Famine Irish," however, came ashore pallid and weak, half-starved, disease-ridden, and impoverished. Few had any skills at all, and the recent investment of a substantial part of Boston's financial resources in the cotton mills at Lowell and Lawrence left few opportunities in the city for unskilled laborers.

By the 1840s, the Yankee-dominated city of Boston was no more hospitable to Irish Catholics than it had been during the 1820s or the 1830s. The traditional contempt of Anglo-Saxons for the Irish people had not subsided to any great degree, and the Anglo-Saxons' abhorrence of Roman Catholicism was as intense as ever. As unskilled laborers, the new immigrants posed an even greater threat to a local labor market that could not possibly absorb them; as impecunious squatters they were seen as a serious danger to social standards and cultural attainments. The Irish had the misfortune of coming to a city that was already more than two hundred years old—positively ancient in terms of American cities—with a reputation that was awesome and a civic identity that was truly intimidating. The Yankee past, as William V. Shannon has observed, had produced the American Revolution, the Old North Church, Faneuil Hall, and Bunker Hill, along with families like the Otises, the Hancocks, and the Adamses. And in more recent years, the transcendentalist movement had turned out such incomparable literary talents as Emerson, Longfellow, Hawthorne, and Thoreau. "The weight of this history," writes Shannon, "could not help but produce in the Irish a massive inferiority complex. At every turn, society seemed to be looming up and asking: What achievements and leaders do you have to compare with these?"[7] The Irish immigrants who traveled to Chicago, St. Louis, Cincinnati, and other new cities of the West, Shannon reminds us, had the advantage of being in at the start and growing up with their cities. Those who settled in New York and Philadelphia lived among social, economic, and ethnic groups that were much more diverse in their origins and more receptive in their attitudes. The Irish who came to Boston, however, found themselves among homogeneous and prestigious native families that were justly proud of their accomplishments, strongly attached to their history, and staunchly determined not to share their heritage with those they did not deem worthy.[8]

The city's financial hierarchy was as rigidly defined and as tightly closed as its social structure. By the time the Irish were arriving in significant numbers, a great many of Boston's oldest and most prestigious mercantile families, which had grown fabulously rich on the trade they had conducted for generations with Europe and the Orient, had begun to share their fortunes with the new textile manufacturers of cotton cloth and fancy fabrics. In a very short time, old money merged with new money and old blood mixed with new blood, as the children of the Lowells, the Cabots, and the Amorys joined in marriage with the children of the Jacksons, the Lawrences, and the Appletons to create a new generation of urban aristocrats, which Oliver Wendell Holmes labeled "Brahmins."[9] With their "houses by Bulfinch, their monopoly of Beacon Street, their ancestral portraits and Chinese porcelains, humanitarianism, Unitarian faith in the march of the mind, Yankee shrewdness, and New England exclusiveness," this new generation combined the pride of place, the prestige of family, and the power of money to form an established order that would influence the course of the city's history for generations to come. Like the priestly Brahmin class of the ancient Hindus of India—the exalted persons who performed the sacred rites and set the moral standards—the new leaders of Boston society assumed a leading role in a modern caste system in which they were indisputably the superior force. Having combined their capital, their enterprises, and their talents in a profitable association of commercial trade and industrial textile production—completing what Samuel Eliot Morison described as the shift from the wharf to the waterfall—old mercantile families found the new diversification not at all unacceptable.[10] As Robert Dalzell has observed in his *Enterprising Elite*, many Bostonians found that manufacturing offered a steadier income than trade, and it provided more leisure to pursue political careers, patronize the arts, or engage in philanthropic and humanitarian enterprises. Members of the Boston Associates provided endowments to Harvard College and generously supported the Massachusetts General

Hospital; they subsidized the Massachusetts Historical Society and maintained the New England Genealogical Society; they subscribed to the Boston Athenaeum and contributed to the construction of the Bunker Hill monument. As the Irish flooded into the city during the mid-1850s they confronted the solid ranks of a Brahmin class that dominated virtually the whole range of the city's civic, cultural, and educational institutions.

Faced with a world in which they could never hope to be accepted, and encountering a social order they could never expect to penetrate, most of the newly arrived Irish simply stayed by themselves. They moved in with friends and relatives in congested districts along the waterfront, close to the docks and the wharves, where men might find occasional work and extra scraps of food while their wives and sisters took jobs as domestics in nearby homes and hotels. They became, as Oscar Handlin expressed it in his classic study *Boston's Immigrants*, "a massive lump in the community, undigested and undigestible."[11]

Native Bostonians might have been willing to send money and food to aid the starving Irish as long as they remained in Ireland, but they certainly didn't want them coming to America. And when the Irish did arrive, their impact on the community sent local residents into violent reactions. The native Bostonians were appalled at the unsanitary living conditions of the newcomers and complained that they were turning Massachusetts into a "moral cesspool." "Foreign paupers are rapidly accumulating on our hands," warned Mayor John Prescott Bigelow in 1850, telling sympathetic taxpayers about the large numbers of "aged, blind, paralytic, and lunatic immigrants who have become charges on our public charities." He complained that the immigrants were living in "filth and wretchedness," all crowded together in "foul and confined apartments."[12] "The increase in foreign-born pauperism in our midst is an evil," agreed the *Boston Daily Advertiser*, "the consideration of which we adjourn until it will, perhaps, be too late to apply a remedy."[13] And the crimes! The increase in drunkenness and violence, the failure of judges to hand down tough sentences, and the easy access to pardons, complained Mayor Bigelow, showed how the city's lenient and "philanthropic" society benefited the criminal rather than safeguarding the innocent.[14] The Reverend Theodore Parker found the Irish to be "idle, thriftless, poor, intemperate, and barbarian," little more than "wild bison" ready to leap over the fences that usually restrained the "civilized domestic cattle."[15] Horrified Bostonians read of two stillborn infants found buried in a rubbish heap, placed there by Irish parents ignorant of American burial laws. They read of one Irishman in Charlestown killing another over a card game, and of another who beat his wife to death with a barrel stave.[16] Editorials in the *Advertiser* expressed particular alarm over the increase in juvenile crime, with nearly three thousand children, "vicious, criminal, profligate, and abandoned," reported to be leading infamous lives of begging, pilfering, and other "degrading practices." The children committing these crimes were mostly the children of Irish immigrants, charged the paper, "who imported their vile propensities and habits from across the water" and who were now passing them along to their "wretched offspring."[17]

The bitter words of editorials like these point out clearly that one of the characteristics native Bostonians found most repulsive in the immigrants who were fast populating the town was their propensity for public drinking. As early as the sixteenth century, travelers who made their way through the countryside of Ireland invariably commented the grinding poverty of the malnourished and half-naked peasants. Visitors also expressed shock at the widespread drunkenness, which was a crippling problem in the everyday lives of poor Irish families. In recent years, scholars have attempted to analyze the factors that made alcohol so prominent in Irish culture. Economists have emphasized the depressing effects of life in a rural society in which there was so little land, work, or incentive that the escape into drink often seemed the only solace available to the poor. Sociologists have pointed out the behavioral influences of a society where the shortage of land discouraged early marriage, where the sexes were carefully separated before marriage, and where male bonding was encouraged by rowdy horseplay and copious bouts of drinking. And historians have underlined the serious consequences of what Kerby Miller calls the "creeping Anglicanization" that moved through Ireland during the late eighteenth and early nineteenth centuries. In many parts of Ireland, the growing distance between the poorer classes, which clung to the Irish language and the traditional customs of the rural countryside, and the more affluent classes, which adopted the English language, the modern ways, and the more rational methods of the Enlightenment, mirrored a generational gap so wide that in some districts that parents and children could scarcely communicate with each other. Miller suggests that the resulting "cultural demoralization" may help explain why, during the 1820s and 1830s, especially, whiskey drinking among the poor people of Ireland appears to have assumed almost "pathological proportions."[18]

To a great extent, the Irish brought their drinking habits with them when they came to America. Grog shops, barrooms, and saloons sprang up overnight in the East Coast cities populated by the Irish. Boston felt the impact almost immediately. In 1846, for example, the city had 850 licensed liquor dealers; three years later, it had 1,200 dealers, most of whom were Irish. The following year, the mayor of Boston reported that two-thirds of the local grog shops were owned by the Irish and pointed out that almost half of those shops were concentrated in the area between Fort Hill and the North End, where the immigrant population was at its greatest.[19] In a country where they found themselves rejected and isolated, Irishmen looked upon the saloon as "the poor man's club," a natural transfer of the familiar pub that had always played such an important role in the social life of the Irish countryside. It was seen as one way of humanizing the cold, impersonal, and hostile urban environment in which the immigrants found themselves without work, without money, and without status. The saloon quickly became the social center of most Irish neighborhoods. It was one of the few places where a poor, tired Irishman could go on his way home from work or job hunting, receive a warm welcome, rest his weary bones, forget about his problems, and experience a few hours of joy and laughter.[20] In Boston, as in most American cities, the saloon also came to be recognized as a key center of political activity—a veritable "political powerhouse." Party leaders recruited new voters, indoctrinated inexperienced ward heelers, and prepared newcomers for eventual citizenship. Bartenders handed out application forms for naturalization, provided free legal advice, and loaned out money to those in need. And it was certainly no coincidence that a number of Boston's future political bosses would start their careers as saloon keepers, pub owners, and purveyors of alcoholic beverages.[21]

Local Catholic church leaders in Boston, however, were only too conscious of how local Yankees saw excessive drinking as further proof of the instability of the Irish people and a serious obstacle to their eventual assimilation. *The Pilot* constantly warned about the dangers of intemperate drinking among Catholics and on one occasion described the disgraceful effects of alcohol at some Irish wakes, where crowds of people stood around "drinking and smoking as they would in a common bar room." Just as bad were the hack drivers returning from funerals roaring drunk, driving at a furious "neck-breaking speed," singing and screaming at the top of their lungs. The road to success in America, advised the Catholic weekly, was not through talking, singing, and dancing but through hard work, perseverance, prudence, and—above all—sobriety.[22] In these editorials, the paper echoed the sentiments of Bishop John Fitzpatrick, who strongly encouraged temperance and who regularly urged the members of his flock to become good Americans and behave properly, so that no one could accuse them of being lazy, apathetic, or careless.[23] During the 1830s and 1840s, a number of Catholic temperance societies were established in Boston, and several priests made energetic efforts to warn their parishioners about the dangers of "the fruit of the bewitching glass" and rescue them from "the premature grave of intemperance."[24]

Although he deplored the effects of alcoholism among the Irish and especially among many of his own priests, Bishop Fitzpatrick did not look kindly upon the visit in 1849 of the famous Irish temperance priest, Father Theobald Mathew. The charismatic Capuchin friar had proved to be such a powerful lecturer on the evils of liquor, persuading thousands of his countrymen to take the solemn pledge of total abstinence, that Protestant temperance leaders invited him to come to America to preach. Fitzpatrick had serious reservations about Father Mathew's cooperation with non-Catholic groups that had moved beyond mere temperance and were promoting state-regulated prohibition. The true remedy, he believed, lay in individual moderation or abstinence—not in government regulation or prohibition. As long as the use of alcoholic beverages was not an evil *per* se, he argued, then Catholics should have the opportunity to use their free will and exercise "individual conscience" without the interposition of the government.[25] Then, too, the conservative bishop of Boston was always suspicious of extremist reformers and liberal agitators who sought to change the established order—especially when most of them were notoriously anti-Catholic and anti-Irish. Because Father Mathew was a guest in the United States, Bishop Fitzpatrick feared the Irish priest would fall under the controlling influence of the "public authorities" as well as the "ultra reformers" and the "pseudo philanthropists." The sight of a Roman Catholic priest like Father Mathew appearing on a public platform in Boston with "sectarian fanatics, calvinist preachers, idolaters, and other such," offended Fitzpatrick's sensibilities and caused him to conclude that such associations would inevitably produce "evil results." If there were reforms to be made and weaknesses to be overcome, he was determined that the Irish should achieve their purposes in their own time and in their own way, without joining forces with the Protestants.[26]

A generation earlier, the Irish working classes had generally ignored the conservative appeals of Bishop Cheverus and Father Matignon, who had asked them to support Hamiltonian programs and to vote for Federalist candidates. The parishioners made it clear that they favored Jeffersonian policies and Democratic principles. Similarly, the Irish ignored Fitzpatrick's arguments on behalf of well-bred and well-educated Whig candidates and favored Jacksonian Democrats and popular causes. Except for an occasional incident when the immigrant voters shifted their allegiance to gain a specific objective or a momentary advantage, the rank and file continued to show that the political preference of the church hierarchy had little or no effect on the way they marked their ballots. Fitzpatrick obviously regretted the short-sighted tendency of his parishioners to support uncouth demagogues for public office, but he hoped that with time, education, and experience they would see the light.[27]

But if Bishop Fitzpatrick failed to have much of a direct influence on the political decisions of his parishioners in terms of individual candidates and day-to-day issues, he may have had an indirect, subtle, and significant influence on the long-range political attitudes of the Boston Irish. Fitzpatrick assumed office in 1846, at a time in history when Western Europe was convulsed by radical uprisings, socialist upheavals, and republican revolutions. Secret societies, subversive groups, and underground organizations—the Freemasons in France, the *Carbonari* in the Italian states, the *Tugenbund* in the German states—conspired to overthrow monarchies and bring down the Church. As a Catholic bishop with traditional views and establishment leanings, Fitzpatrick was determined that no such radical movements or liberal organizations would get a foothold in his diocese. He was obviously pleased when the Sixth Provincial Council of Baltimore officially condemned all "secret societies," and in the columns of *The Pilot* he urged immigrants in Boston to avoid all clubs, societies, and associations that encouraged bigotry, clannishness, or separatism. He was constantly on the alert against signs of any group that might violate his standing rule that no "secret society" would be tolerated in his diocese; on one occasion he refused to approve a charter for the Ancient Order of Hibernians because he felt its wording was suggestive of a secret society.[28] His emphasis on Americanism, loyalty, and the maintenance of good order, together with his obsessive opposition to anything he considered liberal, radical, or "red," may well have accentuated an already well-defined strain of political conservatism among the Boston Irish. For an immigrant people whose loyalty was constantly under attack, whose patriotism was always subject to question, and whose ability to become fully assimilated into the American democratic system was flatly denied— especially in the homogeneous Anglo-Saxon society of Boston—the warning words of Bishop Fitzpatrick may well have pointed out the road that eventually led to their acceptance in the larger society. In his view, by avoiding liberal causes and radical associations, by disassociating themselves from reform movements and social agitations, by refraining from activities that might disturb the prevailing class structure and promote economic discontent, by refusing to question the views of duly elected officials or ecclesiastical superiors, the Irish might establish themselves as good, loyal, obedient, trustworthy citizens of the Republic who would eventually be fully accepted as true "Americans." The terrible fears and pressures that overwhelmed the Irish immigrants in mid-nineteenth-century Boston can be seen as helping to shape the distinctive character of their defensive and parochial political attitudes well into the twentieth century. For the time being, however, it was doubtful whether the immigrants would be given even an initial opportunity to establish a place for themselves in Boston.

In the face of continued problems of public intoxication, increasing numbers of arrests and imprisonments, and a growing tax rate, local residents readily agreed that the immigrants were placing undue burdens on the city's social and charitable institutions, hospitals and asylums, and police and fire departments and were forcing up tax rates and pulling down property values. The fact that so many of the newcomers were members of the despised Roman Catholic Church was an additional source of anxiety to those who believed that few of the immigrants would ever escape the influence of their foreign-born church leaders and become responsible members of a democratic society. The new citizens, it appeared, were incapable of leaving behind them their native land and its numerous problems. Immigrants followed events in the Old Country through special columns and features in *The Pilot*; joined organizations such as the Irish Repeal Association, the American League for the Redemption of Ireland, the United Friends of Ireland; and frequently urged the United States government to become involved in Ireland's continuing

WANTED—A good, reliable woman to take the care of a boy two years old, in a small family in Brookline. Good wages and a permanent situation given. No washing or ironing will be required, but good recommendations as to character and capacity demanded. Postively no Irish need apply. Call at 224 Washington street, corner of Summer street.
6t   jy 28

Coming to Boston in the nineteenth century, the Irish were confronted by rejection, segregation, and discrimination. Here one Boston newspaper prints an advertisement for a reliable housekeeper for a home in Brookline, but warns that "Positively no Irish need apply." This was the attitude faced by both men and women in their search for jobs in the New World.

struggle for independence. Native-born Americans constantly cited these activities as proof of the Irishman's inability to free himself of his past loyalties. Unable to think like an American, they said, the Irishman would never have America's interests uppermost in his heart.[29] Already, there were local native-born Americans who opposed providing public funds to assist immigrants any further and who were spoiling for trouble. Early in June 1847, some nativists distributed handbills calling for the destruction of the hospital facilities on nearby Deer Island that were used to treat incoming "FOREIGN PAUPERS." They called upon "AMERICAN CITIZENS" to be "IN AT THE DEATH" when local patriotic groups tried to provoke another uprising like the one that had led to the burning of the Ursuline convent thirteen years earlier.[30]

Fortunately, the confrontation failed to materialize, but the handbills were indicative of the angry mood of a city with solid Puritan values watching as the number of Irish Catholic immigrants increased every day. Between 1850 and 1855, the Irish accounted for almost half of the total increase in the state's population, a ratio that was reflected in the city's voting statistics. In Boston, during the same five-year period, the native-born vote grew only 14.7 percent while the foreign-born vote, largely Irish, rose at the incredible rate of 194.6 percent—a development that caused native Bostonians to take more seriously the threat of a solid Irish voting bloc.[31]

In his dispensable work dealing with the settlement of the Irish in nineteenth-century Boston, Oscar Handlin argued that during the decade from 1845 to 1855, the breakdown of the old political parties "yielded to the unified Irish the balance of power." While some contemporary observers may have believed this to be true, the Boston Irish were, in fact, no more unified as a political entity than either of the major parties. Although their growing numbers occasionally created an opportunity to exercise a swing vote, the Irish had not at all reached the point where they were capable of playing a decisive role in Boston's politics. They had no leaders, no political funds, and no machine of any sort to help them organize a campaign or to mobilize voters. No Irish names appeared on the membership rolls of either the city's Board of Aldermen or the Common Council. Handlin's

suggestion that Irish leaders encouraged "group solidarity and the maintenance of a virtual party" gives far too much credit to a disorganized group
of immigrants who had not yet established a political base and were not
yet ready to engage in effective or cohesive action.[32]

But in history, as in real life, perception is often more important than
reality, and there were certainly enough frightened nativists who believed
that the Irish had become a significant force in Boston politics to make
that image come to life. In the battle over the Massachusetts constitution
in 1853, an emotional reaction to a momentary display of Irish Catholic
political power mushroomed into a terrifying spectre of foreign influence
and papal intimidation.

By the late 1840s, the older established leaders of the Whig party in
Massachusetts, popularly known as "Cotton Whigs" because of their investments in the cotton industry, found their political base threatened.
Younger and more radical members of the party, called "Conscience
Whigs" because of their desire to make slavery an official party issue,
created a schism. More than that, they formed an alliance with members
of the recently formed Free-Soil party, along with a number of local antislavery Democrats who saw a chance to divide the Whigs and garner a
little more political power for themselves. The result of this unlikely coalition was a defeat for the old-line Whigs in the elections of 1850, which
sent the articulate Charles Sumner to the United States Senate to crusade
against slavery and gave the Democrats a rare chance at patronage at the
state level.[33]

In an effort to transform their momentary victory into long-range results, the Democrats decided to seize the opportunity and change the prevailing system of representation in the state. They wanted to give more
votes to the smaller towns in the outlying rural areas, where Democratic
power was greater, and take votes away from the larger urban districts
(especially Boston), where Whig power had been traditionally concentrated. To accomplish this, the Democrats made plans to revise the Massachusetts constitution.[34]

In the meantime, however, the coalition between the Democrats and
the Free-Soilers proved to be a short-lived affair. It was not able to survive

the presidential contest of 1852 between Whig candidate General Winfield Scott and his Democratic rival, Franklin Pierce of New Hampshire. During this campaign, local Whigs charged that Pierce was a spokesman for the anti-Catholic forces. This was an obvious attempt to capture some Irish votes for their own candidate, General Scott, who had already shown himself to be anti-Catholic in his attitudes but who was making some "last gasp appeals to the Irish voters" anyway.[35] Indeed, the "sweet, soft, mellifluous, musical Irish brogue has caught the fancy of General Scott," laughed the *Irish American* in a tone of obvious sarcasm. "He likes it, he hugs it, he presses it to his heart. . . ."[36] Although Scott lost the national vote to Pierce, the local Whigs were able to ride back into power on the old general's coattails, regaining control of the state legislature and putting their candidate in the governor's chair. "The coalition is completely dead," moaned one antislavery writer who had hoped to keep the alliance going long enough to weaken the Cotton Whigs even further. "The Whig party remains in complete control of Boston, and the money-bags of Boston rule the State."[37]

Despite their victory, however, the Whigs could not derail the movement for a state constitutional convention. The Democrats won over enough legislators on both sides of the aisle to authorize a convention, which met from May to August 1853 and produced a series of proposed changes to be submitted to Massachusetts voters at the November elections. A number of these proposals were distinctly progressive in nature and would have substantially democratized the state constitution— broadening habeas corpus, for example, expanding the responsibility of juries, reforming the county system, and opening many state offices to popular election in the Jacksonian Democratic manner (replacing political appointment in the conservative Whig tradition). On closer inspection, however, the thrust of the revisions appears to have been in the direction of partisan politics—an effort by the Democrats to break the Whig stranglehold on state politics. The proposed changes in the representative structure to give smaller towns more members in the House of Representatives at the expense of the cities and larger towns were obviously designed not so much to bring the blessings of democracy to Massachusetts as to break the legislative power of the Whigs. Another proposition calling for state judges to be appointed by the governor every three to seven years instead of receiving life tenure was just as obviously designed to dislodge Whig judges from their lifetime posts and replace them with deserving Democrats.[38] Whig leaders loudly protested the political motives of the Democrats, while opposition newspapers poked fun at the sight of Whig businessman Abbott Lawrence walking down State Street "drenching his pocket handkerchief with tears at the bare idea of being disfranchised."[39]

One of the most surprising reactions to the proposals to change the state constitution came from Irish Catholics, who abandoned their traditional allegiance to the Democratic party and joined forces with the upper-class Whigs over this particular issue. While the Boston Irish may have been poor and illiterate, they were by no means politically naive. They realized right away that the constitutional changes proposed by the Democrats, giving political power to the western towns and rural communities, would not only work to the disadvantage of the Whigs (which did not particularly concern the Irish) but would also effectively reduced the representation of the large urban centers where the largest numbers of immigrants were concentrated. The Irish saw themselves about to be gerrymandered out of existence because they happened to live in cities. *The Pilot* called the proposed changes "unfair, unjust, and undemocratic" and accused both the Democrats and the Free-Soilers of trying to deprive the immigrant population of its rightful voice in the governance of the community. "No Catholic, no adopted citizen," it claimed, "could possibly vote for this Constitution."[40]

A significant figure in this controversy was Bishop Fitzpatrick, a native of Boston and a graduate of the Boston Latin School, who had won the love of his immigrant flock as well as the respect of the Brahmin community. In the absence of any demonstrable political leadership among the Irish-Catholic population, the bishop assumed the role of counselor and adviser, instructing his parishioners to become naturalized citizens as soon as possible, to exercise their right to vote, and to become an integral part of the American political system.[41] Firmly committed to the process of representative government and to civil rights as protected by the Constitution of the United States, Fitzpatrick called upon all newcomers to forget about political dissension back home and focus on their responsibilities to their adopted country. "We should make ourselves American as much as we can," he urged through the pages of *The Pilot*. "This is our country now. Ireland is only a recollection." There should be no divided loyalties, no fighting old wars in new lands, no viewing the United States as a mere temporary stopover, a base for an eventual return to the "old country." Unless they were willing to leave their internal bickering and traditional hatreds behind them, the newcomers would be "pushed out of the way, trampled upon, laughed at, pitied, and ground into the dust."[42] Fitzpatrick himself was clearly and unabashedly Whiggish in his social and political views. In the columns of *The Pilot* he attempted to persuade the Irish to disregard the popular Democratic favorites they usually supported in favor of the conservative and well-bred Whig candidates he himself greatly admired, and who were often among his personal friends and acquaintances. These efforts were generally unsuccessful, but in the matter of the proposed constitutional amendments, the Irish viewed the Whig position as closer to their interests than that of the Democrats and the Free-Soilers.

When the proposed revisions to the constitution were eventually voted down in November 1853, it was assumed by nearly everyone that the Irish-Catholic vote in general, and the personal influence of Bishop Fitzpatrick in particular, had played a major role in the defeat of the Democratic proposals. Former governor George Boutwell observed that, although it had always been recognized that the Boston Irish were good and loyal Democrats, when it came to ratifying the proposed constitution they had swung over to the other side in great numbers. "To this result," he complained bitterly, "the influence of Bishop Fitzpatrick has contributed essentially."[43] Although some recent studies have raised questions about whether the Irish were responsible for the defeat of the constitutional reforms or whether it was the well-organized, well-financed "united stand" of the Whigs themselves that turned the tide, contemporary opinion was in no doubt that the Irish vote had done the trick. Certainly, the Irish themselves did nothing to disguise their delight at the outcome, with

The Pilot joyfully exulting: "The New Constituion Rejected! Waterloo Defeat of the Coalition!"[44]

This apparent substantial shifting of votes, with its unsatisfactory outcome, convinced the nativist Boston community (if any convincing was necessary) that the Irish-Catholic vote was no longer a hypothetical factor in Boston politics. The exercise of Irish power in the defeat of the 1853 proposals made it real and unmistakable. "For the first time in the history of the State," observed the *Daily Commonwealth*, "the Catholic Church has taken the field as a power."[45] The role that the newly enfranchised Irish-Catholic voters played—or were thought to have played—in the constitutional convention supplied nativists throughout the Commonwealth with an urgent motive for immediate and direct political counter-reaction. The defeat of the proposals, observed lawyer-politician Benjamin F. Butler, "invoked a bitterness among the people against the Catholic religion, such as had never before been, to any considerable degree, felt or foreshadowed in the State of Massachusetts."[46] This bitterness over the apparent strength of a hostile immigrant voting bloc in 1853 was only one more reason for nativists to conclude that extraordinary measures had to be taken to save the Commonwealth and the nation from the growing power of immigrant voters.

During the 1830s and 1840s, in response to the increase in immigrant populations, there had developed in East Coast cities like New York, Philadelphia, and Boston a variety of local nativist organizations with elaborate patriotic names. "The Sons of Sires," "The Sons of '76," "The Druids," "The Order of United Americans," "The Order of the Star Spangled Banner," and similar groups were pledged to protect Anglo-Saxon-Protestant supremacy in the United States by controlling state governments and passing restrictive legislation. During 1852–53, convinced that the danger of foreign influence had reached national proportions, a number of these local patriotic groups came together to form the "American Party," a national political organization designed to protect the United States from the "insidious wiles of foreigners." The party was highly secret, complete with passwords, handshakes, and other rituals. It was commonly referred to as the "Know-Nothing Party" because its members were pledged not to give out a single word of information about the organization, the funding, or the membership of the party. Any such questions were greeted with the stock reply: "I know nothing."[47]

Almost overnight, voters in a number of major East Coast states cast their ballots in favor of candidates representing the new party. By the spring of 1854, the Know-Nothings had swept into power in Pennsylvania, demonstrating not only a pent-up reaction against Catholic immigrants but also a desire among political leaders to form a new political organization to replace the old Whig party that had been pushed into obscurity after the passage of the Kansas-Nebraska Act. Into the sudden political vacuum created by the issue of slavery in Kansas, the new American party moved with amazing speed. By the fall of 1854, New York was estimated to have upwards of seventy thousand registered "American" voters; the states of Delaware, Rhode Island, Connecticut, Maryland, and Kentucky also fell into line; and the new party made serious inroads into California, Pennsylvania, Virginia, Georgia, Mississippi, and Alabama. In Massachusetts, the Know-Nothings succeeded in electing all the state officers, the entire membership of the state senate, and all but four seats in the house. Henry J. Gardner, a former Whig who had gone over to the American party, was elected governor, and Jerome Van Crowninshield Smith, a longtime nativist, became mayor of Boston. Sparked by religious bigotry and ethnic prejudice, the Know-Nothing party also provided an opportunity for political leaders to survive the party restructuring that followed the passage of the Kansas-Nebraska Act, as well as a chance for rank-and-file, working-class Democrats to undertake another effort to break the Brahmin stranglehold in Boston and introduce more reforms into the state's political system.[48]

Once they took office the members of the Know-Nothing legislature lost little time in pushing forward a program of "Temperance, Liberty, and Protestantism," in the name of the people of Massachusetts who, according to one house member, were ready to eliminate "Rome, Rum, and Robbery."[49] In addition to proposing a so-called Twenty-One-Year Law that would have prevented any immigrant from voting until he had been a resident of the Commonwealth for twenty-one years, the legislature dissolved all Irish militia companies, occupied their armories, and confiscated all their military equipment. The new legislature made the reading of the Protestant version of the Bible (the King James version) compulsory in all public schools and deprived diocesan officials of all control over church property. Some members wanted a law denying certain public offices to anyone who owed spiritual allegiance to a "foreign prince" (such as the pope); others wanted Catholic schools to be inspected by public school authorities. In February 1855, a joint committee of the state legislature was formed to inquire into "certain practices" alleged to be taking place in nunneries and in Catholic schools. The so-called Nunnery Committee undertook three separate investigations—one at Holy Cross College in Worcester; another at a school run by the Sisters of Notre Dame in Lowell; a third at a school in Roxbury operated by nuns of the same order. The investigation at the Roxbury site was especially offensive, as some two dozen men suddenly appeared at the school, announced they were on state business, and proceeded to tramp through the building. They poked into closets, searched cellars, intimidated the nuns, frightened the children—and found absolutely nothing. A number of fair-minded Bostonians were as disgusted as was Bishop Fitzpatrick at this outrageous behavior. When local newspapers began publicizing the unsavory personal conduct of several of its members, the committee lost all credibility and was quickly dissolved.[50]

In 1854 the political influence of the Know-Nothing party in Massachusetts was so overpowering that a number of Catholic leaders suggested that Irish immigrants would do better to fade into the background for the time being, stay away from the polls, and behave in a more subordinate manner—like polite guests in someone else's home. Bishop Fitzpatrick would have none of it, however. He called upon his parishioners to continue to exercise their constitutional right to vote, regardless of the outcome at the polls. Be prepared to use prudence and caution; avoid trouble, he advised in *The Pilot*. Go to the polls singly rather than in groups; cause no commotion; keep the peace; don't get into fights. But by all means vote in the November elections, so that everyone can see that you are ready to

In the absence of effective political leadership during the famine years, responsible direction for the immigrant community was provided by Bishop John Bernard Fitzpatrick. A native of the city and a graduate of the Boston Latin School, Fitzpatrick urged the newcomers to become naturalized, to exercise the franchise, to avoid violence, and to resort to the Constitution and the courts to resolve their problems. Archdiocese of Boston.

exercise your rights as American citizens. If Catholics failed to vote, he insisted, it would work to the advantage of the Know-Nothings, by creating a dangerous and totally artificial "wall of separation" between naturalized citizens and members of the native population.[51]

Fortunately for the newcomers, the Know-Nothing movement collapsed at both the national and state levels almost as suddenly as it had begun. The breakup must be credited in part to the patient work of Bishop Fitzpatrick, as well as to the political ineptness of local American party leaders (many of whom were holding public office for the first time), the outbreak of bloody violence in Kansas beween the Free-Soil and pro-slavery forces, and the emergence of the new Republican party. The city of Boston, with its unusually large Irish-Catholic population and its traditionally hostile anti-Catholic bias, was a powder keg ready to explode. In other American cities during the mid–1850s, tensions between nativists and immigrants often produced violent and even bloody confrontations. In Baltimore there were pitched battles at the polling places; in New Orleans at least four people were killed in religious clashes; in St. Louis the election of 1854 produced a major riot in which ten people were killed; in Louisville, Kentucky, a series of bloody conflicts left some twenty people dead and several hundred wounded.[52] No such violence occurred in Boston. Fitzpatrick restrained the volatile emotions of his Celtic parishioners, warned them to avoid even the occasions of trouble, refused to sanction violence in any form, and patiently appealed to the law and the courts. To later generations the bishop's efforts may have seemed ineffective and even deferential compared, for example, to the explosive outbursts of Archbishop John Hughes of New York, who warned municipal authorities that he would turn the city of New York into a "second Moscow" if nativists attacked a single Catholic Church.[53] By keeping his own calm, however, and by holding the passions of his people in check, the bishop of Boston actually undermined the Know-Nothing cause in Boston by depriving it of combustible materials to fuel the flames of hatred and prejudice.

The Know-Nothing party may have disappeared, but the spirit of anti-Catholicism had not. The nativist press continued to publish articles describing the poverty, sickness, and squalor that had accompanied the influx of immigrants to the city and providing statistics from jails and houses of correction demonstrating the high incidence of crime among the Irish.[54] Although the attempt to require a residency of twenty-one years for naturalization had failed, 63 percent of the voters approved an

1857 referendum requiring a literacy test for voting. Although this "reading-and-writing" amendment to the state constitution was supposed to apply to all voters, it was based on the assumption that the Irish could not read and therefore would be the group most affected.[55] Two years later, another law was passed preventing immigrants from voting until two years after they had been granted citizenship. This last law was so outrageous that it even angered members of the national Republican party, which was in the process of courting the German immigrant vote throughout the West in anticipation of the election of 1860. From Illinois, Abraham Lincoln wrote to Indiana congressman Schuyler Colfax in July 1859 complaining that, if Republicans in Massachusetts would only look "beyond their noses," they would see that "tilting against foreigners" was bound to ruin the party's efforts in the Northwest.[56] Even conservative Henry Wilson attacked the inconsistency of the law by pointing out that while Massachusetts allowed the "ignorant, brutalized, fugitive negro" to vote after a residence of only one year, it was imposing a seven-year residency requirement on the "English, Scot, Irish, and Germans."[57]

The nativist element harassed the immigrant population in other ways, too. Catholic patients were discriminated against in hospitals; children were proselytized by religious groups in orphanages; and priests were granted only very limited access to the sick and the poor at the South Boston Almshouse and the Deer Island House of Correction. Several bills were passed to stop Catholics from burying their dead in public cemeteries, and city authorities even set up restrictive statues concerning burial procedures in the Catholics' own religious cemeteries.[58] And in the Boston public schools, there were constant complaints among Irish parents about the ways in which teachers were using educational techniques to undermine the traditional Roman Catholic faith of their children. Protestant hymns were sung in the classrooms, Protestant prayers were said regularly, and the King James version of the Bible was read daily. Textbooks presented a Protestant view of world history that was decidedly anti-Catholic; primers were critical of Papist ideas and practices; geography books made disparaging remarks about Catholic countries; literary works almost always portrayed Catholics in disrespectful terms. While he urged angry parents to obey the law and send their children to school, Bishop Fitzpatrick sought redress through the courts and through the state legislature to change a system he regarded as both un-American and unconstitutional.[59]

But while religion continued to be a constant source of friction, by the late 1850s it was clear that slavery was becoming the central issue in American politics. In Boston the slavery question not only became a volatile topic in its own right but created even further emotional divisions between the Irish-Catholic and Yankee-Protestant communities.

Ever since 1831, when William Lloyd Garrison ran off the first issue of his antislavery newspaper, *The Liberator*, Boston had been the storm center of a militant abolition movement that denounced slavery as a moral evil and called for the total and immediate emancipation of all slaves. Although in the early years the movement was small and its members few, the growing controversy during the 1840s over whether slavery should expand into the new territories of the Southwest caused more and more people to join the abolitionist crusade. Well-educated sons and daughters of Boston's Brahmin establishment became zealous members of the movement. They held meetings, wrote pamphlets, organized demonstrations, exerted pressure on public officials, and demanded that the major political parties adopt antislavery platforms.

Arriving from their famine-stricken homeland during the mid-1840s, the Irish immigrants paid little attention to an institution that had been firmly established in the American South for some two hundred years. Strangers in a new land, confronted by a hostile environment and preoccupied with their own survival, most immigrants gave little thought to the country's "peculiar institution." Their own deplorable living conditions in shacks and cellars along the Boston waterfront left them with little sympathy for the plight of black people living either in slavery or in freedom, and on numerous occasions *The Pilot* expressed the opinion that most slaves were in far better conditions than the poor starving people of Ireland. Although the Boston Irish gave no indication of wanting such an institution for themselves, they generally conceded the right of citizens in other parts of the country to hold their slave property until some way could be found to eliminate the institution in a peaceful and gradual manner—an attitude that was in general accordance with the principles of the Democratic party.[60] Most Irish Catholics rejected the radical approach of Garrison and his abolitionist followers, especially when they denounced the Constitution of the United States as "a covenant with death and an agreement with hell" because it sanctioned the institution of slavery. In coming to America the Irish had transferred their allegiance to the government of their adopted country and could not countenance a movement that placed some "higher law" above the authority of the Constitution, which the Irish regarded as a sacred guarantee of their liberties. Furthermore, observing that a number of abolitionist leaders were active supporters of the Know-Nothing party, Catholics regarded the antislavery reformers as hypocrites who preached liberty and equality for black people while they worked to take basic rights away from poor white immigrants.[61]

Like numerous American institutions, organized religion was deeply affected by the controversy over slavery. Despite efforts to reconcile differences, violent disputes about slavery caused deep divisions within many established denominations. Southern Baptists, for example, withdrew from the northern memberships and formed their own Southern Baptist Convention. Southern Methodists and Presbyterians, too, formed separate branches in their own region. Conscious of the weak position of their young immigrant church, already under nativist assault, Catholic leaders made a conscious effort to keep the explosive issue of slavery from dividing their congregations. They avoided the subject as much as possible in private conversations as well as in public forums, treating it as a matter of private conscience, the eventual disposition of which was best left to political leaders at the state and local levels. In taking this approach, members of the hierarchy were supported by their immigrant congregations, who generally believed that black people were members of an inferior race—ignorant, savage, and brutish, given to uncontrollable impulses and animal passions—who were much better off under the paternalism of slavery than they would be in freedom. Most Irish protested against the "insane radicalism" of abolitionists and expressed the fear that if the slaves were ever freed they would not only move north and take away the menial jobs of the immigrants but would also create racial turmoil throughout the nation.[62]

There is no question that Irish immigrants were as racist as were most white people in America in the nineteenth century, when the French visitor Alexis de Tocqueville observed that racial prejudice appeared stronger in the North than in the South. At that time, according to the modern historian Eric Foner, "racial prejudice was all but universal in the antebellum North."[63] But there was a difference. While the greater part of the New England population during the late 1850s was showing distinct signs of becoming more antagonistic toward the slaveholding South and less opposed to the idea of emancipating the slaves, the Irish did not budge. In contrast to the angry Boston businessmen, some quite conservative, who raged against the actions of Senator Stephen A. Douglas and the "nefarious" Kansas-Nebraska Act he helped pass in 1854, leaders of the Catholic community urged their people to remain steadfast in their traditional views. Slavery was still protected by the Constitution, and southern citizens still had the right to take their personal property with them wherever they went. Indeed, the refusal of northern Catholics to get involved in the slavery issue was so noticeable that Senator Alexander Stephens of Georgia pointed out that not a single Roman Catholic clergyman had signed a recent anti-Nebraska memorial that had been sent to the Senate. "Their pulpits," he wrote with evident approval, "are not desecrated every Sabbath with anathemas against slavery."[64] Nothing, perhaps, could demonstrate more dramatically how far the Irish were out of step with the changing social consciousness of Massachusetts than an incident in June 1854 associated with the return of a runaway slave named Anthony Burns. Captured in Boston under the terms of the Fugitive Slave Act, Burns was marched down State Street to a waiting vessel through a cordon of some two thousand uniformed troops assembled to prevent any rescue by the outraged populace that lined the street. Conspicuous among the troops assigned to enforce Burns's return was the Columbian Artillery, a unit composed almost entirely of Irish Catholics and commanded by Captain Thomas Cass. Townspeople felt that the presence of Irish troops was simply one more instance of Catholic collaboration with the forces of "slavocracy." One critic accused the Catholics of using the "shallow pretext of upholding the law" to force black people back into slavery.[65] This was the beginning of a bitter antagonism between working-class Irish Catholics and upper-class Yankee liberals over social and racial issues that would continue to divide the two groups well into the twentieth century.

Still, the Irish persisted in their position on the slavery issue and considered their consistency justified when, in March 1857, Chief Justice Roger B. Taney handed down the Dred Scott decision declaring black people to be "beings of an inferior order, and altogether unfit to associate with the white race." Taney wrote that Negroes possessed "no rights which the white man was bound to respect" and that they had never been included under the term "citizen" in the Constitution.[66] *The Pilot* clearly took great satisfaction in pointing out that its own position on slavery over the years was now vindicated by Taney's judicial reasoning. The editors urged all Americans to set aside their personal feelings and accept the verdict of the Supreme Court as the law of the land.[67] Reinforced in their racial attitudes and rededicated to the states'-rights principles of the Democratic party, the Irish made it clear that they admired Senator Douglas, supported his Kansas-Nebraska Act, accepted the provisions of the Fugitive Slave Act, and agreed with the Dred Scott decision.

Buoyed by the election in November 1856 of the Democratic candidate, James Buchanan, the Irish were confident that they had stopped the momentum of the new Republican party, and they looked forward to an even greater victory in 1860. Local nativists were frustrated by the Democratic victory, which they blamed, once again, on Irish votes. The nativists urged Republicans to give up on their unsuccessful efforts to attract foreign immigrants into the antislavery fold. "The Republican Party would be much wiser," said one nativist newspaper, "if it would distinctly understand and accept the fact that the Roman Catholic Church in this country is their declared and uncompromising foe." Reemphasizing the image of the Irish as racists, opposed to emancipation, it concluded: "Catholicism and slavery are twin sisters."[68] Even John Brown's electrifying raid on Harpers Ferry in October 1859 failed to produce any appreciable change in the Irish position. The quixotic attack and Brown's subsequent execution certainly increased sympathy for the abolitionist cause among some segments of the New England population, but the Irish showed not the slightest indication of moving any closer to the Republican party. *The Pilot* wrote Brown off as a fanatical tool of the Republicans—another hypocritical extremist in the tradition of those who had passed the Alien and Sedition Acts, those who had denounced foreigners at the Hartford Convention, and those who had sympathized with "convent burnings."[69]

As the nation prepared for the presidential election of 1860, the Irish lined up solidly behind the Democratic party. After the various party conventions had taken place, the election became a contest involving four major candidates. Abraham Lincoln came out of Chicago as the nominee of the Republicans; Stephen A. Douglas of Illinois was the candidate of the mainstream Democrats; John C. Breckinridge of Kentucky was the choice of the Southern Democrats who had broken away from their own party over the slavery question; and John Bell of Tennessee was the nominee of the Constitutional Union party, which hoped to capture the moderate vote in a deeply divided contest. Reports of Douglas's nomination, observed *The Pilot*, were hailed with "irrepressible bursts of enthusiasm from the hearts of the people—the Union-loving people in every section of this wide extended country." The "Black Republican party," on the other hand, which was now supported by "scattered and broken forces of the know-nothing party," according to the newspaper, represented "hatred and prejudice and injustice to the Irish particularly."[70] While Republican papers were glorifying Lincoln as a young giant from the West, *The Pilot* came out publicly in favor of Douglas and steadfastly refused to support either the rail-splitter or his antislavery party. The paper expressed the hope that none of its readers would vote for Abraham Lincoln, whom it described as a "very weak man intellectually," although it acknowledged him to be a "tough and persevering" campaigner.[71] Douglas, in fact, was so clearly the favorite among Irish-Catholic voters that the *Railsplitter*, a Republican campaign sheet, suggested that Democratic senator from Illinois was actually a secret Catholic who had even paid a visit to the pope.[72]

In what was undoubtedly the highlight of the local campaign as far as

Boston Democrats were concerned, Douglas himself came to Boston in July 1860 and spoke to a large crowd gathered in the square on Bowdoin Street. Thousands came to hear the famed "little giant" give one of his patented speeches, which one Boston newspaper said "set the crowd afire" with the enthusiasm of his oratory.[73] Afterward, *The Pilot* expressed the fear that if Douglas's rival Abraham Lincoln managed to get himself elected, he would not set any crowds on fire but might set the *nation* on fire. The paper predicted that if Lincoln won the election, the South would be driven into secession and the nation divided in two.[74]

Although by the end of the summer even Douglas and his supporters recognized that the Democrats could not possibly win against solid Republican strength throughout the northern states, the Boston Irish refused to admit defeat. On October 25, only a week before election day, the Irish of Ward 7 held a giant rally for Douglas on Fort Hill, where close to ten thousand people reportedly came to hear speeches, sing songs, and march in torchlight processions.[75] And on November 3, in its final edition before the polls opened, *The Pilot* gave its readers a last-minute admonition that "the support of Lincoln is not to be thought of by any Democrat." Any naturalized citizen who would vote for a party that "proscribes" his race, announced the paper in somber tones, "does not deserve the rights of citizenship."[76]

But the cause was lost. Although Douglas swept the two heavily Irish-Catholic wards in the city—Wards 1 and 7—Lincoln carried the ten other wards by substantial margins, as did John A. Andrew, the Republican candidate for governor that year.[77] Before most voters could fully digest the outcome of the election, the Union was in the process of disintegration. On December 20, the state of South Carolina seceded from the Union, and by the end of the following month Mississippi, Florida, Alabama, Georgia, Louisiana, and Texas had also seceded. On February 4, 1861, delegates from all the seceded states except Texas convened in Montgomery, Alabama, where they made their separation from the United States official by forming the new, independent government of the Confederate States of America.

Like most other northerners, Bostonians were shocked and confused by the suddenness and magnitude of the critical events that were taking place. The Irish, especially, were confronted with a bothersome dilemma: On the one hand, for nearly thirty years they had consistently denounced the abolitionists, defended slavery, and sympathized with the southern point of view. On the other hand, as patriotic citizens, they had just as consistently proclaimed their loyalty to the Constitution and their support of the Union. How could they possibly reconcile these two positions now that secession had brought them into open conflict? For a short time the Boston Irish tried to resolve their dilemma by straddling the political fence. They continued to insist upon their loyalty to the national government and made it clear that in the event of war they would fight to preserve the Union. "We Catholics have only one course to adopt, only one line to follow," stated *The Pilot* on January 12, 1861. "Stand by the Union; fight for the Union; die by the Union."[78] At the same time, the Irish expressed sympathy for those southerners who had been victimized by the "malign, brutal conceit" of local abolitionists, and who were merely seeking to have "their lives and property protected against encroachment from the North."[79] The main theme of *The Pilot* during the secession winter was the hope for a peaceful resolution so that both sides would "stack their rifles" rather than embark on a fratricidal war.[80] However, after the Confederate attack on Fort Sumter on April 12, 1861, there was no further talk about peaceful resolution or reconciliation. In one editorial entitled "The Irish and the Republic," *The Pilot* declared that "the Irish adopted citizens are true, to a man, to the Constitution"; in a companion piece entitled "The Civil War," the paper formally denounced the South for putting itself "in the wrong" and announced that from now on *The Pilot* would support the national government. "We have hoisted the American Stars and Stripes over THE PILOT Establishment," wrote the editor, "and there they shall wave till the 'star of peace' returns."[81]

Almost without exception, the Catholics of the city followed their paper's lead and came out in support of the Lincoln administration. Thomas Cass, formerly commander of the Columbian Artillery (which had been forced to disband by the Know-Nothings seven years earlier), offered his services to Governor John Andrew to organize a regiment of Irishmen.

With the governor's enthusiastic permission, Cass used the nucleus of the old Columbian Artillery to recruit the Ninth Regiment, Massachusetts Volunteer Infantry, during April and May 1861. Patrick Donahoe, publisher of *The Pilot*, enlisted the weekly newspaper in the Union cause, took an active part in recruiting volunteers for Cass's Ninth Regiment, and also served as treasurer of a citizens' committee organized to raise funds to furnish equipment for the new Irish regiment. Throughout his activities, however, he continued to emphasize that Irish Catholics were fighting to save the Union, not to free the slaves. "The white men of the free states do not wish to labor side by side with the Negro," he wrote. "Not one volunteer in a hundred has gone forth . . . to liberate slaves."[82] On June 24, the newly organized Ninth Regiment—which would become the famous "Fighting Ninth"—paraded through the streets of Boston to the State House on Beacon Hill, where it was officially received by Governor John Andrew. The governor thanked Colonel Cass for raising "this splendid regiment" and presented him with a flag bearing the emblem of the Bay State. The United States knows no distinction between "its native-born citizens and those born in other countries," the governor said. He predicted that future generations would remember the patriotism demonstrated by the "adopted citizens" of Boston.[83]

Although Boston Catholics continued unshaken in their defense of the Union, their political support of the Lincoln administration, shaky at best, broke down completely in the fall of 1862 because of two administration measures to which they took great exception. The first was the Emancipation Proclamation, which President Lincoln issued in September after the Union victory at Antietam, and which went into effect in January 1863. Although there were many in the North who greeted the proclamation with wild rejoicing as a great humanitarian gesture, the Irish saw it as one more tragic blunder by the "incompetent, fanatic, radical administration of Abraham Lincoln," which had sold out the poor people of the country in order to placate the radical abolitionist wing of the party.[84] Not only would the proclamation stiffen the resistance of the South, prolong the war, and ruin any chance for a negotiated peace, declared *The Pilot*, but it would also cause a massive flood of black workers into the North to take

The Civil War provided the Irish with an opportunity to display loyalty to their adopted country and devotion to the Constitution. Boston's Bishop Fitzpatrick insisted that Catholic soldiers in Irish regiments have their own chaplains and have the opportunity to attend Mass, as shown in this unidentified photograph. Courtesy of the Boston Public Library, Print Department.

much-needed jobs from white laborers. Most blacks didn't want to be emancipated, anyway, argued the Catholic weekly. They were devoted to their owners and satisfied with their lot in life; only "negrophilists" and "nigger-worshippers" would try to convince blacks that they were the equals of whites. "At one time we did support Lincoln," said *The Pilot* bitterly, but "he changed, and so have we."[85]

The other source of friction was the conscription law that Congress passed in March 1863. The vagueness of the terms of the law, the fact that rich men were allowed to hire substitutes or to purchase outright exemption, and the many abuses that occurred when local authorities tried to administer it resulted in widespread protest and outright violence.

All through the North—in Ohio, New Jersey, Pennsylvania, Wisconsin, Indiana, Illinois—there were disturbances and "insurrections" against a law under which poor men would be drafted to fight a "rich man's war."[86] The most violent outburst took place in New York City during the hot summer of 1863, when a mob of predominantly Irish workingmen went on a three-day rampage from July 13 to July 15. With hideous brutality they plundered houses, looted stores, hunted innocent black people through the city streets, and left a number of their unfortunate victims hanging from lampposts. Only when federal troops were brought up from the battlefield at Gettysburg was the bloody rioting finally brought to a halt.[87]

The city of Boston had its own version of a "draft riot" on the afternoon of July 14, when local residents of the largely Irish North End began a scuffle with two provost marshals who had come to serve conscription papers. The fighting became more general when the police were sent into the neighborhood, and by nightfall the lower end of the city was involved in a full-scale riot between angry residents and the city's police force, which had been augmented by units of the state militia and by regular army troops. By morning, however, it was all over. Although the tensions took several days to dissipate, the spontaneous outbreak of tempers lacked the destructive and racial aspects of the New York City riots. Six people had been killed during a nighttime skirmish with the police, but the riot involved no looting of shops, no destruction of property, and no attacks on the city's black population.[88] For the most part, the Boston Irish settled back in a spirit of sullen resentment against the Lincoln administration, waiting for the end of the war and hoping that Lincoln would be defeated in the 1864 election. True to their political tradition, the Irish remained solidly Democratic and gave their support to General George B. McClellan. *The Pilot* came out strongly for the Democratic candidate, taking the opportunity to criticize Lincoln as an incompetent and a "boob"; on one occasion it even likened the president to Mephistopheles because of what it regarded as his guile and deceit.[89] The paper also accused Lincoln of having tried to bribe McClellan to drop out of the presidential race by offering him another high military command. Only if the Democrats got back in control of the national government, argued *The Pilot*, would the Union be restored. Only the Democrats would be willing to stop the terrible war and receive the defeated South back into the Union without a spirit of vindictiveness.[90]

The popular vote in the election of 1864 was fairly close, with Lincoln ahead by only four hundred thousand out of a total of four million votes cast. But the incumbent president easily carried all the northern states except New Jersey and took Maryland and Missouri as well—polling 202 electoral votes to the paltry 21 garnered by McClellan. Carried along by General William T. Sherman's victory at Atlanta and the news of his successful march to the sea, Lincoln won an important political victory and appeared to have solidified his base of power for another four years. *The Pilot*, despite its disappointment at the poor showing of the Democrats, accepted the political outcome with good grace, publicly congratulated President Lincoln on his reelection, and promised to support the national administration in its efforts to bring the war to a close.[91] The paper continued to ask, however, that the North soften the harshness of its surrender terms and enter into negotiations with the Confederacy. At this point, said the paper, the North could well afford to be magnanimous, since the South was virtually helpless in the face of northern military supremacy and since the end of the institution of slavery was already an accomplished fact. The South had nothing more to fight for. "It was the stake the South played for," wrote the editor, "and the stake is lost."[92] And the stake, indeed, was lost. On April 9, 1865, General Robert E. Lee surrendered to General Ulysses S. Grant at Appomattox Courthouse, Virginia, beginning a sequence of military surrenders throughout the South that would finally bring the hostilities of the Brothers' War to a close.

Overall, the Civil War had significant and positive effects on the social and economic status of the Boston Irish. For the first time, after years of nativist charges that they could never become dedicated American citizens or be assimilated into the American culture, the immigrants had a golden opportunity to demonstrate their loyalty to their adopted country, either by joining the Union army or by doing war work in the nearby armories, factories, and shipyards. For the first time, too, they had a chance to make a little money, improve their depressed economic status, and gain a greater measure of acceptance in the New England community. While the names of many skilled Irish craftsmen appear on the rolls of trade unions of that time for longshoremen, carpenters, tailors, granite cutters, and waiters, most immigrants were still untrained and unskilled. By 1860, however, the invention of the sewing machine and the introduction of other new mechanical devices had made it possible even for "greenhorns" to perform tasks once the exclusive province of highly skilled craftsmen. This development brought more Irish workers into garment shops, textile mills, and shoe factories throughout the area by the time the Civil War began, and by the time the war was over Irish workers had joined several more trade unions. The Knights of St. Crispin and the Daughters of St. Crispin elected Catholic as well as Protestant shoe workers as officers in their associations.[93] By the late 1850s and early 1860s, extensive construction projects in various parts of the city provided additional jobs for Irish workers. In the downtown area, Bulfinch's handsome Tontine Crescent and Franklin Place were torn down to make room for blocks of stores and warehouses in an expanding business district. The South End was also the scene of ambitious building projects as new streets, parks, and squares were laid out and attractive blocks of apartment buildings anticipated a new wave of occupants.[94] Boston City Hospital, which the historian Walter Muir Whitehill has described as the "handsomest development of the South End," was under construction from 1861 to 1864, about the same time a new Gothic cathedral was going up to replace the small church on Franklin Street that could no longer contain the city's growing Roman Catholic population. Work on the Jesuit Church of the Immaculate Conception on nearby Harrison Avenue was completed in 1861; and three years later Boston College began classes in the new brick building next door, with only three teachers and with forty-eight students whose parents were able to pay the first semester's tuition of thirty dollars to provide their sons with a Catholic education.[95] Across town, work had already begun on the immense Back Bay landfill project that would continue during the 1860s and 1870s, creating more jobs for Irish workers on the construction site as well as in the factories in South Boston that provided a number of the steam shovels and locomotives used on the project.[96] The outbreak of the Civil War in 1861 opened up even greater opportunities for work. Many Irish women took their place on assembly lines making ammunition at the Watertown arsenal, while others worked in factories in the city. Irish men found war jobs just across the channel in the lower end of the South Boston peninsula, where several large iron foundries turned out guns, cannon, and artillery shells for the Union army and where shipyards were busy constructing new ironclad monitors for the navy.[97] While the work was hard, the hours long, and the wages low—most women earned less than $1.50 a day—this was the first real opportunity for most of the Irish workers to bring home a day's pay on a regular basis.

The remarkable contribution by the Irish to the nation's war effort and the much-heralded courage of their regiments on the battlefields caused even dyed-in-the-wool Yankees to relax their defensive posture and show a much greater degree of tolerance. In 1861, for example, Harvard College conferred an honorary Doctor of Divinity degree on Bishop Fitzpatrick. Although Fitzpatrick had several good friends among the members of Harvard's board of overseers, none would have dared propose the prelate's name for such an honor during the turbulent 1850s when the school question, the slavery issue, and the Know-Nothing movement were causing so much controversy. And even in 1861 it might not have been possible, according to Amos A. Lawrence, had it not been for "the loyalty shown by him and by the Irish who offered . . . themselves freely for the army."[98]

The new attitude was expressed in other ways as well. The Massachusetts state legislature, for example, passed a bill instructing the school committees of the various cities and towns to have daily readings of the Bible conducted "without written note or oral comment" and further stipulated that no students be required to read from any particular version of the Bible if it went against "the conscientious scruples" of their parents or guardians. This piece of legislation, *The Pilot* was happy to observe, was a "long stride" from the Know-Nothingism of 1854 and was a clear acknowledgment of the loyalty displayed by "the adopted citizens in this hour of national trial."[99] The legislature also repealed the 1859 law that had required a two-year waiting period for new citizens seeking to vote, and a short time later, city authorities announced that patients in the Boston City Hospital could now be attended by a clergyman of their own choosing. These were tangible signs that the Irish had entered a new and less hostile phase of their history as residents of Boston.

At the same time, however, the traumatic decades of humiliation and discrimination, of ridicule and contempt, of nativist slanders and Know-Nothing bruises, became a permanent part of the Irish-Catholic heritage in Boston. Although religious and cultural clashes took place in other nineteenth-century American cities such as New York, Philadelphia, and Baltimore, the age and strong traditions of the Boston community, the homogeneous character of its Anglo-Saxon population, and the un-matched Puritan revulsion toward all things Roman Catholic, raised the intensity of anti-Irish sentiment in Boston to incredible levels. For genera-tions to come, Catholic children in Irish neighborhoods would be reared in the catechism of hate that instructed them never to forget the bigotry of Protestants, who had confined them to institutions and asylums, and the cruelty of Brahmins, who had posted on factory gates and workshop doors the signs that proclaimed for all to see: "No Irish Need Apply." The bitter antagonisms of the 1840s and 1850s created a wall of separation that would continue to keep the two communities at arm's length until well into the second half of the twentieth century.

Furthermore, it was by no means clear in 1865 that the Civil War had improved the political status or influence of the Boston Irish in any per-manent fashion. On the contrary, it could be argued that as the war came to an end their prospects for the future seemed worse than before. As stubborn Democrats who had supported Douglas and rejected Lincoln, as opponents of emancipation who had persisted in their racist views, and as members of a loyal (and sometimes not so loyal) opposition that had favored McClellan over Lincoln in 1864, the Irish emerged from the war in political defeat. They belonged to a political organization that at both the national and state levels appeared to possess as little credibility as the old Federalists after the War of 1812. Indeed, it was questionable whether the Democrats in the northern states could continue to exist after 1865 as a bona fide political party.

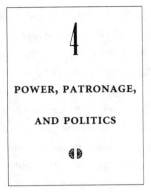

4

POWER, PATRONAGE,

AND POLITICS

BY THE TIME the Civil War was over, the Democratic party in Massachusetts was in an absolute shambles. The Republicans were riding high. The
election of Abraham Lincoln to the presidency in 1860 and again in 1864,
the emancipation of the slaves, the successful prosecution of the war, and
the salvation of the Union had elevated the Republican party to a position
of almost unassailable power.[1]

The Democratic party, by contrast, became the political underdog in
the Bay State and would continue as such for decades to come. Castigated
on all sides for their support of slavery, their sympathy for secession, and
their continued opposition to the Lincoln administration, the Democrats
were further weakened by the defection of former party reliables such as
Nathaniel Banks and Caleb Cushing. There still remained a solid core of
well-established Yankees—lawyers, merchants, bankers, shippers, "gentlemen of property and standing"—many of them former Whigs, whose
traditional role as community leaders had been usurped during the late
1850s by the new antislavery Republicans. These were native-born, upper-
class, Harvard-educated Brahmins like Nathaniel S. Shurtleff, a prominent
physician; Frederick Octavius Prince, class poet at Harvard, active in law
and in Democratic politics; Nathan Matthews, Jr., lecturer in government
at Harvard; and Josiah Quincy, the last in Boston's long line of famous
Quincys and a dedicated Democrat. They all saw themselves as holding

out against the radical social experiments and militant demagogic tactics of those holier-than-thou reformers and arrogant do-gooders who would grant equality to Negroes, liberate women, and otherwise disturb the conservative nature of human society. And as born-again Puritans, these Yankees were repelled by the vulgar ostentation of Johnny-come-lately industrialists and millionaires as well as by the shocking scandals that riddled the Grant administration, demonstrating the unholy alliance between dishonest businessmen and corrupt Republican politicians. They looked to the Democratic party to restore the old-fashioned virtues of individual integrity and personal morality by emphasizing states' rights, local issues, low taxes, limited expenditures, and freedom from the expanded powers of an overgrown federal government.[2]

Their lineage was long and their pedigrees impeccable, but in order to get the sort of numbers they needed to make any kind of political impact in the postwar era, the Brahmin-Democrats needed to make more efficient use of the loyal Irish stalwarts who, for more than two decades, had made up the silent rank and file of the Democratic party. But even that possibility became uncertain because of the changing relationships that characterized the postwar years, when the Republicans were making attempts to bring over some of the Irish, especially those who had fought in the Union army during the war. For example, General Thomas F. Meagher, commander of the famous Irish Brigade, expressed the view that the Democratic party no longer held out any hope either for national independence in Ireland or for the political advancement of the Irish in the United States. Another local hero was young Patrick R. Guiney, who returned from the war to join the Irish Republican Brotherhood and the Sumner wing of the Republican party. Born in Tipperary in 1835, Guiney had originally migrated to New Brunswick and then to Massachusetts, where he worked for a time as a machinist in Lawrence. After a brief term at Holy Cross College, he studied for the bar, practiced law in Boston, and, like so many other young Irish immigrants, became active in the Democratic party. When the Civil War began, he volunteered for duty in the Irish Ninth Regiment. He fought valiantly through many campaigns, lost the sight in one eye, and was mustered out as a brevet brigadier general. By that time, Guiney had become a staunch supporter of the Radical wing of the Republicans because of their support of the free slaves and their sympathy for the Fenian cause.[3] Seeing the example of such enthusiastic Irish converts, Republican leaders began to express sympathy openly for the goals of Fenianism, not only to attract more Irish voters but also to drive a wedge between the Irish and the Democratic party.[4]

As the Irish continued their struggle to achieve home rule for their native land, some became impatient with soft-talking statesmen in frock coats and silk hats whose elaborate parliamentary maneuvers and endless political collaborations never seemed to produce visible results. Convinced that only armed and violent resistance would force Great Britain to loosen its grip on Ireland, groups of nationalists formed the Irish Republican Brotherhood—better known as the Fenians, after a mythic Celtic hero—with branches created simultaneously in Dublin and New York in 1858. This highly secret organization, essentially a secular movement with little clerical support, encouraged Irish soldiers in the United States to use the military training and experience they had acquired in the Union army to advance the cause of Irish home rule once the Civil War was over. Federal authorities intercepted one attempt by Fenian troops to invade Canada in April 1866 but failed to prevent a second attempt two months later when "General" John O'Neil led a rag-tag army of fifteen hundred armed men across the Niagara River. Although the second effort also collapsed almost as soon as it had begun, the Fenians continued to raise money and collect arms for a third assault, which took place in the spring of 1870 when their armies moved on Canada from St. Albans, Vermont, and from Malone, New York. This time, both the American and Canadian governments were ready. After United States marshals arrested the Fenian ringleaders, the invading forces disintegrated.[5]

Despite the disappointing results and the often comic character of its nationalist crusade, the Fenian movement attracted the support of thousands in the United States and was a source of considerable pride among the Irish of Massachusetts.[6] Although it was denounced by most leaders of the Catholic Church in Boston, the Brotherhood nevertheless attracted ambitious young men, rallied the more adventurous elements in the immigrant community, and threatened the traditional alliance between the Irish voters and the Democratic party.[7] Republican leaders spotted this immediately and played up the Fenian cause for all it was worth in an effort to get Irish-American support. In 1866, for example, Senator Henry Wilson, a former Whig and Know-Nothing who had turned Republican, addressed a Fenian picnic, where he defined the movement as being for "the cause of liberty everywhere." At that point he declared: "Well, if that be Fenianism, then I am a Fenian."[8] Benjamin F. Butler, a former Democrat and controversial Union general, now a Radical Republican, was another who courted the Irish vote. Representing an Essex County congressional district, Butler offered a resolution expressing sympathy for the Fenian cause and calling upon the leaders of the nation to adopt an anti-British foreign policy.[9]

Democratic spokesmen, of course, made every effort to counteract Republican appeals and keep the Irish loyal to the old Jackson party. *The Pilot* urged the Irish to give their support to Lincoln's successor, President Andrew Johnson, "the early and constant friend of Ireland," and to hold out against the Radical Republicans who had assumed "a bloodthirsty and vindictive spirit towards the South."[10] Johnson himself actively cultivated Irish support by directing Secretary of State William Seward to petition the Canadian government for clemency for those Fenians who had been captured in the course of their unsuccessful attempt to invade Canada.[11]

Torn between their traditional allegiance to the Democratic party and ongoing attempts by Republicans to lure them away, more than one-third of the Irish voters of Massachusetts resolved the dilemma by sitting out the 1866 congressional elections. The majority of Irish who did go to the polls ignored *The Pilot* and voted in favor of Republicans for both houses of Congress. But the decline in Irish support for the Democrats, at least at the local level, proved to be only temporary. *The Pilot* cut its losses and stopped backing Andrew Johnson, agreeing that the Democrat from Tennessee had "forfeited his place in the party" but maintaining that he should not be impeached.[12] At the national level in 1868 the Irish voted overwhelmingly in favor of the Republican war-hero candidate, Ulysses S. Grant. Back in Massachusetts, however, they returned to their old party and voted for the Democratic gubernatorial candidate by a margin of two to one—even though he eventually lost badly.

At the local level as well as at the national level, it was still a struggle for the Democrats to maintain even a semblance of party organization. Year after year their leaders came together at political conventions for the obligatory ritual of putting up candidates for the various state offices, even though defeat was practically a foregone conclusion. Looking for new issues to turn public attention away from slavery, secession, and the war, they attempted to focus on local topics involving states' rights and individual liberties, such as the controversy over the repeal of the state's prohibition law, proposed literacy tests for voting, and the ever-present school question. But the painful wounds of the Civil War were still too tender for northern voters to reconcile themselves to the Democratic party. In 1867 Alexander Bullock, the Republican nominee, was reelected for a third term as governor of Massachusetts; all the state officers, along with most members of the state legislature, were also members of the Republican party. The Democrats didn't have a chance.

Clearly, something would have to be done to reorganize the party throughout the state, revitalize the membership, and establish new objectives in keeping with the demands of the postwar era. A major figure in this undertaking was a young Irishman named Patrick A. Collins, born on March 12, 1844, in Ballinfauna near Fermoy in County Cork. Collins and his mother joined the thousands bound for the United States after his father died of pneumonia at the height of the Great Famine. Young Collins became one in a line of prominent Irish-Catholic politicians in Boston— Martin Lomasney, Patrick Kennedy, John F. Fitzgerald, James Michael Curley, John W. McCormack, John E. Powers—who lost their fathers at an early age and dropped out of school to earn money at menial jobs to help their working mothers keep the family together. This is an observable pattern in immigrant life so striking that it is impossible to dismiss as mere coincidence. Positions for unskilled laborers in early nineteenth-century Boston were so scarce that fathers in most immigrant families took jobs no one else would take, working at projects that were rugged and usually dangerous. They wore themselves out digging, shoveling, lifting, hauling, and dragging, laboring for ten, twelve, fourteen hours a day with seldom a break and never a vacation. Ralph Waldo Emerson once wrote to his friend Henry David Thoreau telling him how astonished he was to discover Irish laborers who regularly worked a fifteen-hour day for no more than fifty cents.[13] Considering the nature of the jobs, the long hours, and the general inexperience of the immigrant workers, it is not surprising that they fell victim to industrial accidents at a staggering rate. One Irishman was struck by the almost daily litany of disasters reported in the newspapers: "an Irishman drowned—an Irishman crushed by a beam—an Irishman suffocated in a pit—an Irishman blown to atoms by a steam-engine—ten, twenty Irishmen buried alive by the sinking of a bank." These were typical of the perils to which "honest Pat" was constantly exposed in what he called, sadly, "the hard toils for his daily bread."[14] The long working hours, the grinding poverty, the oppressive overcrowding, and the unsanitary conditions in which such workers were forced to live caused outbreaks of tuberculosis, influenza, cholera, typhus, and other illnesses that carried off additional young immigrant fathers; cardiovascular disease took an extraordinary toll of Irish-American males and continued to do so for generations. Indeed, the death of Irish fathers in their late thirties or early forties was such a common occurrence that Boston's Theodore Parker referred to those men as a "perishing class" and observed on one occasion that he rarely encountered a "gray-haired Irishman."[15]

The premature deaths of so many heads of families left a tragic mark on the community, especially because there was seldom enough insurance or other financial assistance to support the widows and children. The mother usually became central to a family's will to survive and to keep the home together after the father's death, impressing upon all the children the absolute necessity to "stick together." The mother usually found some form of employment, scrubbing floors in downtown buildings at night, making beds in a nearby hotel or rooming house during the daytime, or taking up lodgings in a private home in the Back Bay or nearby Brookline as a domestic servant.[16] The children accepted their responsibility to help maintain the family as a fact of life—the inevitable consequence of living in this "vale of tears." They went out into the streets at the age of five or six to peddle newspapers, run errands, shine shoes, pick coal, or rummage through the junkyards for salable items. At the age of twelve or thirteen, they usually left school and took on full-time jobs handling freight on the piers or carrying hods of bricks on construction projects.[17]

Although in most cases, with everybody working and with help and care from aunts, uncles, and cousins, families were able to survive and even occasionally prosper, the impact of this kind of personal trauma and social dislocation must have produced incalculable psychological effects. For one thing, as William Shannon has suggested, it "pulled the family inward."[18] The death of the father focused the children more intensely than ever on the importance of the family in their lives and often made family the single most important consideration upon which they based decisions for the rest of their lives. It also centered the love and devotion of the children on the mother, who assumed a heroic and almost mythical position in Irish-Catholic society. With this collective history, many Irish Americans in Boston persisted in the kind of personal insecurity and national parochialism their ancestors brought with them from Ireland long after the same characteristics had begun to disappear among other ethnic groups and among the Irish in other parts of the country. Then, too, at a time in American history when individual ambition was encouraged and personal achievement was applauded as the criterion for success, the loss of an immigrant father caused many young men and women to subordinate their personal and professional aspirations to the interests of the family as a whole.[19] Tied to the family, rooted in the neighborhood, devoted to the mother, committed to siblings, the emerging Irish American in Boston was more concerned than ever with the immediate comforts of friendship, security, and close family ties than with the more distant prospects of riches, refinement, and renown.

It was in this tradition of fatherless sons and heroic mothers that Patrick Collins came to Boston. As an immigrant boy in a Chelsea public school, he experienced at first hand the intolerance of the Know-Nothing movement when a half-crazed evangelist calling himself "the Angel Gabriel" led a mob through the Catholic section of town, tearing the cross off the roof of the local church, breaking windows, smashing doors, and beating up young Patrick in the process. The Collins family moved briefly to Ohio where, for two years, Patrick worked in the fields and the coal mines; they then returned to South Boston, where Patrick is reported to have continued his education by walking into town to the Boston Public Library after his day's work as an upholsterer's apprentice.[20] In 1864 Collins joined the South Boston Fenian Circle, and two years later he took a full-time job as a recruiting agent for the Brotherhood. Working out of the New York office, he traveled extensively throughout New England until he became disillusioned and returned to his old job in the furniture warehouse.[21]

In the fall of 1867, Collins's career took a political turn when he "accidentally strolled" into the Democratic caucus in South Boston. Because in the course of his travels for the Fenians he had acquired a reputation as a good speaker, he was invited to give a talk to the gathering. His remarks were so well received that he won not only a hearty round of applause but also a place as a delegate to the upcoming Democratic state convention.[22] Several months later, at another caucus meeting, he was nominated to run for the state's house of representatives, won the election, and was reelected the following year. As a state legislator, Collins made it his special concern to ease the various restrictions that still plagued Catholics in hospitals and other public institutions. "I can cite numerous instances in which bigotry has cropped out in the management of our institutions," he charged.[23] Because of his activities, the Massachusetts General Hospital agreed to admit a greater number of Irish people to its wards, and his work in the legislature helped provide increased public funding for the House of the Angel Guardian and for the Sisters of the Good Shepherd. It was some time, however, before his repeated attempts to have Masses said for Catholic patients in penal and charitable institutions were enacted into law. While serving as a state representative, he attended Harvard Law School, earned his law degree in 1871, and passed the Massachusetts bar examination the same year.[24]

On August 18, 1868, while Collins was serving as a member of the General Court—one of only nineteen Democrats—he and Thomas Gargan held a meeting of young Irish political colleagues at the Parker House.

Gargan, then a young man the same age as Collins, was born in the West End of Irish parents who had arrived in Boston in 1825. After attending the public schools, Gargan eventually received a law degree from Boston University Law School before enlisting in the Irish regiment during the Civil War. After the war he returned to his law practice and became a prosperous corporate lawyer, an outstanding public speaker, and a Democratic member of the state legislature.[25] The Parker House meeting arranged by Gargan and Collins proved to be the initial organizational session of the Young Men's Democratic Club, of which Patrick Collins was elected first president, making this twenty-five-year-old Irishman a political figure to be taken seriously.

Obviously encouraged by signs of vitality and aggressiveness among their fellow countrymen throughout the city, Collins, Gargan, and members of the Young Men's Democratic Club began holding weekly meetings to plan campaign strategy, causing the *Boston Post* to remark that never before in the history of Boston had young Democrats shown such interest in a party ticket.[26] The club's first public demonstration took the form of a mammoth rally at Faneuil Hall on October 20, 1868. Seated on the stage of this historic gathering was Patrick Collins as presiding officer, along with such prominent Brahmin-Democrats as John Quincy Adams, Reuben Noble, William Gaston, and Edward Avery. Not in the least intimidated by the prestigious company, the slender young Irishman confidently announced to the audience that the Democrats of the state were now "organized and at work," and that their leaders were dedicated to the party that was the defender of the Constitution and the champion of the people. He urged all the young men of the state to join in a "ballot-box revolution" in order to rescue the state from Republican control.[27]

As the presidential election of 1872 approached, Collins and the Democrats were encouraged by the support they received from a new and unexpected quarter. A number of so-called Liberal Republicans had become disgusted with the ineffectiveness of President Ulysses S. Grant and the scandalous corruption going on within what Senator Grimes of Iowa called "the most corrupt and debauched political party that ever existed." In a desperate effort to defeat the Grant wing, the reformists abandoned the Republican candidate, Charles Francis Adams of Massachusetts, and threw their support to the Democratic candidate, Horace Greeley, crusading editor of the *New York Tribune*. As his platform called for civil service reform and universal amnesty, Greeley seemed the lesser of two evils as far as the Liberals were concerned. The Democrats, hungry for victory at any price and willing to do whatever it took to defeat the Republicans, joined forces with the Liberal Republicans and welcomed their support of Greeley. Massachusetts, therefore, saw some strange bedfellows, as Brahmin-Democrats and Irish-Democrats formed a bizarre coalition with upper-class Liberal Republicans. At the state convention at Worcester on September 11, 1872, the coalition members agreed to support Democrat Horace Greeley on the national ticket, while backing Liberal Republican Frank W. Bird for the post of governor of Massachusetts.[28]

After a bitter presidential campaign that featured ugly mudslinging and name-calling, Grant and his mainline Republican supporters inflicted a devastating defeat on Greeley and the Liberal Republican-Democratic coalition. From one point of view, the election of 1872 marked a new low in the history of the Democratic party, Not only had the party gone down once again to ignominious defeat, but it had lost all semblance of credibility by selling out to the Republicans. As Patrick Collins observed, the Democrats were in a state of "party demoralization."[29] From another point of view, however, the coalition formed in 1872, though temporary and obviously ineffective, provided the new members of the young Irish wing of the state's Democratic party with a degree of visibility, stature, and respectability they had never experienced before.

In the wake of the Democratic defeat in 1872, it was clear to Patrick Collins that young Irishmen like himself would have to work even harder to build their own political version of the Democratic party. They would, of course, continue to work with the old Brahmin-Democrats, whose social and political influence Collins regarded as essential to success. But the Brahmins dominated the Irish in party policy decisions and long-range planning. Collins came to realize that while it was flattering for an Irishman to hold an occasional office in the state legislature or serve one or two terms on the city's Board of Aldermen or the Common Council, this temporary and often random office-holding at the sufferance of the old-time Yankee party leaders was not going to upgrade the political power and status of the Irish in Massachusetts in any permanent fashion. Certainly, he was conscious of the increase in the city's Irish population—to the point where *The Pilot* suggested that the day was not far away when "the last descendant of the Puritans would be exhibited in a glass case at the United States Patent Office as a national curiosity."[30] Under these demographic circumstances, it seemed inappropriate that the Irish were still kept at arm's length by the party hierarchy and denied influence in the formulation of aims and policy. Collins complained that "the population of Boston is Democratic but its rule is Republican."[31] If the Irish were to become effective, he insisted, their politicians must forget about small, localized, and extraneous issues that used up a great deal of time but produced few tangible results. Democrats, he said, should stop fighting against the prohibition issue and debating the technicalities of "this miserable liquor law." They should get on with such practical matters as reorganizing the City Committee, establishing new ward headquarters, holding regular meetings, canvassing districts, and developing effective voter-registration procedures.[32]

Collins's chairmanship of the Democratic City Committee gave him the strategic opportunity to revitalize the party. In June 1874 he helped reorganize the old City Committee by having delegates elected from each of the city's wards.[33] At the first meeting of the new central committee, Collins was chosen president by a large plurality. From that moment on, he hammered home the point that effective organization and party solidarity were the keys to electoral success.[34] In appealing to Boston Democrats to overlook present losses and to organize for the future, Collins spelled out his basic political principle: "We are Democrats not because we are successful," he said, "but because we believe we are right."[35]

Collins and the other Democrats saw signs that the off-year elections in 1874 would bring a resurgence of the Democratic party throughout the country. The dreadful failures of Reconstruction, the disturbing economic dislocations of the Panic of 1873, and the corruption of the Grant administration as seen in the cases of the Crédit Mobilier, the Whiskey Ring, and

Patrick A. Collins was the second Irish-born Catholic to be elected mayor of Boston. Although he was never able to attend high school, he eventually graduated from the Harvard Law School, served in the U.S. Congress, and held the post of U.S. consul general at London. Collins proved such a popular mayor that the city fathers erected a monument in his honor on the Commonwealth Avenue mall. The Bostonian Society.

the Salary Grab Act all worked to the advantage of the Democrats, who won twenty-three of thirty-five states in November elections. In addition, Democrats won control of the House of Representativs in Washington, with 169 of their own members to only 109 Republicans. In the Massachusetts elections, Collins led the opposition to the Republican candidate and the prohibition ticket, while supporting the candidacy of Democrat William Gaston.[36] Although the Republicans still managed to keep control of the state legislature, Gaston was elected governor and rewarded Collins with an appointment as Judge Advocate of the state militia. This earned Collins the title of "General," which he personally claimed to dislike but which his friends and followers invariably used in referring to him.[37]

The hopes of the Democrats were revived by their off-year victory. They approached the presidential election with an air of confidence. Not since the election of James Buchanan in 1856—twenty years earlier—had Democrats seen the inside of the White House. When Democratic leaders in Massachusetts named four delegates to the national convention, Patrick Collins found himself on the same panel as old-line Brahmin-Democrats Judge Josiah Abbott, Edward Avery, and George W. Gill.[38] At the national level Collins and the Irish Democrats had no problem supporting Samuel J. Tilden, the Democratic governor of New York, as their presidential candidate now that Ulysses S. Grant was no longer available. At the state level, however, the Democrats faced some difficulties. William Gaston, their previous choice for governor, had decided to withdraw from the gubernatorial race in favor of the Liberal Republican Charles Francis Adams. This was the result of pressure from party leaders, who believed that the Adams name would enhance the Democratic ticket. Collins and most other Irish-American spokesmen disliked Adams, not only because of his party affiliation but also because they believed he had not done enough to help Fenian prisoners while he had been minister to the Court of St. James. In the interest of party unity, however, Collins set his personal feelings aside and urged his followers to do likewise and support the ticket. "In this fight Charles Francis Adams is with us," said Collins. "That is enough for me."[39] And with that, Collins went out and campaigned for the whole

Democratic ticket in a speaking tour that took him through Massachusetts, Connecticut, New York, New Jersey, and Ohio.

Despite their efforts, however, the Democrats failed once again to put a Democrat in the White House: Republican Rutherford B. Hayes won a close and bitterly contested victory over Samuel J. Tilden. On the state level, Republican Alexander Rice easily defeated Charles Francis Adams, who did even worse in Massachusetts than Tilden had done throughout the country. The defeat of Adams, however, could not be blamed on the Irish. Despite angry denunciations from groups of Irish nationalists, most Irish voters were kept in line by such leaders as Patrick Collins, Patrick Maguire, and Michael Cunniff, another young Irish immigrant whose successful career in banking, land development, and public utilities made him a valuable political asset.[40] The Irish swallowed their nationalist pride, maintained their party allegiance, and voted the straight Democratic ticket. While 1876 was clearly another disastrous year for the Democrats, it witnessed the revival of the party in Massachusetts, not only because of the prominent role played by local Irish leaders in reorganizing the party and getting out the vote, but also because of the remarkable degree of control these leaders exercised over their people during the election itself. Clearly, the Irish had turned the Democratic party around and would be the dominant influence in shaping its future policies.

Someone who recognized this subtle but significant party realignment in Massachusetts was Benjamin F. Butler. A complex and controversial personality, Butler had started out in Lowell before the Civil War as a registered Democrat, an active legislator, and a candidate for governor. He was an apologist for slavery, and in 1860 he attended the Democratic convention in Charleston, South Carolina; he subsequently endorsed Jefferson Davis for president. One year later, Butler became a brigadier general in the Union army, a member of the Radical Republicans, and one of the most hated men in the South because of the high-handed way in which he managed the military occupation of New Orleans. After the war, he was elected on the Republican ticket to the United States House of Representatives, where he supported the rights of freedmen, pressed for an eight-hour work day, and persistently called for the impeachment of President Andrew Johnson.[41]

From the outset, Ben Butler was a thorn in the side of Boston Brahmin politicians, Democrats and Republicans alike. They disliked his combative style of politicking as well as what they considered his vulgar behavior. He was simply not the kind of well-mannered gentleman they liked to see representing the interests of the Bay State. They also resented the way he pandered to the interests of the Irish and shrewdly cultivated the immigrant vote. As a member of the state legislature before the Civil War, for example, Butler led the fight to obtain compensation for the Ursuline convent fire; after the war he supported a congressional appropriation bill on behalf of the Little Sisters of the Poor. Recalling the valiant work of the nuns who aided the sick and wounded Union soldiers on the battlefield, Butler announced he would rather "cut off his right hand" than vote against such an appropriation because of any "religious prejudice against the Catholic faith."[42] Such sentiments were warmly received by the Irish, who continued to view Butler as their champion in the face of nativist attacks. "What public man in America has ever undergone such a swish of filthy abuse as General Butler?" asked one emotional reader of the *Irish World*, which agreed that "his enemies are our enemies."[43] Most Brahmins, however, dismissed this sort of rhetoric as typical of Butler's outrageous demagoguery. Butler had broken with the "sound traditions" of New England, they said, and they were sure that in extending his appeals to "the slums of the cities" he would be giving the liquor dealers of the state a free hand. One observer complained that Massachusetts had thrown the state open to the Irish only to have them, "like the snake in the fable, reward us by a Butler bite."[44]

Butler could afford to ignore the contempt of his upper-class Republican colleagues as long as his old comrade-in-arms, Ulysses S. Grant, was still president of the United States and a generous source of federal patronage. When Grant finally departed from the White House in March 1877, however, Butler's role as patronage boss within Bay State Republican circles came to an abrupt end, and he headed for greener pastures.[45]

Within a year, the political chameleon had returned to his roots in the Democratic party, and he had pulled together his own coalition of Civil War veterans, grateful Irish Americans, aggrieved workingmen, and a handful of black voters. At the Worcester convention on September 16, 1879, ebullient Butler supporters showed up at the crack of dawn, filled all the seats in the convention hall, and promptly nominated Butler for governor.[46] A week later the regular Democrats, furious at Butler's improper tactics, held their own convention in Boston and nominated Josiah Abbott for governor. Among those supporting Abbott and arguing in favor of the mainline Democratic ticket was Patrick Collins, who had been working for a decade to solidify the Brahmin-Irish Democratic coalition only to see it disrupted by Butler for the sake of personal ambition. Collins became even more upset as he watched the Republicans take advantage of the split in the Democratic ranks and put their own candidate in the governor's chair.[47]

The Democratic split continued for the next five years, with Butler and his supporters pitting their slate of candidates against those sponsored by such regular party leaders as Patrick Collins, Thomas Gargan, John Quincy Adams, Josiah Abbott, Frederick O. Prince, and Leverett Saltonstall.[48] With his eyes always on the governorship, Butler refused to yield his place to any of the regulars. He saw his chance in 1882, when Republican governor John D. Long decided not to run for reelection. Taking advantage of a factional split among the Republicans, Butler ran as both a Democrat and as a member of the new Greenback party. With votes from two parties, he was finally able to enjoy the year 1883 as governor of Massachusetts. The following year he was unseated by another Republican.[49]

The election of 1884 not only ended Butler's political career but also marked the end of an important phase of Irish-American politics in Boston. By aligning themselves with Ben Butler, a figure scorned and despised by the Yankee establishment, the Irish had badly damaged their credibility in the political community. For years Patrick Collins had worked to establish good relations between Brahmin-Democrats and Irish-Democrats in order to fashion a disciplined and harmonious political organization through which the Irish could eventually move into power. By abandoning such established party candidates as Adams and Abbott for a maverick like Butler, the Irish embarrassed Collins and convinced many old-time Brahmins that they had been right to distrust the Irish as disruptive and undependable malcontents.

While trying to hold together the statewide Brahmin-Irish coalition, Patrick Collins had also become involved with larger political concerns at the national level and even at the international level. In addition to his activities in the national Democratic party, Collins assumed the active presidency of the American Land League in a short-lived attempt to get Irish-American support for a program of Irish land reform as a step toward eventual home rule.[50] In 1881 Collins announced his candidacy for the new congressional seat produced by the redistricting of sections of the North End, the South End, and South Boston. He easily won the 1882 election and in March 1883 took his seat in the House of Representatives, where he continued to serve through two more terms until 1889.[51] During his years in Washington, Collins worked with Patrick Maguire and Michael Cunniff back in Boston to support the presidential candidacy of New York governor Grover Cleveland. Seeing an opportunity to establish better relations with the Massachusetts Brahmins now that the disruptive Ben Butler had left the scene, Collins welcomed the support of a group of upper-class Republican reformers popularly known as Mugwumps. These idealists had defected from their party for many of the same reasons that had led the old Liberal Republicans to abandon the Grant regime twelve years earlier. Convinced that the Republicans were on the wrong course and that their candidate, James G. Blaine of Maine, was the living embodiment of "venality, corruption, and demagoguery," the Mugwumps agreed to back Cleveland. Collins welcomed the liberal defectors, certain that the Mugwump votes would augment the support of the old-time Brahmin-Democrats, whose confidence he wanted to restore and whose influence he still believed was absolutely essential to the future growth of Irish power in Massachusetts.[52]

Although Grover Cleveland succeeded in winning the presidency for the Democrats in November 1884—he was the first Democratic president in twenty-eight years—back in Massachusetts the Democrats lost both the electoral vote and the governor's race.[53] The fact that more than one-third of Cleveland's statewide vote came from Irish-American Democrats, while a paltry 4 percent came from Republican Mugwumps, destroyed forever the belief of Collins and other Irish leaders that Irish political fortunes were dependent on the support of Yankee Democrats and occasional Republican defectors like the Liberals and the Mugwumps.[54] The election of 1884 demonstrated in dramatic fashion to Irish political leaders, especially to those in the Boston area, that such outside support was illusory at best and subject to the vagaries of statewide forces and pressures. It was clear that the Yankee Democrats needed the Irish much more than the Irish needed the Yankees. From then on, the Boston Irish set about developing their own organizational structure at the local level, from the ground up, regardless of movements in other parts of the state and independent of whatever sympathy or support their Yankee colleagues might provide.

As Patrick Collins moved into national affairs after the election of Grover Cleveland, political leadership in the City of Boston was taken over by Patrick J. Maguire, who saw opportunities for greater Irish political power in a city whose population had changed dramatically over the past quarter century. By the 1880s, after thirty or forty years in the city, the Boston Irish were no longer the impoverished and infirm exiles who had dragged themselves ashore during the 1840s and 1850s. Numbering well over seventy thousand, they constituted a large and maturing community that was becoming increasingly conscious of its size and assertive of its power. Every year the Irish increased their meager incomes, boosted themselves a notch higher on the economic ladder, and took more visible roles in municipal affairs. Before the Civil War there had been only one Irish policeman in the entire city—a man named Barney McGinniskin from "the bogs of Ireland," as he boldly announced to his fellow officers at their first meeting—and he had lasted only a short time on the force. By 1869, however, there were nearly forty Irish-born members of the Boston police force; by 1871 there were forty-five Irish Catholics in uniform.[55]

As their numbers rapidly grew, the first generation of immigrants began moving away from densely populated waterfront areas such as Fort Hill, the North End, and the West End. As new waves of immigrants arrived during the 1840s and 1850s, settling down in the same crowded tenements, shacks, and waterfront cellars, older families moved into the newly developed South End or crossed the water to the peninsulas of South Boston, East Boston, and Charlestown, where better jobs could be found. "By 1875, only a small immigrant community was left on Fort Hill," writes James B. Walsh, "and even the foreign-born population of the South Cove amounted to one-half that of South Boston. Within one generation of the heavy Irish influx of the late forties and fifties, South Boston had replaced Fort Hill as the most populous Irish district in the city."[56]

Then, by the late 1860s and early 1870s, when new forms of transportation such as the horse-drawn streetcar became available, many traveled farther out, to places like Dorchester, Roxbury, and Jamaica Plain and eventually to suburban rural areas such as Brighton and West Roxbury. To accommodate this substantial population shift, it was necessary to build more houses, schools, and churches, provide better playgrounds, enlarge police and fire departments, furnish water supplies, lay down new sewer lines, and develop a complete range of municipal services to meet the needs of incoming families.[57] A series of new public utilities were incorporated during the 1880s—the New England Telephone and Telegraph Company, the Edison Electric Illuminating Company, the Massachusetts Electric Company, the Boston Consolidated Gas Company—to bring in the gas, the electricity, and the telephone lines required to light the lamps, supply the power, and provide the communication systems for the homes and the offices, the schools and the stores, the churches and the hospitals. The new public utility companies and a vast array of municipal service projects offered badly needed employment on a scale never before seen in Boston. These were new occupational opportunities that did not take jobs away from native-born Bostonians and for which Irish Americans, desperate for work, considered themselves eminently qualified. In large numbers they rushed to fill the enormous labor vacuum. Providing needed services for their friends and neighbors in a quasi-official capacity as members of a municipal bureaucracy or employees of a huge corporation like the telephone company or the gas company gave them social status in their community as well as economic security. At first, of course, most of the

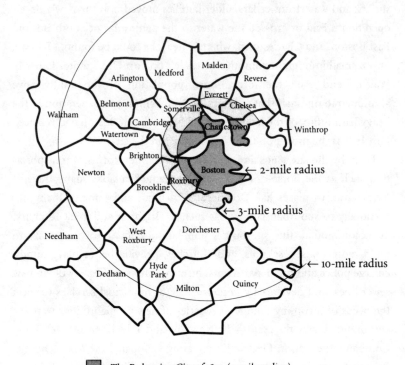

The map shows the following labeled areas:

Waltham, Arlington, Medford, Malden, Revere, Belmont, Everett, Chelsea, Somerville, Cambridge, Watertown, Charlestown, Winthrop, Brighton, Boston ← 2-mile radius, Newton, Roxbury, Brookline ← 3-mile radius, Needham, West Roxbury, Dorchester, ← 10-mile radius, Dedham, Hyde Park, Milton, Quincy

The Pedestrian City of 1850 (2-mile radius)
Boston Proper
East Boston
South Boston
Cambridge
Charlestown
Roxbury

The Peripheral Towns in 1850 (3-mile radius)
Brookline
Chelsea
Dorchester
Somerville

The New Suburbs in 1900 (10-mile radius)

Source: Sam Bass Warner, Jr., *Streetcar Suburbs* (Cambridge, 1962), p. 2.

Irish worked at the more menial jobs as ditchdiggers, hod carriers, pile drivers, cement mixers, and maintenance men. But those with quicker wits, shrewder minds, or better political connections soon became successful real-estate investors, public-works contractors, owners of trucking companies, and managers of construction corporations.[58]

But the demographic expansion during the 1870s and 1880s produced more than social and economic benefits for the Boston Irish; it had important political repercussions as well. The city's population had doubled in the twenty years between 1860 and 1880. Half this growth came from a rising birth rate and continuing immigration; the other half came from the physical expansion of such downtown areas as the South End and the Back Bay and from the legal absorption of outlying neighborhoods such as Roxbury, Dorchester, Brighton, Charlestown, and West Roxbury.[59] With their substantial growth in numbers and their extraordinary movement into the outer neighborhoods and suburbs in the course of a single generation, the Boston Irish now formed a larger and more influential political constituency than ever before. The population increase meant that old wards would have to be subdivided; the addition of new land meant that it was necessary for entirely new wards to be authorized. Back in 1854 there had been only twelve wards in the city; the number increased to twenty-four by 1875 and to twenty-five by 1876, when Ward 22 was divided in two. From that point until the city charter was revised in 1909, the Common Council had seventy-five members.[60] At a time when a whole new political infrastructure needed to be created in a vastly expanded city, young Patrick J. Maguire was in a position to oversee the political organization of Boston's tremendous number of Irish immigrant voters.

Born in Ireland, Patrick Maguire landed at Prince Edward Island in 1838 and spent his youthful years working there as a printer's apprentice. At the age of fourteen he moved to Boston, where he continued his work as a journeyman printer until he was twenty-seven years old, when he went into real estate. By 1882 he had built up a successful business that was profitable enough to allow him to establish *The Republic,* an Irish-Catholic newspaper that became an immediate success. Since the day in 1860 when he cast his first vote as an American citizen for Stephen A. Douglas, Maguire was a confirmed Democrat. Although he chose not to run for any elective public office himself, he became a longtime member of the Democratic City Committee, served on a variety of executive boards, attended Democratic conventions at the state and national levels, and for many years was a major power behind the scenes in Boston politics.[61]

Occasionally, a strong-willed individual like Boston's second mayor, Josiah Quincy ("the Great Mayor") made the office a significant instrument for change through sheer force of personality. But the office of Mayor of Boston was actually designed to be a ceremonial position with little authority. The city was run by the Board of Aldermen, with twelve members, and the Common Council, consisting of seventy-five representatives from the various wards of the city. The real power over the city's executive departments lay in the hands of the city councilors who chaired the committees that organized budgets, arranged finances, determined appropriations, made committee assignments, and distributed patronage for public-works projects.[62] A place on the Common Council, therefore, became a choice position for any aspiring Boston politician, and as the number of wards increased, the competition among candidates to control their own wards became much more active.

Every ward in each Irish neighborhood soon had factions that formed political networks operating out of neighborhood clubs or associations. At first the clubs and associations were primarily social and fraternal organizations, like the Red Berry Club, made up of older residents of the North End, or the Neptune Associates, one of numerous boat clubs in the waterfront wards. These were chiefly recreational centers, reminiscent of the old Irish pubs, where friends gathered to socialize, play cards, drink beer, exchange gossip, and compare notes about the politics of the district.[63] At first, according to historian Paul Kleppner, except for occasions when members came together to support one or another of their friends who happened to be running for public office, the involvement of these local clubs and associations in the formal political process was "sporadic" and "peripheral to their original and major purposes."[64] Ward leadership continued to change hands frequently, with the balance of power shifting back and forth between rival factions. Like ancient feudal barons (Paul Kleppner calls them "ward barons"), or perhaps like old Celtic chieftains, local leaders gathered loyal followers around them, fought for supremacy over would-be competitors, and spread the word as to how much protection they could offer the members of their tribe and how many benefits they could deliver in the shortest possible time.

As new Irish-Catholic political communities came into being in the outlying neighborhoods of the city, Patrick J. Maguire felt that it was not yet necessary to press for the election of a pro-Irish mayor. He was satisfied with getting more Irishmen elected to the Board of Aldermen and the Common Council, where they could take advantage of the numerous opportunities offered by the municipal bureaucracy. However, as the Irish political structure continued to expand and take more definitive shape, Maguire used his influence as a member of the Democratic City Committee to persuade his colleagues to nominate a well-known Brahmin-Democrat, Frederick O. Prince, for mayor in 1876. When Prince defeated his Republican opponent and moved into the mayor's office, Maguire emerged as the city's acknowledged political leader—"the only city-wide boss Boston ever had," according to political historian John T. Galvin. For the next twenty years, Galvin observes, "party decisions were made in the back rooms of Maguire's real estate office."[65] Capitalizing on his influence with Mayor Prince, Maguire was now able to put many more Irish Democrats on the city payroll and give out additional seats on the municipal boards charged with the management of police and the licensing of liquor. Mayor Prince, himself, named Thomas Gargan to the city's board of police, the highest municipal office yet held by an Irishman in Boston. Prince added more immigrants to the ranks of the police force and even found a job as a "light extinguisher" (of street lamps) for an enterprising seventeen-year-old youth in the West End named Martin Lomasney.[66] The parceling-out of jobs to Irish Democrats became a major campaign issue in 1877, when the Republican *Herald* denounced what it called "the ring" for seeking office in order to "aggrandize its own power at the expense of the people."[67] "Give him [Prince] another year," complained the conservative *Boston Evening Transcript*, "and our Irish fellow citizens would have no cause for complaint."[68] Mayor Prince stoutly defended his appointments, however, pointing out that there were still only a hundred Irishmen on a police force that totalled 715 members. Although Prince suffered a defeat in 1877, Maguire moved up to become president of the City Committee the following year and energetically orchestrated Prince's return to City Hall for three successive terms. At the same time, Maguire arranged for a highly respected physician, Dr. Samuel Abbott Greene, to succeed Prince and keep the seat warm for the Democrats.

Maguire was hard at work using his own newspaper, *The Republic*, to champion "all things Irish" and to attack "all things Republican as anti-Irish" and gearing up his city organization for its boldest move yet— putting forward an Irish-born Roman Catholic to become mayor of City.[69] Maguire's hand-picked candidate was Hugh O'Brien, whose parents had come over from Ireland in 1832 when he was five years old. O'Brien attended public school until he was twelve and then became a printer's apprentice on the *Boston Courier* before moving on to the printing firm of Tuttle, Dennett, and Chisholm on School Street. In contrast to Patrick Collins, who was straight, slender, and clean-shaven, O'Brien weighed a good 200 pounds and sported a moustache and a substantial beard. Working his way up in the financial world with his own publication, *Shipping and Commercial List*, which became an important source of information for mercantile and commercial interests throughout the city, O'Brien acquired a reputation in his own right as an able administrator and an effective financier. In 1875, at the age of forty-nine, he was elected to Boston's Board of Aldermen, where he served for seven years and distinguished himself by "conscientious hard work."[70] Solid, successful, and loyal, O'Brien appeared to Maguire to be the ideal candidate, one who had worked his way up the ladder and was ready to make the historic transition to the office of chief executive.

The City Committee officially endorsed Hugh O'Brien at its meeting on November 24, 1883, and Maguire's *Republic* came out in support. The paper warned Irish Americans against voting for the Republican candidate, Augustus P. Martin, on the grounds that this would provide "aid and comfort" to a person who had insulted the Irish people.[71] Although

Born in Ireland, Hugh O'Brien was a successful businessman before becoming the first Roman Catholic elected mayor of Boston. Holding down the tax rate, he managed to widen the streets, improve the park system, and promote the construction of the new Boston Public Library. O'Brien was considered such an efficient executive that he was elected to four consecutive terms as mayor. The Bostonian Society.

there were few public signs of religious or ethnic bigotry in the campaign, the *Boston Post* insisted that O'Brien's candidacy had produced "ringing discourses from the Protestant pulpits in all parts of the city."[72] The conservative *Transcript*, in coming out against O'Brien, denied that his Irish background offered any reason for voting either for or against him. Instead, it focused on his earlier political career as an alderman. O'Brien, charged the *Transcript*, had not only engaged in "junketeering" while in office but had also been responsible for removing a number of "faithful and competent" public officials in order to satisfy the political appetites of Patrick Maguire and the Democratic City Committee.[73] Apparently these charges produced some negative reactions because O'Brien lost to Augustus Martin by a vote of 27,494 to 25,950.

Mayor Martin had hardly settled into office before Maguire's *Republic* accused him of "gross unfitness for the place he occupies." Not only had Martin held back promotions for certain city employees because they were Irish, charged Maguire, but he had also been responsible for careless fiscal policies in managing the affairs of the city.[74] For the most part, however, the City Committee avoided ethnic and religious arguments in supporting Hugh O'Brien's second run at the mayor's office. This was the year when Republican presidential candidate James G. Blaine lost many Irish votes in New York by failing to disavow an insulting remark by a Protestant clergyman to the effect that Democrats were the party of "Rum, Romanism, and Rebellion," but serious religious controversy failed to materialize in Boston.[75] Local Democrats concentrated almost exclusively on the city's "excessive tax rate" and O'Brien's experience as an effective manager and administrator. Shrewdly appealing to the old Yankee virtues of thrift, probity, and limited taxation, the Democrats charged that Mayor Martin had failed to maintain a strict economy.[76] Pointing to the fact that O'Brien had voted against every appropriation bill that came before him during his seven years as alderman, the Committee assured voters that their candidate would reduce the tax rate without cutting needed services.[77] Despite Republican warnings that O'Brien's election would reestablish the kind of "ring rule" at City Hall that had existed when Patrick Maguire pulled the strings that manipulated Mayor Prince, O'Brien rode the Democratic wave that swept Grover Cleveland into the White House, taking fifteen wards to Martin's ten and capturing Charlestown and South Boston. On Tuesday, December 10, 1884, the city of Boston elected its first Irish-born, Roman Catholic mayor by a margin of 3,124 votes.[78]

In the mid-1880s, as a result of a decade of political maturation and perhaps encouraged by O'Brien's election, a number of powerful and ambitious figures known as "bosses" emerged from the pack in the city's Irish wards. Each boss moved to the forefront as the acknowledged political chieftain, the recognized center of power in his particular ward and the distributor of favors to those who accepted his rule. After a few years in the public schools, these bosses—all immigrants or the sons of immigrants—had worked their way up to jobs that enabled them to meet a wide variety of people and hone their talents at influence and persuasion before moving into the larger world of politics. Some owned grocery stores; others operated barrooms and saloons; still others made their living as funeral directors. They occupied strategic positions that allowed them to meet people and offer assistance, to lend money and extend credit, to do favors and express compassion, and to gradually become as well known and highly regarded in their neighborhoods as the parish priest. As the bosses in each ward elbowed out their political rivals and accumulated power and influence, they maintained their influence through a system of local organization that soon became the accepted pattern throughout the city, starting with the older wards in the inner city, such as the North End and the South End, and branching out to the newer neighborhoods and the suburbs. Once a local leader was accepted and installed, even temporarily, his ward was divided into precincts, each with a presiding captain. Each captain supervised perhaps a dozen lieutenants, who, in turn, supervised workers assigned to specific streets. Comparing police lists with voting lists, these workers were expected to check each house on the street to make sure that every party member voted in every election. Each worker had to account to his lieutenant for the failure of even one voter to show up at the polls.[79] To ensure maximum efficiency, personal loyalty was emphasized and party discipline strictly enforced. When the boss held meetings with his captains and lieutenants, the discussions were generally open and a variety of views and opinions could be expressed. Once the leader arrived at a decision, however, no word could be raised against it.[80]

For many an Irish ward boss, politics was more than a means of attaining personal power and social advancement. It was an opportunity to help family, friends, and neighbors at a time when they could not obtain what they needed anywhere but from the crusty Yankee guardians of public charity. It was precisely to relieve thousands of his people of what he aptly called "the inquisitorial terrors of organized charity" that Martin Lomasney, one of the new ward bosses making a name for himself in the West End's Ward 8, worked so hard at his headquarters every day of the year.[81] The needs of poor, uneducated, unemployed immigrant people were basic but mostly unattainable at that time: food and clothing, dentures and eyeglasses, jobs and pardons, medical care and legal advice. The reward for political support was the ward boss's assurances that he would somehow fill these needs. In his perceptive study of urban development from 1870 to 1890, historian Jon Teaford questions the long-held belief that during that period American cities were in a state of "municipal disarray." Teaford insists that the picture of urban rule as a "place of shame" has been greatly exaggerated and the ill effects of ward politics unduly magnified. Most city governments, he maintains, were not only surprisingly well run but, in places like Boston, could claim "grand achievements" like the building of the new Boston Public Library and the construction of Frederick Law Olmsted's impressive park system.[82] From the vantage point of history, the Gilded Age certainly produced remarkable civic improvements and upgraded municipal services; in the reality of the moment, however, these institutional achievements had little effect on the drab daily lives of the poor immigrant families living in squalor in the lower wards of the city. Hungry and cold, lonely and sick, living in ramshackle tenements with dirt-floored basements and no running water, without access to economic benefits or charitable aid, the poor turned to local ward politician as their only source of personal compassion and practical assistance. As Lomasney once philosophized: "The great mass of people are interested in only three things—food, clothing, and shelter. A politician in a district like mine sees to it that his people get these things.

If he does, then he doesn't have to worry about their loyalty and support."[83] It was as simple as that. Power and patronage went hand in hand in the Irish neighborhoods; this was a fact of everyday life that everyone knew and accepted. The underlying political attitude of Irish immigrants differed substantially from that of the old Yankees. The difference was not merely a matter of background, nationality, or culture; it was also a fundamental difference of philosophy with regard to the very nature of the human person and the essential purpose of government.

In 1980 in a lecture series at the John F. Kennedy Library commemorating the 350th anniversary of the founding of Boston, the historian John William Ward distinguished two major strains of political thought in Boston history. The traditional Puritan-Yankee-Brahmin strain he called "rational politics." By this term he meant a coherent system of bureaucratic politics that is designed to work in the "public interest" and that seeks out a political leader who will steadfastly pursue the "general good." Such a leader resists selfish interests, pressure groups, and single-issue constituencies in his sworn duty to serve the "common weal." Rational politics, according to Ward, has usually had a special appeal for administrators, corporate managers, and salaried intellectuals. To the Yankees, the Brahmins, and other native-born Bostonians who have generally believed in the efficacy of such a system, the function of government is to establish the rule of law for the community as a whole in a rational and equitable manner, to operate the financial system with honesty and frugality, and to ensure that the political leaders chosen to head city government are gentlemen of background, breeding, education, and experience.[84]

The second strain—newer in Boston history—Ward called "ethnic politics," an approach characteristic not only of the Irish but of most immigrant groups who came to America. This he described as a political culture that celebrates the personal and individual rather than the general and the universal, that emphasizes family and friendship, and that strongly rejects the notion that human beings merit affection "only if they have earned it by their achievement and performance." The emotional appeal of the ethnic politician, he said, is to a realm of "human values" usually considered irrelevant and often even "illegitimate" in the rational bureaucratic world.

To illustrate this difference, Ward repeated a well-known anecdote about a proper lady from Beacon Hill who went ringing doorbells in an Irish neighborhood on behalf of her candidate for the school committee—a candidate with a Harvard degree and a distinguished pedigree. One Irish housewife listened politely to the lady's appeal, then asked, "But doesn't he have a sister who works for the schools or is somehow involved with the school system?" The Beacon Hill lady drew herself up and said, "I assure you, Madam, my candidate is *not* the sort of man who would use his position to advance the cause of his own sister." Whereupon the housewife replied, "Well, if the son of a bitch wouldn't help his own sister, then why would I vote for him?" and slammed the door in her face.[85]

Although this story is one of Boston's oldest chestnuts, it captures precisely the city's opposing attitudes toward government's role in civic affairs. The typical Yankee, on the one hand, is shocked by the idea that government should be used for the benefit of particular individuals, that an exception should be made for a relative or close friend. Such an approach violates an equitable system of political management and is palpably unfair, in the Yankee view. The typical Irishman, on the other hand, is shocked by the idea that a humane official should overlook the plight of a constituent or the needs of a friend. Newly arrived immigrants took it for granted that a major function of government in America was to provide them with sanctuary, to help them acquire the basic necessities of life, and to offer them opportunities for social and economic advancement. After all, what was government for, if not to help people in this way? "I think that there's got to be in every ward somebody that any bloke can come to—no matter what he's done—and get help," Martin Lomasney is reported to have told the writer and social critic Lincoln Steffens in the course of his research into the plight of American cities. "Help, you understand," said the ward boss, emphasizing the particularistic nature of the ethnic philosophy, "none of your law and justice, but *help.*"

There was a stylistic difference, too, in the way the two cultures approached the process of politics. To the native-born Yankee, politics was a serious business, a civic responsibility that a member of the more fortunate classes assumed with sober reflection and objective concern for the general welfare. Involvement in political affairs was based on a heritage of Anglo-Saxon constitutional precedent and conducted with gentlemanly observance of the rules of proper conduct and fair play. To the immigrant Irish, on the other hand, politics was a practical means to a practical end, fought with the enthusiasm of tribal warfare and the passion of a major theatrical production. All was fair in Boston politics as far as the Irish were concerned, and although they tried to work within the law they were seldom perturbed if their efforts exceeded legal limits. What counted, of course, was winning—but it was also important to win with a measure of ingenuity and drama that would capture the imagination of the electorate and the rank and file of the party. Strategies were planned, rivals outwitted, enemies outmaneuvered, legalities bypassed, and dirty tricks carried out in dramas that became part of the city's political folklore for generations to come. Over the years, politicians regaled each other with classic stories of candidates who turned the tables on one another through ingenious deceptions and uproarious chicaneries. Some political victories were achieved through the prosaic techniques of bribery, extortion, blackmail, physical intimidation (both Martin Lomasney and his brother Joseph were shot in the course of bitter campaigns), or the gift of a welcome bottle of whiskey. Others were won by clever deceptions, blatant forgeries, or just plain dirty tricks, which gained a certain legitimacy as nostalgic reminiscence embellished original facts. Carefully placed reports that a rival candidate was planning to divorce his wife, had run away with a young girl, had converted to Protestantism, or had been seen eating meat on Friday were always good for damaging a reputation in Catholic Boston. Ward bosses made it common practice to send members disguised as Protestant clergymen campaigning for rival candidates in Irish neighborhoods.[86] Occasionally stories became legends, as in the case of Martin Lomasney's envelope trick in 1898. Faced with a challenge to one of his candidates in a senatorial contest, Lomasney called for a party convention at 4:30 P.M. on October 20 at the Maverick House in East Boston. This location was directly across the harbor from the State House on Beacon Hill, where the deadline for filing nomination papers had been set for 5:00 P.M. the same day. Holding a meeting with his supporters in one room while his fellow Irish opponents gathered in another, Lomasney quickly got his candidate nominated and then threw an envelope out the window to a confederate below, who led supporters of the opposing candidate in wild pursuit through the streets of East Boston. Meanwhile, Lomasney threw an envelope with the real nomination papers to a second confederate, who drove off in a hack to a waiting ferry boat. When the vessel reached the other side of the harbor, the envelope was handed to a waiting cyclist who raced madly through the streets of Boston to the State House. There he delivered the nomination papers to the Secretary of State's office at precisely 4:49 P.M.[87] Politics, to the Irish, was not simply dignified posturing and orderly procedure. It was a life-and-death struggle to gain power, status, and reputation in a city that despised them and relegated them to a permanent underclass. Politics was one path to success in the New World, dependent only on the nature of one's talents and the extent of one's ambitions; it was a path the Irish chose with gusto and determination.

The practical political philosophy of the Boston Irish, based on the assumption that it was the responsibility of government to take an active role in the lives of its citizens, was more than an interesting aberration that would moderate over the years. It produced a fundamental change in the political philosophy of the Democratic party itself, a change that would extend to the national level in the twentieth century. Upon their arrival in America, the Irish became part of a Democratic party that in the early part of the nineteenth century, especially before the Civil War, was essentially a rural organization, with significant southern support. Its Jeffersonian philosophy of strict construction emphasized such policies as limited central government, states' rights, local controls, limited taxation, and restrictive appropriations. Through the greater part of the nineteenth century, Democrats advocated the prevailing political philosophy of laissez-faire and free trade, regularly opposing a national banking system, protective tariffs, federal assistance for manufacturing, and any other program involving a direct relationship between the federal government and the economic, social, or cultural life of the nation. The party hailed the Dred Scott decision, which denied the power of the federal government to authorize national citizenship or limit the territorial expansion of slavery, and the Democrats' insistence on the right of a state to secede from the Union eventually contributed to the catastrophe of civil war. Even after the war, there were no immediate signs that the Democratic party had substantially altered its outlook. It still held to the dictum that the business of government was government, strictly defined. Only time would tell how long the urban-based Irish, given their growing political base and their view of the larger social purposes of government, would be willing to accept this essentially rural, anti-urban, and limited view of government.

For the time being, the Irish Democrats faced an immediate and pressing dilemma in their gradual but seemingly inevitable movement to take over the reins of city government. By the mid-1880s, a conflict had developed between the two layers of Irish influence in Boston politics. The outcome would determine whether the Irish moved into more influential positions throughout the city or were forced to continue as a minority faction operating at the neighborhood level.

One layer was represented in the remarkable achievement of Patrick J. Maguire, Michael Cunniff, and the other members of the City Committee in getting Hugh O'Brien elected as mayor of Boston. After nearly two decades of slow, steady, and often painful work, the election of the city's first Irish-born candidate was evidence of the organizational talents of local leaders as well as the degree to which such leaders were prepared to take over control of city politics. The second layer, making its appearance at about the same time, consisted of independent neighborhood wards, controlled by powerful, ambitious, and determined men who exercised extraordinary control over the districts in which they lived and the people with whom they associated.

Where, then, would the power lie after 1884? Would it be at the city-wide level, with Maguire and his City Committee establishing their influence throughout the municipal government by means of strategic appointments and carefully crafted city elections? Or would it be in the hands of the ward bosses, contending for power within their respective districts and bargaining for municipal patronage to enhance their authority and satisfy their grateful constituents? Clearly, the next decade would be crucial for the political future of the Boston Irish.

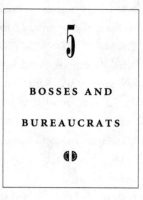

5

BOSSES AND

BUREAUCRATS

ON JANUARY 5, 1885, a little after ten o'clock in the morning, Chief Justice Marcus Morton of the Supreme Judicial Court of Massachusettes administered the oath of office to Hugh O'Brien, making him the first Irish-born mayor of Boston.[1] Irish Democrats, of course, were delighted that after generations of scorn and derision one of "their own" had attained the pinnacle of success in terms of both political power and personal stature. Many members of the city's Protestant-Yankee community agreed that Mr. O'Brien was a suitable man for the job and that he appeared to be assuming his executive duties in a commendable fashion.

Although he covered a whole range of topics in his inaugural address, delivered before the assembled aldermen and members of the Common Council—population and economics, bridges and streets, police and fire, schools and parks, health and sewerage—Mayor O'Brien concentrated on the campaign themes of prudent fiscal management and scheduled tax relief. Deploring the fact that his predecessor had allowed the property tax rate to increase from $14.50 to $17.00 per thousand, he insisted that there was no reason why a $15.00 tax rate could not remain in place for the next ten years despite the city's remarkable growth in area and population. Having gained considerable experience in managing extensive park lands during his years as alderman, O'Brien called for the city to develop a comprehensive plan for a system of streets in the outlying suburban sections that would soon become part of the metropolitan area.[2]

True to his word, during his first year in office O'Brien cut the tax rate 24 percent and maintained it below $15.00 for the next four years. Beyond an occasional gesture to please his Irish constituency—like ordering the Boston Public Library closed on St. Patrick's Day—his preoccupation with holding down the tax rate and widening the streets made him almost indistinguishable from the procession of Yankee mayors who had preceded him. His position on the question of civil service reform was strong enough to placate his liberal Mugwump supporters but ambiguous enough to satisfy Patrick Maguire, with whom he quietly cooperated in handing out a number of "party" jobs to deserving Democrats.[3]

Even in dealing with controversial matters, O'Brien conducted himself in a manner that reduced the level of anxiety that most Yankees felt in seeing an Irishman in charge of city affairs. A good example of this is his approach to the planning of Boston's park system, which also illustrates what historian Jon Teaford describes as a subtle but significant change in the style of late nineteenth-century urban politics. Although businessman-mayors and plutocrat park commissioners may have continued to look down their noses at ward politicians and immigrant voters, says Teaford, they nevertheless found themselves working with them in order to bring about some measure of civic improvement.[4] In 1875 when Samuel C. Cobb was mayor, a park bill was presented to the Common Council requesting the mayor to petition the state legislature to authorize the taking of lands within the city limits. Despite considerable opposition, the vigorous efforts of councilor George A. Shaw and then-alderman Hugh O'Brien resulted in passage of the Park Act of 1875, which established a three-man municipal commission appointed by the mayor and approved by the Common Council. Mayor Cobb subsequently named a park board consisting of three prominent Yankee businessmen—Charles H. Dalton, treasurer of the Manchester Print Works; William Gray, Jr., treasurer of the Atlantic Cotton Mills; and T. Jefferson Coolidge, treasurer of the Lawrence and Amoskeag Manufacturing Companies.[5] Frederick Law Olmsted was invited to create for Boston a new park system to rival the one he had recently designed for New York City.

After his inauguration as mayor in 1885, Hugh O'Brien continued to support the ambitious park program but replaced the original three members of the Park Commission with three new members who better represented the city's new Democratic coalition: Patrick Maguire, the powerful political boss and editor of the weekly *Republic;* John F. Andrew, a liberal Republican Mugwump and son of the late Civil War governor; and Benjamin Dean, a well-known Yankee Democrat. No one was quite certain what this change meant, but it was obvious that many feared the worst—especially since Republicans regarded the appointment of Maguire as a flagrant example of the spoils system in action.[6] Early in 1885, Charles Eliot Norton, professor of fine arts at Harvard, wrote to his friend Frederick Law Olmsted informing him in ominous terms that "the Irish dynasty has fairly settled itself upon the throne in Boston." Olmsted's fears that his project had fallen into the hands of political appointees with no interest in it must have been confirmed when he learned that the new board had rescinded the resolution under which he had been employed. A few weeks later, however, the board approved a new contract with substantially the same terms, and from then on relations between Olmsted and the new commissioners were effective and cooperative. On January 30, 1886, Commissioners Andrew, Dean, and Maguire invited Mayor O'Brien to a board meeting at the Olmsted firm's field office in Franklin Park, where Olmsted presented a plan to incorporate Franklin Park as an integral part of his interconnected park system, which later became known as "the Emerald Necklace." In February of the following year, the commissioners agreed to adopt Olmsted's plan and asked him to prepare a statement for publication. In 1889, in an address to the New England Club, Olmsted described his decade of association with the Boston Park Commission in very positive terms.[7] Clearly, as Olmsted's recent biographer states, "O'Brien's administration proved to be intelligent, honest, economical, and reform-oriented."[8]

As O'Brien came to the end of his first term, there seemed to be a consensus that he had done a good job and deserved a chance to continue.

He was supported for reelection by the *Boston Post,* and both the *Globe* and the *Herald* agreed that the incumbent would be acceptable for another term. The *Boston Daily Advertiser* ran a front-page advertisement listing the names of one hundred prominent Bostonians from distinguished families such as the Bowditches, the Danas, the Pingrees, the Quincys, and the Sargents, who endorsed O'Brien for reelection. O'Brien was promptly returned to office in December 1885 with the largest majority in any city-wide Boston election.[9] "The slaughter was terrific and the Democratic triumph sweeping," commented the *Globe,* as O'Brien's party won majorities in both the Board of Aldermen and the Common Council. Now that the "liberal-minded citizens of Boston" had spoken out in favor of the Irish-Catholic candidate, Maguire's *Republic* went so far as to declare that intolerance in Boston was a thing of the past.[10]

A year later, O'Brien won a third term as mayor, defeating Thomas Norton Hart, president of the Mount Vernon National Bank and a member of the Board of Aldermen. In 1887, O'Brien defeated Hart again, although by a much slimmer margin. At this point O'Brien could point with pride to the fact that the average tax rate for Boston over the past three years had been kept to only $12.98 per thousand; moreover, between 1885 and 1887 he had reduced the net debt by more than a million dollars. In his final inaugural address he reported satisfactory progress on the new courthouse at Pemberton Square but complained of decidedly "slow progress" in the planning of the new Boston Public Library to be built in Copley Square. Asserting that this impressive structure should be a monument "to our intelligence and culture," he urged the Common Council to appropriate additional funds for the library project "even at the risk of being called extravagant."[11] On November 28, 1888, O'Brien had the pleasure of presiding at the laying of the library cornerstone, with eighty-year-old Dr. Oliver Wendell Holmes reading a poem composed for the occasion.

To many native Bostonians, Hugh O'Brien was a pleasant surprise. Businesslike, sober, and cautious, he displayed none of the disturbing characteristics Yankees usually associated with immigrants from Ireland. He contradicted the stereotypes of the day (described by a later historian as follows): "Paddy, the hopeless, witty Irishman, given to drink and quick to tears and laughter, who loved nothing more than 'rows and ructions,' and Bridget, the chaste and prudent but comically ignorant serving girl."[12] There was none of Paddy to be found in the formidable persona of Mayor O'Brien. Furthermore, he was cordial to the Brahmins individually, and deferential to the traditions of the city they personified. He dressed appropriately, spoke correctly, accommodated himself to his surroundings in a dignified manner, and generally displayed the deportment Yankees expected of their public officials. O'Brien could be seen as a role model for his fellow immigrants, an example of what other serious, ambitious, and hard-working members of the Irish race could eventually achieve by abandoning their lazy, happy-go-lucky ways and adapting to the old Yankee principles of thrift, sobriety, and industry. O'Brien, in short, was a "good" Irishman, an "acceptable" Irishman, the kind of Irishman Yankees would seek out and encourage to become the leaders of the Irish and eventually leaders of the city.

Another Irishman of the "better sort," whom the Yankees held in high regard, was Patrick Collins. The Yankees looked favorably upon Collins's rise from humble immigrant origins through hard work, perseverance, and natural talent to graduate from the Harvard Law School and become a successful lawyer, a wealthy gentleman, a director of the International Trust Company, and a rising star in the Democratic party. Collins's career was viewed as a satisfying demonstration of the American work ethic carried to its logical conclusion—a true rags-to-riches story in the Horatio Alger tradition.[13] City leaders saw in his close personal association with Adams, Abbott, Quincy, Gaston, Prince, and the other members of the city's Brahmin hierarchy a clear indication of his belief that by following the traditional Yankee standards of behavior and public service the Irish would be able to raise themselves to new heights.[14]

The Yankees also admired Collins for calling upon his supporters to become full-fledged Americans rather than displaced Irishmen in temporary exile and to devote themselves to the concerns and interests of their adopted country. "Let me say now that there are no Irish voters among us," he said in 1876 to an immigrant audience at Marlboro, Massachusetts, echoing the sentiments expressed by Bishop Fitzpatrick a generation earlier. "There are Irish-born citizens like myself, and there will be many more of us," he continued. "But the moment the seal of the government was impressed upon our papers we ceased to be foreigners and became Americans." "Americans we are," he insisted, "and Americans we will remain."[15] He repeated this theme again and again in public addresses as he urged the Irish to move beyond the parochialism of their past and become contributing participants in their American present. "Those of us born in Ireland or who sprang from the Irish race are here to stay," he reminded his listeners in Albany, New York, during the 1884 campaign. "We and our children and our children's children are here merged in this great, free, composite nationality, true and loyal citizens of the state and federal systems, sharing in the burdens and the blessings of the freest people on the earth."[16]

This was a sincere accommodationist philosophy that gladdened the hearts of native Bostonians, who saw Collins, like O'Brien, as an invaluable ally in bringing the immigrant voters into the mainstream of American society. In 1884, when the loss of income from his former law practice nearly forced Collins to withdraw from the race for a second term as United States congressman, members of the Boston business community were dismayed at the prospect of losing his voice in the Congress and persuaded him to reconsider. Indeed, Collins biographer Michael Curran reports that in commercial and banking circles "a proposition was made to insure his financial independence."[17] Lucius Tuttle, president of the Boston and Maine Railroad, described Collins as "one of the most useful officeholders we ever had in this city." "I say this," he added, "as a Republican and not as a Democrat."[18] For the time being, however, Collins was no longer a factor in the Boston scene, having immersed himself in national politics as an active supporter of Grover Cleveland and a possible candidate for the presidential cabinet. But if, in the future, Patrick Collins should return to Boston, he was just the kind of "acceptable" Irishman the Yankees would support for public office.

At this time another Irishman made his appearance in Boston and rapidly became one of the most articulate and attractive figures on the scene.

John Boyle O'Reilly was born June 28, 1844, in a castle on the outskirts of Drogheda, County Heath, the site of Oliver Cromwell's savage massacre of Catholic women and children. Coming from a family of educators and scholars, O'Reilly traveled to England to work as a printer's apprentice and then enlisted in the British army with the intention of converting Irish-born soldiers to the Fenian cause. When his subterfuge was discovered, he was sent to a penal colony in Australia, but he made a daring escape and eventually found his way to Boston. There, he was befriended by local nationalists such as Patrick Collins and an Irish-American poet named Robert Dwyer Joyce, who helped O'Reilly get an apartment in the West End and a job as a reporter for *The Pilot* in the spring of 1870. During his initial years with the newspaper, O'Reilly displayed an intensely American patriotism, became increasingly critical of the revolutionary aspects of Irish nationalism, and called upon Catholics and Protestants in America to reconcile their differences and work together to present a united front. Although he continued to agitate for home rule in Ireland, he urged Irish Americans to moderate their activities on this side of the Atlantic.[19]

O'Reilly's graceful style of writing, his patriotism, and his conciliatory politics quickly made him a favorite in Brahmin literary and social circles, and in 1872 he was invited to join the exclusive Papyrus Club. The following year, however, perhaps to indicate that he had not gone over to "the other side," O'Reilly helped found the Catholic Union, an organization composed of leading Boston Catholics devoted to the teachings of Pope Pius IX. O'Reilly's future in Boston was prematurely assured when, in 1876 (only six years after his arrival as a fugitive) he and Archbishop John Williams purchased *The Pilot* from Patrick Donahoe. Three years later, O'Reilly was elected president of both the Papyrus Club and the Boston Press Club, and he purchased a summer home in Hull from Amos A. Lawrence, the prominent Boston financier and philanthropist.[20]

By the 1800s, O'Reilly had established himself as one of the leading Irish Americans in the nation. He particularly endeared himself to the New England Yankees, who regarded the young poet as one of the great Celtic bards and also as one of those "acceptable" Irishmen they would like to see leading in city politics. The Yankees installed O'Reilly as a charter

John Boyle O'Reilly, a political refugee from Ireland, won local acclaim for his literary talents, his promotion of American patriotism, and his support of civil rights causes. He was admired not only by his fellow Irishmen, but also by the Brahmins of the city, who invited him to compose the verse for the formal dedication of the Plymouth Rock monument in 1889.
The Bostonian Society.

member of the St. Botolph Club and in June 1881 elected him an honorary member of the Phi Beta Kappa chapter at Dartmouth College. In February 1886 O'Reilly spoke on the Irish question before the Beacon Club, an organization of prominent Boston businessmen; and in November 1888 he published a poem eulogizing Crispus Attucks and his role as a black patriot in the Boston Massacre. In 1889 he was invited to give the main address at the dedication of the national monument to the Pilgrim Fathers at Plymouth Rock. The choice of O'Reilly for this prestigious honor in place of such venerable literary figures as John Greenleaf Whittier and Oliver Wendell Holmes made it clear that he had reached the pinnacle of success in Boston.[21]

There was no question that O'Reilly had won the plaudits of the Brahmins and the admiration of the Irish, but there was considerable doubt about the extent to which he represented the views of the average Irish-Catholic workingman and could play a leadership role in the development of Irish political power in the city. While he involved himself in a wide variety of economic causes, racial issues, and social crusades, he had little to do with the day-to-day problems faced by immigrants in their crowded tenements and miserable workshops. He was a zealous supporter of a Democratic party whose Jeffersonian ideals promoted an independent yeomanry, but he was rarely able to translate the party's agrarian ideals into positive solutions to benefit his city-based countrymen. Without an urban constituency or a neighborhood base, and with virtually no first-hand experience with the intense bigotry under which the Boston Irish had suffered for so many generations, O'Reilly proved to be more of a philosopher and theorist than a political practitioner.[22]

For all their hopes of winnowing from the immigrant chaff a few slender stalks of good wheat, the Yankee community found the pickings depressingly slim. After four terms as mayor, Hugh O'Brien's allotted time was running out; Patrick Collins was still involved with Grover Cleveland and national politics in Washington; John Boyle O'Reilly offered little evidence of the kind of practical leadership the city needed. And if there were no more "acceptable" Irishmen to mold into leaders who would carry on the Yankee tradition, then the city was at the mercy of those "other kinds" of Irishmen who wanted control for the benefit of their own local constituents and for their own selfish ends.

Those "other kinds" of Irishmen were part of that large amorphous mass of immigrants that had grown inexorably to swell Boston's depressed underclass. Those who had come ashore most recently still lived in the shacks, shanties, and cellars of the old waterfront wards of downtown Boston, comprising the North End and the West End. A great many second-generation Irish, however, had moved to better quarters in the neighborhoods of Charlestown, East Boston, South Boston, and Dorchester. There they lived in wooden tenements, inexpensive boarding houses, small clapboard single-family dwellings, and the new two- and three-decker houses that were becoming a distinctive form of architecture in Boston's immigrant neighborhoods.[23] Most of these structures had dirt-floor basements where a single pull-chain toilet was located; few had central heating or running hot water. The main source of heat was the black cast-iron stove in the kitchen, which supplied heat for the house and fire for cooking and for the hot water that was poured from large kettles into galvanized-iron tubs for the family's once-a-week, Saturday-night bath.[24] This may not have been the heaven the Irish had expected to find in America, but it was a great deal better than what most of them had left behind. "It was not rags to riches," observes Stephan Thernstrom, "but it was rags to respectability."[25]

The central unifying force for these Irish neighborhoods was the Catholic Church, which gave the communities their distinctive flavor and unique quality of life. Everything revolved around the Church; the Church, in turn, became an integral part of almost every aspect of family life, literally from the cradle to the grave. In Ireland, the Catholic Church had always been publicly identified with the cause of Irish nationalism and supportive of Irish rebels in their struggle against the imperialism of Great Britain. Unlike many other parts of Western Europe, where the Church was identified with the wealthy landlords and the ruling aristocracy, the priests of Ireland generally came from the ranks of the poor and cast their lot with the aspirations of their people. "The Irish priesthood was poorer and closer to the peasantry than any in Europe," writes the

English historian E. P. Thompson. "In a literal sense they lived off their flocks, taking their meals in the homes of their parishioners and dependent on their goodwill." As the Bishop of Waterford reminded the members of his clergy: "The poor were always your friends. . . . They inflexibly adhered to you, and to their religion, even in the worst times."[26] As a result of this close association, the kind of divisive anticlericalism often found on the Continent was almost unknown among the Irish in America. Most Irish Americans retained an intense faith and looked to their priests and their bishops for guidance and support. They decorated their rooms with pictures of the Sacred Heart of Jesus, the Blessed Mother, and St. Joseph—the Holy Family—and no Irish home was complete without a crucifix prominently displayed.[27] Religious pamphlets and inspirational literature could be found throughout the house; many people went to daily Mass in the dark hours of the morning before work; and entire families knelt together every night to recite in unison the decades of the rosary. Sunday was the big day of the week. The parents would usually go to the early Mass so that the mother could return home to prepare a large breakfast while the youngsters attended the "children's Mass." Later in the day, the children returned to the church for Sunday School. About 3 or 4 P.M. the whole family would sit down together for the main meal of the day, which almost always featured a roast beef, a roast chicken, or a baked ham. In most Irish homes, this large Sunday meal was an absolute necessity, and practically nothing was allowed to change the time of the meal, the character of the menu, or the attendance of every member of the family.[28]

But the influence of Catholicism was not limited to sermons at Mass or the routines of Sunday. The late nineteenth century was the high-water mark of what church historian Thomas Wangler has termed "the Romantic Era" of American Catholicism. This period, he says, was characterized by the proliferation of religious devotions and a semi-religious affirmation of civic identity. Throughout the week, men and women were engaged in activities that kept them closely involved with a religious culture that extended well beyond the formal Sunday requirements. Reports show that almost every parish in the Boston Archdiocese had a rosary society and a scapular society. Some had a St. Vincent de Paul conference and a Confraternity of the Sacred Heart, while an increasing number had sodalities for both married and single women. May devotions to the Blessed Mother, June devotions to the Sacred Heart, and First Friday devotions were extremely popular in most parishes.[29] Through these and many other activities, Catholics unwittingly created what Wangler calls a "second" devotional calendar, which competed with (but did not conflict with) the regular church calendar, with its traditional Easter-Christmas focus. These activities, with which the faithful were all familiar and which they all shared in common, provided local neighborhoods with a distinctive socioreligious society of their own. For generations, Irish Catholics from Boston identified themselves to others by the parish to which they belonged. "What parish are you from?" was the first question asked of any newcomer.

These commonly accepted practices gave members of the neighborhoods a set of moral ideals and ethical principles that served as a practical guide for generations to come. Irish families clung to their church, revered their priests, memorized their catechisms, obeyed their doctrines, and followed their rituals to the letter. The Holy Family—with the obedient Jesus, the devoted mother Mary, and the strong carpenter Joseph—became the universal ideal for working-class families.[30] The sacredness of life, the sanctity of the home, and the permanence of the matrimonial bond were constant themes in the church, in the confessional, and in the home. The importance of unqualified sexual abstinence outside the formal married state was a social as well as a religious tenet of the community, while the virtues of purity, modesty, and virginity were accepted as articles of faith, without question or condition. The Irish might tolerate fighting, swearing, and intemperate drinking as unfortunate yet understandable (and excusable) weaknesses, but they found it impossible to countenance "sins of the flesh" such as premarital sex, birth control, or the bearing of illegitimate children.[31]

The influence of the Catholic Church on a day-to-day basis was strengthened by the almost incessant involvement of the pastor and his curates in the activities of their parishioners, young and old. In addition to saying Mass every morning and on Sundays, the parish priests heard confessions every Saturday afternoon and evening, usually staying in the confessional late into the night until the last penitent had been heard. The priests operated small clubhouses close to the church, where religious and social activities took place during the week. They organized choirs for the church, marching bands for the youngsters, minstrel shows and operettas for those in the parish with musical aspirations. They ran colorful outdoor bazaars during the spring to pay off the parish debt and give members an opportunity to socialize after the long season of Lent. The priests strongly encouraged sports, not only for the health and well-being of their parishioners but also as a moral influence in keeping vigorous young men away from the temptations of crime, the barroom, the pool halls, and the opposite sex. Many neighborhood parishes had their own baseball and football teams, which drew large crowds and provided a healthy outlet for both players and spectators. The typical priest was constantly on the streets of his neighborhood, plainly visible in his long cassock and biretta, talking to the women of the parish during the day, meeting with fathers on their way home from work at night, buying penny candy for the children at the corner store, and making sure that teenagers were not loitering in the doorways after dark or spoiling for a fight with gangs from some other neighborhood.[32]

The main change in the role of the clergy as the Irish became better established in America was a decline of influence in matters of politics. In the decades before the Civil War, when the Irish had virtually no access to political power and practically no political spokesmen of their own, it had been the clergy who exercised whatever civic guidance was possible under the circumstances. Bishop John Fitzpatrick, expecially, had been a major force in helping the small immigrant population of his diocese make the transition from the status of displaced aliens to that of bona fide Americans. For nearly twenty years, he advised them to forget the battles in their homeland, learn about the constitutional system, become naturalized citizens, exercise their right to vote, and become full-fledged participants in the American system. With his Whiggish views and his conservative social attitudes, Fitzpatrick steered his insecure parishioners away from social activism and political extremism, curbed their inclination toward violence, and urged recourse to the law. As a consequence, the Irish of Boston, although steadfastly loyal to the principles of the Democratic party, continued to be a remarkably docile and accommodating element of the city's political structure.[33]

By the 1880s, however, the docility of the Irish in political matters was fast becoming a thing of the past. The Irish American population was not only growing in size, income, and social status, but was becoming more articulate in its desire for an appropriate and responsible role in municipal politics. No longer content to be passive recipients of the city's largesse and silent partners in a civic process dominated by a Yankee minority, the Irish-American voters were ready to assume a positive and vocal role in city government. This was the theme that the ward bosses played upon in their neighborhoods. By this time, political leaders had emerged in many of the city's twenty-five wards, each man vying to be the undisputed boss of his territory.

In the West End's Ward 8 on the northern tip of the Boston peninsula (extending from Cambridge Street to the North Station and across to the Charlestown bridges), Martin Lomasney exercised extraordinary power. Born December 3, 1859, of immigrant parents from County Cork, Martin was forced to leave grammar school at the age of eleven when both his father and his mother died within the same year. He earned money selling newspapers, shining shoes, running errands, and working in a small machine shop until a local politician provided him with a series of city jobs as a laborer, a lamplighter, and a health inspector. In 1885 Martin and his brother Joseph, together with a few friends, founded the Hendricks Club as a gathering place for men of the ward to gossip, exchange information, play cards (however, no dice-playing was allowed, and liquor was strictly forbidden), and talk politics.[34] Lomasney kept an office on the second floor of the building, which originally was located near the North Station but was later moved to Bowdoin Square. From his office he worked day and night caring for the needs of the people who came to see him, serving as an employment agency, creating a virtual charitable bureau, planning political strategy, and turning the Hendricks Club into what he called a "machine for getting votes."[35]

Lomasney was a thickset, well-muscled man with a "massive dome," a small mustache, and a jaw that stuck out "at a pugnacious angle."[36] Gold-rimmed spectacles accentuated the keenness of his gray-blue eyes. He could easily be identified at a distance by his distinctive batwing bow tie and the battered old straw hat he wore throughout the year. A perennial bachelor, he lived a simple life in a modest rooming house, attended church regularly but quietly, neither drank nor smoked, avoided banquets and public functions whenever possible, took long walks at a brisk pace, and spoke in a plain and straightforward manner. His power was based on his skill in manipulating political advantages and on the absolute loyalty and the enduring gratitude of his workers and supporters—the people of his ward whose needs he fulfilled and whose anxieties he soothed. Dubbed "the Mahatma" as a tribute to his exalted rank in the community, he was absolutely devoted to "his people" and expected them to be equally devoted to him.[37]

In addition to establishing himself as undisputed boss of the West End—and thereby as a decisive factor in the success or failure of the ward's candidates in city elections—he decided who would, and who would not, receive the support of his powerful political machine in running for city office. Lomasney was active in public affairs at both the city-wide and state levels. He ran successfully for two terms in the state Senate (beginning in 1896), served another year in the state House of Representatives, and then sat on the city's Board of Aldermen, where he became a powerful voice, from 1901 to 1903. He later returned to Beacon Hill to resume his seat in the House, where he remained for the greater part of the next twenty years.[38]

Meanwhile, in the nearby North End an energetic young man named John F. Fitzgerald had risen to a position similar to Lomasney's. The third of nine sons of Thomas and Rosanna Fitzgerald (two other children had died in infancy), John Francis was born February 12, 1863, in a small wooden North End tenement. His father worked in a small grocery and

MARTIN
LOMASNEY

*A caricature of Martin Lomasney, the legendary boss of Ward 8,
the West End, by the cartoonist "Norman" of the Boston Post.
The drawing captures the "massive dome," the small mustache,
the gold-rimmed spectacles, and the prominent jaw that jutted
out at a pugnacious angle. Born of immigrant parents, Lomasney
became popularly known as "the Mahatma," as he worked day
and night caring for the people of his district.*
The Bostonian Society.

package-goods store on North Street, keeping the family in comfortable circumstances by selling flour, milk, and foodstuffs by day and operating a popular saloon by night. Young John was bright, bustling, and competitive. He graduated from the Eliot School, attended the Boston Latin School, and because of his excellent record was admitted to Harvard Medical School without examination. Two weeks before his first-year final examinations in the spring of 1885, however, his father died, and John left medical school to find a job and keep his family together. The local ward boss, Matthew Keany, took a liking to the feisty young man and offered him a job as his assistant. This gave John Fitzgerald a chance to make a little money, learn about the processes of government, improve his skills at public speaking, and prepare himself for a career in Boston politics. An appointment to a Customs House job gave him the opportunity to marry Mary Josephine ("Josie") Hannon of Acton, and a year later he became the proud father of a baby girl named Rose. Not long after that, he ran for a seat on the Common Council, and with Keany's support he topped the list. When Keany suddenly died of pneumonia in February 1892, it was young Fitzgerald, only twenty-nine years old, who took his place as the new boss of the North End.[39]

As boss of Ward 6, Fitzgerald was able to bypass both the Board of Aldermen and the state House of Representatives to win a seat in the more prestigious state Senate. Running against the incumbent, George McGahey from Ward 7, Fitzgerald saw the need of a strategic alliance and he paid a visit to Martin Lomasney at his headquarters on Causeway Street. Because the Mahatma had a grudge of his own against McGahey, he agreed to throw his support to the "pink-cheeked youngster" from the North End. As a result, in 1892 John F. Fitzgerald became one of the youngest senators on Beacon Hill. After two years in the state Senate supporting progressive labor legislation, Fitzgerald decided to make a run for the United States House of Representatives from the largely Democratic Ninth Congressional District. This district covered the first nine wards of the city, stretching from East Boston and Charlestown to the North and West Ends and including parts of the South End, Winthrop, and downtown Boston. At the time it was the only solidly Democratic congressional

John F. Fitzgerald, father of Rose Fitzgerald Kennedy and maternal grandfather of President John F. Kennedy. Boss of the North End at the age of twenty-nine, Fitzgerald became a member of the state Senate, and in 1895 was elected to the U.S. House of Representatives. After the death of Patrick Collins in 1905, Fitzgerald became the first Boston-born Irish Catholic to become mayor of the city. The Bostonian Society.

district in all of Massachusetts. It was the district from which Fitzgerald's grandson, John F. Kennedy, would launch his political career half a century later.[40]

Fitzgerald's bid for a congressional seat was a dramatic example of a city-wide split developing at that time in Boston-Irish politics. Coming out of the tenements of the North End, Fitzgerald found himself running against the incumbent, Joseph O'Neil. O'Neil was one of Patrick Maguire's "acceptable" Irish candidates, who were seen as bridging the gap between the Irish in the neighborhoods and the Yankees on Beacon Hill.[41] O'Neil had already completed three terms, had provided a rich source of patronage for Maguire and his associates, and had served as an effective and sympathetic representative for the downtown business interests. In keeping with the Yankees' *laissez-faire* style, O'Neil had shown little interest in the plight of industrial workers, the appeals of organized labor, or proposals for progressive reforms. While the economy was booming, this position was sustainable, but in the wake of the bank failures, industrial collapses, and widespread unemployment brought on by the Panic of 1893, American voters could no longer accept the promises of Republican legislators that philanthropy would fill the gap until the economic situation corrected itself. Billed as "the boy candidate," Fitzgerald took to the streets with torchlight rallies, fireworks displays, and marching bands, promising to speak out against the monied establishment on behalf of the poor and the downtrodden. Although O'Neil had the support of P. J. Kennedy of East Boston, Jim Donovan of the South End, and Joe Corbett of Charlestown—a trio of rival bosses then challenging Martin Lomasney for control of the Democratic city machine—Fitzgerald again received backing from the Mahatma, who used the young man to reestablish a balance of power more favorable to himself. To the amazement of most Bostonians, young Fitzgerald defeated O'Neil for the Democratic nomination. He then went on to defeat the Republican candidate, whom he accused of supporting the anti-Catholic policies of the Republican party, policies he claimed were stabbing in the back "a certain loyal class of citizens." On November 6, 1894, Fitzgerald became the United States Congressman from the Ninth District.[42]

Fitzgerald's counterpart across the harbor in East Boston was Patrick J. Kennedy. While still an infant, Kennedy had lost his thirty-five-year-old father to cholera. He grew up watching his young mother, Bridget, go to work every morning at a small shop at the ferry landing to support her four small children. Like so many of his contemporaries, P. J. left school at an early age to help out the family by loading and unloading cargoes at the East Boston docks. Diligent and prudent, he put aside enough savings from his meager income to purchase a small tavern in Boston's Haymarket Square, and within a few years he had acquired two more establishments. Through hard work and attention to detail, he acquired his own

Patrick J. Kennedy, father of Joseph P. Kennedy and paternal grandfather of President John F. Kennedy. Kennedy was a tavern-keeper, liquor importer, and banker. He also served in the state Senate for eight terms, but spent most of his time as the undisputed ward boss of East Boston. John F. Kennedy Library.

liquor-importing company by the time he was thirty years old. His numerous personal contacts in the liquor business, together with his warm-hearted generosity in extending favors and loans to all kinds of people, became the basis for a successful political career. Tall, lean, and courteous, with a thick shock of dark hair and a handsome black mustache, Kennedy became the acknowledged boss of East Boston, meeting day and night with the people of his district, either at his place of business or in his home.[43]

And so it went throughout the Irish neighborhoods of Boston. In Charlestown, Joe Corbett was kingpin; in Dorchester's sprawling Ward 20, Joe O'Connell was boss; "Smiling Jim" Donovan controlled the immigrants moving into the tenements and boardinghouses of the South End's Ward 9; and P. J. "Pea Jacket" Maguire (not to be confused with Patrick J. Maguire) ruled Roxbury's Ward 17 until he was ousted by a young, up-and-coming politician by the name of James Michael Curley. The ward bosses headed what by this time had become fairly sophisticated political organizations complete with functioning ward committees, eager captains, obedient lieutenants, and companies of ward heelers and loyal volunteers. As in other American cities, most of these machines operated out of neighborhood clubs and associations first organized primarily as social and fraternal meeting places but converted by the mid-1800s into tightly knit political organizations. These organizations engaged almost exclusively in the promotion of political candidates, who in many cases were the organizations' founders. Lomasney's Hendricks Club was one of the earliest of these political clubs. Other ward bosses followed Lomasney's example: In 1888 Thomas W. Flood organized the Somerset Associates in South Boston's Ward 14; in the early 1890s John F. Fitzgerald founded the Jefferson Club in the North End's Ward 6; and in 1901 the Tammany Club of Roxbury's Ward 17 was established to promote the political career of James Michael Curley.[44] With clubs such as these, and the many others that followed, local ward leaders were able to meet regularly for planning and strategy sessions, organize support for legislation of importance to their districts, and provide backing for whatever candidates promised the greatest benefits to their neighborhoods.

All of this was too much for most native-born Bostonians. The recent annexation of Roxbury, Dorchester, Charlestown, West Roxbury, and Brighton made a large number of new ethnic neighborhoods part of Boston, transforming it from a small urban town into a major American metropolis comparable in size to New York, Philadelphia, and Chicago. With the Irish clearly moving up into positions of power in city government, and with powerful bosses making their appearance in practically every ward, the Yankees had good reason to be frightened. They saw a distinct possibility that Boston would soon be subjected to the same kind of corrupt "boss rule" that even at that moment was scandalizing New York City under the powerful grip of Boss Tweed and his political supporters. Clearly, steps would have to be taken by prominent Republican members of the state legislature to safeguard the city from those ward bosses and conniving politicians who would plunder the treasury and use municipal offices for political patronage.

Just before Hugh O'Brien's election as mayor, the state passed its first civil service law to regulate the hiring and promotion of state employees, city workers, and members of the city's fire departments—clearly intending to forestall whatever plans the Irish might have to parcel out such precious offices among their friends and relatives. A short time after O'Brien's election, the state legislature took the police department out of the hands of city government, placing it under a special metropolitan commission appointed by the governor. The new commission controlled not only the hiring of police but the granting of liquor licenses—a role the Yankees were especially anxious to take out of the hands of the Irish. Patrick Maguire lost no time in denouncing what he felt were the bigoted motives of the "venerable hayseed legislators from Podunk and other rural sections," led by "Boston hypocrites and frauds, lay and clerical" in a misguided attempt to create "a moral city."[45] Mayor O'Brien agreed heartily. "Why should Boston be singled out for special legislation?" he asked in his inaugural address, contending that Boston should run its own affairs and that the Common Council was perfectly capable of making whatever decisions were necessary for the city's welfare.

But circumstances during the mid-1880s at both the local and national levels convinced Protestant Yankees that the time had come to make a stand if they hoped to hold back the immigrant tide. The prospects for a Yankee political future were certainly poor, as the demographics clearly favored the Irish and would for generations to come. "New England Protestants will do well to remember that the Catholic population gains on them every year, as well by natural increase as by emigration," observed Francis Parkman, bemoaning the fact that the size of Yankee families along Beacon Hill had "dwindled in numbers generation after generation through all this century."[46] But perhaps even more disconcerting than the numbers was the fact that the Irish-Catholic community was assuming an independent attitude and a positive sense of group consciousness. There was, for the first time, a real possibility that new generations of immigrant children would grow to maturity without the painstaking guidance of Yankee headmasters and schoolmarms who could be counted on to steer them in the "right" direction.[47]

Acting on a call from Rome to improve various aspects of church administration, in 1884 Archbishop James Gibbons presided over a meeting of seventy-two American Catholic prelates in Baltimore, Maryland. This Third Plenary Council brought an end to what historian James Hennesey has called the Church's "organization era" and marked the opening of "a period of conflict."[48] The prelates planned various ecclesiastical changes, the creation of a uniform catechism, and the founding of a Catholic university ("a dark Jesuitical plot," one local newspaper remarked) and instructed each parish to open a primary school within two years. In Boston, Archbishop John Williams had anticipated these instructions. Four years earlier, in response to longstanding complaints that Catholic schoolchildren suffered constant humiliation at the hands of Yankee schoolteachers, Williams had announced that he would establish a parochial school system and would withdraw Catholic children from the public schools wherever practicable.[49]

Protestant leaders of Boston reacted with alarm, fearing short-term and long-term consequences for ethnic relations in the city. Some were certain that Roman Catholics would make their way to the state legislature demanding the same public funding for their parochial schools that Protestants had long received for their own favorite institutions. Others feared that without trained teachers or a standardized curriculum Catholic schools would lower educational standards, undermine Puritan values, subvert republican principles, and provide inferior religious indoctrination. In 1888 and again in 1889, the Yankee-controlled state legislature proposed bills to establish local boards of education to supervise all private schools in the Commonwealth.[50]

Up to this time, the public school system had been one of the most effective instruments by which the Brahmin community kept immigrant children under its surveillance and control. Serious, dedicated, and well-trained teachers could instill in these pupils a proper respect for the Puritan tradition and the Boston heritage. In this way, the sons and daughters of ill-bred, barely educated foreigners could be gradually transformed into disciplined, obedient, and respectful second-generation Bostonians. Yankees feared that, if Catholics built their own parochial school system and took their children out of the public schools, hope would be lost for "the happy ideal of assimilation"—the belief that the native-born Anglo-Saxon people could absorb and transform inferior people who migrated to the United States.[51] As Doris Kearns Goodwin has observed, many Brahmin families had already taken their sons out of the public schools and enrolled them in such newly established private schools as Middlesex, Groton, St. Paul's, and St. Mark's, although they obviously felt that Irish children should remain in the public schools.[52] The fact that so many Roman Catholics were "still essentially foreigners," claimed publisher Edwin D. Mead, constituted a major reason why they, "above all others," should be kept for as long as possible in the public schools.[53] If a large segment of the immigrant children—probably the more intelligent ones from better-off families—moved into a school system of their own, operating in accordance with Catholic social values and religious beliefs, the breach between the Irish and Yankee communities would only widen.

The prospect of having their traditional Puritan town, their cherished "City on a Hill," taken over by hordes of Irish Catholics with no appreciation for the city's distinctive past or for the outstanding virtues of its distinguished ruling families was depressing enough for the Boston Brahmins. Even worse, however, was the fact that in recent years new waves of immigration were bringing people from all parts of Europe who had even less in common with the traditions of Boston and, as far as most native Bostonians were concerned, had practically nothing to contribute to the city's future.

Until recently, most immigrants to America had come from northern and western Europe—mainly from the British Isles, but also from northern France, Germany, and the Scandinavian countries. During the mid-1880s, the character of immigration began to change dramatically. By the 1890s, the bulk of immigrants were coming from southern and eastern Europe—from Italy, Austria-Hungary, Greece, and the Balkan countries as well as Poland, Lithuania, and Russia. Fleeing from high taxes, low wages, drought, famine, political oppression, and religious persecution, the people who made up this "new immigration" contrasted sharply with earlier immigrants whose cultural traditions and political institutions were similar to those of the United States. But the new people, too, had been drawn by America's celebrated image as a land of freedom and opportunity, and they were determined to build for themselves a more hopeful future. Massachusetts received its share of the new immigrants, together with other northeastern states such as New York, New Jersey, and Pennsylvania. In the decade between 1900 and 1910, more than 150,000 Italians entered the Bay State, along with some 80,000 Poles and nearly 25,000 Lithuanians. Most of these newcomers headed for major urban centers like Boston, Brockton, Lowell, and Lawrence in search of jobs and homes.[54]

Boston, especially, was a popular haven during the turn of the century. The newcomers quickly moved into the deteriorating old waterfront wards that had been home to the city's original Irish population. The vast majority of Italian immigrants to Boston arrived during the late 1880s and early 1890s. At first they congregated in the North End, where the Italian population grew from about 1,000 in 1880 to 7,000 in 1895. Gradually, they moved across the harbor into East Boston and settled in other neighborhoods that had once been predominantly Irish. Before long, Italians became an important part of all these local communities, working as barbers, hairdressers, cobblers, and leather craftsmen, and operating nearly all the fruit markets in the districts. During the same period, a large Jewish population came to Boston, reaching 4,000 by 1890 and expanding to nearly 40,000 by 1910. Coming from the ghettoes of Russia and Poland, escaping the pogroms that destroyed their homes and threatened their lives, they expanded from a small triangular section of the North End and moved into the South End, Roxbury, and then across the water to East Boston and Chelsea. A short time later, Jewish immigrants began moving into the city's West End in such impressive numbers that they became an important part of Martin Lomasney's political constituency. The boss of Ward 8 sent his lieutenants to meet the incoming boats at the East Boston docks with large signs reading: "Welcome to America. The Democratic Party Welcomes You to America. Martin Lomasney Welcomes You to Boston." Some 10,000 newcomers from Poland settled near the boundary line separating South Boston and Dorchester, just off Andrew Square, and at the same time about 1,000 Lithuanians made their homes in the lower end of South Boston in the vicinity of C and D Streets. By 1890, the South Cove area near Boston's South Station was home to some 200 Chinese Americans who had made their way across the country after the transcontinental railroads were completed.[55]

Many old-time Yankee natives of Boston were virtually beside themselves as they witnessed this latest inundation of foreigners into their ancient and honorable city. The Irish Catholics had been bad enough, but at least they spoke English, came from familiar territories, and had some acquaintance with Anglo-Saxon laws and customs. But the *new* people—swarthy Italians, black-bearded Jews, inscrutable Orientals, and a motley collection of Poles, Lithuanians, Greeks, and Syrians—spoke a babel of incomprehensible tongues, dressed in weird costumes, consumed strange foods, and followed entirely different customs. Indeed, many did not even profess the Christian religion! Here was further proof, if any were needed, that Boston was being overrun by foreigners who could never be assimilated into American society. Things had reached the point, according to Oliver Wendell Holmes, where a New Englander would feel more as if he were among "his own people" in the city of London "than in one of our seaboard cities."[56]

The prospects of Irish political ascendancy, a separatist parochial school system, and now a frightening influx of foreign immigrants more alien than the first caused many Protestants to revert to defensive nativism reminiscent of the pre–Civil War years. The most ambitious of the new nativist groups, the American Protective Association (A.P.A.), operated mainly in the Protestant heartland of the upper Mississippi Valley, but its repercussions could be felt throughout the nation. Organized in 1887 at Clinton, Iowa, by Henry F. Bowers, a man addicted to bizarre fantasies of Catholic conspiracies, the A.P.A. spread rapidly through the Middle West, promoting restricted immigration and denouncing parochial schools as an imminent danger to all American institutions.[57] A.P.A. members pledged never to vote for a Catholic, never to hire one, and always to promote the teaching of the "American" language in the schools. The organization achieved its greatest prominence in 1893 when it spread the rumor that a papal decree had absolved all oaths of allegiance to the United States and that a massacre of "heretics" was planned for September 5—erroneously believed to be the feast day of St. Ignatius of Loyola, the founder of the Jesuits.[58]

As a national movement, the A.P.A. vanished almost as quickly as the Know-Nothings of the 1850s, swallowed up by the Populist movement and the free-silver agitation that rocked the prairie states during the mid-1890s. Nevertheless, its bitter resentment of foreign immigrants and its fears of the mongrelization of the Anglo-Saxon race found a welcome response throughout the Northeast. In parts of Massachusetts, where its membership consisted largely of British-Americans and Orangemen from Ulster, the A.P.A. grew to considerable strength. Reportedly, the A.P.A. in Massachusetts recruited as many as seventy-five thousand members in some 175 to 200 councils, but the movement appeared to be especially strong in cities and towns north of Boston such as Chelsea, Somerville, Lynn, and Gloucester.[59]

Until the fall of 1892 little A.P.A. activity was reported in Massachusetts, but after that time various political parties (not including the Democrats) began catering to the anti-Catholic agitation by adopting nativist phrases and slogans pertaining to the separation of church and state, the dangers of parochial schools, and the importance of reinvigorating the spirit of Americanism.[60] Even prestigious journals like *Harper's Weekly* and *Atlantic Monthly* began regularly printing anti-Catholic articles and tasteless anti-immigrant cartoons.[61] Things became even uglier in the summer of 1895, when the local chapter of the A.P.A. requested permission to march in East Boston's Fourth of July parade. Boston's Board of Aldermen refused authorization for reasons of safety when it became known that the A.P.A. members planned to carry the inflammatory symbol of the Little Red Schoolhouse (an attack on parochial schools). Denied official sanction, the A.P.A. appealed to the governor for permission to hold a parade of its

The Ignorant Vote—Honors Are Easy.

The cartoonist Thomas Nast, who contributed regularly to Harper's Weekly from 1862 to 1886, was a rabid anti-Catholic who constantly ridiculed the Irish as an ignorant people who undermined American democratic institutions. Here he criticizes the Democratic party for trying to balance the interests of Northern Irish votes with the votes of freed slaves from the South.

own, sponsored by the Patriotic Order, Sons of America. Governor Frederick Greenhalge granted permission on the condition that there would be no requests to block the streets. The event took place as scheduled, and the police were able to maintain order during the parade itself. But after the parade, when the A.P.A. marchers were going home, they were taunted by a hostile crowd. In the midst of a scuffle, members of the A.P.A. drew guns, fired into the crowd, and killed a Catholic named John W. Willis.[62] Charging that peaceful marchers had been attacked by a "murderous gang of thugs," members of the A.P.A. held an "indignation meeting" in protest at Faneuil Hall.[63] An inquest was held in East Boston Court on July 12 and 13. Two A.P.A. members were arrested on suspicion of murder, but both were later discharged. Even *The Pilot* chided the Irish for not recognizing that the A.P.A. had a right to hold its own parade.[64]

In the city of Boston, prominent citizens were sufficiently concerned about the influx of foreigners to seek ways of safeguarding the established order. In 1894, three young Boston Brahmins, Charles Warren, Robert DeCourcy Ward, and Prescott Farnsworth Hall—all recent Harvard graduates, members of old Boston families, and terrified by the prospect of continued immigration—founded the Immigration Restriction League of Boston. The organization attracted immediate support from reform-minded Bostonians, and before long it could boast of influential staff such as Henry Lee, Robert Treat Paine, Henry Parkman, and Leverett Saltonstall.[65] The league found an important ally when Henry Cabot Lodge, then only forty-four years of age, added his voice to the chorus calling for immigration restriction. As a congressman, Lodge had already made his views known when he introduced a bill that would require a literacy test for naturalization. The test would be designed to exclude those races he considered "most alien to the body of the American people." There was a limit, he said, to the capacity of any race to assimilate an "inferior race"; and when you began to bring into the country unlimited numbers of people of "alien or lower races of less social efficiency and less moral force," then you were running the most frightful risk a people can run. "The lowering of a great race," Lodge concluded, "means not only its decline, but that of civilization."[66]

In addition to their efforts to roll back further immigration, nativist groups revived the prohibition movement during the 1880s. As increasing numbers of European immigrants crowded into the East Coast cities, fears were raised about the potential impact of stereotypical whiskey-drinking Irish, beer-swilling Germans, and wine-loving Italians on the traditional social order. Nativists saw the saloon as a uniquely alien institution and a central social evil around which all others revolved, including vice, crime, gambling, political corruption, and the neglect of families. Even sympathetic Yankees saw the drinking problem as a defining weakness among the immigrants, a flaw that would need to be corrected. In supporting the creation of public bathhouses in the poorer sections of the city, for example, Mayor Josiah Quincy expressed the hope that if people could take baths every day then perhaps those men and boys who were spending their time in saloons "might then find the home a fit place in which to spend their evenings."[67] Reform-minded Republicans across New England and the Middle West took up the cause of prohibition as one more way of reducing the disastrous impact of foreign immigration on American institutions. In 1874 the Women's Temperance Union joined the cause of prohibition, and in 1892 the Anti-Saloon League gave its support to a growing movement to mobilize the Protestant churches of the country, elect "dry" candidates, and legalize the prohibition of alcoholic beverages.[68]

Success in almost any of these nativist endeavors depended to a great extent on political power—something that members of the old Bostonian establishment saw slipping away from them. Since ward bosses had emerged as a collective force in Boston politics, there had developed a sort of gentlemen's agreement separating the political power of the bosses, who ruled in the wards, from that of the established Democratic party leaders who arranged for the election of mayors and ruled at the city level. Because the powers of the city government were decentralized, ward leaders were content to control the distribution of city jobs and public contracts through their representatives in the Common Council. They had little interest in involving themselves in the nomination of a mayor who may have had considerable social status but who actually had little power. The ward bosses allowed the members of the Democratic City Committee a free hand to decide on their party's nominee for the office of mayor.[69]

This unwritten balance of political power began to break down after Yankee Democrat Nathan Matthews, Jr., was nominated as the Democratic mayoral candidate in 1890. Matthews won the election and returned to office for three additional one-year terms. Moving to strengthen the office of mayor and thereby enlarge his own authority in city government, Matthews used his power of appointment to exert direct control over the various executive departments. This diminished the responsiveness of his department heads to the members of the Common Council, thereby threatening the access of ward bosses to their usual supply of patronage.[70] Suddenly, the nomination of the city's mayor became extremely important to the bosses. This caused them to challenge the exclusive role the City Committee played in the selection process.

When Matthews's fourth term came to a close in 1894 and he decided to retire to his law practice, Maguire and the Democratic City Committee found themselves unable to dictate routinely their choice for the party's next mayoral candidate, Francis Peabody. In the face of considerable opposition in the wards and neighborhoods to the aristocratic Peabody, the chairman of the City Committee, James Donovan, took an unprecedented step. Before presenting Peabody's name to the City Committee for ratification, he called a conference of the twenty-five ward chairmen in an attempt to quiet the opposition and prevent an open conflict. Donovan was successful, in large measure because three of the most powerful ward leaders—John Fitzgerald, Patrick Kennedy, and Martin Lomasney— agreed to the endorsement of Peabody. When the City Committee held the nominating convention two days later, Peabody received 70 percent of the votes, with most of the opposition coming from loyal Lomasney supporters in the Charlestown and South Boston delegations. Despite the strong show of official Democratic support, it was clear that the working class electorate was unenthusiastic about voting for the man who had started the aristocratic Myopia Hunt Club and whose brother, Endicott Peabody, had founded exclusive Groton preparatory school. Peabody polled only 47.2 percent of the popular vote and lost to Republican Edwin Upton Curtis, who had served as city clerk and secretary of the Republican City Committee.[71]

The election of 1894 saw an important change in local Irish politics. For the first time in at least twenty years, the City Committee had been forced to consult with the ward chairmen about the choice of a mayoral candidate. This immediately expanded the role of the neighborhoods in city affairs and changed the rules of the game. With the defeat of Francis Peabody, the City Committee suffered further embarrassment and the ward bosses quickly moved in for the kill. In 1895 the bosses persuaded the City Committee to change its bylaws and return to the older practice of nominating the mayoral candidate by means of a convention of elected delegates. "Henceforth," writes political scientist Paul Kleppner, "the majority nomination would be thrashed out in the rough and tumble of the ward caucuses."[72] The following year, 1895, Josiah Quincy, the last of Boston's famous Quincy family and a lifelong Yankee Democrat, became the first candidate to go through the lively "thrashing" process. He emerged unscathed and was elected for the city's first two-year term as mayor. Believing in the ideal of an activist municipal government committed to humanitarian social goals, Quincy took a personal interest in expanding Boston's system of public baths, gymnasiums, playgrounds, municipal buildings that usually contained showers and recreational facilities, and public transportation outlets to benefit the masses of the people.[73]

With the resulting increase in city jobs and lucrative construction and public-works contracts, the ward bosses scrambled to take advantage of their new political influence. The death of Patrick Maguire in November 1896 removed an important force for political stability, and a bitter factionalism developed from disputes over the proper distribution of the spoils. One group, including John F. Fitzgerald of the North End, Patrick Kennedy of East Boston, Joseph Corbett of Charlestown, and James Donovan of the South End, formed an alliance popularly known as the Board of Strategy. The Board's major objectives were to control the lion's share of the spoils and to prevent the West End's powerful Martin Lomasney from doing so on behalf of his supporters in Charlestown and South Boston.[74]

The backstairs intrigues of the ward factions continued unabated during Josiah Quincy's first term. The chaos showed no signs of letting up until the Yankee mayor decided on a more effective way of handling city finances. After his election to a second term in 1897, Quincy persuaded the state legislature to create what he called a Board of Apportionment that would operate independently of the city's Board of Aldermen and the Common Council in developing and allocating the city budgets. This reformist plan was seen by the ward bosses as a veritable bombshell that would disrupt the prevailing system and take a good part of the patronage out of their hands.[75] Mayor Quincy obviously had outlived his political usefulness. A more deserving Democratic candidate would have to be found, who would be acceptable to the ward chairmen and the City Committee but sufficiently reformist to satisfy the Yankee community.[76]

In an effort to restore order among the feuding factions and to come up with a candidate who had no immediate connections with any particular group, Joe Corbett and some other members of the Board of Strategy turned to Patrick A. Collins, recently returned to the city after almost a decade's absence. During the 1880s Collins had focused on national politics and had advanced rapidly in the party ranks. In 1888 he was named permanent chairman of the Democratic National Convention, and in 1892 he gave the seconding speech for the nomination of Grover Cleveland as president of the United States. After his election to a second term in 1893, Cleveland invited Collins to choose among three jobs: secretary of war, attorney general, or ambassador to Mexico. Unfortunately, however, Collins's political activities had left him little time to make a living at his law practice. As a result, in the words of a friend, he was "broke" and could not afford the luxury of a post that offered considerable prestige but little income. Cleveland eventually appointed Collins consul general at London, a lucrative post where the income from a variety of fees and services made it possible for Collins to earn as much as fifty thousand dollars—a huge sum in those days.[77]

The perquisites of public office do not last forever. In November 1896 the Republicans campaigned successfully for the gold standard and a higher protective tariff. With effective organization and an overflowing war chest, they defeated the Democrats and their Populist allies and put William McKinley, the rocking-chair candidate from Ohio, in the White House. Collins's Washington days were over, and in 1897 he moved back to his Boston law practice and his home on Corey Street in Brighton.[78] Although he had been informed by Governor William Russell as early as 1894 that his party was in bad shape—"at sixes and sevens," as Russell described it—Collins was dismayed to observe at first hand the way Democratic unity in the city had broken down after the death of Patrick Maguire the previous year.[79] Although he professed reluctance, he nevertheless agreed to be the Board of Strategy's mayoral nominee in the 1899 election. Although Collins received 64.1 percent of the delegate votes at the party's nominating convention, he was surprised to discover that his opponent in the primary, John R. Murphy of Charlestown, was supported by Martin Lomasney.[80] Collins went to Lomasney, reminded him that their two families had known each other back in Fermoy, County Cork, and asked him why he was opposing him in this manner. Lomasney explained that he felt obliged to do so not on personal grounds but because Collins was an official Board of Strategy candidate. Lomasney said the Board had been "kicking him around" and trying to "put him out of business" ever since Maguire's death, and now it wanted him to support Collins for mayor. Well, he wasn't going to do it![81] Collins defeated Murphy in the primary elections, but then went on to lose the race in November to Republican Thomas N. Hart, who won by only 2,281 votes.[82]

Collins was not depressed by his defeat; instead, he saw it as an opportunity to unify the party and strengthen his own political base.[83] Over the next two years, he worked tirelessly to heal the wounds within the Democratic party, to line up more supporters on the Board of Strategy, to placate Lomasney and his followers, and to inspire the confidence of the Yankee community. Collins's efforts seemed to bear fruit because by 1901, according to the *Boston Post,* even former Murphy supporters in Charlestown were "vying with each other in the desire to be first in line for General Collins."[84] In November 1901 Collins defeated Hart by the largest majority in the city's history, polling 52,038 votes to Hart's 33,173 and becoming Boston's second Irish-born mayor.[85]

On January 4, 1902, the inauguration ceremony took place in the Council Chambers and was opened with a prayer by Monsignor Denis O'Callaghan, pastor of St. Augustine's Church in South Boston and a longtime friend of the new mayor. The Honorable Oliver Wendell Holmes, Chief Justice of the Supreme Judicial Court, administered the oath of office. After inducting the new aldermen and councillors, Mayor Patrick Collins outlined his policies for the coming year, emphasizing a tight economy in all departments. Despite his emphasis on keeping down expenses, however, he called for the construction of new schools and a new road from the Fort Point channel to the commercial dock areas, the improvement of Boston Harbor, and an expansion of City Hall.[86]

During his first two-year term as mayor of Boston, Patrick Collins ran a businesslike administration that greatly impressed the financial leaders of the Yankee community. At the same time, he used the opportunity to cement good relations with the Lomasney faction. He named Lomasney's brother Joe as Superintendent of Bridges, and he put many Ward 8 men back on the city payroll.[87] He named the Board of Strategy's James Donovan as Superintendent of Streets, a position that controlled more patronage than any other in a city department. This move was an example of the quiet way in which Mayor Collins worked to take the nomination of mayoral candidates out of the hands of the ward chairmen and give it to the Board of Strategy, which he hoped would serve the same city-wide function as the old City Committee. By naming Jim Donovan and several other members of the Board to head his city departments, Collins made it possible for the Board to use the flow of city jobs and municipal contracts to undermine the power of the ward bosses. In this way, he hoped to create a city-wide organization capable of exerting the kind of centralized discipline that he thought necessary for the Democratic party to control the city bureaucracy.[88] And all the while, he navigated the dangerous shoals of city politics, dealing as best he could with a seventy-five-member Common Council and a thirteen-member Board of Aldermen that one local newspaper described as largely composed of "incompetents and nobodies, with a mixture of convicts and notorious grafters."[89]

While Collins's nomination for a second term in 1903 ran into a scattering of opposition among delegates from Dorchester, Roxbury, and Brighton, he was renominated by the Democrats. In December 1903 he was reelected, polling 63 percent of the vote, breaking his own record of two years earlier, and becoming the first Democratic candidate ever to carry every ward in the city.[90] The *Boston Evening Transcript* hailed him as a "strong man and the city's defender against some of the most corrupt schemes that ever menaced it."[91] On the surface, the election of Collins in 1901 and his triumphal reelection in 1903 promised a welcome "Era of Good Feeling" in Boston politics. While the Democratic victories clearly established an Irish-Catholic hegemony in what had been a Yankee-Protestant city, the temporary disappearance of Democratic factionalism, the neutralizing of the ward bosses, the coopting of the Board of Strategy, the absence of malice among Republican political leaders, and the general popularity of Mayor Collins in Protestant circles all seemed to augur well for an inclusive and long-lasting *pax politica* as Boston moved into the twentieth century. It was, therefore, with the greatest of anguish that Bostonians reacted to the startling news on September 14, 1905, that Mayor Patrick Collins was dead. He had never been a man of robust constitution, and many Bostonians had observed when he returned from London in 1897 that he seemed to have grown prematurely old. But as he settled down and became involved in Boston politics, his health appeared to improve. Most people were caught completely by surprise when he died suddenly at the Homestead resort in Hot Springs, Virginia, where he had gone for a brief rest.[92]

The entire city was thrown into public mourning as citizens of all races, creeds, and political affiliations praised the virtues of Patrick Collins and regretted his passing. "He was a manly man among manly men," wrote the *Boston Globe*, "and he filled the public offices to which he was called with high honor." The *Boston Journal* spoke of him as "the recognized leader of his race" in America.[93] Bostonians from all walks of life filled the Holy Cross Cathedral in the South End for the funeral Mass and followed the cortège to Holyhood Cemetery in Brookline, where Collins was buried near the graves of his mother and his close friend, John Boyle O'Reilly.[94] Almost immediately, a committee of prominent citizens headed by Richard B. Olney and James Jackson Storrow took steps to plan a public memorial. Within a month, sufficient funds had been raised for a granite monument to perpetuate the memory of a public servant described in the inscription as "a talented, honest, generous, serviceable man."[95]

Once the eulogies were spoken and the requiems sung, the stricken city confronted an uncertain political future. An era had come to an end. The unexpected death of Patrick Collins brought into stark relief the fact that a generation of impressive Irish-born political leaders had passed away. John Boyle O'Reilly met an untimely end in 1890; Hugh O'Brien passed away in 1895; Patrick J. Maguire expired in 1896. Thomas Gargan would meet his death in 1908 while traveling in Germany. Although Michael Cunniff lasted until 1914, when he died at the age of sixty-five, his active involvement in city politics came to an end with the death of his friend Patrick Collins.[96] These were the men who had worked diligently and consistently at the task of keeping the city's Democratic party unified and disciplined. They maintained a steady keel and steered in the direction of clear-cut objectives. The passing of this cycle of Democratic stalwarts meant not only the loss of a number of dedicated public servants but also a significant change of direction in political philosophy.

O'Brien, Maguire, and Collins were solid party members who believed in the egalitarian principles of the old Jacksonian Democrats. They were determined to see Boston integrated into the Democratic political network throughout the Commonwealth and on the national level. In this way the city of Boston, its mayor, and its political leaders could enjoy a degree of power and patronage that extended far beyond the city limits. By contrast, the younger generation of politicians, especially those who had been born in Boston and had come up through the ranks in the various neighborhoods, showed little interest in the broad implications of Democratic ideology or the activities of party members even as close as Springfield or Worcester, much less in Washington. They were, for the most part, pragmatic in their approach and parochial in their outlook, concerned almost exclusively with what was going on in Boston and its neighborhoods.

The older Irish-born political leaders like O'Brien, Maguire, and Collins had always believed in maintaining a harmonious relationship with the Yankee community, not only with members of the Democratic party like William Gaston, Frederick Octavius Prince, Nathan Matthews, and Josiah Quincy, but also with liberal Mugwumps like Charles Francis Adams who, though nominally Republican, could be expected to vote with the Democrats on certain social issues. The old Irish leaders felt that would provide a broad and inclusive base for their Democratic party and prevent it from being sterotyped as an Irish-Catholic organization. The new young leaders, however, showed little interest in the Yankee community and little enthusiasm for maintaining the traditional alliance with old-family Democrats—especially after the formidable Democratic victories in 1901 and 1903. The Irish had the numbers; now they had the power. There seemed little reason for them to go out of their way to cultivate Brahmin support or rummage for Yankee votes in the narrow, cobblestoned streets of Beacon Hill. At this point, according to William Shannon, the dominant mood was "a cocky, chip-on-the-shoulder self-confidence." The Boston Irish believed that they were better than the Yankees, and if the old Yankees didn't like it, "why then, damn them, they could lump it. Either way it did not matter: their day was done."[97] With the death of Patrick Collins, it was not at all clear where Boston politics was headed—or whether, indeed, it would be able to go anywhere at all.

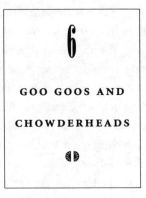

6

GOO GOOS AND

CHOWDERHEADS

ALMOST AS SOON AS Patrick A. Collins had departed the scene, the 1905 election provided an unsettling premonition of what Boston politics would become in the twentieth century. Along with most Bostonians, the members of the Board of Strategy were caught by surprise by the death of the sixty-one-year-old Collins, which left them unprepared for the Democratic primary scheduled for November 14, only eight weeks away.[1] Even more startling was the presence of a Democratic candidate in the race whom the Board had not officially endorsed. Like the champion sprinter he had always wanted to be as a scrappy little boy in the North End, John F. Fitzgerald was first off the mark as soon as he learned of Collins's death. Mobilizing his supporters and his machine, the boss of Ward 6 caught everyone off guard, campaigned seriously, and threatened to take the primary by default.[2] The Board of Strategy looked around for some way to stop Fitzgerald with a candidate more to their liking. They seized upon Edward J. Donovan, a man who not only had served as city clerk for the past five years but who also was Martin Lomasney's closest personal friend. By coaxing "Ned" to become the official Democratic candidate and then persuading Patrick Kennedy of East Boston and Jim Donovan of the South End to support him, the Board brought Lomasney himself into the race against Fitzgerald.[3]

Fitzgerald was stunned by the sudden appearance of Ned Donovan in the race as well as by the unexpected opposition of so many of his fellow ward bosses. But he pulled himself together and waded into a sea of opponents, delighting his supporters with the image of himself as the courageous lone fighter battling "the machine, the bosses, and the corporations." Donovan, an older man not in the best of health, was no match for the energetic forty-two-year-old Fitzgerald, who traveled from one ward to another in the back seat of a large open-air touring car, delivering more than ten speeches a day to enthusiastic crowds. On primary eve, "the Little General" organized the city's first motorcade, complete with honking horns and blazing red flares, during which he spoke in every one of the city's twenty-five wards. The popular "Honey Fitz" ended his barnstorming tour at the Jefferson Club on Hanover Street, in the heart of his old hometown ward, the North End.[4]

In the Democratic primary, Fitzgerald defeated Donovan by some 3,700 votes. Despite the bitter feelings that had been generated among members of the Board of Strategy and the ward bosses, the Democrats patched up their differences in time for the general election in mid-December. Martin Lomasney was the lone exception. Angry at the "dirty tricks" directed against his workers on primary day (during one argument somebody had pulled a gun) and determined to keep up his fight against Fitzgerald and the Board, Lomasney surprised everyone by supporting the Republican candidate.[5] Seeing an opportunity to take advantage of the split in the ranks of the Democrats, the Republicans had chosen Louis Frothingham, a Harvard blue blood and speaker of the state House of Representatives, as their mayoral candidate. Frothingham received backing from the unlikely alliance of Henry Cabot Lodge and Martin Lomasney but met his nemesis in the form of a fellow Republican, Judge Henry M. Dewey of the Municipal Court, who insisted on running as an Independent. Although Lomasney's supporters stood fast and delivered a sizeable bloc of Eighth Ward votes for the Republican candidate, Fitzgerald carried the city with 44,171 votes to Frothingham's 36,028 and Dewey's 11,608. "Thank God for old Dewey," sighed Fitzgerald in relief after the votes had been counted.[6]

At ten o'clock in the morning on January 1, 1906, in the packed Common Council chambers in the old City Hall on School Street, John Francis

Fitzgerald was inducted into office as the city's first Boston-born Irish-Catholic mayor. The opening prayer was offered by the Reverend Dennis J. O'Farrell, pastor of St. Stephen's, the North End church where Fitzgerald had been baptized. Chief Justice Henry Newton Sheldon administered the oath that made Fitzgerald the thirty-fifth mayor of Boston. In an inaugural address that lasted at least an hour and a half and was punctuated at many points by loud applause, Fitzgerald called upon a new generation of leaders to rescue the Boston economy from "stagnation and decline" and begin managing the city with "imagination and risk." Lamenting the political lethargy of certain descendants of old Brahmin families, who lived on the reputation of their forebears, he promised to create "a bigger, better, busier Boston" whose streets would come alive, whose wharves would be active once again, whose factories would provide jobs, and whose schools, hospitals, public parks, and playgrounds would provide benefits to all citizens.[7]

Despite Fitzgerald's frequent assurances that his administration would function on an efficient and "businesslike" basis, his office at City Hall soon became so crowded with throngs of cronies and lobbyists, pensioners and office-seekers, salesmen and contractors, reporters and judges, department heads and city employees, that the new mayor finally had to put off all official city matters until after business hours. He spent his so-called working day talking with tourists and visitors; after five o'clock he met with the heads of his forty-four municipal departments. Evenings were an endless round of parties, banquets, wakes, weddings, athletic events, and public functions. Many evenings Fitzgerald spent in high-spirited camaraderie with his six brothers, joking, arguing, and discussing politics. Some observers saw the brothers as an inner circle of advisers, a sort of kitchen cabinet, and at least one magazine writer referred to Fitzgerald and his brothers as the city's "royal family."[8] Although a number of people feared the mayor would collapse under the strain of so many obligations, he seemed to thrive on the fast pace.

Fitzgerald had also promised Boston voters that there would be no graft or corruption in his administration, that he would be careful in his appointments, and that no person would be placed in public office unless

John ("Honey Fitz") Fitzgerald and his eldest daughter, Rose (b. 1890) during his second term as mayor of Boston. Rose was always her father's favorite child and his chosen companion. She often accompanied her father to dedications, parades, political rallies, and other official functions. Courtesy of the Boston Public Library, Print Department.

"an actual necessity for appointment" arose.[9] However, the traditions of ethnic friendship and neighborhood loyalty, together with the practical requirements of ward politics, proved stronger than Fitzgerald's idealistic pledges. To get around the civil service regulations, the mayor created a new set of job categories, increased the number of positions in old job categories, and provided "emergency" appointments that allowed hundreds of loyal party supporters to be assigned to the city payroll. By expanding the existing pension system he was able to provide old-age security for veteran city workers while at the same time creating new job openings for younger men. And when there were no more public jobs to pass around, he pressured private companies such as the streetcar lines, the telephone company, and the gas and electric companies to hire deserving Democrats. The outburst of criticism that greeted reports of Fitzgerald's payroll padding, whereby the city employed "scores of men who did not labor," according to the *Boston Journal*, grew to violent proportions when he began announcing new department heads in his administration.[10] For the lucrative position of Superintendent of Streets, a gold mine of patronage for thousands of construction jobs, Fitzgerald named James Doyle, a tavern keeper and loyal campaign worker who had been expelled from the state legislature a year earlier for election fraud. The post of Superintendent of Public Buildings went to James Nolan, a popular East Boston liquor dealer with no knowledge or experience in real estate. Tim Crowley of Ward 8, recently acquitted of trying to shoot Martin Lomasney's brother, was appointed Deputy Sealer of Weights and Measures; and a saloon keeper was named to replace a physician on the Board of Health.[11]

Reacting with shock and outrage at the scandalous behavior of Fitzgerald and what the *Boston Herald* called his "wanton mercenaries" at City Hall, Boston's Brahmin community found its worst fears finally realized.[12] The situation had been bad enough before, when the Irish had grown so numerous that they dominated the city and virtually monopolized the job opportunities in the municipal services. But the Brahmins had still been in a position to put one of their own into the mayor's office—or at least to select conservative and compliant Irishmen like Hugh O'Brien and Patrick Collins. The challenge from a ward boss like Fitzgerald, however, was something else again. Not only was he regarded as a brash opportunist and a vulgar upstart but, more to the point, he had the power, as a representative of the neighborhood ward system, to centralize control of Boston's Democratic machine. For a party which up to now had been characterized by a good deal of disunity, with Irish power concentrated in the wards and Brahmin power in central city government, a strong Irish presence in the mayor's office threatened to tip the balance of power throughout the city. The frightening prospect of a complete Irish-Democratic takeover prompted Protestant-Republicans to make renewed efforts to save their city.

For several years, since the beginning of the Collins administration, the upper classes of Boston had been working seriously and thoughtfully on various methods of reforming city management, reducing political corruption, and improving the quality of candidates for public office. On the one hand, this was part of a nationwide "progressive" movement seeking more honest, professional, and efficient approaches to the operations of city government. Liberals and reformers, especially in major urban centers with large immigrant populations, hoped that the movement would encourage a greater sense of civil responsibility and root out big-city crime, corruption, vice, and violence. (These kinds of urban problems were described by Lincoln Steffens in his classic 1903 study, *The Shame of the Cities*.) In such large American cities as Toledo, Detroit, and Milwaukee, reform mayors ousted powerful bosses, broke up corrupt political machines, established municipal ownership of public utilities, and experimented with special commissions and city-manager forms of government. Many people felt that Boston would benefit greatly if the management of complex city departments such as fire, police, health, education, finance, and public works were taken out of the hands of untrained and often uneducated politicians and placed in the more capable hands of experts working on a nonpartisan basis. On the other hand, however, it must be admitted that the local Brahmins also saw bureaucratic reform as a way to keep the less desirable elements of the Irish population out of political life and replace them with middle-class professionals—doctors, lawyers, businessmen, bankers, financiers—who were more acceptable to the local advocates of good government.

One of the first targets of the reformists was Boston's school system. When the election of Thomas Hart in 1888 ushered in a brief but violent outburst of nativism (following Hugh O'Brien's departure from office), all Catholics were ousted from the Boston School Committee. Moderate Protestants in the city wished to avoid further confrontation on religious issues and to reduce the insensitive anti-Catholic rhetoric of the time. But nativist groups, led by an association called the Independent Women Voters, were determined that Catholics should have no policy role in school affairs. This position was warmly supported by members of the business community, who urged Protestant employers of Catholic servants to inform them that, if they intended to vote in the upcoming elections "at the dictation of the priests," they should "look for work elsewhere."[13] Elective membership on the Boston School Committee offered the women of Boston one of their few opportunities to participate in political life and was an especially welcome outlet for Catholic women.

In the complex society of Irish Boston, women asserted their "economic prerogatives" in a number of ways and exercised almost complete control over the running of their households. But according to the modern historian Hasia Diner they never rose to challenge the "public hegemony" of their menfolk.[14] Throughout the nineteenth century, the province of the married woman was circumscribed by the domestic traditions of Irish society as well as by the religious ideals of the Catholic Church, which held up the Holy Family as the only reliable model of family life. The home and the purse strings may have been the province of women, but "politics and saloon life, clubs and organizations belonged to men."[15] Most Irish men believed that women should spend their time and energies mastering the "mysteries of the kitchen, the living room, and the parlor." The men could hardly imagine women crossing the boundary into male activities and involving themselves in public issues.[16] By the turn of the century, however, a number of Irish women had joined their Yankee counterparts in demanding suffrage—much to the disgust of husbands and clerics, who believed that such women had become self-centered and imitative of the Yankee-Protestant women with whom they associated. One such woman was Margaret Lillian Foley, a native of Dorchester, who attended public schools, worked in a hat factory, and eventually became active in the trade union movement. An effective public speaker, telling audiences that women could become a major force for improving factory conditions and cleaning up government, "Maggie" Foley worked strenuously in Massachusetts for women's voting rights and then went west to Nevada, where she continued the struggle.[17] In Nevada, women received the right to vote in 1914, but in Massachusetts the issue was still in doubt. Governor David I. Walsh of Massachusetts became the most ardent Catholic supporter of women's suffrage and fought hard for a voting-rights amendment to the state constitution during his campaign for reelection in 1916. Although both he and the proposed amendment went down to defeat, Walsh continued to argue for women's suffrage in his successful campaign for the United States Senate two years later.[18] Like many priests and politicians of the period, Boston's Cardinal O'Connell expected women to play a limited and essentially passive role in both church affairs and politics. Opposed to secularism and modernism, he was suspicious of a "sinister feminism" that he feared was making women "masculine" and turning men "effeminate" at a time when advocates of birth control were spreading their message.[19] Despite his reservations, however, when the Nineteenth Amendment was finally ratified in 1920, giving women the right to vote, the Cardinal accepted the fact and urged Catholic women to go to the polls and exercise their franchise wisely.[20] Only at this time did the state legislature finally relent and permit women to vote for the mayor of Boston and for members of the city council.

As early as 1879, however, the state of Massachusetts had allowed women to vote in school committee elections and also to run for elective office on the twenty-four-member board. By the turn of the century, therefore, the Protestant Republicans who dominated the educational affairs of the city were both male and female.[21] It was at this time that a group of local activists decided that Boston's educational system would benefit from the same kind of professional reform that they advocated for other aspects of municipal government. The reformers included well-known personalities such as lawyer-educator A. Lawrence Lowell, banker-philanthropist John F. Moors, lawyer-activist Louis Brandeis, women's rights leader Mary Morton Kehew, and social worker Robert Woods. In 1898 they formed the Public School Association (PSA) and put up their own slate of candidates for election to the Boston School Committee in order to replace members they considered politically motivated and professionally unqualified. By 1901 PSA candidates had won a majority of the twenty-four school committee seats. Because the PSA candidates were almost universally Protestant, however, Catholic leaders in the city protested violently against what they saw as a deliberate policy of religious discrimination disguised as reform. Local politicians saw their positions threatened; neighborhood constituents saw job possibilities jeopardized; parents saw opportunities for professional advancement closed to their children. Mrs. Julia Duff of Charlestown, a former schoolteacher and a member of the school committee, loudly championed the cause of "Boston Schools for Boston Girls" and called upon members of the Irish-dominated Democratic City Committee to denounce the so-called reformers, confront the PSA, and nominate their own slate of antireform candidates. Carried along by Mrs. Duff's powerful energies and impressed by her popular support in the neighborhoods, Democratic political leaders agreed to her demands. In 1902 and again in 1903 they endorsed slates of candidates organized by Mrs. Duff, and within two years they were able to overturn the PSA majority and elect a majority of her candidates. In 1904 Mrs. Duff won a signal victory when her supporters on the school committee voted out veteran superintendent Edwin Seaver, a Protestant, in favor of his deputy, George Conley, a Catholic. Although both were competent men, the religious implications of the power transfer were obvious.[22]

Forced to reconsider practical realities, the PSA modified its program and offered a compromise ticket for the next school committee election, nominating four Irish Democrats along with four Yankee Republicans— all nonpolitical figures. In spite of bitter cries of betrayal from Mrs. Duff, the Democratic City Committee agreed to support the list of Democrats endorsed by the compromise ticket. Mrs. Duff angrily nominated her own slate of Irish-Catholic candidates; the Independent Women Voters drew up their own list of rival Yankee-Protestant candidates; but both were defeated. In the election of 1904, the losses by extremists on both sides and the election of moderate Democrats to the school committee seemed to set the stage for a greater measure of reason and good will.[23] One proper Bostonian saw this as a golden opportunity to step in boldly and reform the school system along more centralized and professionalized lines. James Jackson Storrow was an able, public-spirited banker, one of the leading organizers of the Boston Chamber of Commerce, president of the Boy Scouts of America, founder of the West End Club, and a highly respected model of municipal responsibility. In January 1905, he petitioned the state legislature for a new charter for the Boston School Committee. He proposed a smaller committee of only five members, elected at large, which would set overall educational policy. The committee would yield many of its traditional administrative responsibilities to a staff of professionals. Storrow's proposals were vehemently opposed by Mrs. Duff and by many other Irish Catholics, who saw the elimination of the large elective committee with its subcommittees as a serious loss in neighborhood power, patronage benefits, and job prospects for young Catholic teachers. Storrow's personal prestige was so great, however, that the state legislature authorized his proposed changes even though John Fitzgerald had won the election as mayor of Boston. Boston voters elected the PSA's balanced slate of two Protestants (including Storrow himself), two Catholics, and one Jew in an apparent desire to end a decade of bitter rivalry and create a nonpolitical school committee that would concentrate on educational matters.[24]

Representing a more comprehensive aspect of turn-of-the-century progressive reformism, in 1903 a number of Boston's most distinguished men and women banded together to form what they called the "Good Government Association" (GGA). The aim of these old Bostonians was to translate the theoretical ideals of "progressive" government into a practical form of control over the political future of the city. Funded by the Chamber of Commerce, the Merchants Association, the Associated Board of Trade, the Fruit and Produce Association, and the Massachusetts Bar Association, the GGA attracted the support of Brahmins like James Jackson Storrow and Robert Treat Paine, businessmen like Edward A. Filene and Laurence Minot, professional activists like Louis Brandeis and Mary Morton Kehew, social workers like Robert Woods and Edmund Billings, and journalists like Edward Clement of the *Boston Evening Transcript* and Edward Grozier of the *Boston Post*. Calling for reform, efficiency in administration, lower expenditures and taxes, and an end to corruption, these men and women represented the conservative financial interests of the downtown community. Bankers and financiers, lawyers and realtors, social reformers and academics, urban planners and social activists, nearly all of them Yankees, the members of the GGA saw it as their responsibility to support candidates for public office who possessed breeding, education, experience, and integrity. They believed it their duty to oppose the type of Irish politician who was more interested in jobs, contracts, and personal favors than in good, honest government. Adherents of what John William Ward calls "rational politics," the GGA members backed public officials they believed would work for the interests of the city as a whole—not those who would concern themselves with particularistic issues or the immediate needs of their neighborhood constituents.[25]

The alarming reports of Fitzgerald's scandalous "payroll graft" during his first two-year term as mayor prompted the GGA to seek authorization from the state legislature to conduct a full-scale investigation of the administration's financial record. To head off a state-sponsored probe, Fitzgerald quickly proposed that the city create an independent commission to undertake "a comprehensive inquiry." By making this proposal, Fitzgerald obviously hoped to sidestep the Republican thrust, coopt the process, name the members of the commission himself, and manipulate the investigation to show him in the most favorable light.[26]

With considerable apprehension and a certain degree of skepticism, seven well-known and "representative" Bostonians accepted Mayor Fitzgerald's invitation to serve as members of the newly established Finance Commission and convened under the chairmanship of former Democratic mayor Nathan Matthews. Although he had retired from office in 1895, Matthews continued to be a respected force in the city, with his extensive real estate holdings and his considerable municipal experience. Convinced that political corruption had caused real estate values to decline and business opportunities to stagnate, Matthews accepted a place on the "Fin Com," as the group came to be called.[27] After assembling a staff of lawyers, accountants, and engineers, the Fin Com began a series of well-publicized investigations during the summer and fall of 1906, exposing examples of collusion and shoddy deals between city officials and various vendors and contractors. Especially embarrassing to the administration was the inept testimony of Michael Mitchell, a good-hearted Charlestown undertaker and a close personal friend whom Mayor Fitzgerald had persuaded to head up the Supply Department. Under cross-examination, Mitchell showed that he knew painfully little about the operations of his own department and even less about city coal contracting. The administration became an object of ridicule and poor Mitchell was forced to resign.[28]

Although the minor patronage, payroll padding, and inefficiency uncovered by the Fin Com were petty compared with the shocking revelations of wholesale corruption in cities like New York, St. Louis, and San Francisco during the same period, they were enough to cut into Fitzgerald's political support. In 1908 the Republican mayoral candidate was George Albee Hibbard, an unsuccessful businessman who had served in the state legislature and been a highly respected city postmaster for several years. Despite support from Martin Lomasney and other ward bosses such as P. J. Kennedy, Joe Corbett, and James Donovan, Fitzgerald lost to Hibbard by a margin of slightly more than two thousand votes. Upon assuming office, Mayor Hibbard proceeded to reverse the course of city government by operating a cost-conscious administration, reducing expenditures, and removing from the city payrolls all unnecessary political appointees. "His parrotlike nose," recalled journalist Joe Dinneen, "was a gift to cruel cartoonists."[29]

In the meantime, having achieved their first goal in removing Fitzgerald from office, the progressive members of the Fin Com set about to make sure that neither he, nor anyone like him, would return to that office. To that end, they asked the state legislature to authorize a new city charter that would change the basic structure of city government. The eight-man Board of Aldermen would be abolished; the seventy-five-member Common Council, with three members representing each of the twenty-five wards in the city, would be replaced by a single City Council whose nine members would be elected at large. The members of this greatly reduced body would serve terms of two years—half as long as the mayor, whose term would be expanded to four years. The mayor would become a much stronger figure, with veto power over all acts of the City Countil and with all department heads certified by the Civil Service Commission. In a further effort to take municipal administration out of party politics—and to cripple the growing Democratic machine before it could become more effectively organized and put another ward boss like Fitzgerald into the mayor's office—the Fin Com stipulated that city elections be conducted on a nonpartisan basis. A new city charter, incorporating the proposed changes, was passed by the Massachusetts state legislature in 1909. With the vigorous support of the members of the GGA, the new charter was adopted by the voters of Boston in November 1909, just in time for the mayoral elections of January 1910.[30]

The passage of the new city charter made liberals, reformers, Mugwumps, progressives, and good-government advocates more optimistic than ever about their chances of putting one of their own candidates into the mayor's office and changing the course of Boston's history. For some time they had been grooming James Jackson Storrow, whose credentials were impeccable, whose integrity was unquestioned, and who seemed unbeatable, especially after his constructive reorganization of the school committee.[31] To supply Storrow with experienced political workers and an effective campaign strategy, the GGA organized the "Citizens Municipal League," composed of representatives of the GGA and the Fin Com and other members of the Yankee political establishment. Expecting the continued support of mainline Republicans once Fitzgerald had announced his candidacy for another term, Storrow's campaigners plastered walls and lampposts throughout the city with posters denouncing the "Evils of Fitzgeraldism" in hopes of capturing enough respectable middle-class Irish votes to tip the scales in Storrow's favor.[32]

But prim, proper, polished Storrow didn't have a chance. Never an effective public speaker, he was no match for the two-fisted attack of his blustery Irish opponent. Fitzgerald launched a whirlwind campaign with a spectacular motorcade that brought him to every ward in the city. He denounced Storrow as a tool of the "merchants of Boston," called for "Manhood against Money," and promised his supporters "A Bigger, Better, Busier Boston." Before he left each gathering, he would sing "Sweet Adeline" at the top of his voice, to the delight of his partisan supporters (this tradition continued through the remainder of his career). To their chagrin, the Yankees saw Fitzgerald win the election of 1910 by a plurality of 1,402 votes and become the first Boston-born Irish Democrat to hold a four-year term as mayor of Boston—the honor the Yankees had so carefully designed for one of their own.[34] The one ray of hope left to the downtown establishment was that when Fitzgerald finally completed his

The political survival of the ward boss depended on his ability to provide for the basic needs of the people in his district, who would respond with their loyalty and their votes. In this photograph, John F. ("Honey Fitz") Fitzgerald personally hands out baskets containing turkeys and groceries to grateful residents of the North End at Christmastime. John F. Kennedy Library.

four-year term of office he would not try for another. Fitzgerald had already indicated that he was ready to move on to greener pastures, and neither the City Committee nor the ward bosses appeared to have any other candidate with the spirited vote-getting appeal of "Honey Fitz."[35]

It came as a surprise, therefore, when early in 1913 thirty-nine-year-old James Michael Curley announced that he would attempt to succeed Fitzgerald in the 1914 mayoral election. Born November 20, 1874, on Northampton Street in Boston's South End to immigrant parents from Galway, Curley grew up in the mudflats behind the City Hospital. When his father died suddenly, ten-year-old Jim worked at a variety of jobs—delivering groceries, peddling newspapers, sweeping streets, working at the local drugstore—while attending public school. He spent most evenings at a local tobacco shop, where old-timers lounged around the potbellied stove smoking cigars, swapping yarns, and exchanging information about political shenanigans in Ward 17. As young Curley was drawn into the fascinating world of politics, he saw the value of education and began working to improve his public speaking. Before the age of twenty he had made a conscious decision that politics would be his career.[36]

When Patrick J. ("Pea Jacket") Maguire relinquished his post as boss of Ward 17 to become chairman of the Democratic City Committee, Curley supported John F. Dever, the new boss, but also began quietly organizing his own group of followers. He made it a point to meet people, do favors, provide assistance, and make his name known in the South End. He sold tickets for church functions, served on the entertainment committee for the Ancient Order of Hibernians, hired bands for the St. Patrick's Day parade, and organized neighborhood picnics. After failing in his first run for the Common Council, he only worked harder to improve his skills and make himself better known. He cultivated his speaking voice, refined his diction, expanded his memory, and haunted the public library to analyze the speeches of famous orators. In 1899, better known, better dressed, and better prepared, he ran again for the Common Council. To the surprise of boss John Dever and the Ward 17 gang, young Curley not only won the seat handily but also showed that he intended to use it as a stepping-stone for further advancement. In 1900, while still serving on the council, Curley announced himself as a candidate for chairman of the Ward 17 Democratic committee. Attacking both the old Pea Jacket faction and the new Dever faction, Curley divided and demoralized the enemy so badly that he won the election and became the youngest ward boss in the city.[37]

After a brief trip to New York to study the operations of the legendary Tammany Club, Curley returned to the South End to establish his own Tammany Club on Hampden Street. Attending Common Council meetings by day, he spent most of his evenings at the club headquarters doing what a successful ward boss was supposed to do. He supplied food, clothing, and coal for indigent families, arranged for medical care, legal services, and welfare assistance for those who needed it, and located jobs for hundreds of grateful constituents. At the same time, young Curley kept his eye on the larger political picture. In 1901, when his term as councillor ended, he moved up the political ladder to become state representative for the 1902–3 term. Concentrating on union issues involving strikes, picketing, industrial accidents, and overtime pay (he told his Tammany supporters he wanted to be "right on labor measures"), he continued to travel back and forth between the State House on Beacon Hill and his Tammany Club in Roxbury, which was fast becoming a well-oiled ward machine.[38]

One term in the state legislature was enough for Curley, and in 1903 he offered himself as a candidate for the city's Board of Aldermen. During the campaign he was approached by two young Irish immigrants looking for jobs as letter carriers. They were healthy and hearty "boyos," ready for hard work, but had serious doubts about their ability to pass the written Post Office examination. To help these two "deserving" applicants, Curley and his good friend Thomas Curley (no relation) went to the examination site at the Federal Building, passed themselves off as the two young men, and took the examination. But the Curleys were recognized by a court attendant and promptly found themselves in federal court before Judge James Cabot Lowell. They were found guilty of "combining, conspiring, confederating, and agreeing together to defraud the United States." Sentenced to two months at the Charles Street Jail, James Curley was released on bail pending an appeal and immediately resumed his campaign for a seat on the Board of Aldermen. In this effort he was ignored by the downtown Brahmins, who assumed that the pending criminal charges had destroyed the headstrong young man's political career forever. He was also abandoned by Lomasney, Fitzgerald, and most of the other ward bosses, who saw him as an ambitious young upstart who had gotten what he deserved. But Curley used his conviction to promote sympathy and support among the Irish voters. In a classic demonstration of Ward's "ethnic politics," Curley did not minimize what he had done, and he did not apologize for it—indeed, he glorified and romanticized it. Invoking bitter memories of injustices done to the Irish people under English rule, he claimed this had been his chance to strike a blow against the kind of unjust law that enabled the rich Yankees to keep good jobs for themselves and deny them to the poor Irish. Yes, he had done it, he told the voters, and he would do it again if necessary. And it was perfectly moral, he insisted, because he "had done it for a friend." Curley's maneuvering was a classic throwback to the ways of the old country, where the Irish consistently displayed a good-humored but irritating contempt for Anglo-Saxon authority. As British labor historian E. P. Thompson has observed, the Irish adhered to a "different value-system" and, in deliberately shocking English proprieties, often "enjoyed themselves and acted up the part." In court, they would usually play up to the spectators, recalls one English attorney, bringing forward a tribe of countrymen as "character witnesses," showing an acute knowledge of legal procedure, and making the magistrate "dizzy with their blarney."[39] That certainly was the case with Curley in his dealings with Judge Lowell. In all probability, if Curley had tried to hide his transgression or minimize it, he would not have carried the day. But the audacity of his defiance of the wealthy establishment and his stubborn adherence to the traditional code of the Irish—family and friendship above all!—brought delighted voters to the polls. By the time his appeals were exhausted and Judge Lowell was finally ready to impose a sentence, Curley had been elected to the Board of Aldermen and was well into his first year in office. Judge Lowell was confounded and furious at the tactics of the defendant, who not only had failed to display the slightest remorse but had used sympathy votes to win public office. Making it clear that he would have imposed a stiffer sentence had he known Curley would behave in such a disrespectful manner, Judge Lowell sent Curley to the Charles Street Jail. There, the farce continued as Curley basked in the relative comfort of the institution's largest cell, reading large numbers of books, receiving hordes of visitors, and consuming baskets of fruit. On January 6, 1905, he was released and returned home, receiving the kind of jubilant hero's welcome he would receive after being released from a federal penitentiary nearly fifty years later.[40]

Curley continued to serve on the Board of Aldermen until 1909, then moved to one of the nine seats on the City Council that had just been created by the new city charter. By that time, however, he had incurred so many personal responsibilities that he began to consider running for a higher-paid position: United States congressman. The idea had first been proposed to him by William S. McNary of South Boston, who was looking for a way to get back the Tenth Congressional District seat he had lost two years earlier to Joe O'Connell, the ward boss from Dorchester. By using Curley and O'Connell to divide the votes of Roxbury and Dorchester, McNary hoped to walk away with the election on the strength of the South Boston vote. Curley had a different idea, however, and launched a vigorous campaign against both candidates. He canvassed the neighborhoods and captivated the voters with his impressive speaking voice and his irrepressible wit. In an uproarious campaign, he defeated both O'Connell and McNary in the primary and then went on to trounce the Republican opponent, J. Mitchell Galvin, in the general election. In 1910 Curley moved his family to Washington, D.C., where he served two uneventful terms in the United States Congress.[41]

Curley never felt at home in the large fishbowl of the nation's capital, and with the news of John F. Fitzgerald's impending retirement in 1914 he announced himself a candidate for the office of mayor of Boston. In taking this step, Curley made it quite clear from the outset that he was acting on his own, not through the usual tribal nomination channels. He refused to seek the blessings of the influential Democratic City Committee, which he ridiculed as a pack of "empty eggshells" incapable of delivering the vote, and he publicly dispensed with the ward bosses as parasites and hypocrites, a "collection of chowderheads." At the same time, he dismissed the pretigious GGA as a bunch of simple-minded "Goo Goos," referred to the business leaders of the city as the "State Street wrecking crew," and characterized the distinguished Brahmin aristocracy as "clubs of female faddists, old gentlemen with disordered livers, or pessimists croaking over imaginary good old days and ignoring the sunlit present."[42] He made it clear that he rejected all the old forms of political machinery and social legitimacy. Instead, he appealed directly and personally to voters in the various ethnic neighborhoods, on his own terms. He created his own,

Always a colorful campaigner, James Michael Curley was a charismatic figure with a golden speaking voice and a biting wit that people recalled many years later. For nearly forty years he dominated the Boston political scene, appealing to ethnic voters in the various neighborhoods with his continuous flair for the unexpected and the dramatic. Courtesy of the Boston Public Library, Print Department.

personal constituency through a political plebiscite of his own making—claiming the people as his only source of power and legitimacy.

In a panic-stricken attempt to prevent this irreverent upstart from taking office, the bosses and the Brahmins became strange political bedfellows. John R. Murphy, former state legislator from Charlestown and longtime protégé of Martin Lomasney, rushed forward to file nomination papers, as did John A. Kelliher, a former congressman from the South

End, and Ernest Smith, a progressive city councillor running as an independent. The Democratic City Committee nominated Thomas J. Kenny of South Boston, an Irish-Catholic attorney and president of the City Council. Kenny was immediately endorsed by "Honey Fitz," James Jackson Storrow, and the entire GGA. The downtown interests saw Curley as a greater threat than Kenny to the established order because Curley had completely rejected the spirit of accommodation that had maintained at least a semblance of balance between the Yankees and the Irish for many years. By supporting Kenny, the members of the GGA could demonstrate that they were not a group of bigots—that they were opposed not to Irish Catholics as such but only to self-seeking rascals like James Michael Curley and his Tammany Club crowd. "His record," they said flatly, "should make his election impossible."[43] With December 19, 1913, as the final deadline for filing nomination papers, Mayor Fitzgerald unexpectedly changed his mind and decided to run for another term.[44] On December 5, however, while watching firemen putting out a terrible fire in the South End in which twenty-eight people were burned to death, Fitzgerald suddenly collapsed. Three days later, he called upon the candidates to restrict their campaigning until after Christmas—presumably to give him time to get back on his feet and get his own organization started again. This left only three weeks for active campaigning before election day on January 13, 1914.[45] In the interests of fair play, all candidates agreed to comply with the mayor's request—except James Michael Curley. Curley maintained that Fitzgerald was faking, and circulated the story that the real reason Fitzgerald had dropped out of the race was that he had heard that Curley was about to give a series of public lectures. The first lecture, "Graft in Ancient Times and Modern," would call attention to the nepotism Curley charged was rampant in the current city government. The second lecture, titled "Great Lovers, from Cleopatra to Toodles," was a not-too-thinly disguised reference to Fitzgerald's well-known dalliance with a twenty-three-year-old cigarette girl named "Toodles" Ryan. According to Curley, "Honey Fitz" had concluded that discretion was the better part of valor and feigned illness to prevent the campaign from going further.[46] Needless to say, Curley's belligerent tactics widened considerably the already serious rift between him and the ward bosses.

By Christmastime, the field had been whittled down drastically. On December 18 Fitzgerald decided to withdraw from the race completely; Murphy withdrew on December 22; Smith did not get enough signatures to be nominated; and Kelliher withdrew on December 31 when it became evident that he did not have a solid base of support. This left only two candidates: Curley and Kenny.[47] The choice between these two reportedly left the Democratic leaders of the city "in a state of bewilderment."[48] Although many of them regarded Curley as an ambitious young maverick who was liable to build a citywide political machine of his own, they were not entirely happy with Kenny, who seemed to personify the subservient and "acceptable" Irishman admired by the Yankees but suspected by the Irish.[49] A number of bosses feared that if Kenny was elected, with his downtown business support and his Good Government backing, he might well usher in an era of oldtime Yankee dominance.[50] The Democratic City Committee was so badly split over whether to endorse Kenny or Curley that it took no action at all, and ward bosses like John F. Fitzgerald proclaimed themselves "neutral."[51] On the surface, at least, they were content to let the two Irish-Catholic candidates slug it out while they stood on the sidelines and watched.

Curley's superb political showmanship, his grandiloquent speeches, his gigantic outdoor rallies, his appeals to ethnic pride, and his glowing promises of a more prosperous city captivated the voters.[52] He attacked Kenny as a tool of the "vested interests" of downtown Boston, dismissed his political record as "weak" and "puny," and called upon him to explain his connections with "the banking interests, the railroads, and the corporations."[53] Curley found, in responding to Kenny's frenzied counterattacks, that he could produce gales of laughter by holding up his hand, shaking his forefinger reprovingly, and clucking: "Naughty Naughty, Tommy!"[54] The taunt of "Naughty Tommy" plagued Kenny for the rest of the campaign and made it more difficult than ever for voters to take him seriously as a mayoral candidate. Curley defeated Kenny by a vote of

43,000 to 37,000, carrying sixteen of the twenty-six wards and running ahead in all the low-income neighborhoods of the city.[55]

James Michael Curley was destined to have a distinctive and decisive influence on Boston politics for the better part of half a century, and the nature of this influence became immediately evident in the dramatic way in which he heralded his own arrival. Instead of the modest inaugural ceremony that was usually held in the small council chamber in City Hall, attended by family members, close friends, department heads, and a scattering of city hall employees, Curley held his inaugural festivities in Tremont Temple, where some 2,500 of his loyal supporters had an opportunity to salute the champion in person. After the morning's program the new mayor walked around the corner to his office at City Hall and, as his first official act, fired his predecessor's head of the Building Department. After presiding at a luncheon for the members of the City Council, posing for the obligatory photographs and ordering the numerous floral arrangements he'd received sent to the city's hospitals, Curley called in the scrubwomen and gallantly shook hands with each woman personally, as befitted the self-proclaimed "mayor of the people." He then called it a day and went home.[56] Later, he ordered long-handled mops for the scrubwomen in City Hall and announced that the only time a woman would go down on her knees in his administration would be when she was "praying to Almighty God."[57] The legend of Jim Curley was about to begin.

Once installed in office, Curley exceeded the expectations of his gleeful supporters and the fears of his disgruntled opponents. The day after he was sworn in, he sent Yankees into fits of apoplexy by proposing to sell the Public Garden for ten million dollars. He would put half the money in the city coffers, he blandly suggested, and use the other half to purchase new public gardens in sections of the city where they would be "more easily accessible to the general public." Even while the Brahmin community was sputtering at this "outrageous" and "preposterous" suggestion, the newly elected mayor further horrified the guardians of the city's traditions by proposing that a water-pumping station be installed under the sacred grounds of the Boston Common and that a public comfort station be provided for the convenience of visitors from other parts of the city.

Although it is clear that Curley was acting more out of mischief than spite, the battle lines were clearly drawn. If there had been any prospect of even a temporary alliance between Curley and the conservative elements of Boston society, it was gone now. The Brahmin aristocracy would never cooperate with a political leader who openly mocked their institutions and trifled with their proud historical heritage. Curley understood this perfectly and made it clear that he was not at all frightened by the outworn power of the blue bloods. "The day of the Puritan has passed; the Anglo-Saxon is a joke; a new and better America is here," he boasted publicly. What Boston needs, he said, is "men and mothers of men, not gabbing spinsters and dog-raising matrons in federation assembled." The Brahmins must learn, said the new mayor, that "the New England of the Puritans and the Boston of rum, codfish, and slaves are as dead as Julius Caesar."[58]

However, Mayor Curley surprised many observers by putting on a great display of reform during his first months in office. After appointing the honest and highly respected chairman of the Fin Com, John A. Sullivan, as the city's corporation counsel, Curley slashed salaries of city employees, fired more of Fitzgerald's political appointees, and canceled a number of Fitzgerald's "sweetheart" contracts.[59] The Yankees were pleasantly surprised, the Republican *Boston Herald* applauded, and even the GGA declared that the new mayor deserved "the highest praise."[60] In reality, however, Curley was using the pretense of cleaning house as an opportunity to replace Fitzgerald's people with his own appointees and to establish himself as the central focus of political power and patronage. After his announcement that his administration would be open to all the people of the city, the corridors and staircases of City Hall teemed with voters looking for jobs and favors of every description. Curley proceeded to make his own arrangements with the new army of contractors and vendors who came parading through his office at all hours of the day and night.

More than personal showmanship or political demagoguery, the new routine represented a basic realignment of power in the city—the real beginning of the so-called Curley Machine. The ward bosses had always wielded extraordinary power because of their ability to dispense patronage directly to their constituents—patronage was their professional stock in trade, the very foundation upon which their power was based. Curley stripped the bosses of power by making patronage his exclusive domain, thereby cutting their political legs out from under them. A few, like the West End's Martin Lomasney, withstood the force of Curley's attacks and maintained some semblance of control in their districts; most simply withered on the vine. From now on, James Michael Curley alone would dispense favors to his city-wide constituency day and night, fifty-two weeks a year, from his desk at City Hall or from the elegant new home he had built on the Jamaicaway.[61]

Curley walked a fine line in establishing the image he projected to the general public, the images of professional bureaucrat and chief executive on the one hand, and of popular favorite and revered tribal leader on the other. He dressed impeccably, spoke beautifully, attended the symphony, held forth on oriental jade. When the occasion provided an opportunity for him to display the cultivated trappings of a learned Bostonian, he quoted the classics and cited appropriate passages from Shakespeare and Tennyson. At the same time, Curley maintained a warm and intimate relationship with his supporters in the neighborhoods, reassuring them by his words and his demeanor that with all his pomp and elegance he had not abandoned his Celtic roots—he had not "gone over" to the Yankee establishment. He continued to make his home in Jamaica Plain; he appeared regularly at Irish-Catholic wakes, weddings, and christenings; and he could be seen prominently every Sunday morning attending Our Lady of Lourdes Church with his wife and children, the epitome of the "good family man" that every Irish mother hoped her sons would emulate. He may have cultivated a rich and mellifluous speaking voice, but none of his followers—scrubwomen, teamsters, dockworkers, streetcar conductors, policemen, firemen, housewives—doubted for a minute that "Jim" was still "one of us." With a city of devoted followers behind him, Curley did not undertake to develop any kind of complex machinery or organizational structure. Skillfully steering a middle course between outraged Yankee businessmen and vengeful Irish bosses, he depended largely on his own charismatic personality, his absolute control of the patronage system, and his remarkable voice—a "golden baritone," as the *New York Herald Tribune*'s John Hutcheson described it, "touched with a faint Oxonian accent and garnished with classical allusions"—to command the loyalty of his followers."[62]

Mayor Curley had been in office scarcely six months when a general European war broke out in August 1914 and threatened to engulf the world. At first most Americans accepted President Woodrow Wilson's advice to remain neutral "in thought as well as in deed," but as time went on sentiment shifted against Germany. (However, as Jack Beatty has pointed out in his engrossing biography of the "Rascal King," Curley was careful not to allow Boston to turn against its own German-American population, as happened in other American cities during those emotional times.)[63] The startling announcement that after February 1, 1917, German submarines would follow a "sink on sight" policy made hostilities almost inevitable. Then, a series of unarmed American merchant vessels were sent to the bottom of the sea. On the evening of April 2, 1917, President Wilson went before a joint session of Congress, reviewed the hostile actions of the German government, and asked for a declaration of war. Within a week, both the Senate and the House of Representatives had voted overwhelmingly in favor of war with Germany. Almost overnight, Boston became a patriotic city where the word "slacker" was used to characterize any young man who did not rush off immediately to put on a uniform. Recruiting tents went up on Lafayette Mall, "Liberty Bond" drives were launched all over the city, and thousands of young draftees traveled to Camp Devens for their basic training."[64]

In many ways, Mayor Curley looked upon the coming of the war as a godsend. Rumors of scandals and corruption in his administration had begun to erode his political support, even in the districts where he had once been most popular. Proclaiming the war to be a crusade of democracy against despotism, Curley embraced the Allied cause and quickly became a central figure in public demonstrations, bond rallies, and visits of prominent dignitaries to Boston. The arrival of Marshal Joseph Joffre in May 1917 gave Curley an opportunity to appear in a succession of parades, deliver stirring speeches, and proclaim eternal friendship with the French people. In this rush of activities there was the obvious hope that the wartime excitement would obscure the problems of Curley's administration and help him in his bid for reelection in 1918.[65]

But Curley's popularity was clearly waning, and his many political enemies moved in quickly for the kill. Former mayor Fitzgerald encouraged Congressman James A. Gallivan of South Boston, who had served many years in the state legislature and had taken over Curley's congressional seat in 1914, to enter the race. A second rival appeared in the person of Andrew J. Peters: son of a wealthy Yankee family, Harvard graduate, former congressman, and assistant secretary of the treasury under Woodrow Wilson. Peters resigned his Washington post and got the enthusiastic backing of the GGA in his run against Curley. A third contestant was Congressman Peter Tague, whom Martin Lomasney put forward in the hope that Tague would prevent Curley from getting the Irish votes in Charlestown and East Boston.[66]

With his back to the wall, Curley took on all comers and struck back tenaciously. He referred to Gallivan as a "desperado," threatened Fitzgerald again with a disclosure of the embarrassing "Toodles" affair, and advised "the gentleman from Dover," as he called Andrew Peters, to go back to his "old job" in the treasury department.[67] But this time Curley faced too many powerful enemies. With Gallivan taking nearly 20,000 votes and Tague attracting almost 2,000, there were simply not enough Irish votes left over for Curley. Andrew Peters was elected mayor with 39,924 votes, while Curley came in second with 28,850 votes, having won only six of the city's twenty-six wards.[68] In January 1919, Curley walked down the steps of City Hall into private life and a brief period of political obscurity.

It may have been just as well for Curley that he lost in 1918 because he did not have to face a brief but violent episode in the city's history during which his support for the rights of labor might have placed him in an awkward situation. On September 9, 1919, during a year that was marked from one end of the nation to the other with strikes, work stoppages, and labor demonstrations, some nine hundred members of the Boston police department went on strike protesting low wages and poor working conditions. Left without organized police protection, the city of Boston and surrounding neighborhoods were terrorized for several nights by hoodlums and troublemakers who smashed windows and looted stores. Mayor Peters called out the state guard to prevent further violence in the city, and Governor Calvin Coolidge, proclaiming that "there is no right to strike against the public safety anywhere, anytime," called up additional regiments of the national guard. Sporadic vandalism continued for several more days, but the arrival of helmeted troops, equipped with rifles and bayonets, quickly put an end to most incidents. On December 21, 1919, the last units of the state guard were relieved of their patrol duties. All police officers who had participated in the strike were fired and never rehired. An entirely new Boston police force was organized, recruited in large part from young men recently discharged from military service.[69]

The Boston police strike went a long way toward solidifying the division between the Boston Irish and the Yankee blue bloods. For one thing, the strike brought into sharp relief the social and economic differences that continued to separate the ethnic newcomers, who formed the working class of the city, from the upper-class natives, who still made up the city's ruling aristocracy. Most of the police officers who had gone on strike and subsequently lost their jobs were immigrants or sons of immigrants, predominantly Irish Catholic. They had been looking for some way to force an unresponsive city government to provide them with a living wage at a time of high inflation and improve the inhuman working conditions at dilapidated station houses plagued by rats and cockroaches. Most municipal and state leaders who denounced the strike—Governor Calvin Coolidge, Mayor Andrew Peters, Police Commissioner Edward Upton Curtis, members of the Republican state legislature, and most commanders of the national guard—were old-line Protestant Yankees, as were those who eventually discharged the policemen. The absolute refusal of these leaders to respond to the grievances of the patrolmen seemed to represent a complete lack of sympathy and understanding. One can still find Irish families in Boston who recall father, sons, brothers, and uncles on the force losing their jobs forever, and who continue to harbor bitter resentment against the Harvard students who offered their services as scabs and strikebreakers. In their eyes, the outcome of the strike was a realistic indication of the wide gap that still existed between the workers and the owners, between the people and the princes.[70]

In addition to what the strike revealed about the socioeconomic structure of Boston, it brought to the surface sentiments of national and religious bigotry that many people thought had sunk to the bottom but which were, in reality, floating just beneath the waves. Conservative reaction against the leaders of the police strike and the union organizers who encouraged it seemed to follow President Warren G. Harding's nostalgic call for a return to "normalcy." It was clearly in line with the general postwar reaction against all things foreign and in keeping with the isolationist emphasis on loyalty, conformity, and "hundred-percent Americanism." Undoubtedly recalling the role of Irish immigrants in the Draft Riots of 1863, many Bostonians saw the police strike as another outbreak of anarchy that could be attributed to the unstable and untrustworthy character of the "wild" Irish. The strike simply confirmed what many Bostonians already suspected—that there were "too many Irishmen" on the police force. The Irish police would need to be replaced by "husky Yankee boys," "full-blooded Americans," in order to instill more "Americanism" into the force. "Good American Yankees," the Bostonians declared, "do not strike!"[71] The Irish of the city viewed these outspoken sentiments as proof that old-time Bostonians continued to regard them as an inferior group, still not fully assimilated after nearly a century. In the face of the growing paranoia during the 1920s against Reds, radicals, and bolsheviks, buttressed by fierce prejudice against Catholics, Jews, blacks, and others, most residents with immigrant backgrounds pulled back defensively into groups with others of their own religious and national origins, taking refuge in the safety of their own neighborhoods.

These were precisely the antagonistic attitudes upon which Curley established his political base and which he used to solidify his power during his second administration as mayor of Boston. Despite bright promises of honesty and integrity, the administration of Andrew J. Peters from 1918 to 1922 proved to be a major disappointment. Preoccupied with the leisurely pleasures of golf and yachting as well as with the charms of Starr Faithfull, an abandoned eleven-year-old girl who had become his ward and for whom he had developed a morbid attraction, Peters left the details of government to underlings, who sold jobs, gave out promotions, and assigned contracts in a prodigal manner.[72] Curley made a dramatic comeback as a "reform" candidate, charged the Peters administration with wholesale graft and corruption, and called upon voters to "turn the rascals out." Realizing that they could not stop the Curley momentum, the Peters supporters did the next best thing: they submitted a bill to the state legislature barring mayors of Boston from succeeding themselves in office. Although written in general terms and applicable to all mayors, the bill was clearly directed against Curley and was quickly passed by the Republican-controlled legislature in 1918.[73]

The Republicans put up a weak candidate named Charles H. Baxter as their conservative representative in 1922, and Lomasney again put forward his old champion, John R. Murphy. Despite the barbs of Curley, who characterized his veteran opponent as "an old mustard plaster that has been stuck on the back of the people for fifty years," Murphy almost immediately received the endorsement of the GGA and the downtown business interests as the man calculated to defeat Curley. Not intimidated by the well-heeled opposition of the Republicans and vigorous opposition from within the ranks of Irish Democrats, Curley used every trick in his political repertoire and won a second term in 1922 by a slight margin.[74] After a victorious inauguration at Mechanics Hall before twelve thousand cheering spectators, the new mayor prepared to launch the city on a new era of building and expansion, which he promised would benefit the poor, the aged, the homeless, and the disadvantaged—all in keeping with his proud claim to be the "people's mayor."

The devotion of Curley's followers and his magnetic hold on the voters could be sustained only as long as he delivered the two things these people needed most—benefits and jobs. And this was precisely what Curley set out to do, with a zest and efficiency that exhausted newspapermen who dogged his footsteps and frustrated investigators who tried to unravel the financial knots that held together his numerous operations. Using the power of his office and the charm of his personality, Curley produced numerous social, medical, and recreational facilities for his low-income supporters in the neighborhoods that fringed the downtown area. He enlarged the City Hospital, created a series of local health units, developed extensive beaches and bathhouses in the neighborhoods, built recreational facilities such as playgrounds and stadiums, extended the tunnel to East Boston, expanded the subway system, tore down slums, paved streets, built bridges, and widened roads. These construction projects not only produced much-needed benefits for Curley's grateful working-class constituents but also provided the jobs upon which his whole system of personal patronage depended.

The new state law that made it impossible for the sitting mayor to succeed himself resulted in a power vacuum at the end of Curley's term, which brought out an amazing number of would-be successors. Curley put forward his loyal fire commissioner, Theodore ("Teddy") Glynn; Martin Lomasney encouraged "Honey Fitz" to run; former legislator Dan Coakley, a disbarred lawyer, announced his candidacy; World War I hero General Edward Logan considered a run for the position; and, for the first time in the city's history, a woman announced for mayor of Boston. Frances G. Curtis, a social worker and longtime member of the Boston School Committee, said she looked upon the city as little more than a large household. She felt qualified to run it, she said, having successfully brought up nine brothers and sisters. "With women in office," Curtis declared, "there will be no graft. Women will not stand for graft." By the time the ballots were printed, however, Curtis had been dropped from the list because she had failed to gather the required number of signatures. With no fewer than ten candidates in the field, local Republicans turned out in force to support Malcolm E. Nichols of Jamaica Plain, a Harvard-educated lawyer, former legislator, and federal tax collector, whom the GGA endorsed as a means of ridding the city of its "incumbus of misrule and inefficiency." In what historian John T. Galvin has aptly described as a "four-ring circus," with the three major Democratic finalists cutting into each other's votes, Nichols won the race by a comfortable margin.[75]

As the city's last Brahmin mayor, Nichols presided from 1926 to 1930 over a remarkable period of commercial building, civic improvements, and new architectural creativity. Unable to run for a second term (unfortunately for the Republicans, their succession law cut both ways), Nichols had to stand aside while Curley announced his intention to run for a third term as mayor. This time, Curley was supported by most of the ward bosses, even those who had opposed him in previous campaigns. Martin Lomasney, Peter Tague, and William McNary stood shoulder-to-shoulder with their former rival, and even "Honey Fitz" agreed to sing "Sweet Adeline" at Curley's rallies.[76] Curley's opponent was fifty-two-year-old Frederick W. Mansfield, an Irish-Catholic Democrat, president of the Massachusetts Bar Association, former state treasurer, and a previous Democratic candidate for governor. Not only did Mansfield receive the backing of the GGA, which saw the distinguished lawyer as Boston's only hope "to prevent the return of machine rule," but he was also rumored to have the blessing of His Eminence, Cardinal Henry O'Connell. The antagonistic class distinctions and social divisions that Curley had widened even further with his political and fiscal policies were reinforced in an unintended way by O'Connell, the new leader of Boston's substantial Roman Catholic population. In many ways, O'Connell represented in ecclesiastical terms the type of change that had taken place in political terms when the accommodationist policies of Hugh O'Brien, Patrick Collins, and John Boyle O'Reilly gave way to the confrontational policies of John F. Fitzgerald and James Michael Curley.

During the nineteenth century the general tendency of Boston's Catholic hierarchy had been one of friendship, tact, and diplomacy. The town's first bishop, Jean Lefebure de Cheverus, established cordial relations with the Yankee community, and later bishops such as John Fitzpatrick and John Williams continued to work in a defensive, nonaggressive fashion. These early leaders encouraged peaceful coexistence between their insecure immigrant flock and a hostile native-born population through a policy of what the historian Paula Kane calls "withdrawn entrenchment."[77] By 1907, however, when forty-seven-year-old William Henry O'Connell took over as archbishop of Boston, the balance of power had shifted and a policy of religious accommodation seemed outmoded and unnecessary. Irish Catholics were no longer the oppressed minority they had been a half a century earlier. With the election in 1906 of Mayor John F. Fitzgerald, a Boston-born Irish Catholic, with David Ignatius Walsh becoming the Commonwealth's first Irish-Catholic governor in 1914, and with "himself" (as the Irish would say) raised to the exalted rank of cardinal in 1911, O'Connell recognized that the Irish had won considerable power and influence. He urged Catholics to adopt an independent attitude and focus on their own distinctive culture instead of striving to adapt to the traditions of the host society.[78] From the outset, O'Connell insisted that the old Protestantism was receding and that a new tide of Irish Catholicism was sweeping over the region. "The Puritan has passed; the Catholic remains," he announced bluntly in his sermon on the occasion of the archdiocesan centennial in 1908.[79]

Using the impressive dignity of his position and the intimidating force of his personality, Cardinal O'Connell established a pattern of separatism throughout the archdiocese of Boston that was deliberately designed to free Catholics from all forms of Yankee influence. Through this deliberate strategy of "separatist integration," O'Connell shaped a "triumphalist, separatist Catholic subculture," according to Paula Kane, which was "sacred but equal, separate but integrated."[80] He exerted pressure on pastors and curates, mothers and fathers, to make sure that children attended parochial schools.[81] Although he himself maintained close and even affectionate relations with many members of the city's Protestant establishment, he warned the faithful of the archdiocese to avoid Protestant churches and non-Catholic rituals and ceremonies—even semisocial occasions such as marriages and funerals. Youngsters were cautioned not to join Boy Scout or Girl Scout troops, not to participate in YMCA or YWCA activities, and not to attend social gatherings at local neighborhood clubs.[82] Instead, church leaders organized parallel, exclusively Catholic social activities for the young people of the archdiocese. Catholic Boy Scout and Girl Scout troops were created; the Catholic Youth Organization was established to provide opportunities for boys and girls to join sports teams, debating clubs, and marching bands without going outside their parishes. Large numbers of Catholic men were enrolled in the Holy Name Society; Catholic women became members of the Legion of Mary or other sodalities, which existed in every parish.[83] Emphasizing the theme of the "church militant," the cardinal went out of his way to demonstrate in dramatic fashion, in the words of one local journalist, that "the once brow-beaten Irish Catholics have come into possession of Boston."[84]

Cardinal O'Connell was simply making a conscientious effort to preserve the faith and morals of those whose souls had been entrusted to his episcopal care, to help Catholics realize their "full duty to themselves," and to promote in the community at large "a fair attitude toward the Church." He insisted that Boston Catholics, especially young people, should no longer be pale imitations of Yankee role models. By looking into their own heritage and their own history, he believed Catholics would gain a greater awareness of their own values and their own principles. In the process, however, he unwittingly supplied a socioreligious dimension to the political and fiscal policies of James Michael Curley that were dividing Boston into two separate and often antagonistic camps. "The new assertive mood in the church," Curley's biographer Jack Beatty observes, "closely paralleled the new ethnic politics."[85]

This did not mean, however, that O'Connell and Curley liked each other or that they were consciously working toward the same goals. On the contrary, there was no love lost between the two men, although they never allowed their hostility to become public. Having acquired the tastes and bearing of an aristocratic ecclesiastic, an appreciation of the fine arts, and a love of good music, O'Connell thoroughly disapproved of Curley, whom he regarded as a cheap and vulgar mountebank playing to the baser instincts of his working-class constituents. The Cardinal, of course, was too wise to come out with a public endorsement of Frederick Mansfield (later to become the lawyer for the archdiocese). The Irish accepted episcopal pronunciamentos concerning such broad issues as child labor laws, the vote for women, birth control, and public aid for parochial education, but they would not accept the personal intervention by any member of the hierarchy in the give-and-take of neighborhood politics. Nevertheless, practically everyone in Boston knew that Mansfield was O'Connell's "man." Ponderous, methodical, and slow-moving—"as spectacular as a four-day-old codfish and as colorful as a lump of mud," quipped Curley—Mansfield was no match for the fast-talking Curley and lost by a margin of some 21,000 votes.[86]

Three months after the stock market crash of October 1929, Curley was sworn in for a third time as the city's chief executive. By January 6, 1930, when he took the oath of office at Symphony Hall before an overflow crowd of jubilant friends and supporters, it was obvious that extraordinary steps would need to be taken to deal with the economic crisis that was rapidly spreading across the country. In his inaugural address, Curley promised to furnish "work and wages" for those in need of "sustenance and employment" and proposed an ambitious Fifty-Year Plan to combat the effects of the Depression by developing industry, commerce, and municipal construction.[87] As one of President Franklin Delano Roosevelt's earliest and most enthusiastic supporters in the Bay State—at a time when most local Irish-Catholic Democrats still clung loyally to Alfred E. Smith—Curley had every reason to expect both personal rewards and municipal benefits from FDR and his New Deal managers.[88]

However, Curley was never able to get the huge sums of money he wanted to fund his extensive programs of public works. Many of his proposals died in the Republican-controlled state legislature, whose financial watchdogs were disturbed not only by the growing financial crisis but also by the mayor's personal political ambitions.[89] The Bay State's worsening financial condition, combined with his critics' tight-fisted control of the purse strings, forced Curley to cut back severely on his spending plans. Reluctantly, he reduced city salaries by 10 percent and laid off city workers. Not even the emergence of large-scale federal funding in the mid-1930s provided the degree of opportunity for the Curley administration that it did for many other big-city bosses across the nation. Charles Trout's study of the Depression years has shown that Boston never received the amount of federal assistance appropriate for a city of its size and political importance. Administration leaders in Washington had a deep-seated mistrust of Curley and other influential political figures in Boston. Whether the reasons were real or imagined, whether the mistrust was based on first-

*Mayor James Michael Curley presiding at the dedication of Co-
lumbus Park on October 12, 1930. While the dedication of this
new park in South Boston obviously pleased the Irish-American
residents of that community, Curley used the occasion of Columbus Day to appeal to his Italian-American supporters by praising
the virtues of the great Italian explorer and by flying the
Italian flag. The Bostonian Society.*

hand knowledge or on stereotypical allegations, they viewed Curley as
a corrupt political boss whose administration was composed of greedy
embezzlers and incompetent rascals who would waste, steal, or misman-
age whatever federal funds came into their hands.[90] The attitudes of James
Farley, Harry Hopkins, Louis Howe, and other New Deal bureaucrats were
shaped in great part by reports from federal employees in Boston describing the operations of local emergency relief programs as so "blatantly
bad" that even the unemployed classes had become disillusioned with the
New Deal's efforts to improve their conditions. Stories of political feuds,

longstanding neighborhood rivalries, and conflicts among ethnic groups ("the Yankees look down on the Irish. . . . The Irish look down on the Italians. . . .") convinced the administrators of federal funds that Boston would never be able to handle large sums of money honestly, equitably, or responsibly.[91] Boston's hopes for federal funds faded even further in 1933, when Mayor Curley attempted to pressure President Roosevelt into fulfilling a promise the mayor was convinced had been made in return for his early support. Curley wanted to succeed Charles Francis Adams in the prestigious post of secretary of the Navy (what a coup to replace a member of Boston's leading Yankee family!), but he let it be known that he would accept an ambassadorship to France or Italy.[92] When FDR offered to make him ambassador to Poland—an eloquent indication of just how little the New York aristocrat thought of the Irishman from Boston—Curley recognized the insult, exploded in rage, and stormed out of the presidential office. "So ended one phase of a beautiful friendship," concludes Joe Dinneen."[93] A contemporary popular joke suggested that if Curley *had* accepted the appointment he would have given out contracts to pave the Polish Corridor. In the prevailing view, the Boston mayor was little more than a political opportunist.

Mayor Curley was able to generate some municipal assistance by resorting to makeshift measures—hiring unemployed workers to rake leaves on Boston Common, offering snow shovelers five dollars a day to clean the streets for the city's 1930 tercentenary celebration, laying miles of curbstone in public parks, constructing a new causeway to Castle Island. But except for occasional road jobs and subway construction, his long-range plans for housing and building projects never materialized. The Boston Irish were left to suffer the consequences of the worst depression in American history.[94]

According to William Shannon in his perceptive study *The American Irish,* the economic collapse of 1929 and the twelve terrible years of Depression that followed "ended a world for the American Irish" and "broke the rationale they had lived by." Since their arrival in the United States, most working-class Irish had committed themselves to the vision of upward mobility—the Great American Dream. They were fully convinced that if they worked hard, remained sober, obeyed the law, saved their money, sent their children to good schools, and remained true to their religious faith, their future would be bright and their horizons unlimited. The Great Depression shattered their dreams and ambitions; it had took away their hopes for the future. They were at a loss to explain what had happened, how it had happened, or who was responsible for it all. In the midst of this traumatic experience, says Shannon, the appealing voice of a Catholic priest from the Midwest, Father Charles E. Coughlin, captured the attention of "shocked and disoriented millions" of middle-class and working-class Irish Catholics. Coughlin was probably the first person to persuade the stubbornly self-sufficient Irish that the national government should play a more positive role in their lives.[95]

When Father Coughlin began broadcasting in the fall of 1930 from the Shrine of the Little Flower in Royal Oak, Michigan, he attacked the traditional laissez-faire policies of the Republican party and called for a positive program of government action to bring justice and charity into the industrial system. Early in 1931 he appealed to the isolationist mood of ethnic groups such as the Irish Americans and German Americans by denouncing the Versailles Treaty, blaming the Depression on international bankers, and warning that Europeans were plotting to drag the United States into another world war. The "Radio Priest" quickly became a favorite among Irish-Catholic families, who gathered around their radios every Sunday afternoon and listened to his broadcasts with an almost religious devotion. The Irish believed in Coughlin first of all because he was a priest who spoke out boldly on moral and ethical issues the way they thought a priest should. Second, he identified the enemy—J. P. Morgan, Bernard Baruch, the House of Rothschild, and other "international bankers"— playing subtly but effectively on the latent anti-Semitism of many Irish Catholics who feared the unseen power and influence of Jewish financiers. Third, and perhaps most important, Coughlin provided a strong religious justification for obedient Irish Catholics to become openly critical of national political leaders. The Boston Irish traditionally had avoided taking critical positions on public issues for fear of having their patriotism questioned or their loyalty impugned—as had happened during the recent Al

Smith campaign. The priest himself led the way in February 1932 with an assault on President Herbert Hoover as "the Holy Ghost of the rich" and "the protective angel of Wall Street." "Drive the money-changers from the temple!" he cried. Coughlin pointed to Roosevelt's New Deal as consistent with Christian teachings and the principles of papal encyclicals. "It is Roosevelt or ruin!" he exclaimed to his devout listeners in the autumn of 1932.[96]

Even after the election of Roosevelt in November 1932, Coughlin was not satisfied that the New Deal was doing enough to provide relief for the poor, the unemployed, the disabled, and the elderly. By the end of FDR's first term, Coughlin had organized his own political movement—the National Union for Social Justice. In 1936 he began publishing a newspaper called *Social Justice*, which almost immediately became required reading in all of Boston's Catholic neighborhoods. Every Sunday morning after Mass, thousands of parishioners snatched up their copies of *Social Justice* piled alongside the *Globe*, the *Herald*, and the *Post* outside every Catholic church. These working-class people regarded the charismatic priest from Michigan as their champion in the struggle between the rich and the poor, the haves and the have-nots.[97]

Encouraged by the devotion of his followers, Coughlin came out publicly against Roosevelt and organized his own political convention in Cleveland in August 1936. There, Representative William Lemke of North Dakota was nominated for president and Thomas O'Brien of Boston, a former district attorney for Suffolk County, was chosen as the vice-presidential candidate. Despite his boast that he could deliver nine million votes, Coughlin's bid for national power was an embarassing failure. Not only did the lackluster Lemke poll fewer than one million votes, but the radio priest himself lost a good deal of popular support. After this defeat, Coughlin's political views became more extreme, his sermons more strident, and his anti-Semitism more blatant. Some Irish-Catholic supporters were turned off by the priest's personal involvement in party politics, and Cardinal O'Connell spoke out against "hysterical addresses" by priests talking "nonsense" and indulging in "emotionalism."[98] But many other Bostonians continued to listen to the Sunday afternoon broadcasts, con-

tinued to read *Social Justice,* and responded positively to Coughlin's ti-
rades against the alleged machinations of the Jews. The spirit of anti-
Semitism had always been present to some degree in the provincial and
homogeneous city of Boston, but because the Jews were isolated and their
numbers extremely small, the reaction against them was generally abstract
until the turn-of-the-century wave of East European immigrants.[99]
Whether because of the severity of the Great Depression, the frightening
charges by Father Coughlin of an international Jewish conspiracy, the
increasing number of Jewish people moving into Irish neighborhoods, or
reports of Nazi atrocities against the Jews in Hitler's Germany, Boston
experienced an outbreak of anti-Semitic violence during the late 1930s and
early 1940s. Bands of Irish youths ranged up and down Blue Hill Avenue
in the Jewish district of Dorchester (the Irish disparagingly called it "Jew
Hill Avenue"), harassing shop owners, beating up Jewish boys on their
way home from school, scrawling swastikas and ugly graffiti on Jewish
homes and temples.[100] Not until well after World War II did the social and
religious climate in Boston change sufficiently to enable political and
church leaders to speak out against anti-Semitism. For the time being,
Mayor Curley could boast that Boston was "the strongest Coughlin city
in the world."[101]

In the meantime, the economic effects of the Great Depression continued to be felt throughout the city. Although Curley was greatly disap-
pointed that the federal bureaucracy refused him the substantial federal
funding he wanted, he managed to use whatever federal funds he did
receive, together with whatever appropriations he could extract from the
city and state treasuries, to favor the interests of the ethnic neighborhoods
from which he drew his political strength while virtually ignoring the
needs of the downtown areas. He enlarged the Boston City Hospital in
the South End to provide surgical facilities for working-class families and
established seven new health units in various neighborhoods, where poor
people could receive emergency medical treatment and professional medical advice. In communities like Jamaica Plain, Hyde Park, West Roxbury,
and Brighton, Curley built new branch libraries to make available to people in the neighborhoods many of the resources of the Boston Public

Library in downtown Copley Square. He constructed new public schools; developed beaches, roads, and tunnels; expanded parks and playgrounds; and laid out miles of roads, highways, and parkways.[102]

The cost of Curley's city-wide construction projects brought him into a series of bitter confrontations with the conservative financial establishment of the city, which had opposed his rise to political power from the start. Curley brushed aside their protestations with a cavalier wave of his hand. Tax money was supposed to be used to help people, not hoarded away in bank vaults, he insisted. When there were no more funds left in the city treasury to pay bills or to cover salaries, he went to the state legislature to borrow money until he could bring in more tax revenue. If there weren't enough funds on hand to meet current operating expenses, he went to local bankers for loans. More than 90 percent of the banking resources of the city were in conservative hands: Lee, Higginson and Company; Kidder, Peabody and Company; the National Shawmut Bank; the First National Bank of Boston; and twenty-one other banks and trust companies whose directors had prominent Yankee names like Amory, Choate, Gardner, Gaston, Lawrence, Lyman, Saltonstall, Sears, Shaw, and Storrow.[103] The bankers were not at all sympathetic to Curley or to his proposed projects, which would push the tax rate even higher. But the mayor had "ways" of getting the loans he needed. A disarming smile and a gentle reminder that some city inspector might order a certain bank closed for "faulty wiring" or "improper plumbing" was often enough to open the reluctant Yankee pocketbook. Curley himself took great pleasure in describing one exercise in "political banditry" against Philip Stockton, president of the First National Bank. When Stockton balked at loaning the mayor money, Curley reminded him of a water main with floodgates located directly under the bank. If Curley didn't get the money he needed by three o'clock that afternoon, he told the banker, he would see that the gates were opened and the bank vaults flooded. "He acceded to my request," Curley wrote in his autobiography, taking obvious delight in "putting the bankers in their place."[104]

The confrontational relationship that developed between City Hall and Boston's financial community during the 1930s as a result of Curley's high-handed tactics widened the gap between the "inner city" and the "outer city," between the Yankee and the Celt, between the Boston of the Protestants and the Boston of the Catholics. Neighborhoods with distinctive ethnic characteristics and identifiable boundaries had been a feature of Boston's history since the early part of the nineteenth century. What Curley did was to weld the minority groups—the Irish, the Italians, the Jews, the blacks, and others—into one powerful political force devoted to him personally and capable of neutralizing the opposition of the downtown Yankee. The Yankees submitted to his power but denied him the legitimacy he sought as mayor of the entire city. Accepting this division of power as a political fact of life—indeed, often capitalizing on it for his own purposes—Curley left the upper-class residents of the downtown to wallow in Puritan self-righteousness while he turned his attention and his municipal favors to those "other" Bostonians who never failed to give him their loyalty—and their votes. While Curley built playgrounds in Dorchester and Roxbury, he let Scollay Square become a place where ugly tattoo parlors and sleazy burlesque houses blighted the historic landscape. While he planned extensive bathhouses in South Boston, the docks and piers along Atlantic Avenue rotted on the pilings. While he laid out miles of paved sidewalks in Charlestown and East Boston, the cobblestones of Beacon Hill fell apart and the old lampposts came tumbling down.[105] The idea of improving "new" Boston with money extracted from "old" Boston struck Curley as a particularly appropriate way to balance the scales that had, for so long, been weighted against the poor.

On this basis James Michael Curley dominated the Boston political scene for nearly forty years, from before World War I, when he was elected to the United States Congress for the first time, until after the end of World War II. After serving three separate terms as mayor of Boston, in 1935 he finally won a single term as governor of Massachusetts, which earned him the flattering title of "Governor" wherever he went for the rest of his days. But by this time he found it increasingly difficult to maintain his customary hold on the electorate. In 1936 he was beaten by Henry Cabot Lodge, Jr., in a race for the United States Senate. The following year he suffered a particularly disappointing defeat in another bid for the mayor's office at the hands of young Maurice J. Tobin of Roxbury's Mission Hill. Tall and handsome, with the striking good looks of a matinee idol, Tobin had become a protégé of the aging Curley with assurances that he would be the older man's natural successor. But Tobin got tired of waiting. Curley complained that he had been "stabbed in the back" and went down to defeat in a campaign that became a classic part of American political lore, fictionalized in Edwin O'Connor's incomparable novel, *The Last Hurrah*.[106] Curley's loss was all the more bitter because he had become the victim of the kind of dirty trick he had used so often and so successfully against others. Election day, November 2, 1937, fell on All Souls' Day, and as thousands of the faithful came out of morning Mass they saw below the masthead of the *Boston Post* a statement by Cardinal O'Connell declaring: "The walls are raised against honest men in civic life." These words were followed by a ringing endorsement of Maurice Tobin as "an honest, clean, competent young man." Most readers failed to notice that the endorsement was not part of O'Connell's statement—actually made six years earlier—but had been written by the editors of the *Post* and cleverly appended. Voters went to the polls and dutifully voted the way they thought His Eminence had directed, and Curley's try for a fourth term was doomed.[107] Although Curley managed to win the Democratic nomination for governor in 1938, he lost the general election. The winner was the Republican Leverett Saltonstall, who had captured a surprising number of Irish-Catholic votes by capitalizing on the craggy features he laughingly called "my South Boston face." More than one Irish voter was heard to express the belief that the popular Brahmin, who belonged to one of Boston's oldest and most distinguished families, was already so wealthy that he wouldn't need to steal. In 1941 the frustrated Curley made another attempt to become mayor of Boston but, after a bitter campaign, lost to Maurice Tobin by only about 9,000 votes.[108]

The Boston mayoral election was hardly a month past when, on December 7, 1941, the Japanese attacked the American fleet at Pearl Harbor. The United States was at war, and the complex problems of Boston politics were obscured by the exigencies of national survival. With a growing deficit, an unbalanced budget, dishearteningly high taxes, an inability to attract government funding or corporate investment, and a constant state of warfare between the Irish-Catholic political system and the Yankee-Protestant financial establishment, Boston was in trouble. Even the most optimistic observer would have to concede that the postwar future of Boston did not look promising.

7

LACE CURTAINS

AND TWO TOILETS

❧

BY 1945, when the Allied forces defeated Nazi Germany and American bombers destroyed Hiroshima and Nagasaki to bring World War II to an end, the condition of Boston was more depressing than when the war had first begun. The already shaky financial state of the city worsened when Mayor Maurice J. Tobin decided to abandon city politics and retire from the office of mayor in 1944 in order to make what proved to be a successful run for the governorship.[1]

The situation became even more complicated when James Michael Curley returned from his congressional seat in Washington to run for mayor in 1945. Despite being under indictment by a federal grand jury on charges of mail fraud, the seventy-year-old veteran politician swept the field, taking 45 percent of the vote and defeating his nearest rival almost two-to-one. It took more than a year for the embattled mayor to exhaust all his judicial appeals, but finally, in June 1947, he was sentenced to a term of six to eighteen months in the federal penitentiary at Danbury, Connecticut.[2] Embarrassed by the spectacle of its mayor languishing in jail and running on automatic pilot under a temporary mayor appointed by a Yankee governor, postwar Boston faced seemingly insurmountable problems.

What little stimulus World War II had given to local industries disappeared almost before the war was over. Textile plants continued to abandon New England and move southward; the leather and footwear industries went into decline; the shipping industry, once the mainstay of the Boston economy, was a thing of the past; railroads no longer brought shipments of coffee beans, leather, wool, and tropical fruit to the terminals and warehouses along Summer Street. The Bethlehem shipyards in East Boston and the Fore River shipyards in Quincy were closing down, while the huge army base in South Boston was cutting back its operations. War contracts were cancelled; the machinery and tooling industries announced substantial layoffs; the housing shortage became more serious every day; inflation rose steadily. Streets were in a terrible state of disrepair; highways were clogged with traffic; construction was at a standstill. Even long-established Boston business executives recognized the decline of the city: they moved the offices and plants of their growing electronics industry to the western suburbs along Route 128, far from the old downtown of Boston proper.[3]

The circus-like atmosphere of Boston politics became more bizarre when, after five months in prison, Curley was pardoned by President Harry Truman and made a triumphal return to Boston the day before Thanksgiving 1947. As Curley's locomotive chugged noisily into Back Bay Station, thousands of friends, supporters, and well-wishers greeted him, cheering and ringing cowbells while a brass band played "Hail to the Chief." The Great Man was back, and after spending Thanksgiving Day at home with his family, in the house with shamrock shutters on the Jamaicaway, he returned to City Hall bright and early the next morning with his wife on one arm and his daughter on the other. After posing for photographers, he breezed into the mayor's office, signed a series of contracts, and gave out a number of jobs. Later, he emerged from his office with a smart-alecky remark to waiting reporters: "I have accomplished more in one day than has been done in the five months of my absence." This offhand wisecrack, he observed, made temporary mayor John B. Hynes "visibly upset," but Curley undoubtedly viewed it as insignificant at the time—merely the type of humorous witticism the reporters expected of him as he waved good-bye and left City Hall for the weekend.[4]

But Curley's parting shot was a turning point in his career. That cutting remark did more damage than Curley could anticipate. A professional bureaucrat and city clerk for many years, Hynes was a decent, honest, hardworking man who took pride in his accomplishments and had accepted the job as temporary mayor at the request of the governor in order to keep city government on an even keel. Curley's contemptuous insult, casting aspersions on his professional competence, absolutely infuriated Hynes, and it was at that moment that he decided to retaliate by running for mayor in November 1949. Hynes might have returned quietly to his desk as city clerk, and Curley might well have gone on for one or two more terms as mayor of Boston, had it not been for that one flippant remark. Hynes could not let it pass; it hurt too much. And so the fight was on. It would be Hynes against Curley in 1949 in a David-and-Goliath contest that few people could take seriously at first. The idea of an unknown and inexperienced bureaucrat who had no money and no political machine, and who had never run for political office in his life, taking on one of the most charismatic and powerful big-city bosses in the United States seemed laughable.[5]

Before long, however, Curley found he had a serious contest on his hands. Hynes capitalized on a ground swell of dissatisfaction with the prevailing political system in Boston and offered voters the prospect of an honest and enlightened administration. In a surprisingly short time, Hynes drew together a broad-based coalition of reform-minded, middle-class Irish, Jewish, and Italian voters and a scattering of downtown Yankee business and financial leaders to whom anyone was preferable to "that man" Curley. In addition to attracting a significant number of black voters from the South End–Roxbury district and appealing to the city's women voters, whose numbers had become an important factor in Boston politics, Hynes made a special effort to capture thousands of World War II veterans and a whole new generation of college students who would vote for the first time in the 1949 election. Curley ridiculed Hynes as "a little city clerk," a "pawn" of the Republican party, and a "stooge" for "the State Street wrecking crew"—a technique Curley had used successfully against Thomas Kenny in 1914—but his opponent remained cool under fire. Hynes promised to give Boston a "clean, honest, and efficient administration." He played cleverly on the age of Curley—"this tired and battle-scarred war horse" whose votes now rest "in the cemeteries of an era long past"—and won an increasing number of endorsements from the downtown Boston community. As the newspapers had predicted, the turnout was large and the race was close. Hynes defeated Curley by a margin of only 11,000 votes, winning a total of 138,790—the largest number of votes won by any candidate in the city's history. Curley's total of 126,042 was the largest vote in the old warrior's long political career. Despite the closeness of the contest, many people sensed that something significant had taken place in this surprise upset of one of Boston's most famous and colorful political figures. "The decision rendered yesterday by voters of the city of Boston," wrote the editor of the *Boston Daily Globe*, "marks the end of one era and the beginning of another."[6]

Whether he came up with the idea himself or borrowed it from Edwin O'Connor's best-selling novel *The Last Hurrah*, which had been published only a year before he completed his autobiography, *I'd Do It Again*, Curley blamed a good part of his defeat on circumstances over which he had no control—including, especially, the extensive social-welfare programs of Roosevelt's New Deal. These became in Curley's words, his most "formidable competitor as the best friend of the poor."[7] It is certainly true that the New Deal did much to undermine the system of patronage that for years had served as the basis of political power for big-city bosses like Curley. In the past, the lifeblood of any political organization had been the ability of the boss to deliver the greatest number of favors—jobs, cash, housing, medical care, legal assistance—in the shortest amount of time, to the greatest number of friends and supporters. With the passage of New Deal legislation such as social security, unemployment insurance, and workmen's compensation, followed after World War II by the wide-ranging benefits of the G.I. Bill, including temporary employment, housing loans, professional training, and educational benefits, there was little reason for anyone to go to the local ward boss for help. And with more federal offices, courthouses, post offices, banks, and veterans' bureaus appearing on the scene, civil-service appointments provided numerous jobs beyond the control of ward bosses. Increasingly, members of the United States Congress like John W. McCormack, Thomas P. ("Tip") O'Neill, and other federal officials became more influential sources of patronage than their counterparts on the state and local levels. Forty years earlier, when he first became mayor of Boston, Curley had undermined the local bosses by taking personal control of all patronage in the city. Now, in a somewhat parallel process, the federal government was making big-city bosses like Curley obsolete. The citizens of Boston became more dependent on the bottomless largesse of federal agencies than on the limited handouts of city bosses.[8]

To blame the collapse of the Curley regime solely on "the New Deal

Three generations of Boston politicians appear together on the public rostrum. From left to right, Mayor James Michael Curley, Governor Maurice J. Tobin, and congressional candidate John F. Kennedy join forces at the Veterans of Foreign Wars Convention in 1946. Courtesy of the Boston Public Library, Print Department.

factor," however, would be simplistic. Several other factors must be considered in accounting for Curley's "Last Hurrah" in 1949. For one thing, the years had not been kind to James Michael Curley. Behind the imperturbable facade—the grand manner and self-assured posture—his strength had been slowly draining away. In addition to the devastating effects of the death of his beloved first wife and the tragic loss of seven of his nine children, poor health and old age were taking their toll. Many of the loyal followers who had gone to meet "Young Jim" when he returned from prison two years earlier had been visibly shocked by the pallid skin, the rheumy eyes, and the sunken cheeks of a man in his mid-seventies who had clearly passed his prime.[9]

To make matters worse, there existed no organized system capable of continuing the Curley operation. Curley had never really created a political "machine" in the accepted sense of the term, nor had he groomed a cadre of bright, young political lieutenants who could move up the ladder and take over when he relinquished control. Ironically, although Boston was frequently characterized in the national press as the prime example of a city controlled by a "political machine," there never was a professionally organized Irish-Democratic political network that could exercise sufficient control over its members to achieve either short-term or long-term goals. In his biography of "Honey Fitz" John Henry Cutler suggests that, while there were no antagonisms too deep to reconcile, the Democrats failed to come up with a political machine because "there were not enough Boston Irishmen able to agree on a premise long enough to form one."[10] But cussedness alone is not enough to explain why the Irish in the twentieth century could not accomplish what leaders like Maguire and O'Brien and Collins had managed in the nineteenth. Certainly, power politics and ethnic rancor on the part of the city's ruling elite played a decisive role. In 1909 the Yankee establishment had deliberately and successfully undermined any possibility for effective machine politics when they had the state legislature pass the new city charter putting mayoral elections on a nonpartisan basis. To further restrict the activities of any future Irish mayors, Republicans had also used their influence in the Great and General Court to set limits on the city's ability to borrow funds and to spend money on its public schools. The Republicans refused to let Boston raise its own taxes or increase its assessments without permission of the state legislature and even took the appointment of the city's police commissioner out of the hands of the mayor. A state licensing board was set up to regulate liquor sales in Boston and supervise the operations of amusements and dining places in the city.[11]

Nevertheless, although the Boston Irish did not develop a modern political machine and were hampered on many occasions by a hostile state legislature, they had both the numbers and the power to monopolize the agencies of municipal government. This political fact of life Curley turned to his own advantage when he became mayor, exuding a personal magnetism and a one-man appeal that worked better—for him, at least—than any organizational chart or campaign strategy. He bypassed the legitimate sources of power in the city and appealed directly to his Irish-Catholic constituency in a virtual plebiscite of raw political muscle. Now that the Great Man was gone, however, Irish Democrats faced a political vacuum of enormous proportions at a time when the traditional techniques of politicking were undergoing substantial changes. In the old days, when politicians like "Honey Fitz" and Jim Curley had first begun their careers, outdoor festivities were the most conspicuous feature of political campaigns in the Boston neighborhoods, complete with torchlight rallies, fireworks and flares, horse-drawn wagons, sound trucks, banjo players, Irish step dancers, and long drawn-out speeches to arouse the enthusiasm of faithful suppporters. Curley himself was among the first to recognize that these techniques had become obsolete, and that in the postwar era the old-time rally had gone the way of "vaudeville and the hurdy-gurdy man."[12] The advent of radio and television not only kept people indoors but put strict limits on the length of speeches. The new media required careful preparation of brief presentations instead of rambling oratorical polemics in the time-honored Celtic tradition. An accomplished writer who composed most of his own speeches, John Hynes was better at using the radio to put his personality across and drive his message home than was Curley, whose florid style and flamboyant delivery were much better suited to outdoor speeches.

Moreover, by the late 1940s and early 1950s many of Boston's old-time ethnic neighborhoods, which had supplied devoted and enthusiastic support for men like Curley, were losing their ethnic distinctiveness. Sons and daughters of Irish families that had been in America for two or three generations had lost touch with their ethnic heritage and were all but impervious to emotional appeals to the traditions of the "old country." It was pleasant enough for young people to celebrate St. Patrick's Day once a year, to enjoy a bit of Irish music, and to spend an evening with their friends at a local Irish pub, but few of them had any firsthand knowledge of the history or culture of Ireland. Nor did they feel any particular attachment to the old neighborhoods like Charlestown, Dorchester, East Boston, and South Boston. When their fortunes brightened they gladly left the old three-decker houses in districts where their families had lived for generations and moved to new split-levels and ranch houses in the suburbs. With some notable exceptions, such as the heavily Italian North End, by the early 1950s Boston's old neighborhoods were fast losing their original ethnic compositions. Increasingly transient populations showed little evidence of the ethnic solidarity or the political unity that had once made these districts a powerful influence in city politics. The Curley era was ending, it is true, but what would take its place was by no means clear.[13]

John B. Hynes was sworn in as mayor at Symphony Hall on January 2, 1950, with little to indicate that he was much different from his political predecessors or that he would have any significant impact on the city's history. Born in 1897 on East Lenox Street in the South End, the son of immigrant Irish parents, Hynes grew up in the Neponset section of Dorchester. He attended public school, went to work for the telephone company when he was fourteen, and took night courses in typing, stenography, and business at the local high school. After a brief stint in the air corps in World War I, he became a stenographer in the city's health department, then moved to the auditing department and eventually became chief clerk in the mayor's office. After a brief period of military service in World War II, he returned to municipal government and became city clerk in 1945. Hynes was a quiet, gentle, compassionate person with a love of literature and a gift for composing simple poetry. He attended Mass every morning, telephoned his wife regularly at noon, and had a broad range of friendships in the City Hall bureaucracy. At first there seemed no particular reason for Hynes to be any more committed to the general welfare or any more capable of reforming government than earlier mayors. As time went on, however, he gained recognition as a political figure who appealed not only to third-generation Irish-American voters in the neighborhoods but also to members of the Yankee community of downtown Boston.[14]

For one thing, Hynes did not look the part of a typical neighborhood "pol." With his pinstripe suits, his conservative ties, his carefully groomed white hair, and his rimless glasses, he could easily be mistaken for a downtown banker. A calm, reasonable, soft-spoken man, he made no attempt to rekindle old ethnic or religious antagonisms to strengthen his political base. His main appeal was for a new political coalition in which formerly hostile elements could come together and work for the best interests of the city as a whole. Because of this approach, many Boston Yankees warmed to Hynes. They associated him with the tradition of accommodationist mayors like Hugh O'Brien and Patrick Collins rather than with the irreverent and confrontational tradition of "Honey Fitz" or Jim Curley.[15]

Then too, because Hynes had never been part of ward politics at the neighborhood level, there was less fear that he represented an Irish-Democratic political machine that might take advantage of the power vacuum created by Curley's defeat. Although Hynes had been intimately involved in the political system for many years and was well acquainted with both the machinery of government and the personnel who operated it, his position as city clerk distinguished him as a professional bureaucrat rather than a ward politician. He appeared much less dangerous to the established order than most of his peers.[16]

Finally, as a man twenty years younger than Curley and a veteran of World War II, Hynes was able to generate considerable appeal among many young Irish Catholics in the city who were tired of the steady diet of ethnic rivalry, class animosity, and religious antipathy with which they had grown up. Most of these young people were veterans of World War II, and many of them came from middle-class families and were college

graduates. They were less defensive about their ethnic origins, less parochial in their religious convictions, and more sophisticated in their political idealism than their parents. They were embarassed by the boisterous
rhetoric and outmoded antics of old-time bosses and felt that public service in the middle of the twentieth century demanded more than practical
jokes and dirty tricks. True, they were steeped in the traditions of Boston
politics. They thoroughly enjoyed the uproarious anecdotes told by the
old-timers and were still amused by the sight of a typical Boston "pol"
walking down School Street in his chesterfield coat with the black velvet
collar, the pearl grey fedora, the splashy necktie, and the huge cigar stick-
ing out of the corner of his mouth. But they saw the politics of the James
Cagney–Pat O'Brien era as irrelevant in the atomic age. To most American

*After a long and expensive campaign, organized by his younger
brother Bobby, John F. Kennedy defeated prominent Boston blue
blood Henry Cabot Lodge, Jr., in 1952 for a seat in the U.S. Senate. Here Kennedy celebrates his victory with well-wishers at the
Quincy Ship Yard. Courtesy of the Boston Public Library,
Print Department.*

Catholics, and to the Boston Irish especially, the emergence of John F. Kennedy as a political leader of national prominence created a great surge of pride and marked a dramatic turning point in their political consciousness—what William Shannon called a rounded fulfillment of the "long story of Irish adjustment in America."[17] Although the members of the Kennedy family seldom involved themselves in Boston politics, except where their own interests or candidates were directly concerned, young Jack, the grandson of two Boston ward bosses, one of whom served twice as mayor of the city, came to have a special place in the heart of the Boston voters.[18] Still conscious of their immigrant past, they appeared to see in the brilliance of his mind and the flair of his public appeal what was finally needed to wipe away any lingering feelings of social inferiority and political insecurity. As they listened to Joe Kennedy's son preach the familiar doctrines of Democratic progressivism, the Irish were quick to note the air of pragmatic ruthlessness that lay behind the graceful prose and the sparkling humor they loved so well. Power, politics, and poetry marked the progress of the handsome young chieftain on his way to the White House, and the Boston Irish flocked to his banner with a confidence and enthusiasm they had seldom known before. At the national level, a younger generation had found in Jack Kennedy a new political leader who was definitely "something different," and at the local level they were looking for someone with many of the same qualities. For the time being, at least, John B. Hynes seemed to fit the bill.

Another factor that played an important but subtle role in changing the political atmosphere of the city was the emergence in 1945 of Archbishop Richard J. Cushing as the spiritual leader of Boston's Roman Catholic population. Cushing was a crusty and unpredictable cleric from South Boston who had made a name for himself by successfully directing the local office of the Society for the Propagation of the Faith. His informality, his gruff affability, and his down-to-earth common sense contrasted sharply with the rather aloof pomposity of his predecessor, William Cardinal O'Connell, who had dominated the local religious scene for the past thirty years. Little concerned with ceremonies or abstract theology, Cushing was interested in updating the church and making it relevant to the everyday lives of ordinary people. He avoided the ornate vestments of his office except when they were required for church services and usually appeared in public in plain black clerical garb. Breezy and outgoing, he welcomed publicity, courted photographers, and mingled with all sorts of people, from the rich and powerful to the poor and disadvantaged. He said Mass for prison inmates, accompanied groups of nuns to baseball games, administered the sacraments to mentally retarded children, and personally sliced the turkey at annual Thanksgiving dinners for elderly people.[19]

But Cushing was more than a new man in town with a different way of doing things. He helped define a new level of human relations in an archdiocese theretofore noted for bitter and sometimes violent conflicts

The size of the women's vote became an increasingly significant factor in both national and local elections in the years after the Second World War. Here Senator John F. Kennedy takes time out from marching in the 1953 Bunker Hill Day parade to greet enthusiastic female admirers along the route in Charlestown. Courtesy of the Boston Public Library, Print Department.

among people of different religious, ethnic, and racial backgrounds. Distancing himself from the rigid and often confrontational attitudes of his predecessor, who had established a clear-cut policy of religious separatism, Cushing adopted an open and tolerant approach, pledging to refrain from "all arguments with our non-Catholic neighbors and from all purely defensive talk about Catholicism." Working in the spirit of the postwar ecumenical movement and preaching the doctrine of universal brotherhood—more often than not by his own bold example—Cushing unceremoniously knocked aside many of the barriers that for so long had separated his parishioners from their non-Catholic neighbors. By the time he was appointed Cardinal by Pope John XXIII in 1958, Cushing had anticipated many of the changes that would be instituted by the Vatican Council. He preached in Protestant churches, spoke before Jewish audiences, and generally promoted a feeling of fellowship and good will among the ethnic and religious groups in the Greater Boston area. Almost alone in

Dramatic evidence of the changing norms in an old city in which religious prejudices and social differences had long created bitter differences among members of the community was displayed when the Catholic archbishop, Cardinal Richard Cushing, appeared in person, wearing a yarmulke, to address an ecumenical breakfast at a Jewish temple in Brookline. The Boston Globe.

the American Catholic hierarchy, Cushing spoke out on behalf of Israel during the 1967 war and the following year formed a Catholic-Jewish Committee to bring together leaders of both communities to discuss sensitive issues and head off potential conflicts. The new archbishop's influence was clearly in tune with the political exhortations of Mayor Hynes, who urged the citizens of Boston to put aside their differences and work together for the benefit of the city.[20]

With a changing electorate, a new generation of voters, a growing spirit of reform, and a noticeable thaw in the city's religious climate, Mayor Hynes slowly pulled together into a working coalition two of the most hostile elements of the Boston political scene. Since the beginning of the twentieth century, as the immigrant tide grew substantially larger and moved alarmingly higher in wealth, social status, and political power, control of the city had divided into two distinct and antagonistic camps. Irish-Catholic Democrats gradually gained control of all aspects of municipal politics, from grass-roots balloting and patronage to the upper echelons of power. Yankee-Protestant Republicans, on the other hand, controlled all levels of the city's businesses and banking institutions. During the first half of the twentieth century, Boston was a city where political power and financial influence were split right down the middle, with little chance of cordiality or accommodation.

The fact that few if any of the Boston Irish were included in the higher echelons of the city's business establishment did not mean that a number of individual Irishmen had not become quite wealthy or that Irish families had not made remarkable economic progress over the years. The grocery business, for example, proved to be an auspicious starting point for many immigrants during the nineteenth century. The often-attendant liquor industry produced wealthy entrepreneurs such as James Kenney, Michael Doherty, and Lawrence Logan, whom the social historian Dennis Ryan has called "the barons of Boston's liquor business." The necessary work of the undertaker was another profession in which a number of Irishmen, such as Patrick Brady, John McCaffrey, and Frederick Crosby, became proficient and prosperous. With the growing need for roads, houses, sewers, and bridges in the new Irish neighborhoods, the contracting business also flourished. Patrick O'Riorden became a millionaire working on city projects; Charles Logue worked on the construction of Fenway Park; Timothy Hannon helped fill in the Back Bay; and Owen Nawn's trucking company that carried granite from the quarries attracted lucrative contracts from City Hall and the public utility companies. Irishmen also moved steadily into the ranks of the city's legal profession, serving mainly as general practitioners while they explored careers in government service. By the twentieth century, according to Ryan, at least half of the prominent Irish attorneys practicing in the city either held elective office or were otherwise involved in politics. However, although many Irish lawyers went on to become municipal judges (like Joseph D. Fallon, the first Irish Catholic appointed to the South Boston District Court in 1880), they were slow in gaining appointments to the state's higher courts. Irish Catholics encountered similar barriers in the medical profession, which was still dominated by the Yankees. Physicians like William Dunn, John Blake, and George Galvin became well known in the city in great part because of their involvement in public affairs. Doctors Dunn and Blake were active members of the school committee; Galvin helped found the Boston Emergency Hospital. But it would be some time before Irish doctors were admitted to the more exclusive medical societies and professional associations.[21]

On a more modest level, the upward mobility of Irish-Catholic families during the early part of the twentieth century allowed them to save a little money, send a son to college (usually the first in the family's history), and eventually move out of the old two-decker to a single-family home in Milton or West Roxbury, where they became part of the so-called lace-curtain Irish. Bright young men and women from Irish-American families competed for openings as teachers, policemen, firemen, nurses, custodians, librarians, and clerks, while others found equally desirable jobs in the telephone company, the gas company, and the electric company, or as streetcar conductors, motormen for the Boston Elevated Railway, or salesmen in downtown insurance companies. It was not at all surprising that Mayor Maurice Tobin had started out as a clerk and traffic manager in the telephone company, or that Mayor Hynes had spent nearly thirty years as a clerk in the municipal bureaucracy.[22] The choice of such occupations reflected the strong desire of most Irish Catholics to avoid the insecurities of high-risk ventures and uncertain investments as a means of gaining great wealth. They favored lifetime positions with guaranteed employment and comfortable pensions, either in civil service or in public utility companies.

There were great opportunities to be found in government service. By the early part of the twentieth century there had developed a substantial political bureaucracy, tucked quietly away in the offices and back rooms of City Hall: a close-knit, well-established, and hardworking cadre of knowledgeable men and women—by this time predominantly Irish Catholic—whose families usually had solid political connections. An anonymous army of assistants, managers, clerks, secretaries, and administrators, they kept the records, filed the papers, stamped the contracts, typed the correspondence, answered the telephones, maintained the tax records, gave out the licenses, issued the birth certificates, and staffed the hundreds of offices, departments, divisions, and agencies that served the general public. They occupied coveted municipal positions that provided generations of citizens with attractive and well-paying jobs with virtually guaranteed security and comfortable pensions. And beyond the confines of the city itself, extending into the neighborhoods, there grew up an even larger number of bureaucrats, civil servants, technical experts, and professional consultants serving the needs of the municipality. Civil engineers, landscape architects, librarians, archivists, schoolteachers, physicians, scientists, and many others became indispensable elements in the structure of urban government. According to Jon Teaford, who traced the development of this corps of experts and specialists from the turn of the century, these civil servants usually were "more devoted to their professions than to any party."[23]

Despite these accomplishments, however, the Boston Irish still had not moved into the upper levels of corporate management. As late as 1940, according to William Shannon, only four of the thirty directors of the Boston Chamber of Commerce were of Irish descent. Only one small bank, he notes, and not one of the city's major department stores, was headed by people with Irish names. When the journalist John Gunther visited Boston on his tour of American cities near the end of World War II, he was astonished to find that the New England Council, a businessmen's organization formed in 1925 to stimulate the regional economy, had never had an Irishman as an officer, a committee chairman, or a member of the executive committee.[24]

The division between Irish politicians and Yankee businessmen was accentuated by the biting wit of James Michael Curley, who for years made a political career out of poking fun at the downtown establishment (the "State Street wrecking crew"), gleefully blackmailing their banking institutions, and ridiculing their families as the descendants of "rumrunners and slave traders." While these sallies provoked gales of laughter in the ethnic neighborhoods, they were hardly the kind of remarks to inspire a harmonious relationship, much less a friendly coalition, between businessmen and politicians in Boston. The downtown business interests were not at all amused. They hated Curley and all he represented and refused to cooperate in any programs or projects that seemed to have the approval of City Hall. The postwar decade of the 1950s saw major urban renewal taking place in other large American cities, such as Chicago, Albany, Pittsburgh, Philadelphia, and New Haven, largely as the result of "pro-growth" coalitions between ethnic mayors and business associations. The alliance between Mayor David Lawrence of Pittsburgh and the Allegheny Conference on Community Development is only one example of the new socioeconomic relations that were evolving in other urban communities.[25] In Boston, however, it was almost impossible for people even to *conceive* of such a political-business alliance in light of the traditional hostility between the two forces. Downtown industrialists were merely following the national trend when they located their new electronics firms and high-tech agencies outside the city, along the approaches to Route 128 and closer to the younger work force that had moved to the suburbs during the fifties. But this major relocation of human resources and capital investment cast further doubt on the ability of the downtown area to recover its financial viability and confirmed the prevailing image of the city's schizophrenic economic culture.

Gradually, however, by conveying an air of quiet professionalism and personal integrity, John Hynes built bridges to the Boston business community. He met with business leaders, listened to them seriously, and appointed a number of them to special committees and mayoral commissions. Yankee Republicans slowly indicated a willingness to extend to Hynes the political recognition and the financial cooperation they had so long denied Curley. Irish Democrats, in turn, demonstrated a willingness to work with the downtown establishment on a basis of equality and respect. Hynes was also able to solicit the support and cooperation of several leading colleges and universities in the area, whose specialists provided valuable economic studies, financial reports, and urban-planning designs for the projects he had in mind. Working with Boston banks and a variety of federal funding agencies during the prosperous years of the Eisenhower administration, he began renewing the face of a badly scarred city. With a new Central Artery under construction that would allow heavy automobile and truck traffic to bypass the congested downtown area, Hynes exerted pressure to construct an underground garage beneath the Boston Common. He established a commission to design a modern auditorium for conferences and conventions, and a short time later he created the Government Center Commission to plan a new centralized area for city, state, and federal office buildings. With increased federal funding he was able to build a series of new public housing projects in the surrounding neighborhoods. He worked with the Prudential Insurance Company to clear some twenty-eight acres of abandoned railroad yards in the Back Bay and build a regional office and a $75 million commercial complex. With further federal funding, Hynes authorized the transformation of a corner of the South End known as the New York Streets area from a small residential district to an industrial zone. He then went on to a more ambitious project involving the city's West End.[26]

One of the city's oldest waterfront sections, which consecutive waves of immigrants—Irish, Italians, Jews, Greeks, Russians, Albanians, Ukrainians—had turned into a colorful and densely populated melting pot, the West End in the 1950s provoked feelings of both affection and revulsion. To old-time residents, the West End was a warm, friendly, and close-knit community that should be preserved at all costs; younger and more professional observers saw it as an overcrowded and dangerous slum that should be wiped out as soon as possible. Despite emotional appeals and political protests, the residents of the West End—most of them poor and many of them recent immigrants—were evicted from their homes. The entire district was demolished and replaced by a luxury apartment complex designed to attract upper-middle-class residents ("quality shoppers") back to the city.[27] The ruthlessness with which the West End project was carried out, together with the extent of its destruction, aroused such bitter feelings that the future of urban renewal in Boston was very much in doubt. When Mayor Hynes's final term came to an end in 1960, it seemed to many observers that his vision for a newer and brighter Boston might never get off the drawing board.[28]

John Hynes's major contribution during his ten years in office was to change the general perception of Irish-Catholic political leadership in Boston. For half a century, the outrageous scandals of "Fitzgeraldism" and the legendary corruption of "Curleyism" had established an image of Boston in the minds of most outsiders—and quite a few insiders, too—as a city whose political leaders, almost to a man, were venal, criminal, and untrustworthy. Leaders of the business community were convinced that Boston was in the hands of "supercrooks," as one downtown banker later put it. "Nobody had ever seen an honest Irishman around here," he said, expressing the common belief that all Irishmen were "cut from the same cloth."[29] The image of Curley-style manipulation had so long flavored the reputation of the city and its politicians that the state and federal governments hesitated to assign grants to Boston. Private corporations declined to make investments or undertake construction, and local businessmen refused to become associated with the public affairs of the municipality. But Hynes slowly transformed the negative perception of the city, establishing a personal reputation for honesty and integrity, bridging the gap between the Irish political community and the Yankee business establishment, encouraging investment by outside corporations, and restoring pride and satisfaction among the residents of the city. A plain and simple man of limited background, saddled with a traditional bureaucratic structure and a woeful lack of financial support, he was unable to bring about most of the innovative physical changes he felt were needed to create a truly "new" Boston. His early attempts at reconstruction were tentative, piecemeal, and clumsy; and the city's terrifying demolition of the West End came close to bringing the urban renewal process in Boston to an end. Whether the spirit of urban renewal would be revived, whether the new alliance between political leaders and business leaders would be maintained, and whether the integrity of Boston's leadership would be sustained depended in great measure on the next mayor. The trouble was that the political figure most likely to succeed John Hynes as mayor was a man for whom the "good old days" of the Curley era seemed to have a greater attraction than the idealistic vision of Hynes's "New Boston."

It was generally agreed that John E. Powers was Hynes's logical successor. A longtime political leader from South Boston, an expert on parliamentary procedure, and the powerful president of the Massachusetts Senate, Powers had the support of the neighborhoods, the backing of the labor unions, the encouragement of the newspapers, and the personal friendship of Cardinal Cushing. His only opposition came from John Collins of Jamaica Plain, who had served in the Massachusetts legislature as well as on the Boston City Council before being appointed Suffolk County register of probate—certainly not a typical springboard for high office. At first glance, the election of Powers as mayor of Boston seemed assured.[30]

John Frederick Collins was born July 20, 1919, in Boston's Roxbury section, the first of three sons of Frederick and Margaret Collins, both Irish-American Catholics. After attending public schools, Collins graduated first in his class from Suffolk University Law School in 1941 and passed the bar examination the same year. He enlisted as a private in the army a short time later, during World War II, and was discharged in 1946 as a captain. Collins belonged to the generation of veterans who saw Hynes as a viable alternative to Curley and who had supported the dark-horse candidate in his 1949 victory.[31] The following year, Collins himself was elected to the state Senate, where he served two terms. In 1954, while running as the Democratic candidate for state attorney general, he was summoned to the home of James Michael Curley, who wanted to meet the bright young man and give him some sage political advice. In the course of their conversation, Curley recalled that young Collins's father, "Skeets" Collins, had been a catcher on his old Tammany baseball team. Curley wondered why the son had shifted his support to Hynes in 1949. "Did my father work hard for you in your various campaigns?" Collins asked. "He certainly did," Curley replied. "Well, during the depression my father was having a very hard time," explained Collins. "He was working for a sugar company, and because he was a small man he was having trouble hefting those large sugar bags. He went to City Hall to see you about a job, but with no success. He could never get by your man in the front office. So I figured there was no reason for me to remain loyal to someone who did not help a man who had always been loyal to him."[32] Political memories had always run long and deep in Irish Boston ("and dirty," some would add), and even though it was now the middle of the twentieth century, there were few signs that much had changed in that respect. Although Collins lost the attorney-general race to his Republican rival, it was clear that the young man was going places in Massachusetts politics.

In the summer of 1955, however, it looked as though John Collins's promising political career had come to a sudden and tragic end: he was stricken with polio while running for a seat on the city council. Despite dire warnings from his doctors, Collins continued with the campaign, assisted by his wife and his friends, and ended up winning one of the nine council seats. In January he took the oath office at his Jamaica Plain home, but the following day he showed up in a wheelchair at the first council meeting. After a year, Collins accepted an appointment to a vacancy as register of probate for Suffolk County, and a year later he was elected to the position for a full term. It appeared that the thirty-nine-year-old politician would settle down as a career bureaucrat. Therefore, it came as a surprise when in 1959 Collins announced his candidacy against Senator Powers in a race that few people thought he could win.

However, several factors operated in Collins's favor: First, there is little doubt that his courageous comeback from a crippling bout with polio, like that of Franklin Delano Roosevelt, created a measure of sympathy and respect that worked to his political advantage. Second, in the new medium of television, which was becoming a factor in American politics (the famous Kennedy-Nixon television debates were less than a year away), Collins had a distinct advantage. He was able to convey a clean-cut, wholesome, nonpolitical image to Boston voters, in the tradition of Hugh O'Brien and Patrick Collins. Powers, by contrast, came across on television as a tough, arrogant, old-time machine politician in the tradition of "Honey Fitz" and James Michael Curley. In one of the biggest upsets in Boston's political history, Collins defeated Powers for mayor by 24,000 votes. Since both candidates were middle-class Irish-Catholic Democrats

Looking more like two conservative downtown bankers than stereotypical Boston Irish politicians, newly elected Boston mayor John F. Collins (left) meets with retiring Boston mayor John B. Hynes (right) on November 25, 1959. This was Collins's first visit to City Hall since his mayoral victory, and his first opportunity to discuss with the outgoing mayor various aspects of the position he would occupy after January. Courtesy of the Boston Public Library, Print Department.

at a time when race had not yet become a significant factor in city politics, one can only assume that Boston voters continued to favor a moderate, "nonpolitical" candidate without visible attachments to a machine organization, as opposed to a clearly "political" candidate whose backing smacked too much of the old Curley regime.[33]

When he took office in January 1960, John Collins set out to steer the city in a more positive direction and to establish municipal finances on a more stable basis. With a keen political mind and expert managerial skills, he reduced the city budget, reorganized the bureaucracy, and set out to make the unfulfilled vision of the "New Boston" a reality. Almost immediately, Collins reactivated the coalition of bankers, businessmen, politicians, technocrats, and academics that Hynes had first put together, and he brought in Edward J. Logue, an experienced city planner from New Haven, to direct the Boston Redevelopment Authority (BRA). Promoting the evolving coalition between the Irish political structure and the city's business community, Collins gave the merchants of Boston, through the existing Retail Trade Board, the responsibility of planning changes in the central city. He also worked closely with the members of the new Central Business District Committee, an association of downtown business and civic leaders subsidized by Edward R. Mitton of Jordan Marsh and Harold D. Hodgkinson of Filene's. The committee came to a unique agreement with the city administration—a "memo of understanding" signed by Collins, Logue, and Charles Coolidge—that no downtown project would be undertaken by the city without the approval of the Central Business District Committee.[34] With the resulting financial support from the city's business community and with increased federal funding from the Democratic administration of John F. Kennedy (and later under Lyndon B. Johnson, whose "Great Society" program was in full swing during 1964 and 1965), billions of dollars poured into gigantic renewal projects that transformed the face of the old city. The $200 million Prudential Center revitalized the area from Copley Square to Massachusetts Avenue; the Government Center Project, covering some sixty acres previously occupied by Scollay Square, paved the way for a modernistic new City Hall surrounded by new state and federal office buildings. Reconstruction began on the rundown waterfront district along Atlantic Avenue, a state-of-the-art aquarium was constructed, and the Collins administration took the first steps in restoring the granite structures of the historic Quincy Market behind Faneuil Hall.[35]

By this time the city's business community was no longer what it had been a generation earlier. Even after World War II, the financial affairs of Boston were firmly controlled by the same Yankee Brahmins who had dominated the regional economy for as long as anyone could remember. These were the men who in 1959 formed what they called the Boston Coordinating Committee to guide the economic future of the city—an organization reporters dubbed "The Vault" when they learned that its meetings were held near the old vault in Ralph Lowell's Safe Deposit and Trust Company. Headed by prominent business leaders such as Charles Coolidge of Ropes and Gray; Gerald Blakeley of Cabot, Cabot, and Forbes; Lloyd Brace of the First National Bank; Paul Clark of John Hancock; and Erskine White of the New England Telephone Company, the committee offered assistance to Mayor Collins in his efforts to transform the city.[36] But by this time, a number of Irish-Catholic businessmen had begun to work with "The Vault" in a collaborative urban renewal process. The sons and grandsons of immigrant day-laborers had returned from the war, completed their college educations, and worked their way to the upper echelons of corporate management. John J. Bacon became president of Boston Gas; Thomas J. Galligan, Jr., was chairman of Boston Edison; John I. Ahern served as vice president of the New England Electric System; Thomas H. Carens was vice president of the Boston Electric Company; and William H. (Billy) Sullivan, future owner of the New England Patriots, was president of the Metropolitan Coal and Oil Company. Richard Syron moved up to become chairman of the Federal Reserve Bank of Boston; Walter Connolly headed the Bank of New England; and Peter Madden was president of the State Street Bank. Howard Foley was named president of the High Technology Council; Robert Ryan was executive director of the Massachusetts Development Corporation; and James Dowd presided over the Boston Stock Exchange.[37] It was a remarkable shift of economic power in an amazingly brief period. The new Irish-Catholic business leaders quickly took on most of the characteristics of their Yankee counterparts. They worked hard, invested wisely, prospered greatly, joined country clubs, and moved to the suburbs. There, they joined the exalted ranks of the "two-toilet Irish" with expensive homes in Wellesley and summer places in Nantucket. In their Brooks Brothers suits, negotiating business deals over power breakfasts at the Ritz, they became practically indistinguishable from the Boston Brahmins who had once been their mortal enemies. The two groups joined in business as well as in politics to build a truly "New Boston" on the ashes of the run-down old city. By the 1970s the old rivalries between Protestants and Catholics, Yankees and Irish, were largely forgotten. In these more sophisticated and tolerant times, Irish Catholics not only constituted a dominant force in city politics but also exerted a growing influence in the financial affairs of the city.

For his leadership in the creation of the gleaming and prosperous "New Boston," Mayor Collins received the plaudits of the city's downtown business community, the recognition of urban planners throughout the world, and the admiration of tourists coming to the historic city for the first time. However, when he applied many of the same techniques in various neighborhoods that ringed the central city, the mayor received unexpected criticism. These neighborhoods were generally populated by blue-collar families living in two- and three-decker wooden houses and by people of color occupying run-down tenements and shabby rooming houses. The city's urban renewal program was designed to upgrade these valuable locations and transform them into attractive, revenue-producing communities. It was hoped that the shiny new town houses and apartments would draw middle-class families and well-to-do professionals back to the city, where they would make Boston once again an appealing place to live and a convenient place to work. The Hynes administration's West End project had been a first attempt, clumsy, and highly controversial, to accomplish these ends; Collins and his urban planner, Ed Logue, promised to bring greater efficiency, responsibility, and compassion to the process. The question, of course, was where to begin.

By the end of the nineteenth century, there had developed two separate and distinctive lines of authority characterizing Irish political power in

Boston. On the one hand, there were the "city" leaders—men like Patrick Maguire, Hugh O'Brien, and Patrick Collins—who maintained a close relationship with the Democratic party, insisted on a disciplined political organization, and sought city-wide power by associating with various elements of the Yankee community. On the other hand, there were the ward leaders—men like Martin Lomasney, Patrick J. Kennedy, and "Smiling Jim" Donovan—who sought jobs and favors for their constituents, ignored the larger issues of state and national politics, and concentrated on the concerns of their individual neighborhoods. During the first fifty years of the twentieth century, the "city" approach to municipal government was largely overwhelmed by ward politics, first under Fitzgerald and then under Curley. The power of the ethnic vote, the influence of neighborhood concerns, and the appeals of demagogic ward politics played a decisive role in the affairs of Boston for half a century. After World War II, however, and especially after the defeat of Curley in 1949, the "city" approach began to take precedence over ward politics. John B. Hynes and John F. Collins clearly fit the mold of late-nineteenth-century accommodationist mayors like Hugh O'Brien and Patrick Collins. With ambitious goals and explicit agendas, they formed political alliances, cultivated economic coalitions, and worked for city-wide objectives, reestablishing the authority of the mayor as a representative of the city as a whole.

Ward politics did not disappear completely, however, and its continuing influence could be seen in the activities of the Boston City Council. Back in 1909, the revised city charter had replaced the original seventy-five-member elected Common Council with a nine-member city council to be elected at large. Seeking to stem the tide of Irish power and to take city business out of the hands of local ward bosses, the Republican-dominated state legislature deliberately strengthened the executive power of the mayor, under the assumption that James Jackson Storrow would defeat "Honey Fitz" in the 1910 election. The Yankees extended the mayor's term of office to four years, expanded his veto power over council action, and freed his power of appointment from council approval. At the same time, they reduced the term of a city councillor to only two years and greatly limited the council's quasi-legislative influence in municipal affairs.[38] The unexpected victory of Fitzgerald, however, ruined the Yankees' well-laid plans. With the Irish firmly in control of City Hall, it was too much to expect that neighborhood politics would continue to be denied access to municipal power, and in 1924, during Curley's second term, a twenty-two-member city council was adopted, with members representing each of the city's twenty-two wards. From that point until 1951, the council was largely a ceremonial institution whose members were not held in very high regard by the general public.[39] The councillors met regularly and ineffectually, enjoyed the benefits of generous patronage, and used their positions as little more than stepping-stones to higher office. The anonymity of the council was especially pronounced during the Curley years, when the powerful mayor's free-wheeling executive style and unorthodox budgetary maneuvers left little room for action by the council.

In 1951, after the defeat of Curley by Hynes and his reformist supporters, a revised city charter put into effect a so-called Plan A system that reduced the twenty-two-member city council to nine members elected at large, thereby once again reducing the power of the neighborhoods. The five members of the school committee, who had served staggered terms of four years, would be elected all at once but for two-year terms. Many Bostonians assumed that these changes would enhance the power of the mayor while reducing the influence of neighborhood representatives. During the Hynes years, councilmen such as Joseph White, Francis X. Ahearn, Michael Ward, and Frederick Hailer tended to work cooperatively with the city administration. Their election was largely attributable to the efforts of a liberal political-action group called the New Boston Committee, which organized slates of progressive, reform-minded candidates.[40] However, during the last four years of Hynes's administration, the New Boston Committee began to disintegrate because of internal conflict. As a result, more-independent candidates were elected to the city council. The demolition of the West End and disturbing reports of the heartless displacement of the poor residents did much to promote a more confrontational attitude among the newly elected members of the city council after John Collins was elected to office in 1959. Conscious of their diminished powers and resentful of being deliberately excluded from the process of government, first by Collins and later by Kevin White, the councillors used every means at their disposal to interfere with the budgetary plans and personnel policies of the mayors. Many councillors found that, despite their limited powers, the increasing presence of radio and television in politics gave them more public visibility than in the past. The fact, too, that they were now elected at large allowed them to go beyond the concerns of their own districts and involve themselves in city-wide affairs. And the realization that they could depend on a solid base of political support in the larger Irish and Italian neighborhoods, which were becoming disenchanted with the mayors and looking for someone to champion the concerns of the white ethnic communities, permitted the councillors (and, at times, encouraged them) to ignore the growing demands of the city's African-American population, which was still largely unrepresented. As the mayors became more expansive and ambitious, the members of the council seemed to become more insistent and extreme in their opposition. Colorful and eccentric, defiant and bombastic, council members were clearly pledged to the interests of the constituents in their wards rather than to the general concerns of the city. All too often, city council meetings became shouting matches that centered around the irresponsible and shocking behavior of the councillors. Sometimes the incidents were spontaneous: At the climax of one heated exchange, Councillor Katherine ("Kitty") Craven hurled a huge ashtray across the chamber, narrowly missing the head of Councillor George Foley. More often than not, however, the dramatic displays were calculated. Increasingly, council members found that by opposing the plans and policies of the mayor in a provocative and outrageous manner, they could get front-page publicity and additional votes from their gleeful supporters. As a result, many city council meetings took on the theatrical characteristics of broad Irish farce, with a touch of Italian comic opera. By the late 1960s and early 1970s, most members of the city council had established themselves as protectors of the neighborhoods against the unwarranted intrusions of the mayor, his urban planners, and his real-estate developers. It was hardly a coincidence that Mayor Collins and Edward Logue scheduled no major urban renewal projects for the larger and more heavily populated wards with strong representation in the city council—certainly not for the Italian districts of East Boston or the North End, with councillors Freddie Langone and Chris Iannella on the alert.[41] Plans for extensive urban renewal in Irish South Boston were called off in the face of bitter opposition from city councillors Bill Foley and Johnny Kerrigan against professional reformers and idealistic do-gooders who went into working-class neighborhoods and tried to tell people how to live, how to fix up their homes, and how to run their schools.[42] One of the more colorful examples of old-fashioned Irish ward politics at the end of the twentieth century was seventy-five-year-old Albert Leo "Dapper" O'Neil, who served more than twenty years as a member of the Boston City Council. Like a character out of the pages of *The Last Hurrah*, the popular old "pol" boasted that he never had to pay for things like campaign literature or poll workers because the voters could see him at work "seven days and seven nights a week."[43] While younger voters dismissed him as a political dinosaur, older voters found him delightfully reminiscent of the old style of Irish politician, with a golden voice and a personal touch. Walking the streets, shaking hands, doing favors, attending wakes, and defending the "little people" against the encroachments of liberal bureaucracy, "Dapper" became the darling of his elderly Boston constituents, who saw him as a powerful voice on their behalf at City Hall.

Taking the path of least political resistance, therefore, Logue and the BRA turned their efforts to areas like Charlestown and Allston-Brighton, which lacked personal representation in the city council. In both cases, however, longtime residents—the "townies"—rose up in angry protest against the plans of city bureaucrats, "social engineers," and outside real-estate developers to demolish their neighborhoods, displace their families, and put up fashionable housing developments where the local people could never afford to live. Although Collins, Logue, and the BRA eventually succeeded in getting most of their projects through, the result was a growing and bitter antagonism between the Irish-Catholic residents of the ethnic neighborhoods and the Irish-Catholic politicians who ran the city government.[44]

The conflict over urban renewal was only one indication to neighborhood residents that city government was doing very little for them. Many neighborhoods, already in trouble as a result of the postwar decline in jobs and the departure of younger families to the suburbs, were left with disproportionate numbers of elderly residents, retired persons living on pensions and social security, and low-income transients taking advantage of depressed rental prices. Many such communities saw alarming increases in crime, vandalism, and violence, caused in great part by poor street lighting, inadequate fire and police protection, and inefficient street cleaning and garbage disposal.[45] The conviction that the neighborhoods were being ignored while the downtown was being refurbished brought to the surface, once again, the class antagonisms that had led such neighborhoods to support James Michael Curley during the 1920s and 1930s. But now it was upper-middle-class Irish-Catholic politicians and businessmen who were looked upon as the enemies—turncoats who had forgotten their roots, who either ignored the old Irish and Italian neighborhoods entirely or used them selfishly for investment or real-estate opportunities.[46]

Feeling themselves caught between the indifference of municipal authorities and the greed of urban developers, neighborhood residents decided to do what residents in other parts of the country were doing at the time—take political control of events in their own districts. They would establish their own priorities, develop their own political strength, plan their own improvements, and force city authorities and business leaders to consult with neighborhood representatives before taking any action that might endanger their communities. Local groups fought against plans to construct a multilane Southeast Corridor through densely populated Roxbury, to increase the number of medical institutions in the Mission Hill district, to expand Logan Airport despite the opposition of the residents of East Boston, and to build a gala "Expo" center in South Boston for national bicentennial observances. On a more positive note, many neighborhoods formed local organizations to rehabilitate their old housing stock, develop new housing, stimulate new industrial enterprises, promote local trade, and force downtown banks to invest in local neighborhoods.[47] As Mayor John Collins's second four-year term came to a close, community-based groups were well on their way toward becoming the kind of countervailing political force—reacting against the policies of the central city government—that the ward bosses had constituted half a century earlier.

But the adversarial relationship between city government and the white ethnic neighborhoods was not the only political complication Collins faced during the mid-1960s. He was also confronted by a rising tide of discontent among the black residents of the city.

Through most of its history, Boston had one of the smallest African-American communities of all major American cities. Numbering somewhere between 1,800 and 2,000 by the middle of the nineteenth century, the city's black citizens lived a self-contained existence on the back slope of Beacon Hill.[48] At the turn of the century, after a Democratic gerrymander took away their small political representation (the blacks were staunch Republicans) and made them more vulnerable to the flood of East European immigrants settling in the old waterfront wards, the black citizens moved en masse to the South End. Eventually, they constituted a distinct and well-established community extending from Columbus Avenue and Tremont Street across Massachusetts Avenue to Dudley Street in lower Roxbury. Although the black population rose to about 20,000 by 1940, it was generally assumed that blacks would continue living in a stable and separate community confined to the South End–Roxbury area.[49]

During the 1930s and 1940s the African-American community, like other ethnic and national groups in the city, accepted the unwritten law of residential segregation. According to this law, it was possible for all kinds of people to live together in peace and harmony as long as members of each group remained within clearly defined geographical boundaries and socialized only with other members of the same group. At work, in political affairs, and in community activities, people were all expected to meet together, associate on a democratic basis, and work together on an equal footing. In personal affairs, however, and in social arrangements, each group was expected to reside in its "own place" and associate with its "own kind." Many Jewish merchants, for example, came into Irish neighborhoods every morning to operate meat markets, clothing shops, and variety stores, where they associated freely and congenially with their

Gentile customers. Each evening, however, they closed up their shops and returned to their homes in the self-contained Jewish district of Mattapan along Blue Hill Avenue. There, Julius ("Julie") Ansel, boss of Ward 14, a supporter of the Curley machine, and the only Jew on the Boston City Council, operated from a corner table at the G&G delicatessen.[50] It was understood that Jews did business in Irish neighborhoods but were not welcome to live there. Those were the rules of the game, clearly understood by everyone—Italians, Germans, Poles, Lithuanians, Syrians, Armenians, and African Americans. In the South End, a group of local black political leaders traded power for patronage much as the Irish ward bosses had done some years earlier. Dr. Silas F. ("Shag") Taylor, a pharmacist, became boss of Ward 9 with the help of his organization, the Massachusetts Colored League. During the prewar years, Shag and his brother Balcom ("Bal") worked with the Curley machine: They set up meetings, organized rallies, ran ads in the local newspapers, and pressured their constituents to support white candidates. The Taylors were among the many black politicians who switched to the Democratic party in the 1930s when Roosevelt's New Deal offered them a chance for social and economic security. Beyond this, however, they accepted the segregated system as a political fact of life, assuming, like everyone else, that in Boston you had to "go along to get along." Within the ethnic and racial "cluster" system, it was understood that the spoils of city office and the benefits of municipal patronage would be distributed appropriately. Every locality would share according to its size, the strength of its political influence, and the loyalty of its voters to the incumbent mayor.

During the course of World War II, however, large numbers of skilled and unskilled black workers from all parts of the country came to New England to work in factories, industrial plants, army bases, navy shipyards, and armories. As a consequence, Boston's black population doubled by 1950 to more than 40,000 and continued to rise steadily during the postwar years. Since no new construction had taken place in the South End for at least thirty years, the expanding black population literally burst out of its traditional boundaries and began settling along the fringes of formerly all-white (and predominantly Irish-Catholic) neighborhoods such as Dorchester, Jamaica Plain, Roslindale, and Hyde Park.[51] The old rules had been broken; the unwritten laws had been repealed. For the first time on any large scale, people from one community were moving out of "their own" neighborhoods into other communities. The whites saw the influx of blacks as a direct threat to their welfare and security.

In need of economic support, community assistance, expanded housing, and better schools for the rapidly expanding African-American population, prominent black leaders such as Otto and Muriel Snowden, political spokesman Royal Bolling, Sr., education activist Ruth Batson, and attorneys Harry and Clarence Elam looked to Mayor Collins, Ed Logue, and the BRA to bring the benefits of urban renewal to the South End and revitalize their multiracial community.[52] In a very short time, the BRA moved in with bulldozers and steam shovels and began to reduce the old wood-frame houses to "splinters" and to transform many of the familiar brick houses of the district into "clouds of rubble," according to one longtime black resident of the South End. He watched with dismay as wrecking crews demolished the streets that were once "alive with children and the chatter of black people, the cries of vendors of fruits and vegetables and fish, and ice, wood, and coal and oil."[53] The object of the renewal program was clearly to upgrade what had become a run-down and neglected community so that well-to-do professionals and upper-middle-class families could move in, purchase expensive apartments or town houses, contribute to rising real-estate values, and increase the city's tax revenues. Residents of the South End, many of them African Americans, Puerto Ricans, Hispanics, East Europeans, and people who were poor, elderly, or disadvantaged, quickly became disenchanted with what they saw happening. Instead of helping them, the white-dominated establishment took away their land, evicted them from their homes, demolished the neighborhood, built fashionable apartments for white "gentry," and pushed the original residents into less desirable sections of Roxbury. "We did the dirty work," said Ralph Smith, a local community organizer, "and now everybody with their education and their fancy, fancy degrees told us to get out of the way."[54]

Stimulated by the successes of the civil rights movement in the South, inspired by the words of the Reverend Martin Luther King, Jr., and encouraged by the passage of the Civil Rights Act of 1964 and the Voting Rights Act of 1965, black residents of the South End resolved to take matters into their own hands and fight back.[55] In the mid-1960s a new wave of young, assertive black community activists replaced the older and more established figures in agitating for the needs of the black community. The new activists spoke out boldly against Mayor Collins, accusing his administration of ignoring poor people living in what the local black newspaper called "the worst slum conditions in Massachusetts."[56] Early in 1966, a group of Roxbury welfare mothers, accompanied by their children, staged a sit-in at Mayor Collins's office at City Hall to demand action against the infestation of roaches and rodents in their housing project; on another occasion, a group of Roxbury residents dumped a huge pile of trash and garbage on the front steps of City Hall to protest inadequate rubbish collection in their district.[57]

Collins's second term as mayor was coming to an end. Because he had stated categorically in June 1967 that he would not run for a third term in the upcoming November election, the political future of Boston was very much in doubt. As was typical in Boston politics in the twentieth century, no clearcut successor had emerged. In the absence of any controlling mechanism like the old Democratic City Committee or the ward bosses' Board of Strategy, the number and variety of candidates threatened to divide the vote. Hoping to keep his urban renewal program going, Collins encouraged Ed Logue to run as his successor, but there were plenty of local competitors ready to block his progress. Three well-known city councillors had already decided that the time was right: council president Peter Hines, veteran councillor Christopher Iannella, and Barry Hynes, son of former mayor John B. Hynes, all became candidates. Louise Day Hicks of South Boston, the city's top vote-getter in her recent bid for a seat on the school committee, became one of the leading contenders for the mayor's office. Kevin Hagan White, secretary of state for the Commonwealth, announced his own candidacy, recognizing the mayor's job as a strategic stepping-stone to the governorship. Even John Winthrop Sears decided to run, reasoning that with so many Irish Democrats in the race, an old-time

As Massachusetts secretary of state, Kevin H. White greets sup-porters as he arrives at the G & G Delicatessen on Blue Hill Ave-nue in Mattapan, November 6, 1967, the traditional end of the mayoral campaign the night before the election. Running against Louise Day Hicks of South Boston, White was making his first bid for the office of mayor in a move he hoped would eventually bring him to the governor's office. Courtesy of the Boston Public Library, Print Department.

Yankee Republican might have a good chance. No one felt able to predict what would happen.[58]

Compounding the political confusion in 1967 was a series of economic complications resulting from American involvement in the Vietnam war. The Boston financial community's funding for Collins's ambitious urban renewal program had been greatly augmented by the extensive federal funding Ed Logue obtained from supportive Democratic administrations during the early 1960s.[59] But halfway through Collins's second term, the steady flow of federal funds began to dry up at an alarming rate, causing an observable slowdown in many of the publicly financed renewal projects. This was due in part to the costs of the Vietnam war, which had begun to skyrocket during the mid-1960s. With the total military budget rising from $51.6 billion in 1964 to $82.5 billion in 1969, Congress was forced to cut appropriations for all kinds of domestic programs. This not only affected Boston's renewal and housing projects but also caused local colleges and universities to discontinue many of the bureaus, institutes, and planning centers that had been providing valuable assistance to municipal authorities. Whoever would be elected mayor of Boston in November 1967 would take on extensive commitments to construction projects and social welfare programs without the necessary federal funding. Whether this would mean the decline of urban renewal in Boston, the breakup of the pro-growth coalition between the political and financial elements of the city, and the end of a new period of prosperity would depend to a great extent on the person who became the next mayor of Boston.

For eight years, from 1960 to 1968, John F. Collins proved to be a skillful leader and an effective manager. He ran the city administration in an efficient manner, balanced the city budget with courage and determination, and produced a comprehensive program for urban renewal that created the "New Boston" he had promised at the outset. Collins further enhanced the reputation of the city as a place where the mayor was honest and capable, where the business community was encouraged to participate in the process of revitalization, where public funds were spent wisely, and where private investments were actively sought and enthusiastically received. Soaring structures of reflecting glass and shining steel supplanted time-worn buildings of outmoded design; the irregular silhouette of a new skyline replaced the familiar monotony of the old low-lying waterfront; banks, insurance companies, brokerage houses, real-estate firms, and advertising agencies took up residence in the downtown canyons of State Street. Transformed into a center of high-tech, service-oriented enterprise, Boston's financial structure took on a new vitality capable of meeting the challenges of a changing national and international economy. Applauding the "bridge of confidence" Collins had built between the financial community and the body politic, the *Boston Globe* praised him as one of the city's "greatest mayors." The *Globe* credited Collins with transforming the face of Boston and changing forever the city's entire contour and configuration.[60]

But there were those who did not approve, either of the vast changes Collins brought to the city or of the means by which he effected those changes. Many people saw Collins as the originator of the entire urban renewal process, and he was often held responsible for projects that had been executed before he took office. Many Bostonians, especially in the neighborhoods, could never be shaken in their belief that Ed Logue had masterminded the destruction of the old West End; others blamed Collins for the high-speed expressway that cut through the heart of old Boston, isolating the North End and the Atlantic Avenue waterfront from the rest of the city. Preservationists protested the demolition of small streets and historic alleyways to make way for orderly roads and wind-swept open spaces that did not encourage leisurely strolls or casual sightseeing. In the stately Back Bay area, the fifty-two-story Prudential Building rose from a concrete platform some sixteen feet above street level, bringing what one BRA official proudly called a "new, slick, and shiny image" to the city.[61] Across town, the new City Hall sparked violent controversy with its massive "Mycenaean" design, which many critics felt bore no relationship to the architectural environment in which it was built.[62] Collins, Logue, and the BRA were accused of destroying a number of quaint, old-fashioned, and often eccentric architectural treasures, which residents and visitors had valued as charming and distinctive aspects of the three-hundred-year-old city. Critics complained that the new array of undistinguished modern skyscrapers had transformed a rare historical urban district into a sanitized and homogenized copy of hundreds of other American cities.

When Collins tried to bring the benefits of urban renewal to the ethnic neighborhoods that surrounded the downtown area, he ran into further difficulties and louder criticism. In the central city, there had been a general consensus on the need for radical change; there had been no significant concentrations of residents to be displaced; and the desire to achieve profitable real-estate values and increased tax revenues had motivated businessmen and politicians alike. In most neighborhoods, on the other hand, there was no consensus for significant change. The persistent memory of wholesale destruction in the West End created fears of similar catastrophes in other densely populated neighborhoods. And the vision of higher rents from modernized townhouses and expensive apartment complexes had little attraction for working-class families, who enjoyed their two- and three-decker wooden houses, took comfort in the close proximity of friends and neighbors, and saw little need for outside professionals to come in and change their way of life. Efforts by the Collins administration to extend the modernizing effects of urban renewal into the white neighborhoods produced a stormy relationship with community leaders. Large numbers of middle- and working-class white ethnics—long the solid core of the Democratic party—now began to view the city government as their enemy. They no longer saw it providing the helpful services to the poor and the elderly, the widows and the orphans, the homeless and the disadvantaged, that Irish Catholics and other European immigrants had always assumed to be the logical and natural role of government. Instead, they saw it as it as an overgrown establishment that was continually oppressing them, taxing them, conspiring to take away their land and knock down their houses, telling them where to go, how to behave, how to dress, how to raise their standard of living. In anger and frustration, the white neighborhoods rejected the BRA's lure of better housing, cleaner streets, and better schools, in great part because they suspected that an alien liberal agenda would accompany these changes and ultimately threaten their family values, their religious ideals, and their working-class traditions. Perceiving a common enemy in the wealthy professional classes of real-estate developers, downtown bankers, City Hall politicians, university professors, and suburban do-gooders, a number of the old neighborhoods came back to life, rediscovered their ethnic roots, developed community action groups, and formed a solid line of defense against the Collinses and the Logues. "Not in my neighborhood you don't" became the battle cry of the "townies," who were determined to force the city not only to furnish their basic municipal needs—streetlights, clean streets, fire protection, police protection—but also to refrain from unwarranted intrusion into their neighborhood concerns.

In Boston's black community, with its expanding numbers and its increasing sense of identity and pride, the city's urban renewal programs produced similar reactions of fear and resentment. Initial hopes that urban renewal would revitalize the community were quickly dashed when residents found that few of them could ever become the beneficiaries of the expensive improvements that were taking place. At the same time, the black residents of the South End and Roxbury were not convinced that Mayor John Collins and his city administration were doing enough to meet their basic needs: health care, low-income housing, employment opportunities, and upgraded schools. A diverse group of ministers, poverty program employees, social workers, and community organizers came together and formed political action groups to oppose the BRA, halt demolition and relocation, and push for more subsidized housing. It was becoming evident that the black community expected to play a greater role in its own development, in the face of what it regarded as neglect and abandonment by the predominently white political power structure. This was perhaps the most important issue the new mayor of Boston would confront when taking office in January 1968—clearly a critical time in the city's long political history.

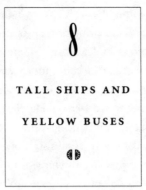

8

TALL SHIPS AND

YELLOW BUSES

BEFORE 1967 all candidates in Boston's mayoral elections were male and none were anything but white. The first seriously divisive issue related to group identity appeared in the late nineteenth century, when ethnic origin and religious persuasion became decisive factors at the polls. For most of the twentieth century, political contests in the city pitted working-class Irish Catholics against upper-class Yankee Protestants. Boston's mayoral election in 1967, however, was different from all previous mayoral elections in at least two significant respects. First, it was the first election in which a female was a serious candidate for the city's highest office.[1] Second, it was the first election in which the issue of race played a decisive role. Interestingly enough, it was the female candidate who figured most prominently in the racial controversy.

Louise Day Hicks was the daughter of Judge William J. Day, justice of the South Boston district court, a highly respected lawyer, banker, and real-estate investor. Louise attended local schools, married John Hicks during the war, lived in the City Point section of South Boston, and clerked part-time in her father's downtown law office until his sudden death in 1950. Although she was then thirty-six years old, married, and the mother of two children, she returned to the Boston University Law School, completed her law degree, and in 1956 passed the bar examination. In an era before it had become fashionable, she was an independent professional woman and a working mother. For a time she went into a law partnership with her brother, John, but she soon became active in various civic organizations. In 1961 she ran successfully for a seat on the Boston School Committee. Elected for a second term in 1963, Hicks was chosen as committee chairman and became a popular and effective advocate for neighborhood schools, consistently denying charges by black parents that Boston's schools were racially segregated. She was quickly acknowledged as the champion of Boston's white working class, which gave her over-whelming support in the municipal elections. By claiming to defend the interests of "the little people" of the neighborhoods against the unreason-able demands of black "outsiders" and their liberal, Ivy League allies, Hicks gathered enough support in Irish-Catholic and other white ethnic neighborhoods to become the first serious female contender in a Boston mayoral contest.[2] With the three city councillors cutting into each other's votes in the September primary election, and with John Sears neutralizing Ed Logue's silk-stocking votes in the Beacon Hill district, Louise Day Hicks demonstrated again her vote-getting prowess by coming in first with 43,719 votes—just over 28 percent of the votes cast. Kevin White came in second with 30,497 votes—about 20 percent of the total vote.[3] Under the Plan A system, only the top two candidates would fight it out in the final election in November. This meant that in two months, Boston could well have a woman mayor for the first time in its history.

Hicks's rival in November 1967 was Kevin Hagan White, who repre-sented a second generation of Boston politicians typifying the city's Irish-Catholic population. White's maternal grandfather, Henry Hagan, had spent his life in city politics. White's father, Joe, the son of an immigrant from Galway, became a star quarterback at Boston College and played semipro ball for the Providence Steamrollers before going into politics as a full-time career. After four terms in the state House of Representatives and another four in the state Senate, Joe served fourteen years on the Boston School Committee, and then ten years on the Boston City Council. During most of these years, in the bureaucratic tradition of Maurice J. Tobin and John B. Hynes, he also served as director of the telephone and telegraph division in the Department of Public Utilities. Joe made a respectable name for himself in the so-called upper wards of the city, where many second- and third-generation Irish families had moved. Because he was generally regarded as a progressive politician, he was able to draw votes from a wide variety of ethnic constituencies—even serving for a time as regional chairman of the National Conference of Christians and Jews.[4] When Joe's son, Kevin, married Kathryn Galvin of Charlestown in 1956, the young man joined a second family with a history in the Boston Irish political tradition. Kathryn's father, William Galvin, had worked at a variety of enterprises during the Depression years before gravitating into politics. He became a member of the Boston City Council in 1937, where he remained four years, the last two as council president. He served as acting mayor on occasions when Mayor Maurice Tobin was out of town; in return, Tobin eventually named him city superintendent of markets, an appointment that provided his family with a comfortable living for a quarter of a century. A colorful, affable, and flashy politician, Galvin served for many years as a sort of elder statesman for Charlestown, becoming familiarly known as "Mother" Galvin because of the favors and considerations he bestowed upon his many friends and constituents.[5]

With experienced veterans like Joe White and Bill Galvin running political interference for him in the streets of the neighborhoods and the corridors of City Hall, Kevin White garnered substantial support not only among Irish Catholics but also among downtown Brahmin businessmen. His undergraduate degree from Williams College and his law degree from Boston College made him acceptable to upper-middle-class groups in the city, who saw him as a capable and articulate administrator. After serving as an assistant to the Suffolk County district attorney, White ran for elective office in 1960 and defeated Republican Edward W. Brooke to become Massachusetts secretary of state. After four terms in that office, and as the only Democrat who had survived the Republican sweep in 1966, White was viewed by older members of the Yankee community as an appealing "nonpolitical" candidate in the tradition of Hugh O'Brien, Patrick Collins, John Hynes, and John Collins. The Yankees saw in White a business-oriented professional who could be depended on to keep the process of urban renewal rolling now that Ed Logue was out of the picture. And finally, as a reputed liberal progressive in the flamboyant style of New York's popular mayor, John Lindsay, White was more than acceptable to Boston's African-American community. In any case, he was the only viable alternative to Louise Day Hicks—making him the only game in town from the African-American perspective. "Kevin White, candidate for Boston's top office, has realistically met the issues of this campaign and the issues and problems that confront the city of Boston with a candid and believable approach," declared the black community's *Bay State Banner* in its election-eve endorsement of the former secretary of state.[6]

The contest between Kevin White and Louise Day Hicks was a tight race, a bitter fight, with the outcome very much in doubt until the end. Hicks more than held her own despite vocal opposition from civil-rights groups, black associations, the downtown business establishment, the academic world, and most newspaper reporters, who made fun of her hats, laughed at her beehive hairdo, joked about her blue-collar supporters as "characters in a Moon Mullins comic strip," and dismissed her as an inconsequential "tea party candidate."[7] In the rock'em-sock'em tradition of "Honey Fitz," Jim Curley, and Johnny Powers, she rallied her loyal constituents in support of local autonomy and neighborhood schools ("You know where I stand," she repeated), and called upon "the little people"—white, tax-paying, working-class residents of the neighborhoods—to stand up for their rights and defend their local institutions against the social experiments of black "outsiders," the meddling of suburban reformers, and the greed of downtown real-estate developers. She won considerable admiration in traditional ethnic communities for standing up to powerful forces that threatened to disrupt their close-knit neighborhoods. Indeed, Hicks proved such a strong candidate that the *Boston Globe* broke tradition by coming out with an endorsement of Kevin White.[8] Although her supporters in South Boston's Wards 6 and 7 gave Hicks a whopping 11,335 votes to a meager 4,489 for her opponent, Kevin White was able to pile up enough votes in the other wards to take the election. From a total of 192,673 votes cast, he defeated Hicks by a margin of 12,000.

Kevin White took office during one of the most chaotic and disruptive

"All politics is local," Speaker Thomas P. ("Tip") O'Neill was fond of saying. This is especially true of Irish politics in Boston, where candidates are expected to take to the streets and meet with voters in person. In these two photos Mayor Kevin White speaks with constituents in different parts of the city. Courtesy of the Boston Public Library, Print Department.

periods in American history. Protests against the Vietnam War grew in number and intensity; civil-rights demonstrations multiplied at a prodigious rate; and student upheavals paralyzed colleges and universities from Berkeley to Cambridge. The city of Boston, as a major academic center, as a focal point of antiwar resistance, and as an urban community whose black population was growing increasingly militant, could easily have been ripped apart.[9]

White worked long and exhaustively to keep the city under wraps during those frenzied years by placating as many of the varied and often conflicting constituencies as possible. For one thing, he maintained good relations with the bankers and businessmen of the financial establishment by indicating that he would push ahead with plans for urban renewal and

commercial development that had been in the works during the last stages of the Collins administration. He used his energy and talents to dramatize the "New Boston," publicizing its physical advantages for financial and commercial purposes, its unique educational and cultural opportunities, and its appeal to potential home owners as a "livable city." White was aware that urban renewal over the past decade had improved the financial standing of Boston and enhanced its reputation as a model of progressive modernization. He did not intend to lose the momentum that prosperous enterprise had brought to the city.[10]

At the same time, however, the new mayor kept his promise to involve himself more closely in the affairs of the neighborhoods. White established "Little City Halls" throughout the wards, staffed by members of his administration, to make city government more responsive to the needs of the people and to give local representatives an opportunity to participate in the political process. The Little City Halls served as strategic political bases from which to send out foot soldiers and volunteers to canvass all parts of the wards and solidify political support for Kevin White. This helped White to undercut the power of the Boston City Council, whose attempts to stall his budgets and interfere with his personnel appointments he fiercely resented.[11] White spent much more money than previous administrations had on neighborhood capital improvements, engaging in highly publicized efforts to provide better lighting and improved fire and police protection to help reduce crime and vandalism.[12]

White also appreciated the political realities of the racial issues that had appeared for the first time in Boston politics during the election of 1967. As mayor he worked hard to calm the restive black community. The brutal murder of the Reverend Martin Luther King, Jr., in April 1968, only three months after White's inauguration, followed by the killing of Senator Robert F. Kennedy two months later, created shock waves of violence that were felt throughout the country. These events fueled the resentment of local black citizens, who were demanding adequate housing, better employment opportunities, and integrated schools. With his jacket slung over his shoulder, his necktie loosened around his button-down oxford-cloth shirt, Kevin White became a frequent visitor in the black neighborhoods during his early years in office, sauntering through the playgrounds, talking with groups of mothers, maintaining personal contacts with local black leaders. He increased the number of black policemen assigned to the Roxbury area to counteract charges of police brutality, made an effort to include black people as full members of the Boston community, and supported a mobile program called "Summerthing" to supply music and entertainment for young people during the long, hot, dangerous summer months.[13]

In November 1971 White had nearly completed his first four-year term and defeated Hicks a second time by a more comfortable margin. It must have seemed to him then, as it did to most Bostonians, that the old city had weathered the worst of the storm and that his second term would be less stressful than his first. The Vietnam War was winding down and racial tensions seemed to be easing up. By the time the official cease-fire agreement was signed in August 1973, effectively ending the American combat role in Vietnam, the city showed signs of returning to a normal and peaceful routine. There appeared to be little more trouble on the horizon than deciding how to celebrate the bicentennial of the nation's independence in 1976.[14]

Mayor White decided to use the bicentennial as an opportunity to put the "New Boston" on display, not only to the citizens of Boston but to people all over the country. The breathtaking arrival of the Tall Ships in full sail, the historic visit of Queen Elizabeth II, and the spectacular Fourth of July concert on the Esplanade with the bells of the city ringing out the final chords of Tchaikovsky's 1812 Overture as skyrockets lit up the night sky, made for a memorable celebration. Another major public festivity took place only a few years later when Boston celebrated its 350th anniversary in 1980. Throughout that year the city sponsored special events commemorating its long history, beginning with the founding of Boston in 1630 by John Winthrop and his Puritan followers. The Tall Ships made a return appearance; two bronze statues of James Michael Curley were erected behind the new City Hall; and a series of lectures, festivals, and concerts celebrated various aspects of the city's impressive history. In keeping with Mayor White's insistence that the "New Boston" was now a "world class city," mayors from thirty-six major cities around the world were invited to a Great Cities of the World Conference to discuss urban issues in the last half of the twentieth century.[15]

Ironically, one of those urban issues was rapidly catching up with the city of Boston. It soon became evident that the air of festivity that marked the celebrations of historic events during the early 1970s was largely superficial. From beneath the tranquil surface the explosive issue of race was about to emerge. It had already begun to divide the urban community into bitter factions; shortly, it would create one of the most serious confrontations the city had ever faced.

Although the number of black residents in Boston had more than doubled during the World War II period and continued to rise steadily in the years that followed, by 1960 blacks still constituted a small 10 percent of the city's population. For this reason, black citizens were unable to translate their growing pressure into sufficient political power to address their needs or bring about changes in the way they were treated. Despite the early promises of urban renewal, most black people continued to live in dilapidated housing, with rents continually rising. As runaway inflation during the mid-1970s sent the prices of food, clothing, heating fuel, and gasoline soaring to undreamed-of heights, the recession worked its most distressing effects on the black community. There unemployment climbed to levels not seen since the days of the Great Depression. Entire districts were abandoned, and redlining by banks and insurance companies hastened the decline of black neighborhoods. As the predominantly white political establishment failed to come up with reasonable or effective solutions to these problems and, indeed, seemed oblivious to the unusual impact they were having on minority groups, the black population became increasingly angry. The boiling point was reached in the mid-1970s, after the Boston branch of the NAACP focused on what it regarded as a particularly egregious example of the injustices to which the city allowed its black citizens to be subjected.[16]

It was a decade earlier, in June 1963, that the NAACP had first pointed out that there were many schools in Boston whose pupils were predominantly white, while there were other schools where pupils were predominantly black. According to the 1954 ruling of the Supreme Court of the United States in the case of *Brown v. Board of Education of Topeka* (handed down nearly ten years before the NAACP's action), segregation in public schools was unconstitutional. On the basis of this decision, the NAACP demanded that steps be taken to desegregate the Boston schools as soon as possible in accordance with the Court's ruling.[17] The Boston School Committee, however, insisted that there was no deliberate segregation in its public school system. The fact that some schools were predominantly white and others predominantly black was simply the result of parents' wishing to send their children to the nearest neighborhood school. Committee chair Louise Day Hicks and the other members of the school committee, all of whom were white, denied the charges of de facto segregation. They virtually ignored the terms of the *Brown* decision as well as the implications of the Racial Imbalance Act, passed by the state legislature in 1965, which stated that any school that was more than 50 percent black would be considered racially imbalanced. For nearly twenty years, despite constant pressure by the state Department of Education, the Boston School Committee insisted that the *Brown* decision did not apply to Boston schools and refused to design any comprehensive plan for integration. White voters clearly approved. They elected to the school committee a succession of white, Irish-Catholic candidates—Louise Day Hicks, William O'Connor, John McDonough, John Craven, Paul Ellison, James Hennigan—who spoke out publicly and consistently against any change in the existing system.[18]

In 1971 the state Board of Education insisted that the school committee transfer a number of white children from an all-white school near their homes to a newly constructed school in Dorchester in order to achieve a satisfactory racial balance. When the school committee refused, the state board withdrew some $14 million in state aid from the city, and the NAACP decided to file a class-action suit against the Boston School Committee. The case became known as *Morgan v. Hennigan* (the mother named in the suit was Tallulah Morgan, and James Hennigan was school committee chairman at the time).[19] Early in 1972, the *Morgan* case was assigned by lot to Judge W. Arthur Garrity, Jr., an Irish Catholic from Worcester, a graduate of Holy Cross College and the Harvard Law School, a staunch supporter of John F. Kennedy, and a highly respected member of the Massachusetts bar. For nearly two years, Garrity studied the literature and listened to the arguments in the case. On June 21, 1974, he finally handed down his decision, declaring that the Boston School Committee had "knowingly carried out a systematic program of segregation" and had "intentionally brought about and maintained a dual system." For these reasons, he concluded that the entire school system of Boston was unconstitutionally segregated. The judge then ordered a program, to go into effect at the opening of school in September, under which some 18,000 schoolchildren would be bused to achieve racial balance in the schools.[20]

The residents of white neighborhoods were furious at Judge Garrity's decision and determined to resist to the bitter end the court-ordered program that would bus white children to schools in black neighborhoods and bring black students into white neighborhoods.[21] Encouraged by public officials on the school committee and spurred on by members of the city council, who called Judge Garrity's decision the "death knell of the city," community leaders prepared to defend the integrity of their neighborhoods and the sanctity of their "neighborhood schools."[22] In South Boston, Charlestown, and East Boston, especially, communities where the Irish and Italian ethnic pride burned most fiercely, the old "neighborhood spirit" was amazingly revitalized by the busing issue, which provided a common danger and a common enemy against which residents could unite.[23]

Strikes, boycotts, harassment, and outright violence attended the city's busing program, starting with the opening of school in September 1974 and continuing unabated until the close of school in June 1975.[24] Hundreds of city and state police had to be called in to patrol the streets, monitor the schools, and protect the yellow buses that carried black students to schools in white neighborhoods.[25] As well-established white neighborhoods that still took pride in their Irish-Catholic roots, their traditional neighborhood loyalties, and their sense of local self-determination, communities such as Charlestown and South Boston became storm centers of white protest. The residents of these communities expressed unabashed opposition to the aspirations of those they regarded as dangerous black militants. The high schools in these districts became the focal points of the most serious racial disturbances.[26] The fact that Charlestown and South Boston were virtually isolated peninsulas, approachable from the downtown area only by bridges, had made the process of gradual integration practically impossible in the past. In 1974, it created serious logistical problems for state and local police in enforcing court-ordered busing.

Despite the tumult that characterized the first year of mandatory busing, Judge Garrity refused to be deterred from his objective. When the school committee ignored a direct order to develop a city-wide integration plan, the judge held the offending officials in contempt of court. He then produced his own desegregation plan for September 1975, which called for the busing of 3,000 more students than under his 1974 plan. On May 10, 1975, the United States Supreme Court gave support to Judge Garrity by

In 1967, Louise Day Hicks was the first woman in the history of Boston to be a candidate for the office of mayor. Mrs. Hicks had won a seat on the Boston School Committee in 1961, where she subsequently became a vocal critic of plans to desegregate the Boston school system. She won widespread support in the ethnic communities for her support of neighborhood schools and her opposition to court-ordered busing. Mrs. Hicks was defeated by Kevin White in 1967, and lost to him again by a wider margin in 1971. Courtesy of the Boston Public Library, Print Department.

refusing to review his original finding that the Boston schools were unconstitutionally segregated.[27]

Judge Garrity's actions inflamed neighborhood opposition. A coalition of neighborhood groups known as ROAR (Restore Our Alienated Rights) was formed by Louise Day Hicks to lead the fight against busing. Encouraged by the sympathetic remarks of President Gerald L. Ford, the local groups tried to organize support for a constitutional amendment to outlaw enforced busing. In this effort, however, they were discouraged by such national political leaders as Senator Edward Kennedy, Senator Edward Brooke, and Congressman Thomas ("Tip") O'Neill, who tried to show them the futility of their undertaking.[28] A short time later, they suffered another setback when the U.S. attorney general refused to order a Justice Department review of the Boston situation. For the time being, at least, it was painfully clear to the opponents of court-ordered busing that they would have to rely on their own resources if they were to maintain control of their neighborhoods and determine the racial composition of neighborhood schools. The busing issue had created a major schism, not only between white people and black people, but also between working-class Irish Catholics and their more affluent friends and relatives who had moved away to the suburbs. Working-class families in neighborhoods like South Boston, East Boston, and Charlestown felt they were being forced to face the full impact of racial desegregation all by themselves. These neighborhood residents were the ones who had to watch their children bused away every morning to predominantly black neighborhoods, while their friends and relatives in the suburbs drove their children to white schools that were unaffected by the judge's ruling. The neighborhood residents were the ones whose husbands, fathers, brothers, and uncles were denied jobs or promotions in the police, fire, and public works departments because of new affirmative action policies, while doctors, lawyers, and bankers in the suburbs were far removed from the effects of such liberal social experiments.[29] Irish and Italian blue-color workers and their families felt betrayed, ignored, and abandoned by "their own kind," by people they had looked up to and counted on—political leaders, social workers, educators, lawyers, judges, even priests and bishops—who now seemed more concerned with the problems of newly arrived black people than with the needs of poor white people whose families had lived in Boston for generations. Feeling themselves at the mercy of outside forces and realizing that there was no one to help them, residents of the neighborhoods took matters into their own hands and in the long Celtic tradition of lost causes decided to go down fighting.[30] With hand-painted slogans of "NEVER" and "RESIST" splashed on buildings and fences, parts of Boston's neighborhoods took on the appearance of Belfast under siege. The next two years saw a series of ugly racial incidents, including stonings, beatings, firebombings, and even shootings, as a result of which Boston acquired a reputation as the most racist city in the nation.[31] "Irish history is littered with the bones of rebels and fighters who took on overwhelming foes and insurmountable odds," observes Ronald Formisano in his book *Boston Against Busing.* Formisano quotes the New York journalist Jimmy Breslin, who once called the busing controversy "the perfect fight for the Irish." "They were doomed before they started," Breslin wrote. "Therefore they can be expected to fight on."[32]

While Mayor Kevin White grappled with the busing crisis, his administration came under attack from organized forces in the neighborhoods demanding a greater role in other decisions affecting their communities. In addition to a general sense of alienation and neglect by an administration that had started out by promising them relief, but that now seemed to be catering to the businesspeople, the bankers, and the financiers of downtown Boston, the neighborhood representatives had several specific complaints. One was the tendency of government agencies, private institutions, and real-estate developers to make inroads into local communities, taking over land and housing, displacing inhabitants, and polluting the environment in a variety of ways. The continuing expansion of Logan Airport in East Boston, the spread of the Harvard Medical School complex in the Mission Hill area, and the impact of the Tufts–New England Medical Center on the Chinatown district were only a few examples of the encroachment feared by every neighborhood. The recollection of what had happened to the old West End was still vivid and frightening. Compounding the effects of municipal neglect was the continuing refusal by most downtown banks to grant mortgages or home-improvement loans in districts they declared "blighted" or "bad." As a result, many young families could not afford to purchase two- or three-family houses or to maintain their homes in good condition. Old neighborhoods began to show signs of the blight and decay predicted by the banks. Parks and playgrounds fell into disrepair; vandalism became commonplace; many dwellings were abandoned and boarded up. In densely populated areas like the Fenway, the spectre of arson intensified the growing sense of helplessness and despair.

Another problem in several older neighborhoods was the relatively new process of "gentrification." In a reversal of the post–World War II movement to the suburbs, the late 1960s and early 1970s saw a movement back to the city. Undoubtedly this resulted from two decades of urban renewal that had substantially upgraded the downtown area, attracted investment, and promoted a distinctive service-based economy. Well-educated and affluent young people—engineers, computer specialists, architects, designers, medical technicians, advertising executives—single, or married with few or no children, saw the benefits of living in a city like Boston. They were attracted by the city's cultural and educational institutions, its proximity to rural and recreational areas, and its appeal as a walkable and livable city. In large numbers this young "gentry" moved into convenient and historic locations like the North End, the South End, and the waterfront area. With their professional incomes they inflated local rents and accelerated the conversion of rental units to condominiums. This caused serious financial burdens among the older and poorer inhabitants, forcing many of them to move out of familiar neighborhoods where they had spent their entire lives.[33]

Seeing their neighborhoods transformed by forces beyond their control and convinced that they were cut off from normal channels of assistance by an administration that was either catering to the downtown bankers or pandering to the blacks (local residents were now referring to Kevin White as "Mayor Black"), many neighborhoods formed development corporations of their own. The Codman Square Community Development Corporation, the South Boston Community Development Corporation, and several other agencies worked to preserve their districts from government renewal plans. The Massachusetts Urban Reinvestment Advisory Group was especially influential in forcing banks to invest in local neighborhoods; and the Inquilinos Boricuas en Accion was successful in creating a Hispanic residential development in the South End called Villa Victoria. Longtime residents of Beacon Hill sought to preserve the distinctiveness of their historic neighborhood with the Beacon Hill Civic Association; businessmen in Mattapan worked to stabilize their local commercial district with the Mattapan Square Board of Trade. Parents fought for educational reforms through such coalitions as the Boston Home and School Association and the Federation for Children with Special Needs; and Hispanic parents worked for successful programs in bilingual education through *La Grassa Mancha*. And in the Fenway area, residents formed the Symphony Tenants Organizing Project when they became convinced that city and state authorities were not doing enough to stop the alarming wave of arson in the crowded neighborhood near Symphony Hall. Sometimes these community-action groups failed; sometimes they were forced to compromise. But they quickly became a force that could not be ignored, either by City Hall or by the bankers of State Street. Coalition politics became a new source of power in the city, exercising substantial influence in decisions regarding the social and economic future of Boston's neighborhoods.[34]

Racial conflict that seemed endless, a busing crisis that showed no signs of letting up, neighborhood opposition that got nastier every day, and nagging financial problems worsened by further cutbacks in federal funding badly tarnished Kevin White's image as a liberal, sophisticated big-city mayor. After his runaway victory in the second contest with Louise Day Hicks in 1971, White had begun to be viewed as an asset to the national Democratic party. Indeed, during the 1972 elections he was wooed by several presidential candidates and was seriously considered by Senator George McGovern as his vice-presidential running mate. Although the nominations never materialized, White spent the better part of the next year touring the nation and involving himself in national issues in an attempt to revive the hopes of the Democratic party.[35] However, the mayor's excursions out of town detracted from his personal magnetism for Bostonians and eroded his local political base. With city elections approaching in November 1975, he marshaled his forces in a last-minute effort to head off a surprising challenge by Joseph F. Timilty. Tall and handsome, an ex-Marine and a former city councilman, state senator Timilty claimed to speak for the people in the neighborhoods, and he cut deeply into the political support the mayor had built up in those areas. Fighting charges of political corruption and patronage, White managed to defeat Timilty by an embarrassingly narrow margin. In the same election the voters again chose an all-white school committee to administer what was quickly becoming a predominantly nonwhite school system. This made it almost a certainty that during his third term White would not be able to make any substantial improvements in the school system, the busing crisis, or the city's complex race relations.[36]

After his hard-won 1975 election, White seemed to withdraw further from personal involvement in local issues and neighborhood affairs. Discouraged by repeated failure to solve the busing crisis, weary from grappling with community problems, and perhaps still fascinated by the prospect of national office, White concentrated on affairs at City Hall and on development in the downtown area. He intensified his efforts to publicize the attractions of Boston and continued to emphasize its reputation as a "world class city." Traveling to Europe and the Far East, he created links with "sister cities" in various parts of the world in order to promote tourism and encourage investment. He associated with business leaders and bankers, met with architects and designers, negotiated with planners and developers, greeted foreign diplomats at City Hall, and held receptions for visiting dignitaries at the elegant Parkman House on Beacon Hill. He obviously found such associations more congenial and rewarding than the thankless rough-and-tumble of neighborhood politics.[37]

Although White and his well-oiled political machine of department heads, city workers, ward bosses, and precinct captains combined to defeat Joe Timilty again in 1979, the mayor's fourth term proved to be difficult and sometimes painful. In addition to many pressures from both black and white neighborhoods, White's last years in City Hall were plagued by a troubled economy. During the administration of President Jimmy Carter from 1976 to 1980, inflation reached double-digit rates, unemployment rose to unprecedented heights, and gasoline and heating fuels were scarce and expensive. The situation became even worse for big-city mayors after the Republican victory in 1980, when President Ronald Reagan proceeded to make severe cuts in federal funding for public health, education, welfare and unemployment benefits, and other social services. At the local level, the state referendum known as Proposition 2½ placed a ceiling on property taxes, thereby sharply curtailing city revenues. Because the mayors of Boston traditionally had little or no political influence beyond the confines of the city, and because state representatives from other parts of the Commonwealth traditionally took an unsympathetic view of Boston's economic problems, it was extremely difficult for White to obtain financial assistance from the state legislature on Beacon Hill.[38]

Increasingly, Kevin White found himself battered by one constituency or another in ways that seriously damaged the sources of political power that had sustained him in office for nearly sixteen years. The downtown sections of the city continued to show signs of progress and prosperity: Business and office space increased, new hotels multiplied, the old retail district was revitalized, and the Faneuil Hall Market did a thriving business as a tourist attraction. But in the surrounding neighborhoods working-class families were suffering from the combination of economic recession and government cutbacks—especially after Mayor White responded to fiscal restraints by laying off nearly 4,000 city employees, including fire fighters and police.[39]

The anger and frustration of working-class residents at being deprived of both valuable jobs and needed services further eroded White's political support, not only in traditional white neighborhoods but also among former backers in the black community, who were looking for new leadership of their own. Increasingly, Mayor White was characterized as a self-centered politician, interested only in power and perks. Conservatives in the city complained about his spendthrift ways; the Parkman House on Beacon Hill, where he entertained close friends and visiting dignitaries, became a dramatic symbol of the mayor's extravagant tastes. Neighborhood leaders refused to accept White's explanations for his financial cutbacks and denounced him for endangering their communities by shutting down police and fire stations. Political opponents charged him with flagrant political patronage: forcing city employees to contribute to his political campaigns, parceling out city jobs to loyal political backers, and pressuring city employees to help defray the costs of a birthday party for his wife. Less than a year before the 1984 election, federal investigations into charges of political corruption and financial irregularities further embarrassed White and caused an even more rapid deterioration of his political base.[40] Although his pollsters assured him that he could win a fifth term, White decided not to try, and on May 25, 1983, he delivered a brief television announcement of his retirement. After sixteen consecutive years as mayor of Boston, longer than any person in the city's 350-year history, Kevin White could no longer function effectively as chief executive. There were simply too many forces combining against him.

Even the most skillful fighter gets arm-weary after fifteen rounds of heavy punishment. The breathing gets heavier, the legs no longer respond, it takes longer to get off the ropes. The early rounds had been good ones. White had been bright, fast, and quick, punching and counterpunching with speed and determination. The footwork was agile as "Kevin from Heaven" raced from one neighborhood to another, from one crisis to another, holding the city together during the late 1960s and early 1970s in the face of Vietnam War protests, peace rallies, college riots, and civil rights demonstrations. It is interesting and somewhat frightening to speculate about what might have happened in Boston during those disruptive times if the election of 1967 had turned out differently. It was during the early rounds, too, that White used his high energy and vitality to sell the charms of his bright and shining "New Boston" to local residents and to visitors from all parts of the world.

But the middle rounds turned ugly, as a flurry of uppercuts caught the young mayor by surprise and rocked him back on his heels. When the city's simmering racial hatreds erupted in violence, White found himself pummeled from all sides. He was caught between the demands of the black community and the fears of the white community; between the authority of federal power and the pride of local autonomy; between the judicial gavel of Judge Arthur Garrity and the rosary beads of Louise Day Hicks. No amount of pleading, moderating, cajoling, or threatening could produce any sort of compromise. There was no middle ground, no common ground; and there was little or no support from other elected city officials. Whatever White did was wrong: Blacks accused him of selling out to the whites; whites accused him of pandering to the blacks. The busing crisis hurt White badly, landing body blows that took his breath away and caused his knees to buckle. His reputation as a progressive mayor quickly disappeared, as did any hopes for national office.

By the final rounds, White seemed to be backpedaling, going through the motions, waiting for the bell. Disillusioned with the black community, largely disowned by the white neighborhoods, deprived of state and federal funding, attacked by the press, investigated by federal agencies, he increasingly sought the companionship of family and friends, the stimulation of artists and writers, the solace of quiet dinners at the Parkman House. And when the bell finally sounded, no one knew better than Kevin White that the time had come to hang up the gloves.

With White's withdrawal, the mayoral contest was wide open. A surprising number of candidates announced their intention to follow in White's footsteps. But in the preliminary election in October the choice came down to two men: Raymond Flynn and Melvin King, both of whom represented the interests of the neighborhoods as opposed to the interests of the downtown business and political establishment. Flynn, forty-four, was a three-term member of the Boston City Council, a lifelong resident of South Boston, a devout Roman Catholic, the father of six children, and a spokesman for neighborhood schools. The son of Irish-American parents, Flynn had grown up in a distinctively Catholic neighborhood in the tradition of Martin Lomasney, "Honey Fitz," and James Michael Curley. Flynn's father was a hardworking longshoreman, disabled with tuberculosis, who "left the house each morning on cold winter days . . . not knowing whether he could find work": his mother cleaned downtown office buildings "from eleven at night until seven in the morning." A devoted Catholic, Flynn spent his youth in a household filled with the songs and stories of Old Ireland, the radio tuned either to "The Irish Hour" or the nightly recitation of the rosary. After graduating from South Boston High School, Flynn attended Providence College on a basketball scholarship. He later married his childhood sweetheart, Catherine Coyne, whose family lived only a block away and whose father worked with Ray's father as a long-shoreman on the South Boston docks. For a number of years Flynn spent his days and nights traveling the city as a state representative and city councillor, working with neighborhood groups on a variety of local projects. One of the earliest political spokesmen to oppose the school desegregation program, Flynn took the position that it was an unconstitutional form of judicial activism that had usurped the powers of the legislative branch of government. However, Flynn was adamant in his opposition to violence in any form. On numerous occasions during the busing crisis he was present in the streets of South Boston, counseling restraint and offering nonviolent alternatives. He personally rescued a black couple being chased by whites on Boston Common in 1979 and was the only white politician to attend the funeral of Levi Hart, a black fourteen-year-old killed by a white policeman in 1980.[41] By the end of the decade, he was recognized as a strongly committed political leader with the capacity to see both sides of a troublesome issue. A rather brusque, taciturn, and unsophisticated individual, Flynn made his appeal to the working-class voter and went about the business of politicking in a plodding, determined, and down-to-earth manner.

Flynn's opponent in 1983 was Mel King, fifty-five, a resident of the South End and an established spokesman for the black community. King's father originally came from Barbados, where he had worked as a long-shoreman on sugar boats; his mother came from former British Guiana, now called Guyana. The family lived on Seneca Street in Boston's South End until the death of King's father, when his mother moved to Florian Street and King went on to graduate from Boston Technical High School. In 1951 he graduated from Claflin College in South Carolina and then returned to Boston to earn a master's degree in education from Boston Teacher's College. A teacher, social worker, political organizer, and five-time elected state representative from Lower Roxbury and the South End, Mel King was the first African American in Boston's history to run as a finalist in a mayoral election.[42] Encouraged by the victories of black mayoral candidates in Chicago and Philadelphia during the fall of 1983, King formed a multiracial "Rainbow Coalition" to attract not only black voters and a small number of white liberal voters, but also the increasing number of Hispanic and Asian voters who had become residents of Boston in recent years. Because the number of black voters in Boston was not yet large enough to offset the white votes, King hoped to make up the difference with a coalition of peoples of color—especially drawing upon the "New Bostonians" who were becoming, for the first time, a significant factor in Boston politics.[43]

The emergence of Mel King as a candidate for mayor of Boston and the formation of his Rainbow Coalition were dramatic evidence that continuing change in the composition of Boston's population eventually would influence the nature of the city's political system. In the 1980 census it was reported that the city had more than 87,000 residents who had been born in foreign countries and that nearly 100,000 people spoke a language other than English at home. Some of the newcomers had come from somewhat familiar countries such as Poland, Czechoslovakia, and Russia, fleeing the oppressive Soviet regime during the 1960s and 1970s. Others had arrived from Caribbean countries and from several regions of Central and South America. Earlier arrivals from Puerto Rico, who eventually would constitute about half of Boston's Spanish-speaking people, and large numbers of black people from West Indian islands such as Jamaica and Barbados, were joined by Haitians escaping the excesses of Jean-Claude Duvalier, by Cubans fleeing Fidel Castro's government, and by others seeking to escape the fearful bloodshed in El Salvador, Honduras, Colombia, and Nicaragua. After 1980, Boston neighborhoods received a sizeable number of refugees from the Far East. Some came from Taiwan, mainland China, and Japan; others were refugees from the wars and purges in Vietnam, Cambodia, and Laos.[44] The faces, the colors, and the languages of Boston changed dramatically in a very short period, and several old-time neighborhoods once solidly Irish became kaleidoscopes of various cultures. Dorchester

Avenue, for example, an old, familiar thoroughfare that ran from central Boston through Dorchester to Milton, became a microcosm of the changing city. On the stretch from Andrew Square to Columbia Road, immigrants from Poland and newcomers from Ireland moved into old houses and developed new communities; from Columbia Road to Fields Corner Asians were the new arrivals—especially Vietnamese, Cambodians, and Thais—with restaurants, apothecaries, groceries, and gift shops that displayed colorful signs in strange new languages; from Fields Corner to Ashmont more newcomers from Ireland found comfortable lodgings with friends and families who took them in; Haitians and other Caribbean immigrants clustered further down the avenue. And all along the way, old brick Gothic churches, built and paid for by the sons and daughters of Irish-Catholic immigrants, received parishioners of entirely different origins. Masses were said in Vietnamese at St. Matthew's church; at St. Peter's church Masses were said in Haitian, and the parochial school children were nearly all black.[45] Indeed, although the total population of Boston in 1980 was still nearly 60 percent white, only about 52 percent of school-age children were white. (By 1990 that number would fall to 40 percent, making the number of white children of school age dramatically lower than the total number of black, Hispanic, and Asian children.) During the 1980s, Boston's white population dropped to 59 percent, while the number of blacks rose to 25 percent and the number of Asians more than doubled. By the year 2000 minorities are expected to make up the major portion of Boston's population.[46] Reflecting on such figures, Mel King worked hard during his campaign against Ray Flynn in 1983 to add the New Bostonians to his loyal black constituency as "people of color."

In view of the violence of the school busing controversy, Boston's mayoral election of 1983 was conducted with a surprising degree of civility, tolerance, and restraint on all sides. Mel King and Ray Flynn took generally similar positions on the major issues of the campaign—espousing neighborhood interests, proposing liberal housing programs, and urging increased economic assistance for the unemployed and the disadvantaged. Although King captured an overwhelming percentage of the city's black

Raymond L. Flynn was elected mayor of Boston in 1983, won reelection in 1987 and again in 1991, and then accepted the post of United States ambassador to the Vatican. As mayor, Flynn emphasized the importance of the neighborhoods. He traveled around the city, met with constituents, took care of local problems, and established a reputation as "the people's mayor."

votes, Flynn won an easy victory by sweeping the predominantly white neighborhoods. In his victory statement, Flynn underlined the basic theme of the election by promising to finance neighborhood development from a share of the profits of economic revitalization in downtown Boston. It was time to tip the scales, he said, by creating what he called a "linkage" between downtown prosperity and neighborhood needs.

The city's first mayor from South Boston was sworn in on January 2, 1984. Raymond L. Flynn held the largest inauguration ceremony in Boston history downtown at the Wang Center for the Performing Arts in order to accommodate more than four thousand friends, neighbors, and campaign workers. This was consistent with his image as "the people's mayor"—the representative of the neighborhoods—in the populist tradition of James Michael Curley. From a historical point of view, Flynn's election marked a basic change in the character of Boston's recent mayors. For a quarter of a century, Boston voters had rejected overtly political candidates, representatives of the wards and neighborhoods, in favor of apparently nonpolitical bureaucratic managers such as John B. Hynes, John F. Collins, and Kevin H. White—men who were reminiscent of earlier accommodationist mayors like Hugh O'Brien and Patrick Collins. But Raymond Flynn came out of the wards, proclaiming a grass-roots working-class populism akin to that of "Honey Fitz," Jim Curley, Johnny Powers, and Louise Day Hicks. Whether Flynn was a temporary aberration or the start of a new trend only time would tell. From a practical point of view, the election of Ray Flynn ushered in a period of relative calm, a much-needed breathing spell, after a decade of intense turmoil. In his inaugural address, the new mayor emphasized his determination to create racial harmony within the city and to bring to an end the hatred and bitterness that had marked the past ten years. "The full weight of city government will be brought down," he declared, "on all those who seek, because of race and color, to deny anyone from any street, any school, any park, any home, any job, in any neighborhood of the city."[47]

After the inauguration, Mayor Flynn chased off to a fire at the new Westin Hotel in Copley Square and then attended a gathering at the D

Street housing project in South Boston. Speaking briefly to the audience, which included about a hundred people from public housing projects in Dorchester, Charlestown, and the South End, Flynn reassured them that he would not forget his neighborhood roots now that he was mayor. "The name is still Ray," he joked, "and I'm going to come to D Street to play basketball." The next morning, the new mayor showed up at South Boston High School, from which he had graduated in 1958, to shoot some baskets in the gymnasium. He took the occasion to express support for the school and to announce his decision that the school would not be closed as many opponents of busing had proposed. Such forthright statements and frank gestures could not help easing tensions throughout the city by assuring white communities of Flynn's personal support and sympathies, while giving to black communities his official guarantee that he would do everything to protect their political rights and their civil liberties.[48]

And it seemed to work. According to a research poll conducted early in 1987 by Harvard's Kennedy School of Government, 41 percent of Bostonians agreed that race relations in the city as a whole had improved in recent years. This was true despite the fact that most of the people polled lived in neighborhoods in which one race predominated, and half continued to oppose court-ordered busing. More than 85 percent of the residents of South Boston still opposed busing, but they appeared to be the most optimistic about the new administration—perhaps placated by the fact that one of their own neighbors was now mayor. Some 64 percent of them expressed the belief that race relations had improved over the preceding five years, although a majority said that black people still would not feel comfortable walking through their neighborhood.[49] The results of the Harvard poll appeared to be borne out by the records of the city's own Community Disorders Unit, which reported that the number of civil rights investigations in 1987 showed a marked decline since the early days of the busing crisis. "We had 607 ugly racial incidents back in 1978," recalled Police Commissioner Francis M. Roache. "We had firebombings, we had people wearing the ugly robes of the KKK harassing, intimidating people. Those patterns are no longer there." The number of incidents dropped to 300 in 1980, to 200 in 1985, and to 157 in 1987. "This is not to suggest that we have reached the pinnacle of race relations in the city of Boston," said Mayor Flynn, "but that we're working very hard at it, and that we take this responsibility very seriously."[50] "True to his word," said an editorial in the black community's *Bay State Banner*, "the new mayor, Ray Flynn, has made dramatic moves to bring the city together."[51]

The school situation, too, had quieted down, but not with quite the positive results expected by Judge Garrity and his educational advisers. On September 3, 1985, the day Dr. Laval Wilson assumed office as the city's first black superintendent of schools, Judge Garrity closed the file on thirteen years of hearings, consultations, and orders dealing with the Boston desegregation case. "Mayor Flynn has made a strong public commitment to the continuing vitality of the Boston Public School system," said the judge, "and to desegregation."[52] Garrity then returned control of the schools to the school committee, while retaining standby jurisdiction over student assignments, faculty integration, the condition of school buildings, and parental involvement. The busing crisis was officially over. However, there remained serious questions as to whether the effort had achieved its social objectives. "The dream of integration is gone," commented newspaper columnist Ian Menzies, "burned on the crucible of one of Boston's greatest traumas, school busing."[53] And, indeed, statistics seem to bear out that somber conclusion. Of a total of 59,896 students registered in the Boston school system in 1987, there were 28,551 blacks, 15,852 whites, 10,760 Hispanics, and 4,742 Asians. The number of white students had dropped by nearly 30,000 in the course of fourteen years. In 1987 the system was about 50 percent black, 25 percent white, 16 percent Hispanic, and 8 percent Asian.

In addition to addressing the city's racial problems, Mayor Flynn was required to address the needs of another pair of conflicting constituencies. First, he had to fulfill his pledges to the neighborhoods to provide better low-cost housing, cleaner streets, additional parks and playgrounds, more effective police and fire protection, and greater opportunities for employment. At the beginning of his term, he created a Mayor's Office of Neighborhood Services, appointed liaisons to each community and ethnic group, and encouraged the formation of Neighborhood Councils through which residents could monitor the delivery of basic services.[54] In the old Curley tradition, however, Flynn went out into the neighborhoods in person. In doing so he publicized the needs of the neighborhoods as well as his own personal role in addressing those needs. Capitalizing on local television coverage, the mayor often appeared in the evening news, riding snow plows with the Public Works crews, supervising the filling of potholes, driving to fires, visiting wounded policemen in the hospital, playing basketball with children at local playgrounds, running in the Boston Marathon, marching in parades, rescuing trapped motorists, and performing all sorts of public and civic duties directly related to the interests of his voting constituents in the neighborhoods. Flynn also directed a great deal of time and attention to the growing problems of poverty and homelessness. He established a Mayor's Hunger Commission to help create networks of public and private agencies to distribute meals and groceries to hungry residents throughout the city. He joined with volunteers to produce an annual census of the homeless by conducting all-night surveys of the city's shelters and alleyways. Committing more than $75 million in resources to programs for the homeless, Flynn promised that no one would be denied "a warm bed, transportation to a shelter, food, or quality health care just because they are poor."[55] There may have been those who raised an eyebrow at the new mayor's shirtsleeve politicking, his sweatshirt jogging, his working-class expressions, his appearances at neighborhood bars, wakes, and American Legion halls rather than at the Ritz Carlton or the Copley Plaza. But Flynn knew where the votes came from that kept him in office for ten years. His iconoclastic displays were always well calculated to catch the attention of the news media and to remind the residents of the neighborhoods that he had not "gone over," he had not changed his ways, he was still "one of them."[56]

Flynn also had to convince the downtown bankers, financiers, and real-estate developers that, although he came out of the Irish-Catholic political system, he was not another James Michael Curley. He had to demonstrate that his proposed "linkage" plan to divert a portion of the financial profits from downtown redevelopment to the neighborhoods was not just another "soak the rich" scheme that would once again raise the spectre of class hatred and drive the old wedge between the city's financial and political leaders. He had to show the members of the business community that he understood their problems, that he regarded them as essential to the future prosperity of the city, and that he could work with them in a reasonable and productive manner to continue the expansion and development that had already made Boston one of the leading cities in America. To stimulate greater interaction between the downtown and the neighborhoods, the Flynn administration established a Linked Deposit program requiring that banks holding city funds meet certain standards of investment in minority neighborhoods or face withdrawal of the city deposits. The new administration also supported a $400 million neighborhood reinvestment agreement with the downtown banking community to increase below-market mortgages and business loans to minority neighborhoods. In addition to calling for increased hiring of local residents, members of minority groups, and women on publicly funded construction projects, Flynn pressured construction companies and real-estate developers to contribute one dollar per square foot to support local job training programs.[57] In his first full year in office, Flynn balanced the city's budget; he kept it balanced for nine consecutive years and could boast that Boston's bond rating had risen to "A" grade, the highest rating in the city's history. Moody's Investor Service praised Boston's "commitment to maintaining fiscal balance," and Standard and Poor complimented Boston on its "strong fiscal management."[58]

On November 3, 1987, Flynn was reelected to a second term as mayor of Boston by an even wider margin than in his 1983 victory over Mel King. Flynn won 63,412 votes to Joseph M. Tierney's 30,897, taking twenty of the city's twenty-two wards and more than 67 percent of the total vote. Flynn's margins were particularly impressive in the black sections of the city—in Mattapan's Ward 14, for example, he won by a ratio of 14 to 1. In a stunning turn of events, however, he suffered a setback in—of all places—his home wards in South Boston. In those wards he lost by nearly 400 of the 10,638 votes cast. The source of this deliberate "back-of-the-hand" gesture by local residents to one of their native sons was the simmering issue of race.

In October 1987, only a month before the election, the federal Department of Housing and Urban Development had notified Mayor Flynn that the Boston Housing Authority was maintaining a policy of segregation in its public housing projects and had deliberately excluded black people from projects in South Boston. The federal agency warned the mayor that failure to address this problem could result in a federal lawsuit and could jeopardize millions of dollars in federal and state funding.[59] About a week before the mayoral election, Flynn announced that he would comply with the demands of federal and state agencies and see that the city's housing projects were integrated. Residents of South Boston, angry at the mayor for submitting to another federal desegregation demand, demonstrated their outrage at the polls.[60] In Edwin O'Connor's *The Last Hurrah*, the fictional Mayor Skeffington noted the "virtually bottomless capacity" of Irish-American voters for suspicion and ridicule. He had seen popular men, he recalled, who when suddenly suspected of getting a bit above themselves "had been turned on with a savagery which could scarcely be believed." Ray Flynn became the surprised recipient of such "savagery" from friends and neighbors who were infuriated by his public support of integrated housing.[61] The mayor spoke to groups of irate local residents to explain his position, met with city councillors and administration officials, and was supported publicly by Cardinal Bernard F. Law, who urged peaceful integration of public housing. "There is too much at stake," he said in a pastoral letter read at all Boston Masses, "for us to let our communities become divided by blind emotion."[62] Flynn defused another potentially explosive situation by guaranteeing that no elderly tenants would be displaced from housing projects; that no present tenants would be moved; and that all families on the waiting list would have a "fair opportunity" to live in a public housing project of their own choosing. By calming the fears of neighborhood residents and, at the same time, conforming to the letter of the civil rights requirements, he hoped to avoid a "forced-housing" program under federal supervision.[63] For the remainder of his second term, Flynn mended fences in his home community, rebuilt his alliances throughout the other neighborhoods, and slowly reestablished his popularity as "the people's mayor." When he ran for a third term in 1991, he not only was reelected but won every precinct in every ward in the city—a first in Boston's history.

As Ray Flynn began his third term as mayor of Boston, however, several problems emerged that had been simmering over the previous two years and threatened to upset the social and economic stability he was working so hard to maintain. First and foremost was the collapse of the inflated economy. Throughout the United States during the 1980s, the Republican policy of deregulation had created a high-flying economic mood that was reminiscent of the giddy Roaring Twenties. Banks handed out loans for risky speculative ventures, "junk bonds" achieved a new sense of legitimacy, fast-moving entrepreneurs looked for quick profits, new high-tech companies sprang up everywhere, and real-estate prices went through the roof. Along with most of the rest of the country, the Commonwealth enjoyed an unparalleled degree of prosperity, which led Governor Michael Dukakis, in his unsuccessful run for the presidency in 1988, to boast of the "Massachusetts Miracle."[64] Within a year of the victory of George Bush, however, the collapse of the Massachusetts Miracle reflected the deterioration of the economy throughout the country. Eight years of tax-cutting, combined with massive military spending, an expensive Gulf War, soaring welfare costs, and inflated medical charges, had pushed the federal debt past the $3 trillion mark, while the deficit reached nearly $170 billion in 1991—and continued to climb. By the summer of 1990, the nation was in the midst of a major recession. Banks failed, the savings-and-loan industry collapsed, investments went bad, depositors lost their savings, retail sales slumped, housing construction declined, major industries went out of business, and unemployment rose to new heights. At a time when states were forced to cut back on social services and welfare funding, the number of homeless people became larger than ever. The city of Boston, like other major urban centers with sizeable minority populations and serious social commitments, felt the impact of hard times as industry continued to decline, more banks failed, more companies declared bankruptcy, and more workers became unemployed.

The recession of the nineties exacerbated problems that had festered during the eighties but that now seemed to worsen with disturbing reports of guns, drugs, and indiscriminate violence. Although such lawlessness could be found in any city, any town, any suburb, any socioeconomic community, its worst effects were found in the poor black neighborhoods where unemployment, homelessness, and poverty were most prevalent. Here, in an atmosphere of isolation, desperation, anger, and fear, children sold drugs on street corners; teenagers carried knives, guns, and assault weapons; gangs roamed the streets and murdered innocent people in drive-by shootings. The police department found this flood of violence difficult to fathom and impossible to stop.[65]

All of this spilled over into the city's public school system, which threatened to become more unmanageable than ever. Having barely recovered from the prolonged trauma of court-ordered busing, the city's education system felt the impact of both the economic cutbacks and the urban violence. The lack of adequate funding caused serious shortages in textbooks, laboratory equipment, instructional resources, personnel, and programs in arts, music, and sports. Meanwhile, the increasing presence of guns, knives, and drugs threatened the lives of teachers and students on a daily basis and made a proper educational atmosphere extremely difficult to achieve. In an effort to balance the school department budget, reduce central administration, and increase spending for classroom instruction, Mayor Flynn proposed changes in the existing form of school governance. In 1991 voters approved a referendum calling for the proposed changes, and the elected school committee was replaced with a board appointed by the mayor.[66]

From 1985 to 1991, Ray Flynn served as chair of the United States Conference of Mayors task force on hunger, homelessness, and poverty and attacked the Reagan administration for neglecting the nation's cities and ignoring the needs of the poor. In 1991 he was elected president of the Conference of Mayors and placed urban issues at the top of the national agenda. There can be little doubt that his involvement in national affairs and his association with prominent figures in the federal government opened the Boston mayor's eyes to new political opportunities and whetted his ambitions for higher office. The persistent concern for his own future welfare and that of his family only increased Flynn's efforts to move far beyond the limited confines of city government.

In the midst of burning political issues and sweeping societal events, the prosaic question of how to earn money after leaving office influenced the decisions of Boston's Irish mayors throughout the twentieth century. The earlier Yankee mayors had moved easily in and out of office in the manner of the English gentry, who served in Parliament for an allotted time and then retired to the family estate. But most of Boston's Irish mayors had no financial cushions to ease their retirement into private life. They came from working-class families with neither incomes nor investments to provide security when their years of public service were over. To members of the wealthy establishment, participation in politics was regarded as a civic responsibility, a form of the traditional noblesse oblige that required the gentry to safeguard the interests of what Mayor Josiah Quincy liked to call "the less prosperous classes." But politics for the Irish was not so much a part-time service as a permanent profession, a lifetime preoccupation, through which they could feed their families, help their neighbors, find jobs for their friends, and make their way upward in a world where the cards always seemed stacked against them. "Honey Fitz" eventually might acquire a millionaire son-in-law to make his declining years comfortable, but Curley and those who followed him had no such reassurances. Between his sporadic four-year terms in office Curley, the master politician, struggled vainly to make ends meet, dabbling in risky get-rich-quick schemes that often brought him to the verge of bankruptcy. John Hynes, after ten years as mayor of Boston, was forced to rely on a small law practice and an income as state commissioner of banks and banking to provide for his family in later years. John Collins, after two terms in each house of the state legislature and eight years as one of the nation's most imaginative and successful big-city mayors, failed to gain election to the U.S. Senate and faced the challenge of survival in an inflationary economy. He taught at MIT for several years, resumed a portion of his law practice, appeared regularly on a popular Sunday morning television program, and served as a consultant for several national firms. Kevin White held office as mayor of Boston for an unprecedented sixteen years, steering the city through the wild social turmoil and bitter racial violence of the late sixties and early seventies, only to confront the inevitable question of where to go and what to do as a former city leader. White had always wanted to be governor and was hypnotized by the prospect of becoming George McGovern's running mate in 1972. At quiet dinners at the Parkman house, with insiders such as Robert Strauss and the *Washington Post*'s David Broder, White speculated about the possibilities for a 1976 presidential nomination. When none of these sugar plums materialized, the former mayor settled back in comfortable anonymity, combining his unexpended campaign funds with the substantial income he received as a professor at Boston University. White's long professional experience and his extensive political contacts helped make it possible for Boston University president John Silber to acquire the huge National Guard Armory on Commonwealth Avenue and to expand the university's real-estate holdings in the Kenmore Square area. However, none of the city's retired mayors assumed advisory roles as elder statesmen or contributed in any substantive way to the city's political future—they simply could not afford it. Except for an occasional lecture, newspaper article, or television interview, the former mayors' advice was seldom sought, their ideas largely ignored, their participation rarely welcomed.

In the case of Mayor Ray Flynn, the problem of personal finances took on a frantic and, at times, almost paranoid dimension. A man without a law degree and with little professional experiences, Flynn had been active in city politics most of his adult life. Toward the end of his third term, he faced the nagging question of a postmayoral career. He had no family money, no law practice, no insurance company, no real-estate agency— and relatively little by way of residual campaign funds. The prospect of stepping into empty space was a frightening one, and helps explain Flynn's frenetic search for a reputable and secure source of income after leaving City Hall. Flynn worked energetically for the national Democratic party in the 1992 campaign against Republican George Bush, first announcing his support for Tom Harkins of Iowa, then encouraging New York's Mario Cuomo to run, flirting briefly with Ross Perot, and finally endorsing Arkansas governor Bill Clinton. Flynn clearly hoped that, as an outspoken and frequently televised spokesman for the nation's big-city mayors, he would win a Cabinet post heading either the Department of Housing and Urban Development or the Department of Labor. "He was desperate to get a job," said one Flynn worker. "He did everything he possibly could to get one. He was in everybody's face as often as he could."[67] No Cabinet position was forthcoming for Flynn: instead, in a scenario reminiscent of Roosevelt's offer to Curley of the ambassadorship to Poland, President Clinton offered the Boston mayor the post of ambassador to the Vatican. Flynn was indecisive from March to July, traveling back and forth between Boston and Washington, complaining about the financial allotment, protesting the ceremonial nature of the position, while the city waited to see whether he would continue as mayor. When Flynn finally accepted the ambassadorship, city council president Thomas Menino became temporary mayor, and the stage was set for a mayoral election in November 1993.

Flynn had hardly settled into his post in Rome with his wife and children when he showed renewed signs of indecision, signaling that he might run for the governorship of Massachusetts in November 1994. However, after he made plans to return to the United States in March and participate in several St. Patrick's Day parades, presumably to announce his political intentions, Flynn's credibility suffered a serious setback, even among his close friends and supporters. First, the State Department refused him permission to participate in blatantly political functions while still serving as ambassador—an embarrassing rebuke that did not go unnoticed in political circles. Second, only a short time later it was discovered that an elusive aide had disappeared with some $250,000 of Flynn's campaign funds. The crackdown by the State Department coupled with the unexplained loss of a quarter of a million dollars seriously undermined Flynn's reputation for personal integrity. The resulting loss of political standing led him to withdraw his name from the governor's race. For a

three-term mayor who had left office as a champion of social and economic justice, who had revitalized the neighborhoods, and who had
healed many of the deep racial wounds that had scarred the city during
the 1970s, the passage of a single year marked a tragic and embarrassing
political collapse.[68] In the end, as one local columnist put it, Flynn's conduct disqualified him for any further consideration. "It was a depressing
end to what had once seemed such a promising career."[69]

The problems confronting the leaders of Boston during the postwar
decades of the 1950s and 1960s had been largely tangible and manageable.
They had centered around issues such as blight and slums, clearance and
displacement, highways, public buildings, housing projects, convention
halls, and condominiums. In the face of the city's rapid physical deterioration, old enmities were forgotten and new partnerships were formed. For
the first time, Irish-Catholic political leaders and Yankee-Protestant businessmen and financiers formed an effective pro-growth coalition capable
of dealing with the problems at hand. These were essentially middle-class
problems that produced an effective alliance among significant elements
of the city's white-collar population—professional politicians, bureaucrats, industrialists, bankers, economists, architects, and college presi-
dents, working with a series of managerial mayors like Hynes, Collins, and
White to create a "New Boston." In time, the Vault became the symbol of
a new political-economic relationship that transformed Boston in less
than twenty years from a "hopeless backwater" to one of the most attractive cities in the nation.

By the 1990s, however, the problems facing the leaders of Boston had
become more subtle and complex. They included racial conflicts and cultural differences; hunger, poverty, and homelessness; dysfunctional families and abusive parents; an educational system that left many children
functionally illiterate; an economic system that created a permanent underclass of low-paid workers; and a social order that failed to teach respect
for law and justice and regard for human life, with the result that many
young people aspired only to the material benefits that drugs and crime
could bring. When Raymond Flynn left Boston in the summer of 1993 for
his new assignment in Rome, it was clear that whoever followed him as

mayor would need to seek new solutions and new coalitions. An increasing portion of the city's population no longer believed that the health, welfare, and safety of the people were being adequately safeguarded by the leaders of city government.

9

THE LAST

HURRAH?

ON TUESDAY, JANUARY 18, 1994, Thomas M. Menino became the first Italian-American mayor in Boston's history. The grandson of Italian immigrants who had left the village of Grottaminarda in the province of Avellino to come to America early in the century, Menino was born on December 27, 1942, and grew up in the Hyde Park district, where his parents, Carl and Susan, had lived their entire lives and where his father worked for thirty-five years at the local Westinghouse plant. Thomas acquired a serious interest in politics at the age of thirteen, when he helped one of his father's friends run for state representative. After graduating from St. Thomas Aquinas High School, Thomas almost immediately went into political life. From 1978 to 1983, he was a senior research assistant on the state legislature's Joint Committee on Urban Affairs; from 1983 to 1985, he served as vice-chair of the city council's Committee on Housing; in 1989 he became regional chair for the National Trust for Historic Preservation. A lifelong resident of Hyde Park, Menino represented that district in the Boston City Council for nine years. In 1993 he was elected president of the city council and, as such, became the designated successor to the mayor.

Mayor Ray Flynn was sworn in as U.S. ambassador to the Vatican in a White House ceremony on Friday, July 9, 1993. The following Monday he resigned as mayor and handed the reins of city government to city council president Thomas Menino, who became temporary mayor. At that point the stage was set for a special preliminary election in September. Once again, with no established policy of succession and no city-wide institution to screen prospective candidates, a number of mayoral hopefuls emerged. In addition to Menino himself, the list included Roxbury at-large city councillor Bruce Bolling; James Brett, a state representative from Dorchester; Christopher Lydon, a public television commentator; Francis (Mickey) Roache, Flynn's former police commissioner; Robert Rufo, sheriff of Suffolk County; and Rosaria Salerno, at-large city councillor from Allston-Brighton. Except for Bolling, no other minority candidate appeared. Menino and Brett were the finalists in the September primary, and Menino won in November by a substantial margin. It was clear that most white voters in neighborhoods like Charlestown, East Boston, Hyde Park, South Boston, and West Roxbury, where the ethnic turnout was the greatest, preferred the blunt, plain-spoken, down-to-earth approach of Menino to Brett's more sophisticated manner that detractors associated with the manipulative style of Beacon Hill legislators. Apparently, the voters wanted to continue the low-key, neighborhood-oriented policies of Ray Flynn for at least another four years.

Local and national newspaper columnists and television commentators raised the question whether the victory of Tom Menino was "the Last Hurrah" for the Irish in Boston politics.[1] The city's white population which had dropped more than 11 percent between 1980 and 1990, was now only 59 percent of the total, while the black population had risen by 11.4 percent, the Hispanic population by 39 percent, and the Asian population by 45 percent. Would Ray Flynn go down in history as the city's last Irish-Catholic mayor? While the statistics would certainly point in that direction, reports of the demise of the Boston Irish as a political species may be exaggerated.

Despite changing demographics showing a younger and more diverse population in Boston, political power in 1993 still resided in the hands of the longtime residents—older white, working-class Irish and Italians. This was true especially in neighborhoods like Charlestown, East Boston, and South Boston, which to the present day have remained more or less unchanged, retaining their old ethnic flavor and keeping alive the tradition of political discipline. In these districts you make sure you are registered, you go to the polls rain or shine, and you vote the straight Democratic ticket. While it is true that the "New Boston" attracted considerable numbers of well-educated, upwardly mobile, young white professionals into the central city during the late 1970s and early 1980s, most of the newcomers proved uninterested in city politics. Few wanted to get their hands dirty in what was generally regarded as a corrupt and thankless business. Many spent only a few years in the city before moving to the suburbs in search of larger homes, better schools, and greener lawns. By that time, discarding the ideals of responsible, activist government in favor of a free-market philosophy, many became conservative Reagan Democrats, independents, or free-wheeling libertarians.

Neither were any women elected to prominent public office in 1993, a year hailed by feminists as "The Year of the Woman." There were few encouraging signs that women were moving up into more responsible positions in municipal government. Usually, one or two women sat on the city council; an occasional female was elected to the school committee. But these women generally retired after one or two terms and never moved on to higher political office. During the administration of Kevin White, two women rose to the rank of deputy mayor: Katherine D. Kane, who supervised the arts, public festivities, and cultural events; and Micho Spring, who coordinated urban development, social welfare, housing, and rent control. By the late 1960s and early 1970s, it was clear that Louise Day Hicks had become the most prominent (and controversial) woman in Boston's political history, and the top vote-getter of either sex in school committee campaigns. After her defeat by Kevin White in 1967, however, Hicks lost support on the city-wide level, although she remained popular in neighborhoods like South Boston during the busing years. Throughout the 1980s and 1990s, there was little indication that women candidates were gaining momentum in Boston or that the women's vote effected any significant changes in city policy.

The political abdication of the young professionals and the lack of any demonstrable power on the part of women left effective political power in

Thomas M. Menino, whose grandparents emigrated from Italy, became the first Italian-American mayor in Boston's history. In November 1993 he succeeded to the office after Mayor Flynn left for his post at the Vatican. Governing a city whose population is gradually becoming more diverse and multicultural, Menino has promised to stress education, safety, and economic development. Courtesy of Boston City Hall.

the hands of older, more conservative working-class men. This traditional constituency continued to elect the mayor and the members of the city council and rose to influential positions in the city bureaucracy. The names of the four candidates elected to the Boston City Council in November 1993—Richard Iannella, Peggy Davis-Mullen, Albert "Dapper" O'Neil, and John Nucci (the names of the runners-up were Francis Costello, Stephen Murphy, and Michael Travaglini)—were ample evidence of the power of the neighborhood vote. In his inaugural address, Mayor Menino expressed great pleasure that an Italian-American had been elected mayor of Boston; but he also expressed regret that, for the first time since black candidate John O'Bryant had been elected to the Boston School Committee in 1977, "no African-American holds a city-wide elected position."[2]

The relative power of the white ethnic vote in the city was heightened by the fact that much of the nonwhite population either did not vote at all or did not use the vote effectively. In Boston's black community, for decades voter turnout was consistently lower than in white wards. In part, this was because the black population was younger (people tend to vote more frequently as they get older). But in part, too, it was a reflection of serious disenchantment and alienation in the black community. The black vote in Boston may have reached its most visible and organized form in the 1983 election with Mel King's Rainbow Coalition. With Flynn's strong victory over King and with the persistence of intolerable living conditions in the black community, most black voters lost confidence in the political process. Voter registration fell off badly in the black neighborhoods, strategic plans for political organization were largely ignored, and black candidates ceased to make serious efforts to run for municipal office.

The Hispanic population, too, failed to develop influence in city politics in proportion to its numbers. Some newcomers failed to see the relationship of the political process to their personal circumstances. Many Puerto Ricans, for example, resembled the earlier Italian "birds of passage," traveling back and forth between the United States and Italy without establishing permanent roots in the Boston community. Other Hispanics, especially those from South America, were still distrustful of the governmental process and wary of political authority as a result of their terrible experiences in places like Nicaragua and Colombia. The same was true of many Haitians, who had fled from political oppression on their island. For many immigrant groups, problems of language and education made them hesitant to participate in public affairs. The "New Bostonians" have yet to establish an organized or unified political base in the municipal structure. Older members of the new immigrant communities are still preoccupied with finding homes and establishing businesses; the younger members are busy getting an education and finding employment. It will be some time before they become an effective force in city politics.[3]

Inevitably, however, new national and racial groups will rise to the upper echelons of municipal government. Probably the Irish will never completely relinquish their role in Boston politics, but they will have to work out a future very different from their past.

Although they had been loyal members of the Democratic party in the

United States for nearly half a century, the Boston Irish did not become a significant presence in city politics until well after the Civil War, when the Democratic party had all but ceased to exist as a creditable organization. During the 1870s and 1880s, early Irish organizers like Patrick Collins, Hugh O'Brien, Patrick Maguire, and Thomas Gargan took over the floundering party and established it as a viable base for the political advancement of their people. By insisting on strict loyalty and party discipline, by establishing their personal credentials as trustworthy public servants and successful businessmen, and by creating reciprocal alliances with well-known and highly respected old-time Yankee Democrats, these early organizers were able to move the Irish into positions of power and influence in city government.

During the same period, other Irish-American political leaders exercised their personal influence among clusters of constituents in the surrounding neighborhoods. A number of shrewd, energetic, and ambitious men created new mechanisms of government within their own wards, registering voters, dominating the polls, winning local elections, dispensing patronage, and establishing unquestioned authority as the local "bosses." Martin Lomasney in the West End, John Fitzgerald in the North End, and Patrick Kennedy in East Boston were prime examples of local bosses who used their power in the wards to influence municipal politics and nominate city mayors. By combining the power of their own Board of Strategy with that of the Democratic City Committee, they were able not only to support sympathetic Yankees like Josiah Quincy III but also to elect Irish-born candidates such as Hugh O'Brien in 1884 and Patrick Collins in 1901.

By the turn of the century, the political tide in Boston had clearly turned as the Irish took over the reins of city government and moved into power in their own right. During the first half of the century, Boston-born mayors like John F. Fitzgerald and James Michael Curley brought together the votes of their Irish constituents in the neighborhoods to form a solid basis of loyal support in return for personal patronage from the mayor's office and the considerable benefits of a friendly city government. The Irish maintained a powerful role through a half-century of conflict, with

It's always fair weather when winning Democrats get together. In the foreground, state senator John E. Powers of South Boston shakes hands with Edward M. ("Ted") Kennedy. Looking on in the background, left to right, are Francis L. Bellotti, William M. Bulger, and Endicott ("Chub") Peabody. Courtesy of the Boston Public Library, Print Department.

the forces of Irish-Catholic Democrats in the neighborhoods pitted against the established influence of Yankee-Protestant Republicans in the downtown wards. During this period the Boston Irish became more defensive, more militant, more defiant, and more self-conscious as an oppressed minority that had suddenly come into its own and was thoroughly enjoying the fruits of victory for the first time.

By the end of World War II, however, the modern forces of social change, scientific advancement, and technological development made it painfully evident that Boston could no longer afford the divisiveness that had kept the city from developing a solid financial base, rescuing its failing infrastructure, and revitalizing its communities. The accomplishments of the succession of Irish-Catholic mayors who took office in Boston after 1950 were, to a great degree, measured in terms of their ability to bring together old enemies in a cooperative working coalition. These mayors gradually restructured the city's physical features, attracted new business investments and corporate development, achieved a remarkable measure of financial security, and promoted an image of the city as a national metropolis of worldwide importance. This was the first time in the city's 350-year history that the Irish-Catholic population as a whole played a significant role in shaping the city and defining its future.

Postwar politics displayed a surprising degree of stability and continuity in a city whose Irish-dominated political system had, for years, been almost universally regarded as erratic and unpredictable (shades of the "wild Irish"!). Contrary to the stereotype, twentieth-century Boston politics had followed certain clearly established voting patterns. Starting with the victory of Boston's first Irish-Catholic mayor in 1884, voters chose their candidates from two clearly identifiable categories. On the one hand, there were candidates like Hugh O'Brien and Patrick Collins, who were conservative, managerial types, on good terms with the Yankee community and generally willing to accommodate the needs of the neighborhoods with the interests of the downtown business community. Their style of political leadership reemerged in Boston after World War II with Mayors Hynes, Collins, and White. On the other hand, there were candidates more closely identified with the neighborhood ward system, who enjoyed a confrontational relationship with downtown Yankees and promoted the interests of Irish (and, later, Italian) working-class voters. Their style was represented by John F. Fitzgerald and James Michael Curley and reappeared after the World War II with John E. Powers, Louise Day Hicks, Ray Flynn, and Tom Menino. These stylistic differences were not an indication of either instability or discontinuity. Indeed, the longevity of the city's recent chief executives is truly remarkable for a modern American city. John Hynes served for ten years as mayor, John Collins held office for eight years, Kevin White remained in office for a record sixteen years, and Ray Flynn completed ten years. Together, these four men occupied the mayor's office for forty-four years.

During the mid-1960s and early 1970s, however, at about the time that urban renewal reached its peak, massive social changes were sweeping across the nation and influencing major urban centers such as Boston. Antiwar demonstrators protested the conflict in Vietnam; feminists called for radical changes in traditional gender roles; free-speech advocates demanded new openness in communications; college students organized against established curriculums; civil rights activists asserted the rights and liberties of African Americans. Most Boston Irish were caught off guard by this new series of social protests; they were at a complete loss as to who the protesters were, what they wanted, and how they should be dealt with. The Boston Irish were confronted by a vast wave of societal change whose dimensions they could not grasp, for which history had not prepared them, and to which their limited experience in the isolated world of the ethnic neighborhoods had never conditioned them.

Because most of the protest movements conflicted head-on with the traditional beliefs and values of conservative Irish Catholics, the first and instinctive response was negative. Public opposition to United States government policy in Vietnam, for example, was clearly shocking. Irish Catholics had been brought up to love their flag, to support their country right or wrong, and never to cause scandal by displaying open contempt for established authority. Feminism also ran counter to the traditional ideals of the Irish-Catholic family, modeled after the Holy Family of Jesus, Mary, and Joseph. The father went to work and earned the money while the mother stayed home, kept house, did the cooking, and brought up the children. That was the way God intended it! And most Irish Catholics objected to the methods and the objectives of militant black leaders who demanded better jobs, better homes, and better schools. After generations of degradation and oppression by their English overlords in Ireland, the Irish had fled famine and pestilence in the old country. They came to America huddled in the holds of "coffin ships," and those who arrived in Boston faced years of segregation and intimidation at the hands of Anglo-

Saxon Yankees who despised their race and abhorred their religion. Slowly and painfully, Irish Catholics worked their way up the social and economic ladder, taking the meanest of jobs and the smallest of opportunities to establish a place for themselves in a hostile environment. After a century of struggle, with little or no assistance from private agencies or governmental institutions, surviving only through the self-sacrifice of their family members and the generous patronage of their own political representatives, by the middle of the twentieth century many of the Boston Irish had finally "made it." They had good jobs with secure pensions, they owned their own homes, they had a little money in the bank, they were able to send their children to Boston College or Holy Cross—maybe even to Harvard or Dartmouth. They were enjoying the experience of presiding over the social, economic, and political life of a city they now regarded as their own. Most Irish Catholics resented it furiously therefore, when black leaders denounced them as bigots, defined "their" city of Boston as "the most racist city in America," and demanded that the government assure them access to better jobs, better housing, and better schools. This was asking for "too much, too soon," objected the Boston Irish. Nobody had helped *them,* they protested. Nobody had given *them* jobs, provided *them* with houses, made the schools easier for *their* children. They did all these things themselves, through persistent hard work—and it took them more than a century. As far as the Irish were concerned, the black people should work for it, too; and they should lift themselves up by their own bootstraps the way the Irish, the Italians, the Jews, the Greeks, and other immigrant groups had done in Boston.

With the fierce and unyielding stubbornness for which their people were famous, the Irish refused to budge, seeing the school desegregation controversy as the tip of a liberal iceberg—a conspiracy, in fact—that would use the black civil rights issue to undermine their traditional religious beliefs, their distinctive social institutions, and the independent character of their ethnic communities. It was a classic example of an irresistible force meeting an immovable object. The result was a violent clash in which there was, as J. Anthony Lukas has pointed out, no "common ground." It was a battle to preserve what many Irish regarded as ancient

Celtic values against the unreasonable demands of black militants and the half-baked theories of liberal social engineers.

What made the clash all the more violent and the tension almost unbearable was the fact that the confrontation caused bitter divisions within the Irish-Catholic community itself. While opponents of forced busing struck out against the NAACP, Tom Atkins, Ruth Batson, Mel King, and the other black leaders of the city who led the fight to desegregate the city schools, they at least understood the reasons for the blacks' anger and the basis of their demands. What the Irish could not understand was why so many of "their own kind" could turn against them, side with the liberals, and take up the cause of integration. The most explosive expressions of their outrage, as Lukas has pointed out, were directed principally at such fellow Irishmen as Judge W. Arthur Garrity, Senator Ted Kennedy, Mayor Kevin White, and Congressman Tip O'Neill.[4] By advocating integration and supporting civil rights, these people were committing one of the worst crimes in the lexicon of Irish villainies—the one mortal sin for which there was no forgiveness. They had broken ranks with the Clan; they had betrayed the Family. They had become turncoats and informers; they had gone over to the enemy. With that, the close-knit, competitive world of the Boston Irish was split wide apart. Beyond its purely racial context, this confrontation was a critical challenge to the dominance the Boston Irish had finally achieved over the city's political, social, religious, and educational life. Even twenty years later, as the city observed the anniversary of Garrity's desegregation decision, old enemies heatedly debated the controversial role the Irish-Catholic judge had played in the busing crisis. Ruth Batson of Roxbury, one of the original black activists, praised the decision for ensuring that the "lawless would not be rewarded" and insisted that the judge had unfairly been made scapegoat for all the social ills of the city.[5] William M. Bulger of South Boston, president of the state Senate and a longtime opponent of busing, insisted that Judge Garrity had resorted to "decapitation" to cure Boston's "headache" and was responsible for the ruin of the city's entire school system.[6] The Boston Irish have long memories, as well as an insatiable desire for revenge.

Professor Thomas N. Brown, a specialist in the history of Irish nationalism, suggests that there are two competing traditions at work in the Irish community. The Irish-American politician, he says, can function effectively as an "organization man." Working quietly and skillfully, with charm and tact, on many occasions he has demonstrated an ability to accommodate political differences, to compromise moral controversies, and to adjudicate financial conflicts. On other occasions, however, the Irishman can be a "rebel" who rejects compromise in any form and will pursue a principle "even unto death." The politician, says Brown, functions in the "ancient houses of power"; the rebel finds his place in the streets and in the hills.[7] Over the years, Irish political leaders in Boston have alternated between these two personae. In mayors like Hugh O'Brien and Patrick Collins the organization man was dominant: they accepted established civic virtues and worked to create a harmonious relationship with the Yankee community. James Michael Curley, on the other hand, was the classic Irish rebel. He shattered whatever cultural consensus had existed in Boston by attacking the Yankee community and ridiculing its history. With the departure of Curley in 1949, however, the pendulum swung back again. Hynes, Collins, and White typified the return of the organization man. They established a new and workable balance between opposing social and political forces in the city.

With the busing crisis in the 1970s, the two traditional personae no longer alternated—they clashed. For the most part, the "organization" Irish had become the upper-middle-class, college-educated, upwardly mobile professionals who held high positions in government, served on important corporate boards, and spent their days in the boardrooms and law offices of downtown Boston. Most of them had moved to the suburbs, where they sent their children to private schools. They admonished their Irish-Catholic friends and relatives in the old neighborhoods to modernize their thinking, become more tolerant, allow their children to be bused across town to black communities, and accept black children in their own neighborhood schools. The "rebel" Irish were found in the city council, the school committee, and the lower echelons of city government, as well as in the old ethnic neighborhoods where their families had lived (often in the same house) for generations, where their churches were located, and where their neighborhood schools and sports teams stood as proud standards of an independent spirit. The "rebel" Irish were furious at the hypocrisy of their lace-curtain, two-toilet relatives, who had moved to the wealthy suburbs where there were few, if any, black children in the schools but who now made fun of their narrow "parochialism," criticized their "insular" ways, and chastised them as bigots and racists for refusing to yield to the outside pressures of militants and liberals. The racial divisions in the city were greatly exacerbated by the violent outbursts of hatred that occurred within families—those knock-down, drag-out Irish family fights that pit husband against wife, father against son, with no quarter asked and no quarter given. Seldom, if ever, in the history of Boston had the Irish family experienced such a bitter and heart-rending conflict.

What Ray Flynn did for this troubled city in 1983 was to supply a respite from open racial conflict and establish a tentative balance among the warring factions that had kept Boston divided for the better part of a decade. This time, it was not a matter of balancing the interests of the Yankee and the Celt, the Protestant and the Catholic—those controversies had long since disappeared. Flynn worked to balance the concerns of black people and white people, rich people and poor people, the haves and the have-nots. He paid little attention to the glamour of municipal office and focused instead on prosaic projects essential to the interests of working people, citizens of color, the new minorities, the unemployed, and the homeless. His administration created parks and playgrounds, replaced fire and police equipment, cleaned streets and paved roads, replaced water and sewer pipes, expanded the City Hospital, started youth programs, and built affordable housing. The respite from controversy was welcome, and while some criticized the Flynn administration for not taking on more elaborate renewal programs or engaging in more experimental cultural enterprises, the majority of voters were content to enjoy a period of comparative quiet while they had their streets plowed and their potholes repaired. It was probably because Tom Menino promised a continuation of such meat-and-potato neighborhood programs that he won such a strong mandate in the 1993 election.

But past solutions may not provide future remedies in light of the new and urgent problems that confront the city of Boston. There is a desperate need for a cost-effective system of public education that will be intelligently managed, effectively delivered, and made available to all children regardless of where they happen to live or where their parents come from. An outstanding public educational system is necessary not only to prepare today's children for tomorrow's computerized workplace but also to attract new families to a city where they can be sure that their children will receive a first-class public education. However, success will depend to a great extent on how well city officials cope with the culture of drugs, crime, and violence that has spread through every major urban center in the United States. Until the streets and the schools are safe, politeness, civility, and normal social intercourse cannot be sustained, and the inspiring work of education will inevitably take second place to depressing security measures and police patrols. Older institutions that once took the lead in establishing the patterns of culture and the standards of behavior in Boston society either have disappeared or no longer exercise the influence they once did. It is clear that the Catholic Church, for example, while still a highly respected institution, no longer has the all-pervasive influence it once had among the Irish Catholics of Boston. Membership has fallen off, attendance is down, vocations for priests and nuns have declined dramatically, parochial schools have closed for lack of funding and enrollments, and the hierarchy's positions on controversial issues such as birth control and abortion are widely ignored.

An abrupt change in local church tradition came about in November 1970 with the death of the popular Cardinal Cushing and the surprising appointment of Bishop Humberto Sousa Medeiros as his successor. The son of immigrants from the Portuguese Azores who had supported the cause of Mexican farm workers in Brownsville, Texas, Medeiros was the first bishop of Boston in over a hundred years who was not of Irish descent. Although his formal reception was courteous, there was no great love in the city's hierarchy for this outsider, whom J. Anthony Lukas describes as an "alien graft" on the form of Boston's Irish Catholicism.[8] A gentle, pious, humble pastor, Medeiros lacked the thick skin, the aggressive instincts, and the robust managerial skills to deal effectively with the frustrating complexities of Boston politics—both religious and secular. He was saddled with the enormous financial burdens of Cushing's building programs, hampered by the passive resistance of resentful Irish pastors, and confronted by the bitter school desegregation issue that erupted into violence only a year after Medeiros arrived in Boston. Although he tried, on numerous occasions, to formulate peaceful Christian policies that would satisfy everyone, he ended by alienating almost all parties to the conflict. Discouraged, depressed, and worn out by a badly damaged heart, Cardinal Medeiros died in September 1983. He was succeeded by Bishop Bernard F. Law, who was named eighth bishop and fourth archbishop of Boston. A graduate of Harvard College who had attended seminaries in Louisiana and Ohio before serving in Mississippi and Missouri, Law's appointment was greeted as a welcome return to Boston ecclesiastical tradition. Bright, affable, and compassionate, the young prelate made friends easily, moved about the archdiocese actively, and displayed a serious concern for the needs of the poor, the homeless, and the newer immigrants, mainly Hispanics and Asians, who were becoming part of the city's Roman Catholic population.

Elevated to the rank of Cardinal in 1985, Law was seen by some as rather liberal in his social attitudes, urging greater diocesan support of programs for the impoverished and the underprivileged; others found him conservative in his theological pronouncements. A loyal supporter of the traditional moral positions taken by Pope John Paul II, Cardinal Law articulated the pope's views with great vigor. He spoke out strongly against birth control and abortion, opposed priesthood for married men and for women, and generally supported the male-oriented traditions of the church. Many in the archdioceses, particularly the older parishioners who supported the pope, applauded the outspoken Cardinal Law, and approved of what they regarded as a long-overdue modification of undesirable liberal experiments initiated by the Second Vatican Council. Others, however, usually younger college-educated Catholics, questioned the scriptural basis of the pope's teachings on matters such as family planning and ordination and viewed the cardinal's positions on these matters as regressive and unresponsive. The preoccupation of the Catholic hierarchy

with new moral trends and doctrinal disputes, along with pressing practical responsibilities related to budgets, seminary enrollments, parochial
schools, and social-service programs, left the Church little time to reestablish connections with City Hall or to involve itself in the larger political
issues of the city. Reporters at Boston city desks no longer asked what
"Number One" would say about a piece of legislation or what position
"Lake Street" would take on a troublesome issue. They were interested, of
course. A statement by the cardinal archbishop of Boston is always front-
page news. But it really didn't matter. The old political clout wasn't there
any more. Times had changed.

But such changes were not unique to Boston, nor were they peculiar
to the Roman Catholic Church. By the 1990s most American religious
denominations, especially in the nation's largest cities, exerted very little
influence beyond the confines of their places of worship. Similarly, the
American family, once the major source of counsel, morality, and authority in the lives of its members, had undergone significant changes during
the 1970s and 1980s. By the 1990s it was largely ineffective in the lives of
the younger generation. The complexity of urban life, the rise of a service
economy, the influence of technology, the increase of divorce, the preva-
lence of one-parent families, the rise in the number of illegitimate births,
and the redefinition of the family itself have all reduced the effectiveness
of the institution as a social force. New institutions are desperately needed
to perform many of the functions once served by the church and the
family; new coalitions must be found either to replace institutions that
have disappeared or to reinvigorate those like the church and the family
that are still alive and are redefining themselves in a changing society; new
leadership must emerge to formulate creative ideas and develop realistic
urban agendas to restore the moral values necessary to a free and democratic society.

Perhaps the role of the Boston Irish in the twenty-first century is to
involve themselves in the task of defining and establishing a meaningful
urban society for the growing multicultural population of Boston. It is a
task for which their long and painful struggle would seem to have prepared them in a special way. For generations, Americans have been fasci-

nated by the story of Boston and especially by the role of the Irish in that story. The history of the Boston Irish, from the time of the Great Famine to the age of the Kennedys, has inspired innumerable books, novels, motion pictures, and television productions. There are a number of reasons for the undiminishing interest in Boston: the city's incomparable history, its distinctive architecture, its diversified economy, its colorful mayors, its eccentric political practices. But observers rarely fail to appreciate the overriding drama of Boston as a conflict of opposites. Today's Boston is the product of a confrontation of truly dramatic proportions between a wealthy, powerful, well-established, homogeneous society and a poor, displaced, despised immigrant people who sought—and won—not only the immediate advantages of political asylum and economic security but also eventual acceptance into the full social and cultural life of the community. This is a David-and-Goliath story, a classic struggle between members of a strong group that had it all and wanted to keep it all and a rising tide of newcomers who wanted to share in the American dream without sacrificing their religious faith, their family values, or their ethnic traditions.

For nearly two centuries, the Boston Irish made their presence felt in the old Puritan Boston community, cutting down its hills, excavating its dams, constructing its roadways, building its railroads, bringing laughter, music, and amusing expressions to what could often be a dull and colorless town. The experience of the Irish in Boston was not like that of immigrants to other nineteenth-century American cities such as New York, Philadelphia, Cincinnati, St. Louis, and Chicago, where pioneers, travelers, transients, and immigrants assimilated with native populations that were, themselves, an ethnic and cultural mixture of fairly recent vintage. Boston was old and long settled. Its clash of cultures was immediate and violent; its religious conflicts, bitter and irreconcilable; its social differences, stark and painful. The Irish had to fight against long-established religious beliefs and social prejudices to achieve recognition. The valor they displayed during the Civil War earned them a greater measure of respect and tolerance, and during the postwar years they made their way up the economic ladder to become increasingly important in the city's human infrastructure. But it was in the political life of Boston that the Irish played their most distinctive role: first, by reorganizing and reconstituting the modern Democratic party during the post–Civil War years, when the old Jefferson-Jackson party almost passed into oblivion; and second, by transforming the nature and purpose of that party to meet the pressing needs of a modern industrial society. In the political philosophy of the Federalist-Whig-Republican tradition, the purpose of politics is to establish an impersonal rule of law "without fear or favor," without reference to either individual needs or social privations. The Irish brought to Boston a new sense of what politics could do to raise the level of human compassion. In their view, politics should involve itself directly in the day-to-day problems of the community. Irish neighborhood politics brought a small measure of social and economic security to disabled and impoverished citizens at a time when no government agencies existed to help those who could not help themselves. At first, of course, the efforts were small and were restricted mainly to the confines of the neighborhood ward. The Irish neighborhood leaders were sneered at as "bosses"; their efforts to find jobs for the unemployed were condemned as "cronyism"; and their success in providing food to the hungry and aid to the needy was referred to in contemptuous terms as "patronage." Gradually, however, the "boss" system expanded from the wards into the upper echelons of municipal government. By the early part of the twentieth century the Irish were moving into the major centers of political power in Boston. At this point, in the face of overwhelming Irish numerical superiority, powerful members of the Yankee establishment quietly withdrew to a series of sensitive and strategic positions in business organizations and civic institutions in an effort to preserve aspects of the community that they considered essential to a good social order. After that, the Irish served as the working political base for a city that was growing in size and complexity all the time. They succeeded in naming the mayors, electing the city councillors, and monopolizing practically all the agencies of municipal government. By the mid-1950s and early 1960s, they had also moved into leadership positions in the city's business and financial community. This enabled them to form alliances of mutual respect with the Yankees in order to revitalize the old city and create the "New Boston" of the 1970s and 1980s.

If, with the passing of a generation of postwar political leaders and the rapid growth of an entirely new racial and ethnic population, the Irish can no longer hold on to all the political power they once monopolized, they might do well to concentrate on those areas of city life they feel are most in need of their special knowledge. They are no longer the immigrants and exiles of the Famine era, the street sweepers, hod carriers, and ward bosses of the Gilded Age. The Boston Irish have become people of education, culture, and refinement. They are statesmen and diplomats, physicians and lawyers, businessmen and bankers, artists and musicians, priests and poets. To a great extent, in their prolonged struggle for survival and achievement, they *did* turn Boston into an "Irish" city. For that reason, they now have a special obligation to give back to that city the benefit of the skills, the associations, and the resources they have acquired over the years. In this way they can help preserve the kind of cultivated and responsive community John Winthrop envisioned in 1630, so that new immigrant peoples and their families can share the many advantages of the "City upon a Hill," where the Boston Irish prospered so well, accomplished so much, and endured for so long.

NOTES

❦

INTRODUCTION

1. J. Anthony Lukas, "Melting Pot or Mulligan Stew? Politics and the Process of Assimilation in Boston," *Forum 350* (John F. Kennedy Library, Boston) (October 7, 1980), pp. 41–53.
2. Cited in Kerby Miller, *Emigrants and Exiles: Ireland and the Irish Exodus to North America* (New York, 1985), p. 135.

CHAPTER ONE

1. John P. Marquand, *The Late George Apley* (New York, 1936), p. 154.
2. John Fiske, *The Beginnings of New England; or, The Puritan Theocracy in Its Relations to Civil and Religious Liberty* (Boston, 1889), pp. 40–41.
3. Henry Cabot Lodge, *The Story of the Revolution* (New York, 1898).
4. Michael J. O'Brien, *The Irish at Bunker Hill* (Shannon, Ireland, 1968), pp. 12–13, 19, 33. Also see Thomas H. O'Connor, "The Irish in New England," *New England Historical and Genealogical Register* 139 (July 1985), pp. 187–88.
5. Miller, *Emigrants and Exiles,* pp. 139–40.
6. Ibid., p. 152.
7. Karl Bottigheimer, *Ireland and the Irish: A Short History* (New York, 1982), p. 119.
8. Miller, *Emigrants,* p. 158.
9. Ibid., p. 153.
10. Ibid., pp. 155–56.
11. O'Connor, "Irish in New England," p. 188.
12. Cited in Samuel Eliot Morison, *Builders of the Bay Colony* (Boston, 1981 ed.), p. 37.
13. Ibid., p. 47.
14. Bottigheimer, *Ireland and the Irish,* pp. 109–10.
15. Ibid., pp. 119–21.
16. Ibid., pp. 135–37.
17. Ibid., pp. 137–39.
18. Ibid., pp. 245–46.
19. William V. Shannon, *The American Irish* (New York, 1966), p. 6.
20. Miller, *Emigrants,* p. 163.
21. James B. Cullen, *The Story of the Irish in Boston* (Boston, 1889), p. 24; Carl Bridenbaugh, *Cities in the Wilderness: Urban Life in America, 1625–1742* (New York, 1938), p. 410.

22. Cullen, *The Irish in Boston*, pp. 19, 31 ff. In 1764 a revised copy of the rules and orders omitted the qualification of Protestantism; in 1804 the religious limitation was dropped completely. Also see Carl Bridenbaugh, *Cities in Revolt: Urban Life in America, 1743–1776* (New York, 1955), p. 127.

23. Cullen, *The Irish in Boston*, p. 24. The Town House later became the Old State House, and Long Lane was renamed Federal Street. See Thomas H. O'Connor and Alan Rogers, *This Momentous Affair: Massachusetts and the Ratification of the Constitution of the United States* (Boston, 1987), p. 70.

24. Bridenbaugh, *Cities in Revolt*, pp. 123, 136.

25. Miller, *Emigrants*, pp. 167, 180. Also see James Haltigan, *The Irish in the American Revolution and Their Early Influence in the Colonies* (Washington, D.C., 1907).

26. O'Brien, *The Irish at Bunker Hill*, pp. 17–18; O'Connor, "Irish in New England," p. 188. General John Sullivan, according to his biographer, was not only Protestant but also "violently antagonistic toward Roman Catholicism." See Shannon, *The American Irish*, p. 31.

27. John T. Galvin, "There's Some Irish Green in the Brahmins' Blue Blood," *Boston Globe*, March 17, 1989.

28. Miller, *Emigrants*, pp. 137–38.

29. E. P. Thompson, *The Making of the Working Class* (New York, 1963), p. 429.

30. Miller, *Emigrants*, pp. 140–41.

31. Ibid., p. 146; Cullen, *The Irish in Boston*, pp. 14–15.

32. Massachusetts Court Records, 7:74, May 30, 1700; 7:97, June 17, 1700. Cited in Robert H. Lord, John E. Sexton, and Edward Harrington, *History of the Archdiocese of Boston*, (Boston, 1945), vol. 1, pp. 69–70 (hereafter cited as *Archdiocese of Boston*).

33. Cited in *Archdiocese of Boston*, vol. 1, pp. 158–59.

34. Boston Town Records, 1746, p. 103. Cited in Cullen, *The Irish in Boston*, p. 15.

35. Boston Town Records, 1772, pp. 595–96. Cited in Cullen, *The Irish in Boston*, pp. 15–16.

36. Cullen, *The Irish in Boston*, p. 16; *Archdiocese of Boston*, vol. 1, pp. 237–38.

37. *Archdiocese of Boston*, vol. 1, pp. 235–37.

38. Ibid., pp. 236–37.

39. Ibid., pp. 268–74, 283–84.

40. Ibid., pp. 286–87.

41. Ibid., p. 296.

42. When one of French Admiral Comte Charles Henri d'Estaing's young officers was accidentally killed in a fight with local ruffians, apologetic Bostonians allowed the officer the unusual honor of a burial in the town's venerable King's Chapel. See Allan Forbes and Paul Cadman, *France and New England*, vol. 2 (Boston, 1927), pp. 20–22.

43. *Archdiocese of Boston*, vol. 1, pp. 302–5, 341–42.

44. Ibid., pp. 358–61.

45. Ibid., pp. 354–57. Also see Cullen, *The Irish in Boston*, pp. 68–69.

46. Miller, *Emigrants*, pp. 111–12, 114–15, 174.

47. Shannon, *The American Irish*, p. 9.

48. *The Gonne-Yeats Letters, 1893–1938: Always Your Friend*, ed. Anna MacBridge White and A. Norman Jeffares (London, 1992), pp. 167, 169.

49. Thomas Flanagan, in *The Year of the French* (New York, 1979), provides a fictional but realistic description of the tragic events of 1798, when French troops landed in County Mayo to help the Irish in their unsuccessful rebellion.

50. Bottigheimer, *Ireland and the Irish*, pp. 157–59, 168–69.

51. Annabelle M. Melville, *Jean Lefebvre de Cheverus, 1768–1836* (Milwaukee, 1958); *Archdiocese of Boston*, vol. 1, pp. 525–51.

52. *Archdiocese of Boston*, vol. 1, pp. 585–87.

53. Joseph Charles, *The Origins of the American Party System* (New York, 1956); John C. Miller, *The Federalist Era, 1789–1801* (New York, 1960), pp. 84–98, 99–125.

54. *New England Palladium*, August 13, 1805. Also see *Columbian Centinel*, 3 August 1805.

55. *Independent Chronicle*, August 5, 1806.

56. Melville, *Cheverus*, pp. 127–132.

57. Samuel Eliot Morison, *The Life and Letters of Harrison Gray Otis, Federalist, 1765–1848*, vol. 1 (Boston, 1913), p. 107.

58. Morison, *Otis*, vol. 1, p. 108. Also see James M. Banner, *To the Hartford Convention: The Federalists and the Origins of Party Politics in Massachusetts* (New York, 1970), pp. 90, 98–99.

59. Fisher Ames to Christopher Gore, December 18, 1798, in *The Works of Fisher Ames* vol. 1, ed. Seth Ames (Boston, 1854), pp. 247–48. See Alexander DeConde, *The Quasi-War: The Politics and Diplomacy of the Undeclared War with France, 1797–1801* (New York, 1966), for a scholarly analysis of the strained relations between the United States and France.

60. Stephen G. Kurtz, *The Presidency of John Adams: The Collapse of Federalism, 1795–1800* (Philadelphia, 1957), pp. 306–8; Manning J. Dauer, *The Adams Federalists* (Baltimore, 1968), pp. 152–71; Miller, *The Federalist Era*, pp. 229–32, 240–41.

61. Cullen, *The Irish in Boston*, p. 70.

62. Ibid.

63. Robert W. Tucker and David C. Hendrickson, *Empire of Liberty; The Statecraft of Thomas Jefferson* (New York, 1990), pp. 87–108, 189–222.

64. Marshall Smelser, *The Democratic Republic, 1801–1815* (New York, 1968), pp. 138–50, 151–80; Louis M. Sears, *Jefferson and the Embargo* (New York, 1927).

65. Cullen, *The Irish in Boston*, pp. 69–70. Also see Harry L. Coles, *The War of 1812*

(Chicago, 1965), pp. 14–15; Roger H. Brown, *The Republic in Peril: 1812* (New York, 1971), pp. 93–97.

66. Patrick C. T. White, *A Nation on Trial: America and the War of 1812* (New York, 1965), pp. 121–22; Smelser, *Democratic Republic*, p. 236.

67. Thomas H. O'Connor, *South Boston: My Home Town* (Boston, 1988), pp. 20–21.

CHAPTER TWO

1. Paul Johnson, *The Birth of the Modern: World Society, 1815–1830* (New York, 1991), p. 2.

2. Ibid., p. 83.

3. Robert B. Eckles and Richard W. Hale, Jr., *Britain, Her Peoples, and the Commonwealth* (New York, 1954), p. 266.

4. Miller, *Emigrants*, pp. 170–71.

5. From 1780 to 1821, Ireland's population expanded from four million to nearly seven million—an increase of three million in little more than forty years. See Miller, *Emigrants*, p. 173.

6. Johnson, *Birth of the Modern*, p. 206.

7. Walter Muir Whitehill, *Boston: A Topographical History* (Cambridge, Mass., 1968 ed.), p. 108.

8. Ibid., pp. 107–9.

9. For an analysis of Jackson's views on the ethics of labor, see Marvin Meyers, *The Jacksonian Persuasion: Politics and Belief* (Stanford, Calif., 1957), pp. 21, 23–24.

10. Arthur B. Darling, *Political Changes in Massachusetts, 1824–1848* (New Haven, 1925), p. 2; Arthur B. Schlesinger, Jr., *The Age of Jackson* (Boston, 1945), p. 321; Edward Pessen, *Jacksonian America* (Urbana, Ill., 1969), p. 213.

11. Cited in *Archdiocese of Boston*, vol. 2, p. 190.

12. *Boston Statesman*, March 20, 1828.

13. Ibid., March 24, 1828.

14. *Bunker Hill Aurora*, August 9, 1828.

15. *Boston Courier*, November 3, 1828.

16. John Barton Derby, *Political Reminiscences, Including a Sketch of the Origin and History of the "Statesman Party"* (Boston, 1835), pp. 27, 46. Also see *Archdiocese of Boston*, vol. 2, pp. 190–91.

17. John Bach McMaster, *A History of the People of the United States from the Revolution to the Civil War* (New York, 1906), vol. 6, p. 85. Also see *Archdiocese of Boston*, vol. 2, p. 191.

18. Haltigan, *Irish in the Revolution*, p. 56. Also see Cullen, *The Irish in Boston*, p. 41.

19. Haltigan, *Irish in the Revolution*, p. 57.

20. Ibid., pp. 57–58.

21. Robert V. Remini, *Andrew Jackson and the Course of American Democracy, 1833–1845* (New York, 1984), vol. 3, pp. 78–79.

22. Ibid., p. 75.
23. Samuel F. B. Morse, *Imminent Dangers to the Free Institutions of the United States through Foreign Immigration* (New York, 1854), pp. 15–17.
24. Henry Ward Beecher, *A Plea for the West* (Cincinnati, 1835), pp. 47, 62–63. See Dale T. Knobel, *Paddy and the Republic: Ethnicity and Nationality in Antebellum America* (Middletown, Conn., 1986), for a scholarly analysis of the popular image of the Irish at a time when Americans were trying to define their own national identity.
25. *Boston Daily Advertiser*, July, August 1825, passim. Also see Carleton Beals, *Brass Knuckle Crusade: The Great Know-Nothing Conspiracy, 1820–1860* (New York, 1960), p. 36. Before 1845, says Dale Knobel, Americans concentrated on the "environmental" weaknesses of the Irish—the results of poverty, oppression, and misgovernment. See Knobel, *Paddy and the Republic*, pp. 56–59.
26. Thomas H. O'Connor, *Fitzpatrick's Boston, 1846–1866; John Bernard Fitzpatrick, Third Bishop of Boston* (Boston, 1984), pp. 15–16. Also see Ray Allen Billington, *The Protestant Crusade, 1800–1860* (New York, 1938), for a description of the "no-popery" movement of the late 1820s.
27. *Archdiocese of Boston*, vol. 2, p. 198.
28. Billington, *Protestant Crusade*, p. 120. Also see Samuel F. B. Morse, *Foreign Conspiracy Against the Liberties of the United States* (New York, 1835), pp. 14, 21, for examples of prevailing attitudes toward Jesuits.
29. *Archdiocese of Boston*, vol. 2, p. 198. See Mary Alphonsine Frawley, *Patrick Donahoe* (Washington, D.C., 1946), for a biography of *The Pilot*'s publisher.
30. Knobel, *Paddy and the Republic*, p. 53.
31. Richard Hofstadter, *The Paranoid Style in American Politics* (Chicago, 1979), p. 21.
32. Billington, *Protestant Crusade*, pp. 90–109, provides a documented account of the wide-ranging character of the many works of the period purporting to be revelations of former priests and nuns. Also see O'Connor, *Fitzpatrick's Boston*, p. 17.
33. Billington, *Protestant Crusade*, pp. 72–73. Historians have not been able to demonstrate any direct relationship between Beecher's inflammatory sermons on August 10 and the attack on the Ursuline convent the following night. All agree, however, that these sermons did nothing to calm a dangerous situation.
34. Ibid., pp. 53–57; *Archdiocese of Boston*, vol. 2, pp. 205–39; O'Connor, *Fitzpatrick's Boston*, p. 18; Nancy L. Schultz, "The Ursuline Convent Riot, Charlestown, Massachusetts, 1834," *Sextant: The Journal of Salem State College* 4, no. 2 (1993), pp. 24–29. A compilation of original documents may be found in *The Charlestown Convent: Its Destruction by a Mob on the Night of August 11, 1834: with a History of the Excitement before the Burning and the Strange and Exaggerated Reports Relating Thereto, the Feelings of Regret and Indignation Afterwards; the Proceedings of Meetings, and Expressions of the Contemporary Press* (Boston, 1870).

35. See O'Connor and Rogers, *This Momentous Affair*, pp. 68–71, for a description of the "Grand Procession" in Boston, February 8, 1788, in which laboring groups played a prominent role.
36. John Galvin, "Boston's First Irish Cop," *Boston Magazine*, March 1975, pp. 52–54.
37. *Archdiocese of Boston*, vol. 2, pp. 240–42.
38 Ibid., pp. 243–51; O'Connor, *Fitzpatrick's Boston*, p. 19; Roger Lane, *Policing the City: Boston, 1822–1885* (New York, 1971), p. 33.
39. James C. Johnson, "An Epic Fight in Old Boston," *The Bostonian* 2 (August 1895), p. 537; Paul T. Smith, "The Militia of the United States from 1846 to 1860," *Indiana Magazine of History* 15 (March 1919), p. 47; Fred W. Cross, "Important Events in the Militia History of Massachusetts," *Citizens Service Journal* 3 (1927), pp. 10–15.
40. *Boston Post*, June 28, 1837; *Boston Daily Atlas*, July 5, 1837; O'Connor, *Fitzpatrick's Boston*, p. 20.
41. See *Herald and Star*, July 13, 1837, and *Daily Sentinel and Gazette*, September 19, 1837, for expressions of fear and hostility in response to the arming of immigrants in Boston.
42. O'Connor, *Fitzpatrick's Boston*, p. 21.
43. *Boston Evening Transcript*, September 12, 1837; *Herald and Star*, September 14, 1837; O'Connor, *Fitzpatrick's Boston*, p. 21.
44. *Boston Morning Post*, September 15, 1837; *The Liberator*, September 15, 1837.
45. *Archdiocese of Boston*, vol. 2, pp. 253–57; O'Connor, *Fitzpatrick's Boston*, pp. 21–22.
46. Edward Everett to Archbishop Whatley of Dublin, July 14, 1847, Edward Everett Papers, Massachusetts Historical Society. See O'Connor, *Fitzpatrick's Boston*, pp. 89–90.
47. Edward Everett Hale, *Letters on Irish Emigration* (Boston, 1852), p. 5. Also see Cecil Woodham-Smith, *The Great Hunger: Ireland 1848–1849* (New York, 1962) p. 243.
48. Bishop Fenwick gave up his plans for a Catholic college in Maine and settled for Worcester, Massachusetts, some forty miles west of Boston, where he established the College of the Holy Cross. See O'Connor, *Fitzpatrick's Boston*, pp. 39–41.
49. Ibid., pp. 90–91.
50. *The Pilot*, January 15, 1842.
51. Ibid., March 18, 1843.
52. Ibid., March 25, 1843.
53. Ibid., June 20, 1840; November 12, 1843; June 6, 1844.
54. Ibid., May 20, May 27, July 15, November 11, 1843.
55. Ibid., May 20, 1843.
56. Ibid., January 6, 1844.
57. *Boston Courier*, November 12, 1844.

58. Ibid., November 21, 1844.

59. Ibid.

60. Cited in John R. Mulkern, *The Know-Nothing Party in Massachusetts: The Rise and Fall of a People's Party* (Boston, 1990), p. 8.

61. Ibid., pp. 21–22.

62. *Archdiocese of Boston*, vol 2, pp. 261–63.

63. Cited in Mulkern, *Know-Nothing Party*, p. 22.

CHAPTER THREE

1. *The Pilot*, July 11, 1846.

2. For more information on the Irish famine, see William Adams, *Ireland and Irish Immigration to the New World from 1815 to the Famine* (New Haven, 1932); Marcus Lee Hansen, *The Atlantic Migration* (Cambridge, Mass., 1940); George Potter, *To the Golden Door* (Boston, 1960); Woodham-Smith, *The Great Hunger*; Thomas Gallagher, *Paddy's Lament: Ireland, 1846–1847* (New York, 1982).

3. Edward Wakin, *Enter the Irish-American* (New York, 1976), pp. 28–29.

4. O'Connor, *Fitzpatrick's Boston*, p. 78.

5. Robert B. Forbes, *The Voyage of the Jamestown on Her Errand of Mercy* (Boston, 1847); Woodham-Smith, *The Great Hunger*, pp. 239–40; O'Connor, *Fitzpatrick's Boston*, pp. 78–79.

6. Hale, *Letters on Irish Emigration*, p. 5. See also Woodham-Smith, *The Great Hunger*, p. 243; Adams, *Ireland and Irish Immigration*, pp. 413–14; Potter, *To the Golden Door*, p. 435.

7. Shannon, *The American Irish*, p. 183.

8. Ibid.

9. Oliver Wendell Holmes, *Elsie Venner* (Boston, 1847). In this novel, Holmes describes a young Bostonian: "He comes of the Brahmin caste of New England. This is the harmless, inoffensive, untitled aristocracy."

10. Samuel Eliot Morison, *The Maritime History of Massachusetts, 1783–1860* (Boston, 1921), p. 214.

11. Oscar Handlin, *Boston's Immigrants* (Cambridge, Mass., 1941), pp. 59–66; Woodham-Smith, *The Great Hunger*, pp. 244–45. See also Sir Charles Lyell, *A Second Visit to the United States of North America* (New York, 1849), vol. 1, pp. 124–41.

12. Cited in Alan Lupo, *Liberty's Chosen Home: The Politics of Violence in Boston* (Boston, 1977), p. 22.

13. *Boston Daily Advertiser*, January 18, 1850.

14. Lupo, *Liberty's Chosen Home*, p. 23.

15. Theodore Parker, "A Sermon on the Moral Condition of Boston" (1849), in *The Collected Works of Theodore Parker*, ed. Francis P. Cobbe (London, 1864), vol. 7, p. 136.

16. *Boston Daily Advertiser*, February 1, July 10, 1850.

17. Ibid., January 23, 1850.

18. Miller, *Emigrants*, pp. 77–79; Wakin, *Enter the Irish-American*, pp. 59–60. Also see J. R. Barrett, "Why Paddy Drank: The Social Importance of Whiskey in Pre-Famine Ireland," *Journal of Popular Culture* 11 (1977), pp. 155–66.

19. Handlin, *Boston's Immigrants*, p. 121; Wakin, *Enter the Irish-American*, p. 60.

20. Edward M. Levine, *The Irish and Irish Politicians: A Study of Cultural and Social Alienation* (Notre Dame, 1966), p. 117.

21. Ibid., pp. 117–20. Also see Miller, *Emigrants*, pp. 319–20; Wakin, *Enter the Irish-American*, pp. 60–61.

22. *The Pilot*, January 5, 1850.

23. *Archdiocese of Boston*, vol. 2, p. 347; O'Connor, *Fitzpatrick's Boston*, pp. 95–96. Also see *The Pilot*, April 4, 1840.

24. *The Pilot*, September 9, 1843.

25. O'Connor, *Fitzpatrick's Boston*, p. 95.

26. Ibid., p. 96.

27. Ibid., pp. 233–34.

28. Ibid., pp. 94–95.

29. David H. Bennett, *The Path of Fear from Nativist Movements to the New Right in American History* (Chapel Hill, N.C., 1988), p. 77.

30. Cited in *Archdiocese of Boston*, vol. 2, p. 451. Emphasis in original. See also O'Connor, *Fitzpatrick's Boston*, pp. 86–87.

31. Mulkern, *Know-Nothing Party*, pp. 19-20; *Archdiocese of Boston*, vol. 2, p. 665.

32. Handlin, *Boston's Immigrants*, pp. 191–92.

33. See Thomas H. O'Connor, *Lords of the Loom: The Cotton Whigs and the Coming of the Civil War* (New York, 1968), p. 88; Henry Greenleaf Pearson, "Preliminaries of the Civil War," in *Commonwealth History of Massachusetts*, ed. Albert B. Hart, 5 vols. (New York, 1927–30), vol. 4, pp. 477–78.

34. Samuel Eliot Morison, *A History of the Constitution of Massachusetts* (Boston, 1917), pp. 61–65; Samuel Shapiro, "The Conservative Dilemma: The Massachusetts Constitutional Convention of 1853," *New England Quarterly* 3 (1960), p. 224.

35. Ronald P. Formisano, *The Transformation of Political Culture: Massachusetts Parties, 1790s–1840s* (New York, 1983), p. 297.

36. Cited in Shannon, *The American Irish*, p. 51.

37. William S. Robinson, *"Warrington" Pen Portraits* (Boston, 1877), p. 205.

38. Thomas H. O'Connor, "Irish Votes and Yankee Cotton: The Constitution of 1853," *Proceedings of the Massachusetts Historical Society* 95 (1983), p. 90; Shapiro, "Conservative Dilemma," p. 204.

39. Robinson, *"Warrington" Pen Portraits*, p. 204.

40. *The Pilot*, November 5, 1853.

41. See O'Connor, *Fitzpatrick's Boston*, pp. 91–95, for a discussion of the bishop's political views.

42. *The Pilot*, May 18, 1850.

43. George S. Boutwell, *Reminiscences of Sixty Years in Public Affairs* (New York, 1902), vol. 1, p. 220.

44. *The Pilot*, November 19, 1853.

45. *Daily Commonwealth*, November 22, 1853.

46. Benjamin F. Butler, *Butler's Book* (Boston, 1892), p. 120.

47. See Mulkern, *Know-Nothing Party*, pp. 61–65, for the origins of the American party; Knobel, *Paddy and the Republic*, pp. 134–35.

48. See Mulkern, *Know-Nothing Party*, pp. 83–85, for an analysis of the political impact of the changing party structure in 1854; Knobel, *Paddy and the Republic*, pp. 136–37.

49. William G. Bean, "Party Transformation in Massachusetts, with Special Reference to the Antecedents of Republicanism, 1848–1860" (Ph.D., diss., Harvard University, 1922), p. 293. Also see Knobel, *Paddy and the Republic*, pp. 137–39.

50. John R. Mulkern, "Scandal Behind the Convent Walls: The Know-Nothing Nunnery Committee of 1855," *Historical Journal of Massachusetts* 11 (1983), pp. 22–34; O'Connor, *Fitzpatrick's Boston*, pp. 153–54; Billington, *Protestant Crusade*, pp. 413–15.

51. The idea of getting Catholics to withdraw from local politics was offered by Orestes Brownson, a convert from transcendentalism, and by the young editor of *The Pilot*, Fr. John Roddan, while Bishop Fitzpatrick was away in Europe during the summer of 1854. See Orestes Brownson,, "A Few Words on Native Americanism," *Brownson's Quarterly Review* 2 (July 1854), pp. 339, 341. Also see *Archdiocese of Boston*, vol. 2, p. 371.

52. Billington, *Protestant Crusade*, p. 421.

53. Richard Shaw, *Dagger John: The Unquiet Life and Times of Archbishop John Hughes of New York* (New York, 1977), p. 197.

54. Richard Grozier, "Life and Times of John Bernard Fitzpatrick: Third Roman Catholic Bishop of Boston" (Ph.D. diss., Boston College, 1966), p. 60.

55. Dale Baum, *The Civil War Party System: The Case of Massachusetts, 1848–1876* (Chapel Hill, N.C., 1984), p. 45.

56. Bean, "Puritan versus Celt, 1850–1860," *New England Quarterly* 7 (1934) p. 86.

57. Bean, "Party Transformation," p. 371.

58. O'Connor, *Fitzpatrick's Boston*, pp. 106–8.

59. Ibid., pp. 108–17. See also Raymond Culver, *Horace Mann and Religion in the Massachusetts Public Schools* (New Haven, 1929); Stanley K. Schultz, *The Culture Factory: Boston Public Schools, 1789–1860* (New York, 1973); Michael B. Katz, *The Irony of Early School Reform: Educational Innovation in Mid-Nineteenth Century Massachusetts* (Boston, 1968).

60. For more information on Catholics and slavery, see Madeleine Hooke Rice, *American Catholic Opinion in the Slavery Controversy* (Gloucester, Mass., 1964); Robert Leckie, *American and Catholic* (New York, 1970); John Francis Maxwell, *Slavery and the Catholic Church* (London, 1975).

61. *The Pilot*, April 11, July 11, 1846; November 22, 1856. Also see O'Connor, *Fitzpatrick's Boston*, pp. 165–68.

62. *United States Catholic Intelligencer*, October 1, 1831; *The Pilot*, February 5, 1842. The *Intelligencer* was the new name of Bishop Fenwick's earlier *Jesuit*, until it was renamed a second time as *The Pilot* in 1836.

63. Eric Foner, *Free Soil, Free Labor, Free Men: The Ideology of the Republican Party before the Civil War* (New York, 1970), p. 261.

64. Cited in Rice, *Catholic Opinion*, p. 157.

65. William G. Bean, "An Aspect of Know-Nothingism: The Immigrant and Slavery," *South Atlantic Quarterly* 23 (1924), p. 321. For a description of the excitement over the Anthony Burns episode, see Lawrence Lader, *The Bold Brahmins: New England's War Against Slavery, 1830–1863* (New York, 1961), pp. 155–85; Harold Schwartz, "Fugitive Slave Days in Boston," *New England Quarterly* 27 (1954), pp. 191–212; Samuel Shapiro, "The Rendition of Anthony Burns," *Journal of Negro History* 44 (1959), pp. 34–51.

66. Don E. Fehrenbacher, *The Dred Scott Case: Its Significance in American Law and Politics* (New York, 1978), provides an exhaustive treatment of the case and its historical setting.

67. *The Pilot*, April 11, May 30, 1857.

68. Cited in Bean, "Party Transformation," p. 368, from an editorial in the *The Bee*.

69. *The Pilot*, December 10, 1849. See William F. Hanna, "Abraham Lincoln and the New England Press, 1858–1860" (Ph.D. diss., Boston College, 1980), p. 152, for efforts by the Republicans to woo the Irish.

70. *The Pilot*, November 3, 1860.

71. Ibid.

72. Hanna, "Lincoln," p. 155.

73. *The Herald*, July 19, 1860.

74. *The Pilot*, November 3, 1860.

75. Ibid.

76. Ibid.

77. For statewide election returns, see *Boston Courier*, November 7, 1860. Treatments of the election of 1860 may be found in Emerson D. Fite, *The Presidential Campaign of 1860* (New York, 1911), and Reinhard H. Luthin, *The First Lincoln Campaign* (Cambridge, Mass., 1944).

78. *The Pilot*, January 12, 1861.

79. Ibid.

80. Ibid., February 2, 1861.
81. Ibid., April 27, 1861.
82. Ibid., July 20, 1861.
83. *Boston Post,* June 25, 1861. See William L. Burton, "Irish Regiments in the Union Army: The Massachusetts Experience," *Historical Journal of Massachusetts* 11 (June 1983), pp. 104–15.
84. *The Pilot,* January 17, 1863.
85. *The Pilot,* July 18, September 19, 1863. In the January 24 issue, *The Pilot* maintained that it was "every man's duty" to disagree with Lincoln because he was trying to "destroy the Constitution."
86. Jack Leach, *Conscription in the United States* (Rutland, Vt., 1952); Eugene Murdock, *Patriotism Unlimited: The Civil War Draft and the Bounty System* (New York, 1967); Murdock, *One Million Men: The Civil War Draft in the North* (New York, 1971).
87. Basil Lee, *Discontent in New York City, 1861–1865* (New York, 1943); Irving Weinstein, *July 1863: The Incredible Story of the Bloody New York Draft Riots* (New York, 1952); Adrian Cook, *The Armies of the Streets: The New York City Draft Riots of 1863* (New York, 1974).
88. William F. Hanna, "The Boston Draft Riot," *Civil War History* 36 (September 1990), 262–73.
89. *The Pilot,* June 25, September 3, 1864.
90. Ibid., September 3, October 15, November 5, 1864.
91. Ibid., November 12, November 19, 1864.
92. Ibid., April 15, 1865.
93. James Green and Hugh Donahue, *Boston's Workers: A Labor History* (Boston, 1979), p. 30.
94. Whitehill, *Boston,* p. 127.
95. Charles F. Donovan et al., *A History of Boston College* (Chestnut Hill, Mass., 1990), pp. 52–53; Whitehill, *Boston,* pp. 131–33.
96. See Whitehill, *Boston,* p. 153, for a photograph of steam shovels built at John Souther's South Boston factory loading gravel for the Back Bay landfill.
97. O'Connor, *South Boston,* pp. 62–63.
98. Amos A. Lawrence diary, June 20, 1861, Lawrence Papers, Massachusetts Historical Society. See Francis R. Walsh, "The *Boston Pilot* Reports the Civil War," *Historical Journal of Massachusetts* 9 (June 1981), pp. 5–16.
99. *The Pilot,* March 1, 1862.

CHAPTER FOUR

1. Richard D. Brown, *Massachusetts: A Bicentennial History* (New York, 1978), p. 187; Dale Baum, *The Civil War Party System: The Case of Massachusetts, 1848–1876* (Chapel Hill, N.C., 1984), p. 108.

2. Geoffrey Blodgett, "Yankee Leadership in a Divided City," in *Boston, 1700–1980: The Evolution of Urban Politics*, ed. Ronald Formisano and Constance Burns (Westport, Conn., 1984), pp. 92–93.

3. Cullen, *The Irish in Boston*, pp. 245–49; Green and Donahue, *Boston's Workers*, pp. 50–51.

4. Dale Baum, "The 'Irish Vote' and Party Politics in Massachusetts, 1860–1876," *Civil War History* 26 (1980), pp. 130–31.

5. Thomas N. Brown, *Irish-American Nationalism, 1870–1890* (Philadelphia, 1966), pp. 40–41; Eric Foner, *Politics and Ideology in the Age of the Civil War* (New York, 1980), pp. 153–55. Also see Michael A. Gordon, *The Orange Riots: Irish Political Violence in New York City, 1870 and 1871* (Ithaca, N.Y., 1993) concerning the riots that broke out when Irish Protestants commemorated the 1690 victory of the Battle of the Boyne. Eight persons were killed in the 1870 riots; sixty died in 1871.

6. Dale Baum, *Civil War Party System*, pp. 110-11.

7. Brown, *Irish-American Nationalism*, pp. 40–41.

8. Baum, "The 'Irish Vote,' " p. 131.

9. Ibid., p. 134.

10. *The Pilot*, November 3, 1866.

11. Baum, "The 'Irish Vote,' " p. 112.

12. *The Pilot*, October 26, 1867.

13. Cited in Carl Wittke, *The Irish in America* (Baton Rouge, La., 1956), p. 45.

14. Quoted in Potter, *To the Golden Door*, p. 165.

15. Shannon, *The American Irish*, pp. 28–29.

16. Hasia Diner, *Erin's Daughters in America: Irish Immigrant Women in the Nineteenth Century* (Baltimore, 1983), pp. 60-61.

17. Shannon, *The American Irish*, pp. 37–38.

18. Ibid., p. 37. Also see Diner, *Erin's Daughters*, pp. 60–61.

19. Shannon, *The American Irish*, p. 37.

20. M. Jeanne d'Arc O'Hare, "The Public Career of Patrick Collins" (Ph.D. diss. Boston College, 1959), p. 38.

21. Ibid., pp. 113–26.

22. Michael P. Curran, *The Life of Patrick Collins* (Norwood, Mass., 1906), pp. 32–33.

23. *The Pilot*, June 25, 1870.

24. Cullen, *The Irish in Boston*, pp. 213–16.

25. Ibid., pp. 235–38.

26. *Boston Post*, September 17, 1868.

27. Ibid., October 20, 1868. Also see O'Hare, "Collins," p. 90.

28. Baum, *Civil War Party System*, p. 182; Baum, "The 'Irish Vote,' " p. 138.

29. *The Pilot*, February 7, 1874.

30. Ibid., April 27, 1872.

31. Ibid., February 7, 1874.

32. Ibid.

33. *Boston Globe*, June 27, 1874.

34. Ibid., October 22, 1874; O'Hare, "Collins," p. 113.

35. *The Pilot*, February 7, 1874.

36. *Boston Globe*, November 4, 1874.

37. Curran, *Life of Patrick Collins*, pp. 36–37.

38. *Boston Globe*, September 25, 1875.

39. Patrick Collins, *Charles Francis Adams as Minister to England and an Anti-Know-Nothing* (Boston, 1876), p. 9; O'Hare, "Collins," p. 45.

40. Brown, *Irish-American Nationalism*, p. 138; Cullen, *The Irish in Boston*, pp. 350–51.

41. Margaret Thompson, "Ben Butler versus the Brahmins: Patronage and Politics in Early Gilded Age Massachusetts," *New England Quarterly* 55 (1982), p. 165.

42. Cited in Barbara M. Solomon, *Ancestors and Immigrants: A Changing New England Tradition* (Cambridge, Mass., 1956), pp. 47–48.

43. *Irish World*, October 14, 1876.

44. Cited in Nathan Higgins, *Protestants Against Poverty: Boston's Charities, 1870–1900* (Westport, Conn., 1971), p. 120.

45. Thompson, "Ben Butler versus the Brahmins," p. 185.

46. Dale Baum, "The Massachusetts Voter: Party Loyalty in the Gilded Age," in *Massachusetts in the Gilded Age*, ed. Jack Tager and John Ifkovic (Amherst, Mass., 1985), pp. 50–51.

47. William D. Mallam, "Butlerism in Massachusetts," *New England Quarterly* 33 (1960), p. 206.

48. Brown, *Irish-American Nationalism*, p. 44. "Collins swallowed his pride, worked for the administration, and waited for better days," writes Brown.

49. Wellington Wells, "Political and Governmental Readjustments, 1865–1889," in *Commonwealth History of Massachusetts*, vol. 4, p. 604.

50. Foner, *Politics and Ideology*, pp. 155–57.

51. O'Hare, "Collins," p. 189; Curran, *Life of Patrick Collins*, p. 77.

52. Dale Baum, " 'Noisy but Not Numerous': The Revolt of the Massachusetts Mugwumps," *Historian* 41 (1979), p. 243; Geoffrey Blodgett, *The Gentle Reformers: Massachusetts Democrats in the Cleveland Era* (Cambridge, Mass., 1966), p. 10.

53. Wells, "Political and Governmental Readjustments," p. 606.

54. Baum, " 'Noisy but Not Numerous,' " p. 256.

55. Galvin, "Boston's First Irish Cop," pp. 52–86.

56. James B. Walsh, *The Irish: America's Political Class* (New York, 1976), p. 353.

57. Sam Bass Warner, Jr., *Streetcar Suburbs: The Process of Growth in Boston, 1870–1900* (New York, 1974), pp. 21–23.

58. Jon Teaford, *Unheralded Triumph: City Government in America, 1870–1900* (Baltimore, 1984), pp. 217–25. In chapter 8, "The Triumph of Technology," Teaford describes the many technical innovations that brought "grand achievements" to American cities during the late nineteenth century.

59. Blodgett, "Yankee Leadership in a Divided City," p. 91.

60. Paul Kleppner, "From Party to Factions: The Dissolution of Boston's Majority Party, 1876–1908," in Formisano and Burns, *Boston, 1700–1980*, p. 129.

61. John T. Galvin, "Patrick Maguire: Boston's Last Democratic Boss," *New England Quarterly* 55 (September 1982), pp. 392–97; Cullen, *The Irish in Boston*, pp. 412–13.

62. James M. Bugbee, "The City Government of Boston," *Johns Hopkins Studies in Historical and Political Science*, ed. Herbert B. Adams (Baltimore, 1887), vol. 5, p. 31.

63. Kleppner, "From Party to Factions," pp. 120–21.

64. Ibid., p. 121.

65. Galvin, "Patrick Maguire," pp. 394–95.

66. Blodgett, "Yankee Leadership in a Divided City," pp. 94–95; Lesley Ainley, *Boston Mahatma: Martin Lomasney* (Boston, 1949), p. 27.

67. *Boston Herald*, November 25, 1877.

68. *Boston Evening Transcript*, November 17, 1877.

69. John T. Galvin, "The Dark Ages of Boston Politics," *Proceedings of the Massachusetts Historical Society* 89 (1977), p. 93.

70. Brown, *Massachusetts: A Bicentennial History*, p. 193; Cullen, *The Irish in Boston*, pp. 216–18.

71. *The Republic*, December 8, 1883.

72. *Boston Post*, December 17, 1883.

73. *Boston Evening Transcript*, November 26, 1883.

74. *The Republic*, April 5, 1884.

75. Ray Ginger, *The Age of Excess* (New York, 1975), p. 111.

76. *Boston Globe*, December 7, 1884.

77. *The Republic*, November 29, 1884.

78. *Boston Globe*, December 7, 15, 1884.

79. Ainley, *Boston Mahatma*, pp. 46, 56.

80. Ibid., p. 46.

81. Ibid., p. 14.

82. Teaford, *Unheralded Triumph*, pp. 2–3. Also see Lawrence W. Kennedy, *Planning the City Upon a Hill: Boston Since 1630* (Amherst, Mass., 1992), p. 73.

83. Ainley, *Boston Mahatma*, p. 59.

84. John William Ward, "The Common Weal and the Public Trust," *Forum 350* (John F. Kennedy Library, Boston) (October 21, 1980), pp. 72–73.

85. Ibid., p. 74.

86. See Jack Beatty, *The Rascal King: The Life and Times of James Michael Curley, 1874–1958* (Reading, Mass., 1992) pp. 210–11, 225–26, for examples of the tricks used in Boston political campaigns. Also see Edwin O'Connor, *The Last Hurrah* (Boston, 1956), p. 288. O'Connor's book fictionalizes many famous episodes in campaign strategy.

87. Ainley, *Boston Mahatma*, pp. 86–90.

CHAPTER FIVE

1. *Boston Globe*, January 5, 6, 1885.

2. Hugh O'Brien, *Inaugural Address of Hugh O'Brien, Mayor of Boston, Before the City Council, January 5, 1885* (Boston, 1886).

3. John T. Galvin, "When the Irish Made It to City Hall," *Boston Globe*, December 7, 1984.

4. Teaford, *Unheralded Triumph*, pp. 9–10.

5. Cynthia Zaitzevsky, *Frederick Law Olmsted and the Boston Park System* (Cambridge, Mass., 1982), pp. 41–42. Also see Kennedy, *Planning the City*, pp. 89–97.

6. Galvin, "Patrick Maguire," pp. 399–400.

7. Zaitzevsky, *Olmsted*, pp. 66–67; Kennedy, *Planning the City*, pp. 97–99.

8. Zaitzevsky, *Olmsted*, p. 67.

9. *The Pilot*, December 19, 1885.

10. *The Republic*, December 19, 1885.

11. Cullen, *The Irish in Boston*, p. 218.

12. Brown, *Irish-American Nationalism*, pp. 44–45.

13. Archdiocese of Boston, vol. 3, p. 401. Collins's story, writes the archdiocesan historian, might pass "as a typical saga of a poor immigrant boy who won fame and success."

14. David Montgomery, *Beyond Equality: Labor and the Radical Republicans* (New York, 1967), p. 213.

15. Curran, *Life of Collins*, p. 170.

16. Ibid., p. 228.

17. Ibid., p. 70.

18. Ibid., p. 170.

19. Cullen, *The Irish in Boston*, pp. 207–210.

20. Ibid., p. 210.

21. Ibid., pp. 209–10. Also see Arthur Mann, "Irish Catholic Liberalism," in his *Yankee Reformers in the Urban Age* (New York, 1954), pp. 27–44.

22. Francis R. Walsh, "John Boyle O'Reilly, the *Boston Pilot*, and Irish-American Assimilation, 1870–1890," in *Massachusetts in the Gilded Age*, ed. Jack Tager and John Ifkovic (Amherst, Mass., 1985), pp. 152–54.

23. Warner, *Streetcar Suburbs*, pp. 76–79.

24. O'Connor, *South Boston*, p. 112.

25. Stephan Thernstrom, "Urbanization, Migration, and Social Mobility in Late Nineteenth-Century America," in *American Urban History* 2d ed., ed. Alexander Callow (New York, 1973), p. 401.

26. E. P. Thompson, *The Making of the English Working Class* (New York, 1963), pp. 437–38.

27. Dennis P. Ryan, *Beyond the Ballot Box: A Social History of the Boston Irish, 1845–1917* (Amherst, Mass., 1989), p. 49.

28. O'Connor, *South Boston*, pp. 78–79.

29. Thomas E. Wangler, "Catholic Religious Life in Boston in the Era of Cardinal O'Connell," in *Catholic Boston: Studies in Religion and Community, 1870–1970*, ed. Robert E. Sullivan and James M. O'Toole (Boston, 1985), pp. 240–41.

30. Wangler, "Catholic Religious Life," pp. 250–51; Ryan, *Beyond the Ballot Box*, pp. 49-50.

31. O'Connor, *South Boston*, pp. 80–81.

32. Ibid., p. 80.

33. O'Connor, *Fitzpatrick's Boston*, pp. 233–36.

34. Thomas A. Hendricks, who served as Grover Cleveland's vice president in 1884, was regarded as a stalwart friend of the Irish immigrant. See Ainley, *Boston Mahatma*, p. 21; John T. Galvin, "The Mahatma Called the Shots and Everyone Knew It," *Boston Globe*, June 4, 1990.

35. Ainley, *Boston Mahatma*, p. 13.

36. Ibid., p. 6.

37. Ibid., pp. 8–9, 13.

38. Galvin, "The Mahatma Called the Shots."

39. Doris Kearns Goodwin, *The Fitzgeralds and the Kennedys: An American Saga*, (New York, 1987), pp. 58–72; John Henry Cutler, *"Honey Fitz": Three Steps to the White House* (Indianapolis, 1962), pp. 36–52.

40. Goodwin, *Fitzgeralds and Kennedys*, pp. 96–97; Cutler, *"Honey Fitz,"* pp. 53–56.

41. Goodwin, *Fitzgeralds and Kennedys*, p. 97.

42. Ibid., pp. 98–99; Cutler, *"Honey Fitz,"* pp. 60–68.

43. Goodwin, *Fitzgeralds and Kennedys*, pp. 226–31; Cutler, *"Honey Fitz,"* pp. 72–74.

44. O'Connor, *South Boston*, pp. 88–89.

45. *The Republic*, June 9, 1894.

46. Francis Parkman, *Our Common Schools* (Boston, 1890), pp. 3–4, cited in Solomon, *Ancestors*, p. 43.

47. Solomon, *Ancestors*, pp. 48–49.

48. James Hennesey, *American Catholics: A History of the Roman Catholic Community in the United States* (New York, 1981), p. 182.

49. *Archdiocese of Boston*, vol. 3, pp. 79–85.

50. Solomon, *Ancestors*, pp. 48–49.

51. Ibid., p. 77.

52. Goodwin, *Fitzgeralds and Kennedys*, p. 62.

53. Solomon, *Ancestors*, p. 52.

54. Thomas H. O'Connor, *Bibles, Brahmins, and Bosses: A Short History of Boston*, 3d ed. (Boston, 1991), pp. 155–56.

55. Ibid., pp. 156–62. See James M. O'Toole, " 'The Newer Catholic Races': Ethnic Catholicism in Boston, 1900–1940," *New England Quarterly* 65 (March 1992), pp. 117–34, for a study of the attempts by predominantly Irish-Catholic religious leaders of Boston to meet the demands on their institutions by the influx of new immigrants from central and eastern Europe.

56. Cited in Solomon, *Ancestors*, p. 57.

57. John Higham, "The Mind of a Nativist: Henry F. Bowers and the A.P.A.," *American Quarterly* 4 (1952), pp. 17–23. Higham maintains that Bowers displayed "authentic paranoid tendencies." Also see Humphrey J. Desmond, *The A.P.A. Movement: A Sketch* (Washington, D.C., 1912), pp. 9–10; Gustavus Myers, *History of Bigotry in the United States* (New York, 1943), p. 223.

58. Hennesey, *American Catholics*, pp. 182–83.

59. Desmond, *A.P.A. Sketch*, p. 69; *Archdiocese of Boston*, vol. 3, pp. 140–45.

60. Michael E. Hennessy, *Four Decades of Massachusetts Politics* (Norwood, Mass., 1935), p. 17.

61. Hennesey, *American Catholics*, p. 182.

62. *Boston Globe*, July 5, 6, 1895; *Boston Herald*, July 5, 6, 14, 1895. Also see Blodgett, *Gentle Reformers*, p. 151.

63. *Boston Daily Standard,*, July 5, 1895. The *Standard* was an A.P.A. newspaper that generally ran ten pages in length and carried a great deal of news about city politics.

64. *The Pilot*, July 13, 1895. Also see Walsh, "The *Boston Pilot*," p. 264.

65. Solomon, *Ancestors*, pp. 99–102, 104.

66. Ibid., pp. 111–16.

67. O'Connor, *South Boston*, p. 113.

68. Hennesey, *American Catholics*, pp. 231–32.

69. Paul Kleppner, "From Party to Factions," pp. 117–19.

70. Robert A. Silverman, "Nathan Matthews: The Politics of Reform in Boston, 1890–1910," *New England Quarterly* 50 (March-December 1977), pp. 626–43. Also see Kleppner, "From Party to Factions," p. 123; Constance K. Burns, "The Irony of Progressive Reform: Boston, 1898–1910," *Boston, 1700–1980*, p. 149.

71. Kleppner, "From Party to Factions," p. 123.

72. Ibid., p. 124.

73. Ibid.
74. Ibid., pp. 124–25; Cutler, *"Honey Fitz,"* pp. 69–71.
75. Kleppner, "From Party to Factions," p. 125. Also see Kennedy, *Planning the City,* pp. 104–5.
76. Burns, "Progressive Reform," pp. 136–37.
77. John T. Galvin, "Boston's Eminent Patrick from Ireland," *Boston Globe,* March 17, 1988. Also see O'Hare, "Collins," pp. 251–53.
78. O'Hare, "Collins," p. 255.
79. Ibid., p. 260; Cutler, *"Honey Fitz,"* p. 77.
80. O'Hare, "Collins," pp. 263–64; Kleppner, "From Party to Factions," p. 125.
81. Ainley, *Boston Mahatma,* p. 93.
82. *Boston Herald,* December 13, 1899.
83. *The Republic,* December 16, 1899.
84. *Boston Post,* November 1, 1901.
85. *Boston Herald,* December 11, 1901.
86. O'Hare, "Collins," pp. 267–72.
87. Ainley, *Boston Mahatma,* p. 94.
88. Kleppner, "From Party to Factions," p. 126.
89. Cited by Galvin, "Eminent Patrick."
90. Kleppner, "From Party to Factions," p. 125.
91. Cited by Galvin, "Eminent Patrick."
92. O'Hare, "Collins," p. 289; Galvin, "Eminent Patrick."
93. Curran, *Life of Patrick Collins,* p. 210; O'Hare, "Collins," pp. 289–90.
94. Galvin, "Eminent Patrick."
95. O'Hare, "Collins," p. 290; Galvin, "Eminent Patrick." The monument to Patrick Collins is located on the Commonwealth Avenue Mall between Clarendon and Dartmouth Streets. The granite shaft is topped by a bust of Collins and flanked by two female figures representing Erin and Columbia.
96. *Boston Evening Transcript,* June 22, 1914. Also see Thomas J. Gargan, *Thomas J. Gargan: A Memorial* (Boston, 1910), available at the Boston Athenaeum.
97. Shannon, *The American Irish,* p. 199.

CHAPTER SIX

1. *Boston Herald,* September 15, 1905.
2. Goodwin, *Fitzgeralds and Kennedys,* pp. 21–22, 107; Cutler, *"Honey Fitz,"* pp. 85–86.
3. *Boston Post,* November 9, 13, 1905. Also see Goodwin, *Fitzgeralds and Kennedys,* p. 107.
4. *Boston Globe,* November 16, 1905; Goodwin, *Fitzgeralds and Kennedys,* p. 108; Cutler, *"Honey Fitz,"* pp. 89–92.

5. *Boston Post,* November 17, 1905. See Ainley, *Boston Mahatma,* pp. 96–97; Goodwin, *Fitzgeralds and Kennedys,* p. 109; Cutler, *"Honey Fitz,"* pp. 93–94.

6. *Boston Herald,* December 13, 1905; Goodwin, *Fitzgeralds and Kennedys,* p. 109; Cutler, *"Honey Fitz,"* pp. 95–96.

7. Goodwin, *Fitzgeralds and Kennedys,* pp. 110–13.

8. *Collier's,* November 16, 1907, p. 18, cited in Goodwin, *Fitzgeralds and Kennedys,* p. 125; Cutler, *"Honey Fitz,"* pp. 97–98, 99–100.

9. Cited in Goodwin, *Fitzgeralds and Kennedys,* pp. 115–16.

10. *Boston Journal,* June 1, 1907, cited in Goodwin, *Fitzgeralds and Kennedys,* p. 119.

11. Goodwin, *Fitzgeralds and Kennedys,* pp. 119–20; Cutler, *"Honey Fitz,"* pp. 104–5.

12. *Boston Herald,* December 12, 1905.

13. Cited by Alan Lupo, *Liberty's Chosen Home,* p. 131.

14. Diner, *Erin's Daughters,* p. xiv.

15. Ibid.

16. Ryan, *Beyond the Ballot Box,* p. 50; Diner, *Erin's Daughters,* p. 143.

17. Ryan, *Beyond the Ballot Box,* pp. 51–52.

18. James M. O'Toole, *Militant and Triumphant: William Henry O'Connell and the Catholic Church in Boston, 1859–1944* (Notre Dame, Ind., 1992), p. 130.

19. Ibid., p. 243. Louise Stevenson, "Women Anti-Suffragists in the 1915 Massachusetts Campaign," *New England Quarterly* 52 (March 1979), pp. 80–93, demonstrates the changing social values of the twentieth century that eventually reduced the power of the antisuffragist movement in the Bay State.

20. O'Toole, *Militant and Triumphant,* p. 130.

21. James W. Fraser, "Mayor John F. Fitzgerald and Boston's Schools, 1905–1913," *Historical Journal of Massachusetts* 12 (June 1984), pp. 118–19.

22. Burns, "Progressive Reform," pp. 139–40.

23. Fraser, "Fitzgerald and Boston's Schools," p. 118; Burns, "Progressive Reform," p. 140.

24. Fraser, "Fitzgerald and Boston's Schools," p. 118–19; Burns, "Progressive Reform," p. 143.

25. Beatty, *Rascal King,* pp. 83–84; Cutler, *"Honey Fitz,"* pp. 108–9.

26. Goodwin, *Fitzgeralds and Kennedys,* p. 134, suggests that Fitzgerald thought he might make the Finance Commission a "whitewashing committee" as Boss Tweed had done during a similar investigation in New York. Also see Burns, "Progressive Reform," p. 148.

27. Burns, "Progressive Reform," p. 149; Cutler, *"Honey Fitz,"* pp. 110–12. According to Robert Silverman, "Nathan Matthews," pp. 641–42, Matthews was convinced that the chaotic state of Boston's public affairs was not a failure of democracy but the result of "incompetent, wasteful administration."

28. Goodwin, *Fitzgeralds and Kennedys,* pp. 137–38. During June and July 1909, Mi-

chael Mitchell and Thomas Maher, head of a firm that sold flagstones to the city, stood trial in Superior Court for conspiracy to defraud the city. Both men were found guilty and were sentenced to a year at the House of Correction on Deer Island. See ibid., pp. 151–73. Also see Cutler, *"Honey Fitz,"* pp. 102–4.

29. Joseph F. Dinneen, *The Purple Shamrock: The Hon. James Michael Curley of Boston* (New York, 1949), p. 71. Also see Goodwin, *Fitzgeralds and Kennedys*, p. 150; Cutler, *"Honey Fitz,"* pp. 118–19.

30. Burns, "Progressive Reform," pp. 150–51.

31. Goodwin, *Fitzgeralds and Kennedys*, pp. 191–92; See Henry Greenleaf Pearson, *Son of New England: James Jackson Storrow* (Boston, 1930), for a full-length biography of Storrow.

32. Goodwin, *Fitzgeralds and Kennedys*, pp. 193–94; Cutler, *"Honey Fitz,"* pp. 122–26.

33. Goodwin, *Fitzgeralds and Kennedys*, pp. 195–96; Cutler, *"Honey Fitz,"* p. 82. Cutler insists that close friends did not use the nickname "Honey Fitz." Friends and enemies alike, he says, referred to Fitzgerald as "Fitzie" or "Little Johnny Fitz." Cutler agrees, however, that in later life Fitzgerald was widely known as "Honey Fitz."

34. *Boston Post,* January 12, 1910.

35. Cutler, *"Honey Fitz,"* pp. 142–43.

36. Beatty, *Rascal King,* pp. 37–47; Dinneen, *Purple Shamrock,* pp. 21–29.

37. Beatty, *Rascal King,* pp. 51–69; Dinneen, *Purple Shamrock,* pp. 31–44.

38. Beatty, *Rascal King,* pp. 45–51; Cutler, *"Honey Fitz,"* pp. 184–86.

39. E. P. Thompson, *English Working Class,* pp. 436–37.

40. Beatty, *Rascal King,* pp. 89–91.

41. Ibid., pp. 114–17; Dinneen, *Purple Shamrock,* pp. 74–75, 80–83.

42. James Michael Curley, *I'd Do It Again: A Record of All My Uproarious Years* (Englewood Cliffs, N.J., 1957), pp. 112–14.

43. Beatty, *Rascal King,* p. 83.

44. *Boston Herald,* November 10, 1913.

45. *Boston Evening Transcript,* December 8, 1913; Cutler, *"Honey Fitz,"* p. 194.

46. Goodwin, *Fitzgeralds and Kennedys*, pp. 244–52; Beatty, *Rascal King,* pp. 136–38. Also see Peter Collier and David Horowitz, *The Kennedys: An American Drama* (New York, 1984), p. 37.

47. *Boston Globe,* December 9, 13, 31, 1913; *Boston Journal,* December 18, 1913; *Boston Herald,* December 18, 1913.

48. *Boston Journal,* December 19, 22, 1913.

49. Ibid., December 22, 1913.

50. Ibid.

51. *Boston Record,* December 29, 1913.

52. *Boston Post,* January 6, 1914.

53. *Boston Journal,* January 7, 1914.

54. *Boston Herald,* January 9, 1914.

55. *Boston Globe,* January 14, 1914.

56. Beatty, *Rascal King,* pp. 151–54.

57. Curley, *I'd Do It Again,* p. 36.

58. Cited in Beatty, *Rascal King,* pp. 170–71. Curley's statements were made at a dinner at the Boston City Club in response to derogatory remarks by John Farwell Moors, a banker, a member of the Fin Com, and a charter member of the Immigration Restriction League.

59. Cutler, *"Honey Fitz,"* p. 204.

60. Beatty, *Rascal King,* pp. 156–58.

61. "For the first time, Boston had one boss who had consolidated his power by handing out jobs and making himself personally accessible to everyone from dowager to ragtag and bobtail," wrote John Cutler, *"Honey Fitz,"* p. 199.

62. Cited in Cutler, *"Honey Fitz,"* p. 183.

63. Beatty, *Rascal King,* pp. 200–201.

64. *Boston Globe,* October 21, 1918.

65. Beatty, *Rascal King,* pp. 201–202.

66. Ibid.

67. Ibid., pp. 204–205.

68. Ibid., p. 211; Cutler, *"Honey Fitz,"* pp. 216–17.

69. *Boston Globe,* September 8, 9, 1919. See Francis Russell, *City in Terror: 1919, the Boston Police Strike* (New York, 1975) for the definitive study of the strike. Also see Green and Donahue, *Boston's Workers,* pp. 96–99 for a general labor background of the postwar period.

70. *Boston Globe,* September 11, 12, 13, 1918; Russell *City in Terror,* pp. 161–63.

71. Russell, *City in Terror,* pp. 195–96. Russell cites numerous letters to Police Commissioner Curtis protesting the number of Irishmen on the police force and urging that they be replaced by reliable Yankees.

72. Beatty, *Rascal King,* pp. 206–7. See Francis Russell, *The Knave of Boston & Other Ambiguous Massachusetts Characters* (Boston, 1987), pp. 69–84, for a treatment of Peters's sexual peculiarities in a chapter titled "The Mayor and the Nymphet."

73. Beatty, *Rascal King,* p. 219.

74. Ibid., pp. 221–28.

75. Nichols received 64,492 votes. Teddy Glynn came in second with 42,687 votes; former U.S. Representative Joseph O'Neil ran third with 31,888; Dan Coakley was fourth with 20,144 votes. See John T. Galvin, "The 1925 Campaign for Mayor Was a Four-Ring Circus," *Boston Sunday Globe,* August 21, 1983.

76. Beatty, *Rascal King,* p. 262; Cutler, *"Honey Fitz,"* pp. 240–42.

77. Paula M. Kane, *Separatism and Subculture: Boston Catholicism, 1900–1920* (Chapel Hill, 1994). Also see *Archdiocese of Boston*, vol. 3; Melville, *Cheverus;* O'Connor, *Fitzpatrick's Boston.*

78. Dorothy Wayman, *Cardinal O'Connell of Boston: A Biography of William Henry O'Connell, 1859–1944* (New York, 1955), has been updated by O'Toole, *Militant and Triumphant.*

79. Cited in O'Toole, *Militant and Triumphant*, p. 121. Also see Beatty, *Rascal King*, pp. 103–7.

80. Kane, *Separatism and Subculture*, p. 76.

81. O'Toole, *Militant and Triumphant*, pp. 237–38. Also see James W. Sanders, "Catholics and the School Question in Boston: The Cardinal O'Connell Years," in *Catholic Boston: Studies in Religion and Community, 1870–1970*, ed. Robert E. Sullivan and James M. O'Toole (Boston, 1985), pp. 121–69.

82. O'Toole, *Militant and Triumphant*, pp. 242–44.

83. Wangler, "Catholic Religious Life," pp. 254–56.

84. O'Toole, *Militant and Triumphant*, pp. 229–31.

85. Beatty, *Rascal King*, p. 107.

86. Dinneen, *Purple Shamrock*, pp. 160–63; Cutler, *"Honey Fitz,"* pp. 191–93.

87. Charles H. Trout, *Boston, the Great Depression, and the New Deal* (New York, 1977), pp. 50–52; Beatty, *Rascal King*, pp. 269–70; Curley, *I'd Do It Again*, pp. 246–48.

88. Trout, *Great Depression*, pp. 50–52.

89. Steven P. Erie, *Rainbow's End: Irish-Americans and the Dilemma of Urban Machine Politics, 1840-1985* (Berkeley, 1988), p. 117; Dinneen, *Purple Shamrock*, pp. 227–30.

90. Trout, *Great Depression*, pp. 155–56, 161–62, 171–72; Erie, *Rainbow's End*, pp. 110–11.

91. Trout, *Great Depression*, pp. 191–93; Beatty, *Rascal King*, pp. 368–70. Also see John F. Stack, Jr., *International Conflict in an American City: Boston's Irish, Italians, and Jews, 1934–1944* (Westport, Conn., 1979); W. Lloyd Warner and Leo Srole, *The Social Systems of American Ethnic Groups* (New Haven, 1954), pp. 96–98.

92. Curley, *I'd Do It Again*, pp. 246, 250–51.

93. Dinneen, *Purple Shamrock*, p. 210.

94. Green and Donahue, *Boston's Workers*, p. 106; Beatty, *Rascal King*, p. 366.

95. Shannon, *The American Irish*, pp. 295–96.

96. Ibid., pp. 300–305.

97. Ibid., pp. 310–13.

98. O'Toole, *Militant and Triumphant*, p. 138.

99. Solomon, *Ancestors*, pp. 17–20, 37–41.

100. Theodore H. White, *In Search of History* (New York, 1978), pp. 46–47; Nat Hen-

toff, *Boston Boy: A Memoir* (New York, 1986), pp. 20, 21, 68. Both books provide first-hand accounts of young Jewish boys growing up in the hostile environment of Irish-dominated Dorchester.

101. Beatty, *Rascal King*, p. 395.
102. Curley, *I'd Do It Again*, pp. 225–26; Charles Trout, "Curley of Boston: The Search for Irish Legitimacy," in Formisano and Burns, *Boston, 1700–1980*, p. 181.
103. Frederic Cople Jaher, "The Boston Brahmin in the Age of Industrial Capitalism," in *The Age of Industrial Capitalism in America*, ed. F. C. Jaher (New York, 1968).
104. Curley, *I'd Do It Again*, pp. 220–21.
105. Murray Levin, *The Alienated Voter: Politics in Boston* (New York, 1960), pp. 58–75.
106. Beatty, *Rascal King*, pp. 405–15. For a detailed study of Tobin's career, see Vincent A. Lapomarda, "Maurice Joseph Tobin, 1901–1953: A Political Profile and an Edition of Selected Public Papers" (Ph.D. diss., Boston University, 1968), pp. 38–39.
107. Beatty, *Rascal King*, pp. 414–15; Dinneen, *Purple Shamrock*, pp. 150–251.
108. *Boston Post*, November 2, 1941; Lapomarda, "Maurice Tobin," pp. 52–53.

CHAPTER SEVEN

1. Lapomarda, "Maurice Tobin," pp. 58–60. Also see Alan Lupo, "Beyond V-J Day," *Boston Globe Magazine*, August 11, 1985.
2. The charges against Curley arose from the questionable activities of a wartime consulting firm called Engineers' Group Incorporated. Curley had unwisely allowed this company to use his name. Curley, *I'd Do It Again*, pp. 325–32; Beatty, *Rascal King*, pp. 474–75; Dinneen, *Purple Shamrock*, pp. 296–98.
3. John H. Mollenkopf, *The Contested City* (Princeton, N.J., 1983), pp. 142–44; Robert C. Estall, *New England: A Study in Industrial Adjustment* (New York, 1966), pp. 86–103; National Planning Association, *The Economic State of New England* (New Haven, 1954), pp. 340–41.
4. *Boston Globe*, November 28, 29, 1947; Curley, *I'd Do It Again*, pp. 335–36; Beatty, *Rascal King*, pp. 480–82.
5. Thomas H. O'Connor, *Building a New Boston: Politics and Urban Renewal, 1950–1970* (Boston, 1993), pp. 23–24. The account of Hynes's decision to run against Curley is based on information from Hynes's children.
6. *Boston Globe*, November 9, 1949; Curley, *I'd Do It Again*, pp. 337–39; Beatty, *Rascal King*, pp. 490–96; O'Connor, *New Boston*, pp. 26–28.
7. Curley, *I'd Do It Again*, p. 335; E. O'Connor, *The Last Hurrah*, p. 329. "What really did the job, sport, wasn't McCluskey, or Garvey, or Cass or Amos Force," O'Connor has a reporter explain to Skeffington's nephew after his uncle's defeat. "All you have to remember is one name: Roosevelt."
8. See Steven P. Erie, *Rainbow's End*, for an analysis of the changing role of Irish Americans in big-city politics.

9. Beatty's *Rascal King* provides an accurate and compassionate study of the numerous personal tragedies that plagued Curley throughout his life.

10. Cutler, *"Honey Fitz,"* p. 181.

11. Mollenkopf, *The Contested City*, p. 149. Also see Lupo, *Liberty's Chosen Home*, p. 86.

12. Curley, *I'd Do It Again*, p. 462.

13. O'Connor, *New Boston*, pp. 35–36.

14. Ibid., pp. 37–42. Unfortunately, there is no biography of John B. Hynes, and to date there is no collection of his official documents or personal papers.

15. Ibid., p. 42.

16. Ibid.

17. O'Connor, *Bibles, Brahmins, and Bosses*, pp. 198–200. Shannon, *The American Irish*, p. 431.

18. In his two contests for the U.S. Senate, Kennedy had made it a point to entrust his Boston campaigns to state senator John E. Powers of South Boston. In 1959, Kennedy loyally endorsed Powers for mayor, but saw him defeated by John F. Collins.

19. O'Connor, *Bibles, Brahmins, and Bosses*, pp. 202–3; idem, *South Boston*, p. 202.

20. James M. O'Toole, "Prelates and Politicos," in *Catholic Boston: Studies in Religion and Community, 1870–1970*, ed. Robert E. Sullivan and James M. O'Toole (Boston, 1985), pp. 57–62.

21. Ryan, *Beyond the Ballot Box*, pp. 83–100.

22. Shannon, *The American Irish*, p. 187.

23. Teaford, *Unheralded Triumph*, pp. 132–33.

24. Shannon, *The American Irish*, p. 186; John Gunther, *Inside USA* (New York, 1946), p. 512.

25. Mark Gelfand, *A Nation of Cities: The Federal Government and Urban America, 1933–1965* (New York, 1975), pp. 106–7; Erie, *Rainbow's End*, pp. 145–50; Mollenkopf, *The Contested City*, pp. 139–80.

26. O'Connor, *New Boston*, pp. 98–107, 120–25. Hynes first outlined his vision of a "New Boston" in an address at the first Citizen Seminar at Boston College on October 26, 1954. He called for a Back Bay Center, a Convention Center, a Government Center, a World Trade Center, and a second harbor tunnel. See ibid., pp. 106–7.

27. See Herbert Gans, *The Urban Villagers: Group and Class in the Life of Italian-Americans* (New York, 1962), for a classic sociological study of the West End. For a valuable collection of maps, graphs, illustrations, and scholarly essays, see Sean Fisher and Carolyn Hughes, eds., *The Last Tenement: Confronting Community and Urban Renewal in Boston's West End* (Boston, 1992). Also see O'Connor, *New Boston*, pp. 125–39; and Kennedy, *Planning the City*, pp. 162–63.

28. Whitehill, *Boston*, p. 202.
29. O'Connor, *New Boston*, p. 44, quoting Ephron Catlin of the First National Bank of Boston.
30. Ibid., pp. 150–51.
31. Ibid., pp. 151–52. Although there is currently no biography of John Collins, the official correspondence and personal papers of the former mayor can be found in the Rare Book Room of the Boston Public Library.
32. John Collins, personal interview, February 19, 1991.
33. See Levin, *The Alienated Voter*, for a classic study of the 1959 campaign. Professor Levin and Professor George Blackwood of Boston University conducted some 500 interviews within three days of the election. They concluded that political alienation was a major factor in the outcome of the campaign. Also see O'Connor, *New Boston*, pp. 150–61, for an account of the 1959 election.
34. Harold D. Hodgkinson, "Miracle in Boston," *Proceedings of the Massachusetts Historical Society*, 84 (1972), pp. 75–76. Also see O'Connor, *New Boston*, p. 192. See Jack Tager, "Urban Renewal in Boston," *Historical Journal of Massachusetts* 21 (Winter 1993), pp. 1–32 for an excellent analysis of the role played by municipal entrepreneurs and the urban elite in the renewal of Boston.
35. See O'Connor, *New Boston*, pp. 172 ff, for a description of the major features of Mayor Collins's urban renewal program in Boston. Also see Whitehill, *Boston*, pp. 200–239 for an overview of the changes in Boston's architecture during the 1960s.
36. O'Connor, *New Boston*, pp. 147, 166–68.
37. John Strahinich, "Only Irish Need Apply," *Boston Magazine*, March 1993, pp. 73–74.
38. Blodgett, "Yankee Leadership in a Divided City," pp. 105–6.
39. Beatty, *Rascal King*, p. 485.
40. O'Connor, *New Boston*, pp. 61–63.
41. Tilo Schabert, *Boston Politics: The Creativity of Power* (Berlin, 1989), p. 133, n. 53.
42. O'Connor, *New Boston*, pp. 214–16.
43. William S. Ellis, "Breaking New Ground: Boston," *National Geographic*, July 1994, p. 7.
44. O'Connor, *New Boston*, pp. 216–24.
45. O'Connor, *Bibles, Brahmins, and Bosses*, pp. 229–30.
46. O'Connor, *New Boston*, pp. 234–35.
47. O'Connor, *Bibles, Brahmins, and Bosses*, pp. 230–31.
48. James O. Horton and Lois E. Horton, *Black Bostonians: Family Life and Community Struggle in the Antebellum North* (New York, 1979). This is a valuable survey of the living conditions of black citizens of Boston before the Civil War.
49. Amanda V. Houston, "Beneath the El," *Boston College Magazine* (Summer 1988),

pp. 20–25. Houston recounts the personal experiences of a young black woman growing up in the South End during the 1930s. Also see Ronald Bailey et al., *Lower Roxbury: A Community of Treasures in the City of Boston* (Boston, 1993), pp. 9–19, for an anecdotal description of life in the pre–World War II Roxbury community.

50. Hillel Levine and Lawrence Harmon, *The Death of an American Jewish Community: A Tragedy of Good Intentions* (New York, 1992), pp. 13–23.

51. See J. Anthony Lukas, *Common Ground: A Turbulent Decade in the Lives of Three American Families* (New York, 1985), pp. 57–62, for an admirable summary of the changing nature of Boston's black population over the years.

52. O'Connor, *New Boston*, pp. 224–25. Also see Mel King, *Chain of Change: Struggles for Black Community Development* (Boston, 1981), for an account of the changing character of the South End by a young community activist. Also see Bailey, et al. *Lower Roxbury*, p. 21, for the community's initial reaction to Logue and the BRA.

53. Recollections of the celebrated black artist Allan Rohan Crite, a lifelong resident of the South End, as quoted in the *Boston Globe*, January 23, 1991. Also see Bailey et al., *Lower Roxbury*, pp. 21–22.

54. Quoted in Bailey et al., *Lower Roxbury*, p. 40. Also see O'Connor, *New Boston*, p. 294.

55. Bailey et al., *Lower Roxbury*, pp. 29–38. Also see O'Connor, *Bibles, Brahmins, and Bosses*, p. 216.

56. *Bay State Banner*, February 5, March 12, 1966. See Bailey et al., *Lower Roxbury*, pp. 28–29, for other headlines from the *Bay State Banner* expressing opposition to BRA programs.

57. O'Connor, *New Boston*, p . 237; Bailey et al., *Lower Roxbury*, pp. 28–29.

58. O'Connor, *New Boston*, pp. 257–60.

59. O'Connor, *Bibles, Brahmins, and Bosses*, pp. 209–10.

60. Robert Healy, "Collins Leaves a New Boston," *Boston Globe*, December 29, 1967.

61. O'Connor, *New Boston*, p. 178. Also see Jane Jacobs, *The Death and Life of Great American Cities* (New York, 1961), pp. 4, 21–23, for the critical reactions of a professional planner who argued that urban diversity and vitality were being destroyed by modern city planners.

62. O'Connor, *New Boston*, p. 186. It was Walter Muir Whitehill (*Boston*, p. 208) who described the new City Hall has having "Mycenaean or Aztec overtones."

CHAPTER EIGHT

1. Although Frances Curtis announced herself as a candidate in Boston's 1925 mayoral contest, she did not get her name on the ballot because she failed to get the required number of signatures. See chapter 6, p. 195.

2. O'Connor, *South Boston*, pp. 211–12; O'Connor, *New Boston*, pp. 261–62. Also see Jon Teaford, *The Rough Road to Renaissance: Urban Revitalization in America, 1940–1984* (Baltimore, 1990). Teaford makes the interesting observation that in 1967 two other women followed Hicks's example. Alfreda Slominsk of Buffalo and Mary Beck of Detroit also ran for the office of mayor—and also lost.

3. O'Connor, *New Boston*, pp. 260-61.

4. Lukas, *Common Ground*, p. 590; Alan Lupo, *Liberty's Chosen Home*, pp. 73–79.

5. Lukas, *Common Ground*, pp. 35–41, 140–41; Lupo, *Liberty's Chosen Home*, pp. 79–84.

6. "Kevin White: Boston's Next Mayor?" *Bay State Banner*, November 2, 1967. Also see George V. Higgins, *Style Versus Substance: Boston, Kevin White, and the Politics of Illusion* (New York, 1984), pp. 65–68; O'Connor, *New Boston*, p. 262.

7. Higgins, *Style Versus Substance*, pp. 71–73, 76, 101.

8. Ibid., pp. 103–4.

9. O'Connor, *Bibles, Brahmins, and Bosses*, p. 218; O'Connor, *New Boston*, pp. 262–63; Higgins, *Style Versus Substance*, pp. 106–8.

10. O'Connor, *New Boston*, pp. 268–69.

11. Schabert, *Boston Politics*, pp. 222, 228. According to Schabert, White felt the council threatened the stability of his office and interfered with his freedom to form his own government.

12. Mollenkopf, *The Contested City*, p. 207; O'Connor, *New Boston*, pp. 267–68.

13. O'Connor, *New Boston*, p. 268.

14. Ibid., pp. 279–80. George V. Higgins states that, during the second campaign against Hicks in 1971, at least one-quarter of White's four thousand "volunteers" were on the city payroll. See Higgins, *Style Versus Substance*, pp. 134–35.

15. O'Connor, *Bibles, Brahmins, and Bosses*, pp. 222–23; O'Connor, *New Boston*, pp. 281–82.

16. See Lukas, *Common Ground*, pp. 53–60, for an excellent summary of the growth and development of Boston's black population. Also see Ronald P. Formisano, *Boston Against Busing: Race, Class, and Ethnicity in the 1960s and 1970s* (Chapel Hill, N.C., 1991), pp. 25–28, for a scholarly, well-balanced, and insightful treatment of the busing controversy.

17. Formisano, *Boston Against Busing*, pp. 28–29.

18. Ibid., pp. 30–33, 44–46; Lukas, *Common Ground*, pp. 9–10.

19. Formisano, *Boston Against Busing*, pp. 49–54; Lukas, *Common Ground*, pp. 218–19; Higgins, *Style Versus Substance*, pp. 151–52.

20. Formisano, *Boston Against Busing*, pp. 66–69; Lukas, *Common Ground*, pp. 238–39; Higgins, *Style Versus Substance*, pp. 152–54.

21. See Lupo, *Liberty's Chosen Home*, for a passionate, hour-by-hour account of the busing crisis, written by a liberal Boston journalist from the vantage point of Mayor White and the City Hall administration.

22. O'Connor, *South Boston*, pp. 216–17.

23. Formisano, *Boston Against Busing*, pp. 69–70; Lukas, *Common Ground*, pp. 116–21. Also see Jon Hillson, *The Battle of Boston* (New York, 1977). Hillson was a black journalist and an observer for the NAACP in Charlestown and South Boston during the busing crisis.

24. O'Connor, *South Boston*, pp. 218–19.

25. John Kifner, "The Men in the Middle," *New York Times Magazine*, September 12, 1976, for a perceptive analysis of the conflicting loyalties of Irish-Catholic Boston policemen during the busing crisis.

26. See Formisano, *Boston Against Busing*, pp. 75–78, 81–83, for an account of the violence attending the opening of school during the "Battle of Boston." Also see Ione Malloy, *Southie Won't Go: A Teacher's Diary of the Desegregation of South Boston High School* (Urbana, Ill., 1986), for a sensitive, day-by-day account of what went on in the classrooms and corridors of South Boston High School. See Pamela Bullard and Judith Stoia, *The Hardest Lesson: Personal Accounts of a School Desegregation Crisis* (Boston, 1980), for thirteen personal accounts of the busing crisis by students, parents, and teachers.

27. Formisano, *Boston Against Busing*, pp. 98–101. Also see J. Michael Ross and William M. Berg, *"I Respectfully Disagree with the Judge's Order": The Boston School Desegregation Controversy* (Washington, D.C., 1981), pp. 112–23.

28. Formisano, *Boston Against Busing*, pp. 70–71, 158–62; O'Connor, *South Boston*, pp. 220–21.

29. O'Connor, *South Boston*, pp. 223–25. See Formisano, *Boston Against Busing*, pp. 176–79, on the issue of class in the busing crisis and pp. 190–93 on the sense of powerlessness among the residents of the working-class neighborhoods. See William A. Henry III, "Un-Common Ground," *Boston Magazine*, October 1986, pp. 204, for an exploration of the social and sexual aspects of forced busing in Boston. Also see Richard J. Meister, ed., *Race and Ethnicity in Modern America* (Lexington, Mass., 1974), pp. 180–81.

30. David Mehegan, "What Makes Southie Proud," *Boston Globe Magazine*, January 3, 1982, p. 12.

31. O'Connor, *South Boston*, pp. 218–19.

32. Formisano, *Boston Against Busing*, p. 111.

33. O'Connor, *Bibles, Brahmins, and Bosses*, pp. 228–29.

34. Ibid., pp. 230–31.

35. Higgins, *Style Versus Substance*, pp. 149–50, 212–13; O'Connor, *New Boston*, p. 272.

36. Higgins, *Style Versus Substance*, pp. 174–76.

37. Ibid., pp. 147–148, 203–4; O'Connor, *Bibles, Brahmins, and Bosses*, pp. 231–32.

38. Higgins, *Style Versus Substance*, pp. 196–200; O'Connor, *Bibles, Brahmins, and Bosses*, p. 232.

39. Higgins, *Style Versus Substance*, pp. 201–4; O'Connor, *Bibles, Brahmins, and Bosses*, pp. 232–33.
40. Higgins, *Style Versus Substance*, pp. 221–26, 232–35; O'Connor, *Bibles, Brahmins, and Bosses*, p. 233.
41. O'Connor, *South Boston*, pp. 234–35.
42. Bailey et al., *Lower Roxbury*, p. 60; Robert C. Hayden, *African-Americans in Boston: More than 350 Years* (Boston, 1991), p. 101.
43. O'Connor, *Bibles, Brahmins, and Bosses*, pp. 234–35.
44. David Mehegan, "The New Bostonians," *Boston Globe Magazine*, January 24, 1989.
45. Peter S. Canellos, "Transformations," *Boston Globe Magazine*, September 12, 1993.
46. Bureau of the Census, prepared by Center for Labor Market Studies, Northeastern University and Boston Foundation. Cited in *Boston Globe Magazine*, September 12, 1993, p. 25.
47. O'Connor, *South Boston*, p. 232. Also see *The Flynn Years: A Progress Report on Boston and Its Neighborhoods, 1984–1993* (Boston, 1993), a booklet produced by the Flynn Committee, outlining the accomplishments of the Flynn administration. The booklet was produced after Flynn had resigned as mayor in 1993 to take the position of United States ambassador to the Vatican.
48. O'Connor, *South Boston*, p. 232.
49. The poll was conducted for the *Boston Globe* by Professors Garry Owen and Peter Lemieux. Telephone interviews were conducted from February 22 to March 1, 1987, with about one hundred adults in each of thirteen Boston neighborhoods.
50. *Boston Globe*, February 1, 1987.
51. Cited in Flynn Committee, *The Flynn Years*, p. 12.
52. Ibid., p. 18.
53. *Patriot Ledger*, November 21, 1987.
54. Flynn Committee, *The Flynn Years*, p. 9.
55. Ibid., p. 25.
56. See ibid., pp. 4–5, for photographs showing Flynn in action.
57. Ibid., pp. 13–15.
58. Ibid., p. 35.
59. *New York Times*, December 13, 1987; O'Connor, *South Boston*, p. 241.
60. Andrew Blake, "South Boston Sends Its Mayor a Message," *Boston Globe*, November 4, 1987.
61. E. O'Connor, *The Last Hurrah*, p. 10; *Boston Globe*, November 5, 1987; O'Connor, *South Boston*, p. 242.
62. *Boston Globe*, January 25, 1988; *Patriot Ledger*, January 25, 1988; O'Connor, *South Boston*, p. 243–44.
63. *Patriot Ledger*, January 15, 1988; O'Connor, *South Boston*, p. 243.
64. Jack Tager, "The Massachusetts Miracle," *Historical Journal of Massachusetts* 19

(Summer 1991), pp. 111–32. Tager surveys the period from the late 1970s to 1988, when the Massachusetts economy expanded at a "miraculous rate."

65. Alan Lupo, "Still Yearning for the Great Society," *Boston Sunday Globe*, January 30, 1994.

66. Flynn Committee, *The Flynn Years*, p. 19.

67. Curtis Wilkie, "Behind Flynn's Decision," *Boston Globe*, August 16, 1993.

68. Martin F. Nolan, "Ray Flynn: Revolutionary," *Boston Sunday Globe*, March 21, 1993, Focus section. In his years as mayor of Boston, writes Nolan, Flynn banished "the creative uses of hate that had so often animated city politics."

69. John Ellis, "The Unraveling of a Candidate," *Boston Globe*, April 26, 1994.

CONCLUSION

1. Martin F. Nolan, "Exit the Irish: A Hushed Last Hurrah," *Boston Globe*, November 3, 1993.

2. Thomas M. Menino, Inaugural Speech, January 18, 1995, Office of the Mayor, City Hall, Boston, Massachusetts.

3. John Powers, "Invisible Voters," *Boston Globe Magazine*, August 1, 1993, pp. 16–18.

4. Lukas, "Melting Pot or Mulligan Stew?" pp. 41–53.

5. Ruth Batson, "Scapegoating Judge Garrity Requires Selective Memory," *Boston Sunday Globe*, May 1, 1994.

6. William M. Bulger, "Twenty Years After Busing, the Damage Remains," *Boston Globe*, April 22, 1994.

7. Cited by William V. Shannon, "Shamrocks and Shillelaghs: The Phenomenon of Ethnic Mayors in Boston Politics," *Forum 350* (John F. Kennedy Library, Boston) (September 16, 1980), pp. 1–14.

8. Lukas, *Common Ground*, p. 375. In chapter 20, "The Cardinal," Lukas provides a perceptive and accurate contrast between the outgoing Cardinal Cushing and his successor, Cardinal Medeiros.

BIBLIOGRAPHY

❧

Adams, William. *Ireland and Irish Immigration to the New World from 1815 to the Famine*. New Haven, 1932.

Ainley, Lesley. *Boston Mahatma: Martin Lomasney*. Boston, 1949.

Ames, Seth, ed. *The Works of Fisher Ames*. 2 vols. Boston, 1854.

Bailey, Ronald, et al. *Lower Roxbury: A Community of Treasures in the City of Boston*. Boston, 1993.

Banner, James M. *To the Hartford Convention: The Federalists and the Origins of Party Politics in Massachusetts*. New York, 1970.

Barrett, J. R. "Why Paddy Drank: The Social Importance of Whiskey in Pre-Famine Ireland." *Journal of Popular Culture* 11 (1977), pp. 155–66.

Baum, Dale. *The Civil War Party System: The Case of Massachusetts, 1848–1876*. Chapel Hill, N.C., 1984.

———. "The 'Irish Vote' and Party Politics in Massachusetts, 1860–1876." *Civil War History* 26 (1980), pp. 117–41.

———. "The Massachusetts Voter: Party Loyalty in the Gilded Age." In *Massachusetts in the Gilded Age*, ed. Jack Tager and John Ifkovic. Amherst, Mass., 1985.

———. " 'Noisy but Not Numerous': The Revolt of the Massachusetts Mugwumps." *Historian* 41 (1979), pp. 241–56.

Beals, Carleton. *Brass Knuckle Crusade: The Great Know-Nothing Conspiracy, 1820–1860*. New York, 1960.

Bean, William G. "An Aspect of Know-Nothingism: The Immigrant and Slavery." *South Atlantic Quarterly* 23 (1924).

———. "Party Transformation in Massachusetts, with Special Reference to the Antecedents of Republicanism, 1848–1860." Ph.D. diss., Harvard University, 1922.

———. "Puritan versus Celt, 1850–1860." *New England Quarterly* 7 (1934), pp. 81–92.

Beatty, Jack. *The Rascal King: The Life and Times of James Michael Curley, 1874–1958*. Reading, Mass., 1992.

Beecher, Henry Ward. *A Plea for the West*. Cincinnati, 1835.

Bennett, David H. *The Path of Fear from Nativist Movements to the New Right in American History*. Chapel Hill, N.C., 1988.

Billington, Ray Allen. *The Protestant Crusade, 1800–1860*. New York, 1938.

Blodgett, Geoffrey. *The Gentle Reformers: Massachusetts Democrats in the Cleveland Era*. Cambridge, Mass., 1966.

———. "Yankee Leadership in a Divided City." In *Boston, 1700–1980: The Evolution of Urban Politics,* ed. Ronald Formisano and Constance Burns. Westport, Conn., 1984.

Bottigheimer, Karl. *Ireland and the Irish: A Short History.* New York, 1982.

Boutwell, George S. *Reminiscences of Sixty Years in Public Affairs.* 2 vols. New York, 1902.

Bridenbaugh, Carl. *Cities in the Wilderness: Urban Life in America, 1625–1742.* New York, 1938.

———. *Cities in Revolt: Urban Life in America, 1743–1776.* New York, 1955.

Brown, Richard D. *Massachusetts: A Bicentennial History.* New York, 1978.

Brown, Roger H *The Republic in Peril: 1812.* New York, 1971.

Brown, Thomas N. *Irish-American Nationalism, 1870–1890.* Philadelphia, 1966.

Bugbee, James M. "The City Government of Boston." *Johns Hopkins Studies in Historical and Political Science,* ed. Herbert B. Adams. Baltimore, 1887, vol. V.

Bullard, Pamela, and Judith Stoia. *The Hardest Lesson: Personal Accounts of a School Desegregation Crisis.* Boston, 1980.

Burns, Constance K. "The Irony of Progressive Reform: Boston, 1898–1910." In *Boston, 1700–1980: The Evolution of Urban Politics,* ed. Ronald Formisano and Constance Burns. Westport, Conn., 1984.

Burton, William L. "Irish Regiments in the Union Army: The Massachusetts Experience." *Historical Journal of Massachusetts* (June 1983), pp. 104–15.

Butler, Benjamin F. *Butler's Book.* Boston, 1892.

Canellos, Peter S. "Transformations." *Boston Globe Magazine,* September 12, 1993.

Coles, Harry L. *The War of 1812.* Chicago, 1965.

Collier, Peter, and David Horowitz. *The Kennedys: An American Drama.* New York, 1984.

Collins, Patrick. *Charles Francis Adams as Minister to England and an Anti-Know-Nothing.* Boston, 1876.

Cook, Adrian. *The Armies of the Streets: The New York City Draft Riots of 1863.* New York, 1974.

Cullen, James B. *The Story of the Irish in Boston.* Boston, 1889.

Culver, Raymond. *Horace Mann and Religion in the Massachusetts Public Schools.* New Haven, 1929.

Curley, James Michael. *I'd Do It Again: A Record of All My Uproarious Years.* Englewood Cliffs, N.J., 1957.

Curran, Michael P. *The Life of Patrick Collins.* Norwood, Mass., 1906.

Cutler, John Henry. *"Henry Fitz": Three Steps to the White House.* Indianapolis, 1962.

Darling, Arthur B. *Political Changes in Massachusetts, 1824–1848.* New Haven, 1925.

Dauer, Manning J. *The Adams Federalists.* Baltimore, 1968.

DeConde, Alexander. *The Quasi-War: The Politics and Diplomacy of the Undeclared War with France, 1797–1801.* New York, 1966.

Desmond, Humphrey J. *The A.P.A. Movement: A Sketch.* Washington, D.C., 1912.

Diner, Hasia. *Erin's Daughters in America: Irish Immigrant Women in the Nineteenth Century.* Baltimore, 1983.

Dinneen, Joseph F. *The Purple Shamrock: The Hon. James Michael Curley of Boston.* New York, 1949.

Donovan, Charles F., et al. *A History of Boston College.* Chestnut Hill, Mass., 1990.

Eckles, Robert B., and Richard W. Hale, Jr. *Britain, Her Peoples, and the Commonwealth.* New York, 1954.

Ellis, John. "The Unraveling of a Candidate." *Boston Globe,* April 26, 1994.

Erie, Steven P. *Rainbow's End: Irish-Americans and the Dilemma of Urban Machine Politics, 1840–1985.* Berkeley, 1988.

Estall, Robert C. *New England: A Study in Industrial Adjustment.* New York, 1966.

Fehrenbacher, Don E. *The Dred Scott Case: Its Significance in American Law and Politics.* New York, 1978.

Fisher, Sean, and Carolyn Hughes, eds. *The Last Tenement: Confronting Community and Urban Renewal in Boston's West End.* Boston, 1992.

Fiske, John. *The Beginnings of New England; or, The Puritan Theocracy in Its Relations to Civil and Religious Liberty.* Boston, 1889.

Fite, Emerson D. *The Presidential Campaign of 1860.* New York, 1911.

Flynn Committee. *The Flynn Years: A Progress Report on Boston and Its Neighborhoods, 1984–1993.* Boston, 1993.

Foner, Eric. *Free Soil, Free Labor, Free Men: The Ideology of the Republican Party before the Civil War.* New York, 1970.

———. *Politics and Ideology in the Age of the Civil War.* New York, 1980.

Forbes, Robert B. *The Voyage of the Jamestown on Her Errand of Mercy.* Boston, 1847.

Formisano, Ronald P. *Boston Against Busing: Race, Class, and Ethnicity in the 1960s and 1970s.* Chapel Hill, N.C., 1991.

———. *The Transformation of Political Culture: Massachusetts Parties, 1790s–1840s.* New York, 1983.

Formisano, Ronald P., and Constance Burns, eds. *Boston, 1700–1980: The Evolution of Urban Politics.* Westport, Conn., 1984.

Fraser, James W. "Mayor John F. Fitzgerald and Boston's Schools, 1905–1913." *Historical Journal of Massachusetts* 12 (June 1984), pp. 117–30.

Frawley, Mary Alphonsine. *Patrick Donahoe.* Washington, D.C., 1946.

Gallagher, Thomas. *Paddy's Lament: Ireland, 1846–1847.* New York, 1982.

Galvin, John T. "Boston's Eminent Patrick from Ireland." *Boston Globe,* March 17, 1988.

———. "Boston's First Irish Cop." *Boston Magazine,* March 1975.

———. "The Dark Ages of Boston Politics." *Proceedings of the Massachusetts Historical Society* 89 (1977), pp. 88–111.

————. "The Mahatma Called the Shots and Everyone Knew It." *Boston Globe*, June 4, 1990.

————. "The Mahatma Who Invented Ward 8." *Boston Magazine*, November 1975.

————. "The 1925 Campaign for Mayor Was a Four-Ring Circus." *Boston Sunday Globe*, August 21, 1983.

————. "Patrick Maguire: Boston's Last Democratic Boss." *New England Quarterly* 55 (1982), pp. 392–416.

————. "There's Some Irish Green in the Brahmins' Blue Blood." *Boston Globe*, March 17, 1989.

————. "When the Irish Made It to City Hall." *Boston Globe*, December 7, 1984.

Gans, Herbert. *The Urban Villagers: Group and Class in the Life of Italian-Americans*. New York, 1962.

Gelfand, Mark. *A Nation of Cities: The Federal Government and Urban America, 1933– 1965*. New York, 1975.

Ginger, Ray. *The Age of Excess*. New York, 1975.

Goodwin, Doris Kearns. *The Fitzgeralds and the Kennedys: An American Saga*. New York, 1987.

Gordon, Michael A. *The Orange Riots: Irish Political Violence in New York City, 1870 and 1871*. Ithaca, N.Y., 1993.

Green, James, and Hugh Donahue. *Boston's Workers: A Labor History*. Boston, 1979.

Grozier, Richard. "The Life and Times of John Bernard Fitzpatrick: Third Roman Catholic Bishop of Boston." Ph.D. diss., Boston College, 1966.

Hale, Edward Everett. *Letters on Irish Emigration*. Boston, 1852.

Haltigan, James. *The Irish in the American Revolution and Their Early Influence in the Colonies*. Washington, D.C., 1907.

Handlin, Oscar. *Boston's Immigrants*. Cambridge, Mass., 1941.

Hanna, William F. "Abraham Lincoln and the New England Press," Ph.D. diss., Boston College, 1980.

————. "The Boston Draft Riot." *Civil War History 1858–1860*. 36 (September 1990), pp. 262–73.

Hansen, Marcus Lee. *The Atlantic Migration*. Cambridge, Mass., 1940.

Hart, Albert B., ed. *Commonwealth History of Massachusetts*. 5 vols. New York, 1927–30.

Hayden, Robert C. *African-Americans in Boston: More than 350 Years*. Boston, 1991.

Hennesey, James. *American Catholics: A History of the Roman Catholic Community in the United States*. New York, 1981.

Hennessy, Michael E. *Four Decades of Massachusetts Politics*. Norwood, Mass., 1935.

Higgins, George V. *Style versus Substance: Boston, Kevin White, and the Politics of Illusion*. New York, 1984.

Higgins, Nathan. *Protestants against Poverty: Boston's Charities, 1870–1900*. Westport, Conn., 1971.

Higham, John. "The Mind of a Nativist: Henry F. Bowers and the A.P.A." *American Quarterly* 4 (1952), pp. 16–24.

Hillson, Jon. *The Battle of Boston*. New York, 1977.

Hodgkinson, Harold D. "Miracle in Boston." *Proceedings of the Historical Society* 84 (1972), pp. 71–81.

Hofstadter, Richard. *The Paranoid Style in American Politics*. Chicago, 1979.

Holmes, Oliver Wendell. *Elsie Venner*. Boston, 1847.

Horton, James O., and Lois E. Horton. *Black Bostonians: Family Life and Community Struggle in the Antebellum North*. New York, 1979.

Houston, Amanda V. "Beneath the El." *Boston College Magazine*, Summer 1988, pp. 20–25.

Jaher, Frederic Cople. "The Boston Brahmin in the Age of Industrial Capitalism." In *The Age of Industrial Capitalism in America*, ed. F. C. Jaher. New York, 1968.

Johnson, Paul. *The Birth of the Modern: World Society, 1815–1830*. New York, 1991.

Kane, Paula M. *Separatism and Subculture: Boston Catholicism, 1900–1920*. Chapel Hill, 1994.

Katz, Michael B. *The Irony of Early School Reform: Educational Innovation in Mid-Nineteenth Century Massachusetts*. Boston, 1968.

Kennedy, Lawrence W. *Planning the City upon a Hill: Boston Since 1630*. Amherst, Mass., 1992.

King, Mel. *Chain of Change: Struggles for Black Community Development*. Boston, 1981.

Kleppner, Paul. "From Party to Factions: The Dissolution of Boston's Majority Party, 1876–1908." In *Boston, 1700–1980: The Evolution of Urban Politics*, ed. Ronald Formisano and Constance Burns. Westport, Conn., 1984.

Knobel, Dale T. *Paddy and the Republic: Ethnicity and Nationality in Antebellum America*. Middletown, Conn., 1986.

Kurtz, Stephen G. *The Presidency of John Adams: The Collapse of Federalism, 1795–1800*. Philadelphia, 1957.

Lader, Lawrence. *The Bold Brahmins: New England's War against Slavery, 1830–1863*. New York, 1961.

Lane, Roger. *Policing the City: Boston, 1822–1885*. New York, 1971.

Lapomarda, Vincent A. "Maurice Joseph Tobin, 1901–1953: A Political Profile and an Edition of Selected Public Papers." Ph.D. diss., Boston University, 1968.

Leach, Jack. *Conscription in the United States*. Rutland, Vt., 1952.

Leckie, Robert. *American and Catholic*. New York, 1970.

Lee, Basil. *Discontent in New York City, 1861–1865*. New York, 1943.

Levin, Murray. *The Alienated Voter: Politics in Boston*. New York, 1960.

Levine, Edward M. *The Irish and Irish Politicians: A Study of Cultural and Social Alienation*. Notre Dame, 1966.

Levine, Hillel, and Lawrence Harmon. *The Death of an American Jewish Community: A Tragedy of Good Intentions*. New York, 1992.

Lodge, Henry Cabot. *The Story of the Revolution.* New York, 1898.

Lord, Robert H., John E. Sexton, and Edward Harrington. *History of the Archdiocese of Boston.* 3 vols., Boston, 1945.

Lukas, J. Anthony. *Common Ground: A Turbulent Decade in the Lives of Three American Families.* New York, 1985.

——. "Melting Pot or Mulligan Stew? Politics and the Process of Assimilation in Boston." *Forum 350* (John F. Kennedy Library, Boston) (October 7, 1980).

Lupo. Alan. *Liberty's Chosen Home: The Politics of Violence in Boston.* Boston, 1977.

Luthin, Reinhard H. *The First Lincoln Campaign.* Cambridge, Mass., 1944.

Lyell, Sir Charles. *A Second Visit to the United States of North America.* 2 vols. New York, 1849.

Mallam, William D. "Butlerism in Massachusetts." *New England Quarterly* 33 (1960), pp. 186–206.

Malloy, Ione. *Southie Won't Go: A Teacher's Diary of the Desegregation of South Boston High School.* Urbana, Ill., 1986.

Mann, Arthur. *Yankee Reformers in the Urban Age: Social Reform in Boston, 1880–1900.* New York, 1954.

Marquand, John P. *The Late George Apley.* New York, 1936.

Maxwell, John Francis. *Slavery and the Catholic Church.* London, 1975.

McMaster, John Bach. *A History of the People of the United States from the Revolution to the Civil War.* 8 vols. New York, 1906.

Mehegan, David. "The New Bostonians." *Boston Globe Magazine,* January 24, 1989.

——. "What Makes Southie Proud." *Boston Globe Magazine,* January 3, 1982, pp. 12–15.

Meister, Richard J., ed. *Race and Ethnicity in Modern America.* Lexington, Mass., 1974.

Melville, Annabelle M. *Jean Lefebvre de Cheverus, 1768–1836.* Milwaukee, 1958.

Meyers, Marvin. *The Jacksonian Persuasion: Politics and Belief.* Stanford, Calif., 1957.

Miller, John C. *The Federalist Era, 1789–1801.* New York, 1960.

Miller, Kerby. *Emigrants and Exiles: Ireland and the Irish Exodus to North America.* New York, 1985.

Mollenkopf, John H. *The Contested City.* Princeton, N.J., 1983.

Montgomery, David. *Beyond Equality: Labor and the Radical Republicans.* New York, 1967.

Morison, Samuel Eliot. *Builders of the Bay Colony.* Boston, 1981 ed.

——. *A History of the Constitution of Massachusetts.* Boston, 1917.

——. *The Life and Letters of Harrison Gray Otis, Federalist, 1765–1848.* 2 vols. Boston, 1913.

——. *The Maritime History of Massachusetts, 1783–1860.* Boston, 1921.

Morse, Samuel F. B. *Foreign Conspiracy against the Liberties of the United States.* New York, 1836.

————. *Imminent Dangers to the Free Institutions of the United States Through Foreign Immigration.* New York, 1854.

Mulkern, John R. *The Know-Nothing Party in Massachusetts: The Rise and Fall of a People's Party.* Boston, 1990.

————. "Scandal Behind the Convent Walls: The Know-Nothing Nunnery Committee of 1855." *Historical Journal of Massachusetts* 11 (1983), pp. 22–31.

Murdock, Eugene. *One Million Men: The Civil War Draft in the North.* New York, 1971.

————. *Patriotism Unlimited: The Civil War Draft and the Bounty System.* New York, 1967.

Myers, Gustavus. *History of Bigotry in the United States.* New York, 1943.

Nolan, Martin F. "Exit the Irish: A Hushed Last Hurrah." *Boston Globe,* November 3, 1993.

————. "Ray Flynn: Revolutionary." *Boston Globe,* March 21, 1993, Focus section.

O'Brien, Michael J. *The Irish at Bunker Hill.* Shannon, Ireland, 1968.

O'Connor, Thomas H. *Bibles, Brahmins, and Bosses: A Short History of Boston.* 3d ed. Boston, 1991.

————. *Building a New Boston: Politics and Urban Renewal, 1950–1970.* Boston, 1993.

————. *Fitzpatrick's Boston, 1846–1866: John Bernard Fitzpatrick, Third Bishop of Boston.* Boston, 1984.

————. "The Irish in New England." *New England Historical and Genealogical Register* 139 (July 1985), pp. 187–195.

————. "Irish Votes and Yankee Cotton: The Constitution of 1853." *Proceedings of the Massachusetts Historical Society* 95 (1983), pp. 88–99.

————. *Lords of the Loom: The Cotton Whigs and the Coming of the Civil War.* New York, 1968.

————. *South Boston: My Home Town.* Boston, 1988.

O'Connor, Thomas H., and Alan Rogers. *This Momentous Affair: Massachusetts and the Ratification of the Constitution of the United States.* Boston, 1987.

O'Hare, M. Jeanne d'Arc. "The Public Career of Patrick Collins." Ph.D. diss. Boston College, 1959.

O'Toole, James M. *Militant and Triumphant: William Henry O'Connell and the Catholic Church in Boston, 1859–1944.* Notre Dame, Ind., 1992.

————. " 'The Newer Catholic Races': Ethnic Catholicism in Boston, 1900–1940." *New England Quarterly* 65 (1992), pp. 117–34.

————. "Prelates and Politicos." In *Catholic Boston: Studies in Religion and Community, 1870–1970,* ed. Robert E. Sullivan and James M. O'Toole. Boston,, 1985.

Palfrey, John Gorham. *A History of New England.* Boston, 1865.

Parkman, Francis. *Our Common Schools.* Boston, 1890.

Pearson, Henry Greenleaf. *Son of New England: James Jackson Storrow.* Boston, 1930.

Pessen, Edward. *Jacksonian America.* Urbana, Ill., 1969.

Potter, George. *To the Golden Door*. Boston, 1960.

Powers, John. "Invisible Voters." *Boston Globe Magazine* (August 1, 1993), pp. 16–18.

Remini, Robert V. *Andrew Jackson and the Course of American Democracy, 1833–1845*. 3 vols. New York, 1984.

Rice, Madeleine Hooke. *American Catholic Opinion in the Slavery Controversy*. Gloucester, Mass., 1964.

Robinson, William S. *"Warrington" Pen Portraits*. Boston, 1877.

Ross, J. Michael, and William M. Berg. *"I Respectfully Disagree with the Judge's Order": The Boston School Desegregation Controversy*. Washington, D.C., 1981.

Russell, Francis. *City in Terror: 1919, the Boston Police Strike*. New York, 1975.

———. *The Knave of Boston and Other Ambiguous Massachusetts Characters*. Boston, 1987.

Ryan, Dennis P. *Beyond the Ballot Box: A Social History of the Boston Irish, 1845–1917*. Amherst, Mass., 1989.

Sanders, James W. "Catholics and the School Question in Boston: The Cardinal O'Connell Years." In *Catholic Boston: Studies in Religion and Community, 1870–1970*, ed. Robert E. Sullivan and James M. O'Toole. Boston, 1985.

Schabert, Tilo. *Boston Politics: The Creativity of Power*. Berlin, 1989.

Schlesinger, Arthur B., Jr. *The Age of Jackson*. Boston, 1945.

Schultz, Stanley K. *The Culture Factory: Boston Public Schools, 1789–1860*. New York, 1973.

Schwartz, Harold. "Fugitive Slave Days in Boston." *New England Quarterly* 27 (1954), pp. 191–212.

Sears, Louis M. *Jefferson and the Embargo*. New York, 1927.

Shannon, William V. *The American Irish*. New York, 1966.

———. "Shamrocks and Shillelaghs: The Phenomenon of Ethnic Mayors in Boston Politics." *Forum 350* (John F. Kennedy Library, Boston) (September 16, 1980).

Shapiro, Samuel. "The Conservative Dilemma: The Massachusetts Constitutional Convention of 1853." *New England Quarterly* 3 (1960), pp. 207–24.

Shaw, Richard. *Dagger John: The Unquiet Life and Times of Archbishop John Hughes of New York*. New York, 1977.

Silverman, Robert A. "Nathan Matthews: Politics of Reform in Boston, 1890–1910." *New England Quarterly* 50 (1977), pp. 626–43.

Smelser, Marshall. *The Democratic Republic, 1801–1815*. New York, 1968.

Solomon, Barbara M. *Ancestors and Immigrants: A Changing New England Tradition*. Cambridge, Mass., 1956.

Stack, John F., Jr. *International Conflict in an American City: Boston's Irish, Italians, and Jews, 1934–1944*. Westport, Conn., 1979.

Stevenson, Louise. "Women Anti-Suffragists in the 1915 Massachusetts Campaign." *New England Quarterly* 52 (1979), pp. 80–93.

Strahinich, John. "Only Irish Need Apply." *Boston Magazine,* March 1993.

Sullivan, Robert E., and James M. O'Toole, eds. *Catholic Boston: Studies in Religion and Community, 1870–1970.* Boston, 1985.

Tager, Jack. "The Massachusetts Miracle." *Historical Journal of Massachusetts* 19 (Summer 1991), pp. 111–32.

———. "Urban Renewal in Boston." *Historical Journal of Massachusetts* 21 (Winter 1993), pp. 1–32.

Teaford, Jon. *The Rough Road to Renaissance: Urban Revitalization in America, 1940–1984.* Baltimore, 1990.

———. *Unheralded Triumph: City Government in America, 1870–1900.* Baltimore, 1984.

Thernstrom, Stephan. "Urbanization, Migration, and Social Mobility in Late Nineteenth-Century America." In *American Urban History,* 2d ed., ed. Alexander Callow (New York, 1973).

Thompson, E. P. *The Making of the English Working Class.* New York, 1963.

Thompson, Margaret. "Ben Butler versus the Brahmins: Patronage and Politics in Early Gilded Age Massachusetts." *New England Quarterly* 55 (1982), pp. 163–86.

Trout, Charles H. *Boston, the Great Depression, and the New Deal.* New York, 1977.

Tucker, Robert W., and David C. Hendrickson. *Empire of Liberty: The Statecraft of Thomas Jefferson.* New York, 1990.

Wakin, Edward. *Enter the Irish-American.* New York, 1976.

Walsh, Francis R. "The *Boston Pilot* Reports the Civil War." *Historical Journal of Massachusetts* 9 (June 1981), pp. 5–16.

———. "John Boyle O'Reilly, the *Boston Pilot,* and Irish-American Assimilation, 1870–1890." In *Massachusetts in the Gilded Age,* ed. Jack Tager and John Ifkovic. Amherst, 1985.

Walsh, James B. *The Irish: America's Political Class.* New York, 1976.

Wangler, Thomas E. "Catholic Religious Life in Boston in the Era of Cardinal O'Connell." In *Catholic Boston: Studies in Religion and Community, 1870–1970,* ed. Robert E. Sullivan and James M. O'Toole. Boston, 1985.

Ward, John William. "The Common Weal and the Public Trust." *Forum 350* (John F. Kennedy Library, Boston) (October 21, 1980).

Warner, Sam Bass, Jr. *Streetcar Suburbs: The Process of Growth in Boston, 1870–1900.* New York, 1974.

Warner, W. Lloyd, and Leo Srole. *The Social Systems of American Ethnic Groups.* New Haven, 1954.

Wayman, Dorothy. *Cardinal O'Connell of Boston: A Biography of William Henry O'Connell, 1859–1944.* New York, 1955.

Weinstein, Irving. *July 1863: The Incredible Story of the Bloody New York Draft Riots.* New York, 1952.

Wells, Wellington. "Political and Governmental Readjustments, 1865–1889." Vol. 4 in *Commonwealth History of Massachusetts,* ed. Albert B. Hart. New York, 1930.

White, Anna MacBride, and A. Norman Jeffares, eds. *The Gonne-Yeats Letters, 1893–1938: Always Your Friend.* London, 1992.

White, Patrick C. T. *A Nation on Trial: America and the War of 1812.* New York, 1965.

Whitehill, Walter Muir. *Boston: A Topographical History.* Cambridge, Mass., 1968.

Wittke, Carl. *The Irish in America.* Baton Rouge, 1956.

Woodham-Smith, Cecil. *The Great Hunger: Ireland, 1848–1849.* New York, 1962.

Zaitzevsky, Cynthia. *Frederick Law Olmsted and the Boston Park System.* Cambridge, Mass., 1982.

INDEX